D1287961

Works in English by Wilhelm Reich

THE DISCOVERY OF THE ORGONE: Vol. 1, THE FUNCTION OF THE ORGASM
Orgone Institute Press, 1942. First Edition

CHARACTER-ANALYSIS
Orgone Institute Press, 1945. Second Edition

THE SEXUAL REVOLUTION
Orgone Institute Press, 1945

THE MASS PSYCHOLOGY OF FASCISM
Orgone Institute Press, 1946

THE DISCOVERY OF THE ORGONE: Vol. 1, THE FUNCTION OF THE ORGASM
Orgone Institute Press, 1948. Second Edition

THE DISCOVERY OF THE ORGONE: Vol. 2, THE CANCER BIOPATHY
Orgone Institute Press, 1948

LISTEN, LITTLE MAN!
Orgone Institute Press, 1948

ETHER, GOD AND DEVIL
Orgone Institute Press, 1951

COSMIC SUPERIMPOSITION
Orgone Institute Press, 1951

THE ORGONE ENERGY ACCUMULATOR
Orgone Institute Press, 1951

THE ORANUR EXPERIMENT, First Report (1947-1951)
Orgone Institute Press, 1951

THE EMOTIONAL PLAGUE OF MANKIND: Vol. 1, THE MURDER OF CHRIST
Orgone Institute Press, 1953

THE EMOTIONAL PLAGUE OF MANKIND: Vol. 2, PEOPLE IN TROUBLE
Orgone Institute Press, 1953

CONTACT WITH SPACE, Oranur Second Report (1951-1956)
Core Pilot Press, 1957

WILHELM REICH: SELECTED WRITINGS
Farrar, Straus & Cudahy, 1960

CHARACTER ANALYSIS (Third, enlarged edition)
Farrar, Straus & Cudahy, 1961 (clothbound)
The Noonday Press, 1961 (paperbound)

THE DISCOVERY OF THE ORGONE

THE FUNCTION OF THE ORGASM

WILHELM REICH

THE DISCOVERY OF THE ORGONE

WILHELM REICH

THE FUNCTION OF THE ORGASM

SEX-ECONOMIC PROBLEMS OF BIOLOGICAL ENERGY

Translated from the German Manuscript

By

THEODORE P. WOLFE

THE NOONDAY PRESS
a subsidiary of
FARRAR, STRAUS AND CUDAHY
New York

Library of Congress catalog card no. 61-11057

First printing, 1942
Second printing, 1948
Third printing, 1961

Published simultaneously in Canada by
Ambassador Books, Ltd., Toronto

Manufactured in the U.S.A.

Love, work and knowledge are the well-springs of our life. They should also govern it.

CONTENTS

FOREWORD

In the death of Wilhelm Reich, the Emotional Plague claimed its most formidable opponent. Throughout all of recorded history those who had been killed by the effects of this specifically human disease were invariably its "innocent" victims. Reich, however, did not become a victim innocently. He was the first man to deliberately study and to satisfactorily understand the bio-pathological basis of this scourge which is created by the suppression of genital love life on a mass scale. Throughout his entire life, he sought a practical method of combatting it. He never failed to draw attention to the fact that the Emotional Plague was the one enemy of man which, unless accurately understood and effectively fought, would make impossible the elimination of the agony of the child, the adolescent, and of the masses of bio-physically and emotionally sick human beings. Consequently, when he too fell victim to this disease, it was not unexpected. He realized the risk involved, and with the courage of a true scientist he exposed himself to its destructive effects; seeking in the process, without compromising the scientific truth, to find a way out of the legalistic rigmarole in which the Plague had enmeshed him.

Since Reich's death, there has been an insistent demand for his writings which strongly indicates that the Plague has fallen short of its intention—the concealment of the Truth. The slanderous assaults upon his person, designed to discredit him and, thereby, to divert attention from his significant discoveries, have lost some—unfortunately, not all—of their impact, and it now may be possible to turn to a sober scrutiny of his work.

The Function of the Orgasm was the first of Reich's writings to be translated into English. It is not a textbook. It is rather a scientific biography. "A systematic presentation could not have given the reader a picture of how . . . one problem and its solution led to another; nor would it show that this work is not pure invention; and that every part of it owes its existence to the peculiar course of scientific logic."

That Wilhelm Reich, who was the instrument of this logic, should die in a federal penitentiary is shocking. That those who cared were helpless, and that there were many who knew and who did not care, is tragic. It is no longer possible to stand aside and to say, "Forgive them for they know not what they do." It is time that we all know what we do—and why we do it. It is time that we find a way to end this chronic murder of life and of the knowledge of life. This knowledge exists, and with the republication of Reich's works, it is again made available. We must learn to tolerate the Truth. We must learn to understand and to respect the bio-energetic function of the orgastic convulsion, and we must learn to know what we become and what we do when this function is thwarted and denied.

In this book, there is knowledge; and in this knowledge, there is hope.

Mary Higgins, Trustee
The Wilhelm Reich Infant Trust Fund

New York, 1961

PREFACE TO SECOND EDITION

The discovery of the orgone was the result of a consistent clinical investigation of the concept of "psychic energy," at first in the realm of psychiatry. The present volume may well be considered an extensive introduction to the newly opened field of orgone biophysics. Many of the results of biophysical and physical orgone research, as carried on since about 1934, were published in the *International Journal of Sex-economy and Orgone Research*, 1942-1945, and are being published as the second volume of *The Discovery of the Orgone*, entitled *The Cancer-Biopathy*. Experience has shown beyond any doubt that the knowledge of the *emotional* functions of the biological energy is indispensable for the understanding of its *physiological* and *physical* functions. The biological emotions which govern the psychic processes are in themselves the immediate expression of a strictly physical energy, the cosmic orgone.

The second edition of this volume is unchanged.

W.R.

New York, February 1947

INTRODUCTORY SURVEY

This book summarizes my medical and scientific work with the living organism during the past twenty years. It was not originally intended for publication. The purpose in writing it was merely to set down on paper things which otherwise would not have been expressed owing to such considerations as the concern for my material existence, for my "reputation", as well as the incompleteness of many trains of thought. If I have decided to publish it at this time, it is because the rapid progression of the work from the realm of psychology into that of biology appeared to my co-workers —and even more so to those who were trying to follow my work at a distance—like a sudden jump. It is to be hoped that a presentation of the whole development will help to bridge this seeming gap.

To most people, it is inconceivable how I could possibly work simultaneously in so many diverse fields as psychology, sociology, physiology, and now also biology. Some psychoanalysts would like to see me go back to psychoanalysis; the sociologists would like to relegate me to natural science, and the biologists to psychology.

The problem of sexuality permeates by its very nature every field of scientific investigation. Its central phenomenon, the *orgasm,* is the focal point of problems arising in the fields of psychology as well as physiology, biology and sociology. There is hardly any other field of scientific investigation that would lend itself so well to a demonstration of the *unity of living functioning,* or that would safeguard one so securely against a specialistic narrowing of one's horizon. *Sex-*

economy has become a new, independent branch of science, with research methods and findings of its own. It is a *scientific theory of sexuality based on experimental findings.* It has become necessary to describe its development. In doing so I shall point out what I can claim as my own, what are the historical links with other fields of investigation, and finally, what is behind the empty rumors which have been spread concerning my activity.

Sex-economy originated within the framework of Freud's psychoanalysis between 1919 and 1923. The actual separation from this matrix occurred about 1928, although my severance from the psychoanalytic organization did not occur until 1934.

This is not a textbook, but, rather, a narrative. A systematic presentation could not have given the reader a picture of how, in the course of these twenty years, one problem and its solution led to another; nor would it show that this work is not pure invention; and that every part of it owes its existence to the peculiar course of scientific logic. It is not false modesty when I say that I feel myself only as an executive organ of this logic. The functional method of investigation is like a compass in an uncharted territory. I could not think of any better proof for the fundamental correctness of the theory of sex-economy than the fact that the discovery of the true nature of "*orgastic potency*", the most important part of sex-economy, made in 1922, led to the discovery of the *orgasm reflex* in 1935 and to the discovery of the *orgone radiation*[1] in 1939, this latter finding providing the experimental foundation for the earlier clinical findings. This inherent logic in the development of sex-economy is the fixed point in the maze of opinions, in the struggle against misunderstandings, and in the overcoming of grave doubts at a time when confusion threatens to blur clear vision.

[1] Cf. Glossary, "orgone".

It is a good idea to write scientific biographies in one's younger years, at an age when one has not yet lost certain illusions regarding the readiness of one's fellows to accept revolutionary knowledge. If one still has these illusions, one is able to cleave to the basic truths, to resist all the various temptations to compromise or sacrifice clear-cut findings to laziness in thinking or to the need for peace of mind. The temptation to deny the sexual causation of so many ailments is even greater in the case of sex-economy than it was in the case of psychoanalysis. It was only with difficulty that I succeeded in persuading my co-workers to adopt the term "sex-economy". This term is designed to cover a new field of scientific endeavor: *the investigation of bio-psychic energy*. "Sexuality", according to the prevailing attitude of today, is offensive. It is altogether too easy to relegate its significance for human life to oblivion. It can be safely assumed that it will require the work of many generations for sexuality to be taken seriously by official science as well as by the laity. In all probability, it will not be taken seriously until life and death problems compel *society itself* to consent to the comprehension and mastery of the sexual process and to furnish its protection not only to those who are attempting these tasks but to the undertaking itself. Such a life and death problem is, for example, cancer; another is the psychic pestilence which has made dictatorships possible.

Sex-economy is a branch of natural science. As such, it is not ashamed of the subject of sexuality and rejects as its representative anyone who has not mastered that social anxiety concerning defamation of his character on sexual grounds which has inevitably been a part of his training. The term "vegetotherapy", connoting the sex-economic therapeutic technique, was really a concession to the squeamishness of the world in sexual matters. I would have preferred, and it would have been more correct, to call the therapeutic technique "orgasmo-therapy", for that is what vegetotherapy fundamentally is. The fact had to be taken into consideration that such a term would have meant too much of a social burden to the young sex-economist. People are that way: they laugh embarrassedly or they sneer when the core of their longings and their religious feelings is mentioned.

It is to be feared that in another decade or two the school of sex-economists will split into two groups which will fight each other violently. One group will maintain that the sexual function is subordinated to the general life function, and that, consequently, it *can be discarded.* The other group of sex-economists will radically oppose such a contention and will try to save the honor of scientific sex research. In this struggle, the basic identity of sexual process and life process might easily be forgotten. I might give in myself, and disavow what in youthful years of struggle was honest scientific conviction. For the Fascist world may succeed again, as it did in Europe, in threatening our hard work with extinction at the hands of party politicians and moralistic psychiatrists of the hereditarian school. Those who witnessed the scandal of the Fascist press campaign against sex-economy in Norway know what I am speaking of. For this reason, it is imperative to put down in time what is meant by sex-economy, before I, myself, under the pressure of obsolete social conditions, may begin to think differently and possibly hamper with my authority the coming generation in its search for the truth.

The theory of sex-economy can be put in a few sentences.

Psychic health depends upon *orgastic potency,* that is, on the capacity for surrender in the acme of sexual excitation in the natural sexual act. Its basis is the un-neurotic character attitude of capacity for love. Mental illness is a result of a disturbance in the natural capacity for love. In the case of orgastic impotence, from which a vast majority of humans are suffering, biological energy is dammed up, thus becoming the source of all kinds of irrational behavior. The cure of psychic disturbances requires in the first place the establishment of the natural capacity for love. It depends as much upon social as upon psychic conditions.

Psychic disturbances are the results of the sexual chaos brought about by the nature of our society. This chaos has, for thousands of years, served the function of making people submissive to existing conditions, in other words, of internalizing the external mechanization of life. It serves the purpose of bringing about the *psychic anchoring* of a mechanized and authoritarian civilization by way of making people lack self-confidence.

The vital energies, under natural conditions, regulate themselves spontaneously, without compulsive duty or compulsive morality. The latter are a sure indication of the existence of antisocial tendencies. Antisocial behavior springs from *secondary drives which owe their existence to the suppression of natural sexuality.*

The individual brought up in an atmosphere which negates life and sex acquires a *pleasure-anxiety* (fear of pleasurable excitation) which is represented physiologically in chronic muscular spasms. This pleasure-anxiety is the soil on which the individual re-creates the life-negating ideologies which are the basis of dictatorships. It is the foundation of the fear of a free, independent way of living. This becomes the most potent source of strength for any kind of reactionary political activity and for the domination of majorities of working people by individuals or groups of individuals. It is bio-physiological anxiety and constitutes the central problem of psychosomatic research. Up to now, it has been the greatest obstacle to the investigation of the *involuntary* life functions, which the neurotic person can experience only as something weird and frightening.

The character structure of man of today—who is perpetuating a patriarchal, authoritarian culture some four to six thousand years old—is characterized by *an armoring against nature within himself and against social misery outside himself*. This armoring of the character is the basis of loneliness, helplessness, craving for authority, fear of responsibility, mystical longing, sexual misery, of impotent rebelliousness as well as of resignation of an unnatural and pathological type. Human beings have taken a hostile attitude toward that in themselves which is living, and have alienated themselves from it. This alienation is not of biological, but of social and economic origin. It is not found in human history before the development of the patriarchal social order.

Since then, duty has taken the place of the natural enjoyment of work and activity. The average character structure of human beings has changed in the direction of impotence and fear of living, so that authoritarian dictatorships not only can establish themselves, but can even justify themselves by pointing to existing human attitudes, such as lack of responsibility and infantilism. The international catastrophe we are passing through is the ultimate consequence of this alienation from life.

This formation of character in the authoritarian mold has as its central point, not parental love, but *the authoritarian family*. Its chief instrument is the suppression of sexuality in the infant and the adolescent.

Owing to the split in the human character structure of today, nature and culture, instinct and morality, sexuality and achievement, are considered incompatible. That *unity of culture and nature, work and love, morality and sexuality* for which mankind is forever longing, this unity will remain a dream as long as man does not permit the satisfaction of the biological demands of natural (orgastic) sexual gratification. Until then, true democracy and responsible freedom will remain an illusion, and helpless submission to existing social conditions will characterize human existence. Until then, the extinguishing of life will prevail, be it in compulsive education,[1] in compulsive social institutions, or in wars.

In the field of psychotherapy, I have elaborated the technique of *character-analytic vegetotherapy*. Its fundamental principle is the restoration of bio-psychic motility by means of dissolving rigidities ("armorings") of the character and the musculature. This psychotherapeutic technique was confirmed experimentally through the discovery of *the bio-electrical nature of sexuality and anxiety*. Sexuality and anxiety are opposite directions of excitation in the biological organism: *pleasurable expansion* and *anxious contraction*.

The *orgasm formula* which governs sex-economic investigation is as follows: MECHANICAL TENSION → BIO-ELECTRICAL CHARGE → BIO-ELECTRICAL DISCHARGE → MECHANICAL RELAXATION. This proved to be the formula of living functioning in general. Its discovery led to the investigation of the organizing of living substance out of non-living substance, that is, experimental bion[2] research, and more recently, to the discovery of the orgone radiation. Bion research opened a new avenue of approach to the problem of cancer and certain other disturbances of vegetative life.

The fact that man is the only species which does not fulfil the natural law of sexuality is the immediate cause of a series of devastating disasters. The external social negation of life results in mass death, in the form of wars, as well as in psychic and somatic disturbances of vital functioning.

The sexual process, that is, the expansive biological process of pleasure, is the productive life-process per se.

This is very condensed and sounds almost too simple. This "simplicity" is the mysterious quality which many profess to find in my work. I will attempt in this volume to show in what manner and by what processes I was able to find

---

[1] ***Translator's note.*** "Compulsive", in the sense of psychopathology, and not "compulsory", in the sense of "obligatory".

[2] Cf. Glossary, "bion".

solutions to these problems, which up to now have been hidden from us. I hope to be able to show that there is no wizardry about it; that, on the contrary, my theory amounts to nothing but a formulation of general, though unacknowledged, facts about living matter and its functioning. It was the result of the generally prevalent alienation from life that these facts and interrelationships were overlooked and consistently camouflaged.

The history of sex-economy is incomplete without some statements as to the part played in its development by its friends. My friends and co-workers will understand why I must refrain from giving due credit to their accomplishments here. To all those who have fought and often suffered for sex-economy, I can give the assurance that without their work the entire development would not have been possible. I wish to thank Dr. Wolfe most heartily for the extraordinary care which he has given to the translation of this volume. I may say that such a translation could only have been done by one who is thoroughly acquainted with sex-economy as well as with the problems of psychosomatic research.

This presentation of sex-economy is entirely against the background of European conditions, the conditions that led to the present catastrophe. The victory of the dictatorships was made possible by the ailing mentality of European humanity in general, which the democracies were unable to master either economically, socially or psychologically. I have not been in the United States long enough to be able to say in how far this presentation does or does not apply to American conditions. The conditions I mean are not merely the external human relationships and social conditions, but rather, the *depth structure* of the American individual and his society. To become acquainted with this takes time.

It is to be expected that the American edition of this book will provoke disagreement on various grounds. In Europe, many years of experience had enabled me to judge, from definite indications, the significance of each attack, criticism or praise. As it is to be assumed that the reactions of certain circles here will not differ fundamentally from those on the other side of the ocean, I would like to answer such possible attacks in advance.

Sex-economy has nothing to do with any existing political organization or ideology. The political concepts which separate the various levels and classes of society are not applicable to sex-economy. The social misinterpretation of *natural* love life and its denial to children and adolescents represent a state of affairs which is characteristically human, extending beyond the limits of any state or group.

Sex-economy has been attacked by exponents of *all* political colorings. My publications were banned by the Communists as well as by the Fascists; they were attacked and damned by police agencies as well as by socialists and liberals. On the other hand, they found some recognition and respect in *all* classes of society and in all social groups. The elucidation of the function of the orgasm, in particular, met with the approval of scientific and cultural groups of *every* conceivable kind.

Sexual repression, biological rigidity, moralism and puritanism are not confined to certain classes or groups of the population. They are ubiquitous. I know clergymen who welcome the differentiation between natural and unnatural sex life and who acknowledge the scientific equation of the concept of God with natural law; I know other clergymen who see in the elucidation and practical realization of the sex life of the child and the adolescent a danger to the existence of the church, and thus feel impelled to take drastic countermeasures. *Approval and disapproval,* as the case might be, *were being justified by the same ideology.* Liberalism was considered endangered, as well as the dictatorship of the proletariat, or the honor of socialism or the honor of the German woman. In reality, the elucidation of the function of the living is a threat only to *one* attitude and to *one* kind of social and moral order: *the authoritarian dictatorial regime of any kind, which, by means of compulsive morality and a compulsive attitude toward work, attempts to destroy spontaneous decency and natural self-regulation of the vital forces.*

It is time to be honest: authoritarian dictatorship exists not only in totalitarian states. It is found in the church as well as in academic organizations, among the Communists as well as in parliamentary governments. It is a general human tendency which owes its existence to the suppression of the living function; it forms, in all nations, the mass-psychological basis for the acceptance and establishment of dictatorship. Its basic elements are mystification of the life process; actual helplessness, material and social; fear of the responsibility for shaping one's own life; and, consequently, the craving for illusory security and for authority, passive or active. The age-old, *genuine* striving for a democratization of social life is based on self-determination, on *natural* sociality and morality, on *joyful* work and *earthly* happiness in love. People with this striving consider any illusion a danger. Thus, they will not only be unafraid of the scientific comprehension of the living function, but they will put it to use in mastering decisive problems pertaining to the formation of human character structure; in so doing, they will be able to master these problems in a scientific and practical, instead of in an illusionary manner. Everywhere people are striving to turn formal democracy into a true democracy of all those engaged in productive work, into a *work democracy*,[1] that is, a democracy on the basis of a *natural* organization of the work process.

In the field of mental hygiene, it is a matter of the tremendous task of replacing sexual chaos, prostitution, porno-

---

[1]Cf. Glossary, "work democracy".

graphic literature and sexual racketeering with natural happiness in love, guaranteed by society. This does not imply any intention of "destroying the family" or of "undermining morals". In fact, *family and morals are already undermined by the compulsive family and compulsive morality.* Professionally, we are confronted with the task of repairing the damage done by sexual and familial chaos, in the form of mental disease. If we are to be able to master this psychic plague, we have to distinguish sharply between what is natural love between parents and children, and what is familial compulsion. The universal disease *"familitis"* destroys all that honest human endeavor attempts to bring about.

Though I do not belong to any political or religious organization, I have, nevertheless, a definite concept of social living. This concept is—in contrast to all varieties of political, purely ideological or mystical philosophy—*scientifically rational.* According to this concept, I believe that there will be no lasting peace on our earth, and that all attempts to socialize human beings will be in vain, as long as politicians and dictators of one kind or another, who have not the slightest awareness of the actualities of the life process, continue to lead masses of people who are endemically neurotic and sexually sick. The natural function of the socialization of the human is that of guaranteeing work and natural fulfillment in love. These two biological activities of man have always depended upon scientific searching and thinking. *Knowledge, work and natural love are the sources of life.* They should also be the forces that *govern* our life, the complete responsibility for these being carried by all who are producing by their labor.

If we are asked whether we are for or against democracy, our answer is: We are for democracy, unequivocally and without compromise. But—we are for a genuine democracy, for a democracy in real life, not a democracy on paper. We are for the radical realization of all democratic ideals, be they "government of the people, by the people, for the people", or "liberty, equality, fraternity". We add only one essential point: *Do away with all the obstacles which stand in the way of their realization! Make democracy a living thing! Don't pretend democracy! Otherwise, Fascism will win out everywhere!*

Mental hygiene on a mass scale requires the power of knowledge against the power of ignorance; the power of vital work against parasitism of any kind, be it economic, intellectual, or philosophical. Science alone can, if it takes itself seriously, fight against those forces that attempt to destroy life, wherever this may be happening and through whatsoever agency. Obviously, no man alone can acquire the knowledge necessary to safeguard the natural function of life. *A scientific, rational view of life excludes dictatorship and requires work democracy.*

The social power exercised by the people, through the people and for the people, based on a natural feeling for life, and respect for achievement through work, would be invincible. *But this power will not become manifest and effective until the working and producing masses of the people become psychically independent and capable of taking full responsibility for their social existence, and capable of rationally determining their lives themselves.* What prevents them from doing so is the mass neurosis as it is materialized in dictatorships of whatever kind, as well as in political rigmaroles. If we are to eliminate the mass neurosis and the irrationalism in social life, in other words, if we are to do a real job of mental hygiene, we need a social framework which first of all can eliminate material need and which can guarantee the unhampered development of the vital forces in every individual. This social framework can be no other than a *true* democracy.

This true democracy, however, is not something static, not a *state* of "freedom" which could be given, granted or guaranteed to a group of people by government agencies elected by them or forced upon them. Rather, true democracy is a difficult, slow-working *process,* in which the masses of the people, with the protection of society and law, have—by no means "get"—every possibility of training themselves in the administration of a life, individual and social, that is alive, and of advancing to ever better forms of living. Thus, true democracy is not a finished state enjoying, like an old man, its glorious warrior past; rather, it is a process of constant struggle with the problems presented by the consistent development of *new* thoughts, *new* discoveries and *new* forms of living. The development into the future is consistent and uninterrupted only if that which is old and senescent, after having fulfilled its function in an earlier phase of the democratic development, is now wise enough to make room for what is young and new, wise enough not to stifle it by reason of its dignity and formal authority.

Tradition is important. It is democratic if and when it fulfills the natural function of providing the new generation with the experiences, good and bad, of the past, thus enabling the new generation to learn from past mistakes and to avoid making the same mistakes all over again. On the other hand, tradition turns into the destroyer of democracy if it leaves the coming generations no possibility of making their own choice, if it attempts to dictate what—under changed conditions of life—is to be considered "good" or "bad". Tradition is in the habit of forgetting that it has lost the ability to judge what is *not* tradition. The improvement of the microscope, for example, was not achieved by destroying the first model, but by preserving it and developing it according to a higher level of human knowledge. A microscope from the time of Pasteur does not permit us to see what the virus researcher of today is looking for. But imagine Pasteur's microscope having the authority and the ambition to prohibit the electron microscope!

There would be only the highest respect for that which is handed down, and no hatred of it, if youth, freely and without danger, could say: "*This* we take over from you, for it is strong, honest and still in keeping with our times, and capable of development. But *the other* we cannot take over. It was true and useful in your time, but it has become useless for us." This youth will have to be prepared to hear the same thing from its own children.

The development of pre-war democracy into full and true work democracy means the acquisition of an actual determination of their existence on the part of all, instead of the present formal, partial and incomplete determination. It means the substitution of irrational political drives of the masses by a rational mastery of the social process. This requires continuous self-education of the people to responsible freedom instead of the infantile expectation of having freedom presented on a silver platter or having it guaranteed by somebody else. If democracy is to eradicate the human tendency toward dictatorship, it will have to *prove* that it can eliminate poverty and that it can bring about rational independence in people. This, and only this, deserves the name of organic social development.

It is my belief that the European democracies lost out in their struggle against dictatorship because there was too much in the democratic systems that was formal and much too little that was democratic in an actual and practical way. Fear of that which is alive characterized education in every respect. Democracy was looked upon as a state of guaranteed freedom, and not as a *process of developing mass responsibility*. In the democracies, too, people were, and still are, educated toward submissiveness to authority. This is what the catastrophic events of our times have taught us:

brought up to be mechanically obedient, people *steal* freedom for themselves; they *kill* the giver of freedom, and they elope with the dictator.

I am not a politician and I know nothing of politics, but I am a socially conscious *scientist*. As such, I have the right to say what I have found to be true. If my scientific statements are such as to help to promote a better order of human conditions, then I can feel that the purpose of my work is achieved. After the collapse of the dictatorships, human society will find itself in the need of truths, and particularly, of *unpopular* truths. Those truths that touch upon the unacknowledged reasons of today's social chaos will sooner or later prevail, whether people want it so or not. Such a truth is that dictatorship is rooted in the irrational fear of life on the part of people in general. He who represents such truths is in great danger, but he can wait. He need not fight for power to enforce the truth. His power consists in knowing facts which are generally true for all mankind. No matter how unpopular such facts may be: in times of extreme social necessity society's will to live will force their recognition in spite of everything.

The scientist is in duty bound to preserve the right of freely expressing his opinion under all circumstances, and not to abandon this privilege to the advocates of the suppression of life. There is so much talk about the soldier's duty to give his life for his country. There is too little mention of the scientist's duty to defend, under all circumstances, what has been recognized to be true, no matter at what cost.

The physician or teacher has only *one* obligation, that of practising his profession uncompromisingly, without regard for the powers that attempt to suppress life, and to consider only the welfare of those who are given into his care. He cannot represent ideologies that are in conflict with the true task of the physician or teacher.

He who disputes this right of the scientist, the physician, the teacher, the technician or the writer, and calls himself a democrat, is a hypocrite, or at least a victim of the plague of irrationalism. The struggle against the plague of dictatorship is hopeless without determination and without a serious concern with problems of the life process; for, dictatorship lives—and can only live—in the darkness of *unresolved* problems of the life process. Man is helpless where he lacks knowledge; this helplessness born of ignorance forms the fertile soil for dictatorship. A social order cannot be called democratic if it is afraid of raising decisive questions, of finding unexpected answers, or of the clash of opinions regarding them. If it has such fears, it tumbles under the slightest attack upon its institutions by would-be dictators. This is what happened in Europe.

"Freedom of worship" is dictatorship so long as there is, at the same time, no *freedom of science,* and, consequently, no free competition in the interpretation of the life process. We must once and for all decide whether "God" is an all-powerful, bearded figure in heaven or the cosmic law of nature governing us. Only when God and natural law are identical, can science and religion be reconciled. There is but one step from the dictatorship of those who represent God on earth to that of those who want to replace him on earth.

Morality is also dictatorship if it results in considering people with a natural feeling for life as on the same level with pornography. Whether it wants to or not, it thus prolongs the existence of smut and brings ruin to natural happiness in love. It is necessary to raise a sharp protest against calling a man immoral who bases his social behavior on inner laws instead of external compulsive forms. People are man and wife not because they have received the sacrament but because they feel themselves man and wife. The inner and not the external law is the yardstick of genuine freedom. Moralistic hypocrisy is the most dangerous enemy of natural morality. Moralistic hypocrisy cannot be fought with another kind of compulsive morality, but only with the knowledge of the natural law of the sexual process. *Natural moral behavior presupposes freedom of the natural sexual process.* Conversely, compulsive morality and pathological sexuality go hand in hand.

The line of compulsion is the line of least resistance. It is easier to demand discipline and to enforce it by authority than it is to bring up children to a joyful initiative in their work and to natural sexual behavior. It is easier to declare oneself an omniscient, God-sent Führer and to decree what millions of people should think and do, than it is to expose oneself to the struggle between the rational and irrational in the clash of opinions. It is easier to insist on legally required performance of respect and love than it is to win friendship through genuinely decent behavior. It is easier to sell one's independence for economic security than it is to lead an independent, responsible existence and to be master of oneself. It is easier to dictate to subordinates what they ought to do than it is to *guide* them while respecting their own individuality. This is why dictatorship is always easier than *true* democracy. This is why the indolent democratic leader envies the dictator, and tries, in his inadequate way, to imitate him. It is easy to represent the commonplace, and difficult to represent the truth.

He who does not have confidence in that which is alive, or has lost it, easily falls prey to the subterranean fear of life which begets dictatorship. *That which is alive is in itself reasonable.* It becomes a caricature when it is not allowed to live. If it is a caricature, life can only create terror. This is why knowledge of that which is alive can alone banish terror.

Whatever the outcome of the bloody struggles of our disjointed world may be for the coming centuries: the science of life is more powerful than all the life-negating forces and tyrannies. It was Galileo and not Nero, Pasteur and not Napoleon, Freud and not Schicklgruber, who laid the basis for modern technic, who fought epidemics, who explored the mind; who, in other words, laid a solid foundation for our existence. The others never did anything but misuse the achievements of the great in order to destroy life. We can take comfort in the fact that the roots of science reach down infinitely deeper than the Fascist turmoil of today.

New York, November 1940. W. R.

THE FUNCTION OF THE ORGASM

CHAPTER I

BIOLOGY AND SEXOLOGY BEFORE FREUD

My present scientific position, as just outlined, had its beginnings in the Vienna seminar for sexology (1919-1922). No preconceived idea determined the development of my views. It should not be assumed that here is an individual with a peculiar personal history, who, isolated from "good society" and as a result of "complexes", is trying to foist his phantasies about life upon other people. The fact is that a life vigorous and rich in experience has enabled me to perceive, to utilize and advocate, details and results of research not available to others.

Before joining the Vienna Psychoanalytic Society in 1920, I had acquired as many-sided a knowledge of sexology and psychology as of natural science and natural philosophy. This sounds immodest. But misplaced modesty is no virtue. Starved by the idleness of four years in the war, and equipped with the gift of learning quickly, thoroughly and systematically, I leapt at everything worth knowing that came my way. I spent little time in cafés and social gatherings.

I became acquainted with psychoanalysis by chance. In January, 1919, a slip of paper travelled clandestinely from bench to bench during a lecture. It urged the necessity for a sexological seminar. I was interested and went to a meeting. There were about eight medical students. It was pointed out that a sexological seminar was a necessity for medical students; that this important subject was being neglected by the university. I attended the course regularly but did not take part in the discussion. The manner in which the subject of sexuality was discussed in the first few sessions struck me as peculiar, unnatural. It aroused an aversion in me. An entry in my diary, of March 1, 1919, runs: "Perhaps my own morality objects to it. However, from my own experience, and from observation of myself and others, I have become convinced that sexuality is the center around which revolves the whole of social life as well as the inner life of the individual."

Whence this opposition on my part? I was not to understand it until about ten years later. Sexuality, in my experience, was something different from the thing they discussed. Those first lectures I attended made sexuality seem bizarre and strange. A natural sexuality did not seem to exist. The unconscious was full of nothing but perverse impulses. For example, psychoanalytic doctrine denied the existence of a primary vaginal eroticism in the small girl and thought of female sexuality as something that developed through a complicated combination of other drives.

It was suggested that we invite an experienced psychoanalyst to give a series of talks on sexuality. He spoke well and interestingly, but I instinctively disliked his way of dealing with sexuality. This in spite of the fact that I was very much interested and was learning many new things. Somehow, the speaker did not seem the right person to be talking on this subject. I could not have explained this feeling.

I obtained some works on sexology, such as Bloch, *"Sexualleben unserer Zeit"*, Forel, *"Die sexuelle Frage"*, Back, *"Sexuelle Verirrungen"*, and Taruffi, *"Hermaphroditismus und Zeugungsunfähigkeit"*. Then I read Jung on libido, and finally, Freud. I read much, quickly and thoroughly, many things two or three times. Freud's "Three Contributions to the Theory of Sex" and his "Introductory Lectures" determined my choice of profession. The sexological literature seemed immediately to fall into two categories, the serious and the "moralistic-salacious". I was enthusiastic about Bloch, Forel and Freud. The latter was a great experience.

I did not at once become an exclusive adherent of Freud. I absorbed his discoveries but gradually and along with the thoughts and discoveries of other great men. Before signing myself over to psychoanalysis, I acquired a general knowledge of natural science and natural philosophy. I was impelled to this by my interest in the basic theme of sexuality. Thus, I studied Moll's *"Handbuch der Sexualwissenschaft"* thoroughly. I wished to know what others said about the instinct. That led me to Semon. His theory of the "mnemic sensations" provided food for thought concerning the problems of memory and instinct. Semon stated that all involuntary acts consist in "engrams", i.e., historical imprints of experiences. The protoplasm, which is forever reproducing itself, continues to receive impressions which, in response to appropriate stimuli, are "ecphorized". This biological theory fitted in well with Freud's concept of the unconscious memories, the "memory traces".

The question, *"What is life?"* lay behind everything I learned. Life seemed to be characterized by a peculiar reasonableness and purposefulness of instinctive involuntary action. Forel's research into the rational organization of the ants directed my attention to the problem of vitalism. Between 1919 and 1921 I became acquainted with Driesch's *"Philosophie des Organischen"* and his *"Ordnungslehre"*. The former I understood, but not the latter. It became clear that the mechanistic concept of life, which dominated our study of medicine at that time, was unsatisfactory. There could be no quarrel with Driesch's contention that, whereas in the living organism the whole could be formed out of a part, one could not make a whole machine out of a screw.

However, his explanation of living functioning by means of the concept of "entelechy" was unconvincing. It gave me the feeling that a gigantic problem was being evaded by way of a word.

Thus I learned, in a quite primitive way, to make a strict distinction between facts and theories about facts. I ruminated a good deal about Driesch's three proofs of the specific difference between the organic and the inorganic. They seemed to be sound, but the metaphysical quality of the life principle did not seem quite right to me. Seventeen years later I was able to solve the contradiction on the basis of an energy-function formula. I always had Driesch's concepts in mind when I thought of vitalism. My vague feeling of the irrational nature of his assumption proved to be true. He later found refuge among the spiritists.

I had better luck with Bergson. I studied his writings very thoroughly, especially his *Essai sur les données immédiates de la conscience*, *L'Evolution créatrice*, and *Matière et Mémoire*. I felt instinctively the validity of his effort to reject a mechanistic materialism as well as a finalism. His explanation of the perception of *time-duration* in mental life and of the unity of the self only confirmed my inner perceptions of the non-mechanistic nature of the organism. All this was quite dark and vague, a feeling rather than a knowledge. My present theory of psychophysical identity and unity originated from thoughts of Bergson, though it became a new *functional psychosomatic theory*.

For some time, I was taken for a "crazy Bergsonian", because I agreed with him in principle, without, however, being able to state exactly where his theory left a gap. His *élan vital* was highly reminiscent of Driesch's "entelechy". There was no denying the principle of a creative power governing life; only it was not satisfactory as long as it was not tangible, as long as it could not be described or practically handled. For, rightly, this was considered the supreme goal of natural science. The vitalists seemed to come closer to an understanding of the life principle than the mechanists who dissected life before trying to understand it. On the other hand, the concept of the organism working like a machine was more appealing to the intellect; one could think in terms of what one had learned from physics.

In my medical studies I was a mechanist and in my thinking rather too systematic. In the preclinical subjects I was most interested in systematic and topographic anatomy. I was thoroughly conversant with brain and nervous system; the complexity of the nerve tracts and the ingenious arrangement of the ganglia were fascinating. At the same time, however, I was fascinated by metaphysics. I liked Lange's *"Geschichte des Materialismus"*, because it clearly showed the indispensability of an idealistic philosophy concerning the life process. Many of my colleagues were annoyed by my "desultoriness" and my "illogicality of thought". This "confused" intellectual state I did not understand myself until seventeen years later, when I succeeded—on an experimental basis—in solving the contradiction between mechanism and vitalism. It is easy to think correctly within *known* fields. It is difficult, at times, when one gropingly approaches the unknown and begins to grasp it, *not* to be frightened into flight by a possible confusion of concepts. Fortunately, I recognized in myself at an early date the gift for plunging into complex experiments of thought and thus to arrive at practical results. The orgonoscope in my laboratory, in which biological energy is made visible, owes its existence to this unpopular trait.

The many-sidedness of my sympathies later led me to the principle that "everyone is right in some way"; it is only a matter of finding out in what way. I studied some books on the history of philosophy, and thus became acquainted with the perennial dispute as to which is primary, mind or body.

These early stages of my scientific development are important because they prepared me for the accurate comprehension of Freud's teachings. In the textbooks of biology I found ample material for a science based on exact proof as well as for idealistic wool-gathering. Later, my own research problems forced me to make a clear-cut distinction between fact and hypothesis. Hertwig's "*Allgemeine Biologie*" and his "*Werden der Organismen*" afforded thorough knowledge, but lacked a general connection between the various branches of biological investigation. At that time I was not able to formulate it in this way, but I felt dissatisfied. What disturbed me particularly in biology was the application of the teleological principle. The cell was supposed to have a membrane *in order to* better protect itself against external stimuli; the male sperm cell was so agile *in order to* better get to the ovum. The male animals were bigger and stronger than the females, or more beautifully colored, *in order to* be more attractive to the females; or they had horns *in order to* beat off their rivals. The workers of the ants were sexless *in order to* be able better to do the work; the swallows built their nest *in order to* protect their young; and "nature" had "arranged" this or that in such and such a fashion *in order to* achieve this or that end. In brief, biology also was dominated by a mixture of vitalistic finalism and causal mechanism. I heard Kammerer's most interesting lectures on the heredity of acquired characteristics. He was influenced by Steinach, who came out at that time with his work on the interstitial tissues of the sex glands. I was much impressed by the effect of the implantation experiments on sex and secondary sex characteristics, and the reduction to its proper limits of the mechanical theory of heredity by Kammerer. He was a convinced advocate of the theory of natural organization of living matter from inorganic matter, and of the existence of a specific biological energy. Of course, I was not really capable of forming a valid opinion about all this, but I liked these scientific views. They brought life into material which at the university was presented in a very dry fashion. Steinach as well as Kammerer were being opposed violently. When I visited Steinach one day, I found him tired and worn out. Later I was to understand better how one is maltreated if one does good scientific work. Kammerer later committed suicide.

The "in-order-to" of biology I also found in various religious philosophies. Reading Grimm's "Buddha" I was deeply impressed by the inner logic of this teaching which rejected even joy because it was a source of suffering. The teaching of the migration of souls struck me as ridiculous, but, why did millions of people continue to adhere to it? It could not be for fear of death alone. Rudolf Steiner I never read, but I knew many theosophists and anthroposophists. They were all more or less peculiar, but on the whole more human than the dry materialists. They too must have been right in some way.

During the summer semester of 1919, I read a paper on the concept of libido from Forel to Jung in the sexological seminar. In reading up on the subject, I found that the differences in concepts of sexuality with Forel, Moll, Bloch, Freud and Jung were striking. Except for Freud, they all believed that sexuality was something that, at the time of puberty, descended on the human out of a clear sky. "Sexuality awakens", so they said. Where it had been before, nobody seemed to know. Sexuality and procreation were taken for one and the same thing. What a mountain of psychological and sociological misconception lay behind this *one* mistaken concept! True, Moll spoke of an instinct of "tumescence" and "detumescence", but one did not quite know what was their basis or their function. I failed to recognize then that sexual tension and sexual relaxation were being ascribed to separate instincts. In sexology and psychiatric psychology of that time, there were as many instincts as there were human actions, or nearly as many. There was a hunger instinct, a propagation instinct, an instinct to exhibit, an instinct for power, an instinct for prestige, a nursing instinct, a maternal instinct, an instinct for higher human development, a cultural and a herd instinct; there was, of course, also a social instinct, an egoistic and an altruistic instinct, a special instinct for algolagnia (instinct to suffer pain), one for masochism, sadism, transvestitism, etc., etc. In brief, it seemed all very simple. And yet, terribly complicated; one did not know one's way out. The worst of all was the "moral instinct". Today few people know that morality used to be considered a phylogenetically, even supernaturally determined kind of instinct. But this statement was made entirely in earnest and with great dignity. One was then terribly ethical, anyhow. Sexual perversions were considered something purely diabolical, and were called moral "degeneration". So were mental diseases. Whoever suffered from a depression or a neurasthenia, had a "hereditary taint", in other words, was "bad". The insane and the criminals were believed to be gravely malformed, *biologically* unfit beings, for whom there was no help and no excuse. The man of genius was something like a criminal who had not turned out right, at best a caprice of nature—and not, indeed, a human being who had withdrawn himself from the cultural pseudo-life of his fellows and had maintained his contact with nature. One has only to read Wulffen's book on criminality or the psychiatric texts of Pilcz or any of his contemporaries to ask whether one is dealing with science or with moral theology. Nothing was known then about mental and sexual disorders; their existence aroused moral indignation, and the gaps in science were filled in with sentimental morality. According to the science of that time, everything was hereditary and *biologically* determined, and that was that. The fact that such a hopeless and intellectually cowardly attitude, fourteen years later, was able to take hold of a whole German nation, in spite of all the scientific work in between, is to be ascribed to the indifference of the scientific pioneers in matters related to social living. I rejected intuitively such metaphysics and moral philosophy. I honestly searched for facts to substantiate these teachings, and failed to find them. In the biological works of a Mendel, who had studied the laws of heredity, I found, on the contrary, much more substantiation for the variability of the process of inheritance than for its alleged wooden uniformity. The fact that ninety-nine percent of the theory of heredity is nothing but an alibi, did not even dawn on me then. On the other hand, I liked the mutation theory of de Vries, the experiments of Steinach and Kammerer, and the *Periodenlehre* of Fliess and Swoboda. Darwin's theory of natural selection, also, corresponded to the reasonable expectation that, although life is governed by certain fundamental laws, there is, nevertheless, ample room for the influence of environmental factors. In this theory, nothing was considered eternally immutable, nothing was explained on the basis of invisible hereditary factors; everything was *capable of development.*

I was at that time far from establishing any connection between the sexual instinct and these biological theories. I was not given to speculation. The sexual instinct was regarded by science as a thing *sui generis.*

One has to know the atmosphere prevalent in sexology and psychiatry before Freud in order to understand my enthusiasm and relief when I met him. Freud had built an avenue of approach to the clinical understanding of sexuality. Adult sexuality was seen as originating from stages of infantile sexual development. This finding alone made clear one fact: *Sexuality and procreation are not the same thing.* It followed that the words "sexual" and "genital" could not be used synonymously, and that sexuality was much more inclusive than genitality; if that were not so, perversions, such as coprophagia, fetishism or sadism could not be termed sexual. Freud exposed contradictions in thinking and introduced order and logic.

To the writers before Freud, "*libido*" meant simply the *conscious desire for sexual activity.* "Libido" was a term taken from the psychology of consciousness. One really did not know what it was or what it was supposed to be. Freud stated: The instinct itself we cannot apprehend directly. We experience only *derivatives* of the instinct: *sexual ideas and affects.* The instinct itself is deeply rooted in the biological basis of the organism; it makes itself felt as the urge for release of tension, but not as the instinct itself. This was a profound thought, one which the friends as well as the enemies of psychoanalysis failed to understand, and yet, it was a natural-scientific foundation on which one could safely build.

My interpretation of Freud's statement was as follows: It is altogether logical that the instinct itself cannot be conscious, because it is what governs us. We are its object. Take electricity: we do not know what it is; we only recognize its manifestations, such as light and shock. Though we are able to measure the electric current, it is nothing but a manifestation of what we call electricity and do not really know. As electricity becomes measurable through the manifestations of its energy, so are instincts recognizable only through their emotional manifestations. Freud's "libido", I concluded, is *not* the same thing as the "libido" of the pre-Freudian era. The latter considered libido to be the conscious sexual desire; Freud's "libido" could be nothing else but the energy of the sexual instinct. It might even be possible one day to measure it. The analogy with electricity I used quite unconsciously, without suspecting that sixteen years later I should be fortunate enough to be able to demonstrate the identity of sexual and bio-electric energy. Freud's consistent use of energy concepts derived from natural science fascinated me. His thinking was realistic and clear-cut.

The students of the sexological seminar acclaimed my interpretation. All they had heard of Freud was that he was supposed to interpret symbols, dreams, and such peculiar things. I had succeeded in establishing a connection between Freud's teachings and established theories of sex. Elected leader of the seminar in the fall of 1919, I learned how to bring order into scientific work. Groups were formed for the study of the various branches of sexology: endocrinology, biology, physiology and psychology of sex, and, chiefly, psychoanalysis. Sexual sociology we studied at first chiefly from the books of Müller-Lyer. A medical student gave lectures on social hygiene as taught by Tandler, another taught us embryology. Of the original thirty participants only eight or so were left, but these did serious work. We moved to the basement of the Klinik Hayek. Hayek, in a peculiar tone of voice, asked whether we intended to do "practical sexology" also. I reassured him. The attitude of university professors toward sexuality we were thoroughly familiar with: it no longer disturbed us. We did feel that the omission of sexology from the curriculum was a severe handicap, and we tried to supply this lack as best we could. I learned much in giving a course on the anatomy and physiology of the sex organs. I had drawn from various textbooks. In these, the sexual organs were described merely as being in the service of procreation. This did not even seem striking. The relation to the autonomic nervous system was lacking, that to the sexual hormones inexact and unsatisfactory. In the interstitial tissue of the testicle and the ovary, so we learned, "substances" were produced which determined the secondary sex characteristics and brought about sexual maturity in puberty. These "substances" were also considered to be the cause of sexual excitation. The scientists were unaware of the contradiction which lay in the fact that individuals who are castrated *before* puberty show a diminished sexuality, whereas those castrated *after* puberty do not lose their sexual excitability and are capable of copulation. They did not ask themselves why it was that eunuchs developed a strong sadism. It was only many years later—when I began to see the mechanisms of sexual energy—that I understood these phenomena. After puberty, sexuality is fully developed, and castration takes little effect. *The sexual energy is at work in the whole body and not just in the interstitial tissues of the gonads.* The sadism observed in eunuchs is nothing but the sexual energy which, deprived of its normal genital function, now manifests itself in the body musculature. The concept of sexuality held by sex physiology at that time was limited to a description of individual sexual organs, such as the interstitial tissues, or the description of secondary sex characteristics. For this reason, Freud's explanation of the sexual function was quite a relief. In his "Three Contributions to the Theory of Sex", he himself still assumed the existence of "chemical substances" which were supposed to be the cause of sexual excitation. Nevertheless, he was interested in the phenomena of sexual *excitation,* he spoke of an "organ libido" and ascribed to every cell that peculiar something that influences our lives so much. Later on, I was able to prove the correctness of these intuitive thoughts by way of experiment.

Gradually, psychoanalysis came to assume more importance than all other lines of thought. I started my first analysis with a young man whose chief symptom was that of having to walk fast; he was unable to walk slowly. The symbolism which he presented in his dreams did not strike me as peculiar; it often surprised me by its inherent logic. To most people, the Freudian interpretation of symbols seemed queer. The analysis proceeded well; only too well, as is always the case with beginners, who fail to sense the unfathomable depths and tend to overlook the many-sidedness of the problems. I felt very proud when I succeeded in uncovering the meaning of the compulsion. As a little boy, the patient had once committed a theft in a store and had run away, in fear of being chased. This fact had been repressed, and made its reappearance in the compulsion of "having to walk fast". In this connection, his infantile fear of being caught masturbating could easily be demonstrated. There was even an improvement in his condition.

In my technique, I strictly adhered to the rules laid down in Freud's works. Analysis proceeded thus: The patient lay on the couch, the analyst sitting behind him. The patient was not supposed to look around; his doing so was considered a "resistance". He was asked to do "free association"; he was not to suppress anything that entered his mind. He was to say everything, but *not to do* anything. The main task was that of weaning him away from "acting out" toward "remembering". Dreams were taken apart, and one dream element after the other was interpreted; to each dream element the patient had to give his associations. This procedure was based on a logical concept. The neurotic symptom is the expression of a repressed drive which has succeeded in breaking through the repression in a disguised form. Provided the procedure was correct, the symptom would be shown to contain the unconscious sexual wish as well as the moral defense against it. For example, a hysterical girl's fear of being attacked by a man with a knife is the wish for coitus which has become inhibited by morals and has become unconscious through repression. The symptom owes its existence to the unconsciousness of a forbidden impulse, such as to masturbate, or to have intercourse. The man who chases her represents her conscience-anxiety which prevents a direct expression of the instinct. The drive then seeks disguised modes of expression, such as stealing or the fear of attack. According to the theory, cure takes place because the drive is made conscious and thus subject to rejection by the mature ego. Since the unconscious quality of a desire is the reason for the symptom, making it conscious, so it was said, *must* of necessity cure it. Until Freud himself later questioned this formulation, cure was considered to be dependent upon the *becoming conscious* of repressed instinctual desires, and their *rejection or sublimation.*

This I would like to stress. When I began to develop my genital theory of therapy, it was either ascribed to Freud or else completely rejected. In order to understand my later differences with Freud, one must look for the divergencies which were already appearing in these early stages of my work. Even in those early days of my psychoanalytic work I was able to bring about the improvement or cure of symptoms. This was done by way of making repressed impulses conscious. In 1920, there was no thought of "character" or "character neurosis". On the contrary: *The individual neurotic symptom was explicitly thought of as a foreign body in an otherwise healthy psychic organism.* This is a decisive point. Part of the personality, it was said, had not taken part in the development to maturity, and had remained on an early infantile stage of sexual development. There was a fixation. This part of the personality then came into conflict with the rest of the ego, which kept it in repression. My later characterology, on the contrary, contended that *there are no neurotic symptoms without a disturbance of the total character.* Neurotic symptoms are, as it were, nothing but peaks of a mountain chain representing the neurotic character. I developed this view in full accord with psychoanalytic theory. It necessitated definite changes in technique, and finally led to formulations which were at variance with psychoanalytic theory.

As leader of the sexological seminar I had to procure literature. I visited Kammerer, Steinach, Stekel, Bucura (a professor of biology), Adler, and Freud. Freud's personality made the strongest and most lasting impression. Kammerer was intelligent and amiable, but not particularly interested. Steinach complained about his own difficulties. Stekel tried to please. Adler was disappointing. He scolded at Freud. Really, he, Adler, had achieved it. The Oedipus complex, he said, was nonsense; the castration complex was only a wild phantasy, and furthermore, was contained, in a much better form, in his theory of masculine protest. His finalistic "science" later became a middle-class reform congregation.

Freud was different. To begin with, he was simple and straightforward in his attitude. Each one of the others expressed in his attitude some role; that of the professor, that of the great *Menschenkenner*, or the distinguished scientist. Freud spoke to me like an ordinary human being. He had piercingly intelligent eyes; they did not try to penetrate the listener's eyes in a visionary pose; they simply looked into the world, straight and honest. He asked about our work in the seminar and thought it was very sensible. We were right, he said, and it was a pity that there was no interest in the subject of sexuality, or, if there was any, only a false one. He would be glad to help us out with literature. He knelt in front of his bookshelves and got out some books and pamphlets. They were reprints of "The vicissitudes of instincts", "The Unconscious", "Interpretation of Dreams", "Psychopathology of Everyday Life", etc. His manner of speaking was quick, to the point and lively. The movements of his hands were natural. Everything he did and said was shot through with tints of irony. I had come there in a state of trepidation and left with a feeling of pleasure and friendliness. That was the starting point of fourteen years of intensive work in and for psychoanalysis. At the end, I experienced a bitter disappointment in Freud, a disappointment which, I am happy to say, did not lead to hatred or rejection. On the contrary, today I have a better and higher estimation of Freud's achievement than in those days when I was his worshipful disciple. I am happy to have been his pupil for such a long time without premature criticism, and with a full devotion to his cause.

Unlimited devotion to a cause is the best prerequisite for intellectual independence. In those years of severe struggle for Freud's theory, I saw many characters appear upon the stage and vanish again. Some of them were like comets, seeming to promise much, but performing actually nothing. Others were like moles, working themselves through difficult problems of the unconscious, without ever having the vision of Freud. Others tried to compete with Freud, without grasping the fact that Freud differed from orthodox academic science in that he was maintaining an adherence to the subject of "sexuality". Still others quickly appropriated some piece of psychoanalytic theory and made a profession of it.

But it was in fact not a matter of competing or of inventing a profession. It was a matter of the continuation of a gigantic discovery; it was a matter not only of adding details to what was already known, but it was, primarily, a matter of *giving a foundation to the libido theory through biological experimentation.* It was a matter of taking the responsibility for a piece of important knowledge; knowledge which had to face a world which tried to make everything platitudinous and formalistic. It was necessary to be able to stand alone, and that did not make for friends. Today, many of those who are familiar with this new, biopsychological branch of medicine, understand the fact that the character-analytic theory of structure is the legitimate continuation of the theory of the unconscious. The most important result of a consistent application of the libido concept was the opening of a new avenue of approach to the problem of biogenesis.

The history of science is a long chain of continuation and elaboration, shaping and reshaping, creation and criticism, renewed shaping and reshaping, and new creation. It is a hard, long road, and we are only at the beginning of this history. Including long empty spaces, it stretches over only about 2000 years. It always goes ahead, and, fundamentally, never backwards. The pace of life becomes accelerated, and life becomes more complicated. Honest scientific pioneer work has always been its leader and always will be. Aside from this, everything is *hostile to life*. This places an obligation upon us.

Chapter II

PEER GYNT

The subject of psychoanalysis was great and moving. To the thought of the average man, it came like a slap in the face. You imagine that you can determine your actions by your own free will? Indeed not! Your conscious actions are only a drop on the surface of an ocean of unconscious processes of which you can know nothing, and besides, you would be afraid of knowing them. You pride yourself upon the "individuality of your personality" and the "breadth of your mind"? Naive! Really, you are only the plaything of your instincts, which do with you what *they* want. Of course, this offends your vanity, but—you were just as offended when you had to learn that you had evolved from the monkeys, and that the earth on which you crawled was not the center of the universe, as you once believed. You still believe that the earth is the only star among billions of stars which is inhabited. In brief, you are conditioned by processes which you do not control or even know, which you fear and misinterpret. There is a psychic reality which reaches far beyond your consciousness. Your unconscious is like Kant's "*Ding an sich*": it cannot be itself apprehended, it can only be recognized in its manifestations. Ibsen's Peer Gynt feels this when he says:

"Forward or back, and it's just as far;
Out or in, and it's just as strait!
He is there! And there! And he's round the bend!
No sooner I'm out than I'm back in the ring.
Name who you are! Let me see you! What are you?"[1]

It is the "great Boyg". I read Peer Gynt again and again, as well as many interpretations of it.

The emotional rejection of Freud's theory of the unconscious could not be explained solely on the grounds of a traditional defensiveness against new and great thoughts. Man must exist, materially and psychically; exist in a society which follows a prescribed path. Daily life demands this. Deviation from the known, the usual, the accustomed, may mean chaos and disaster. Man's fear of the uncertain, of the bottomless, of the cosmos, is justified, or at least understandable. He who deviates from the well-trodden path may easily become a Peer Gynt, a dreamer, a lunatic. Peer Gynt seemed to want to divulge a great secret to me, without being quite able to. It is the story of an individual who, insufficiently equipped, gets out of step with the marching column of the human herd. He is not understood. They laugh at him when he is weak; they try to destroy him when he is strong. If he does not understand the infinity of which his thoughts and deeds are part, he automatically goes to pieces.

The world was in a state of transition and uncertainty at the time when I read and understood Peer Gynt, and when I met Freud and grasped his meaning. I felt an outsider, like Peer Gynt. His fate seemed to me the most likely outcome of an attempt to step out of line with official science and traditional thinking. If Freud's theory of the unconscious was correct—which I did not doubt—then one could apprehend the inner, psychic infinity. One became a little worm in the stream of one's own feelings. All this I felt very

[1]From the translation by W. and G. Archer.

vaguely, not at all "scientifically". Scientific theory, seen from the standpoint of life as it is lived, offers something artificial to hold on to in the chaos of empirical phenomena. Thus, it serves as a psychic protection. One is not so much in danger of being submerged in this chaos, if one has neatly subdivided, recorded and described its manifestations and believes one has understood them. By this procedure, one is even able, to some extent, to master the chaos. However, that seemed small consolation. During the past twenty years, the difficulty of seeing one's finite, sharply delimited scientific work in terms of the infinity of life, has been ever with me. In the background of all detailed work was always the feeling of being nothing but a worm in the universe. When one flies in an airplane above a highway at an altitude of a mile, the cars seem to be crawling along.

During the next few years, I studied astronomy, electronics, Planck's quantum theory and Einstein's theory of relativity. Heisenberg and Bohr became living concepts. The similarity between the laws governing the world of the electrons and those governing the planetary systems came to mean more than just scientific theories. Scientific as all this is, one never escapes for a moment the feeling of the magnitude of the universe. The phantasy of being suspended all alone in the universe is more than a phantasy of the maternal womb. The crawling cars as well as the high-sounding treatises on electrons then strike one as very insignificant. I knew that the experience of the insane was fundamentally along those lines. Psychoanalytic theory stated that in the insane, the unconscious breaks through into consciousness. The patient thus loses the barrier against the chaos of his own unconscious as well as the ability to test reality in the world outside himself. In the schizophrenic, the mental breakdown is ushered in by the phantasy, in one form or another, that the world is coming to an end.

I was deeply moved by the earnestness with which Freud

tried to understand the insane. He towered like a mountain above the conceited and conventional opinions on mental disease held by the psychiatrists of the old school. This or the other was "crazy", they said; and that was that. When, as a medical student, I became acquainted with the questionnaire for mental patients, I felt ashamed. I wrote a little play in which I pictured the desperation of a mental patient who cannot master the surging life forces in himself and who looks for help and clarity. Consider the stereotypes of a catatonic patient, such movements as steadily pressing a finger against his forehead, as if in an effort to think; or the deep, searching, far-away look of these patients. And then the psychiatrist asks: "How old are you?" "What is your name?" "How much is 3 x 6?" "What is the difference between a child and a dwarf?" He finds disorientation, splitting of consciousness, and delusions of grandeur, and that's that. The "Steinhof" in Vienna contained about 20,000 such individuals. Each one of them had felt his world tumbling down, and, in order to hold on to something, has created an imaginary world of his own in which he could *exist*. Thus, I could very well understand Freud's concept of the delusion as an attempt to reconstruct the lost ego. However, his views were not altogether satisfactory. It seemed to me that his concept of schizophrenia bogged down in the reduction of the disease to autoerotic regression. He thought that a fixation in the period of primary narcissism during childhood constituted a disposition to schizophrenia. To me this seemed correct, but incomplete. It was not tangible. To me, it seemed that what the self-absorbed infant and the adult schizophrenic had in common was *their manner of experiencing the world.* To the newborn, the outer world with its infinite stimuli can be nothing but a chaos, a chaos of which the sensations from its own body are a part. *Ego and outer world are experienced as a unity.* At first, so I thought, the psychic apparatus distinguishes pleasurable and unpleasurable stimuli. All that is pleasurable belongs to an expanded ego, all that is unpleasurable to the non-ego. As time goes on, this changes. Some parts of the ego-sensations which were localized in the outer world are now recognized as part of the ego. Similarly, parts of the outer world which are pleasurable, such as the maternal nipple, are now recognized as belonging to the outer world. In this way, a unified ego gradually crystallizes from the chaos of internal and external perceptions; it begins to become aware of the boundary between ego and outer world. If now the child experiences a severe shock in this period of orienting himself, the boundaries remain blurred, vague or uncertain.[1] Stimuli from the outer world may then be perceived as inner experiences, or, conversely, inner perceptions may be experienced as coming from the outer world. In the former case we may have melancholic self-reproaches which at one time were experienced as admonitions from the outside. In the latter case the patient may believe himself to be persecuted with electricity by an obscure enemy, whereas in reality he only perceives his own bio-electric currents. However, at that time I knew nothing of the reality of the bodily sensations in mental patients; all I tried to do was to establish a relationship between what is experienced as ego and what is experienced as external world. Nevertheless, it was the nucleus of my later conviction that *the beginning of the loss of reality testing in schizophrenia lies in the patient's misinterpretation of the sensations arising from his own body.* We are all simply a complicated electric machine which has a structure of its own and is in interaction with the energy of the universe. At any rate, I had to assume a harmony of outer world and ego; no other assumption seemed possible. Today I know that mental patients experience this harmony without any boundary between ego and outer world. And that the Bab-

[1]Cf. W. Reich, *Der triebhafte Charakter.*

bits have no idea of this harmony, feeling their beloved egos, sharply circumscribed, to be the center of the universe. The profundity of some mental patients makes them more valuable, from a human point of view, than the Babbits with their nationalistic ideals! The former has at least an inkling of what the universe is like; the latter's ideas of grandeur are all centered around his constipation and his inferior potency.

Such glimmerings made me study Peer Gynt thoroughly. Through him, a great poet expressed his feelings about the world and life. Much later, I realized that Ibsen had simply pictured the misery of the unconventional individual. At first, one is full of phantasies and a feeling of strength. One is exceptional in everyday life, a dreamer and an idler. The others go to school or to work like good boys, and laugh at the dreamer. They are Peer Gynt in the negative. Peer Gynt feels the pulse of life in its strong and undisciplined form. Everyday life is narrow and demands strict discipline. Here is the phantasy of Peer Gynt, there is the practical world. The practical man, for fear of the infinite, isolates himself on a bit of territory and makes certain of security. It is a *modest* problem on which the scientist works all his life; it is a *modest* trade which the cobbler carries on. One does not cogitate about life, one goes to the office, the fields, the factory, the patient, the school. One does one's duty and keeps one's mouth shut. The Peer Gynt in oneself one has long since liquidated. Otherwise, life would be too difficult and too dangerous. Peer Gynts are a danger to peace of mind. There would be too much temptation. True, one dries up, but one has a "critical" though unproductive intelligence, one has ideologies, or Fascist self-assurance. One is a slave and an ordinary worm, but one's own nation is "of a pure race", or "nordic"; the "spirit" is master over the body, and the generals defend "honor".

Peer Gynt is bursting with strength and *joie de vivre*. The others remind one of the baby elephant in Kipling's story "The Elephant's Child". At that time the elephants had as yet no trunks, only a bulgy nose as big as a boot. But there was a baby elephant who was full of insatiable curiosity, and that means he asked ever so many questions. He asked questions about everything that he saw, or heard, or felt, or smelt, or touched, and all his uncles and his aunts spanked him. And *still* he was full of insatiable curiosity. He wanted to know what the Crocodile had for dinner. Finally he went to the river to find out for himself. The Crocodile caught him by his little nose. The little elephant sat back on his haunches and pulled and pulled, and his nose began to stretch, and grew longer and longer. Finally he felt his legs slipping, and he said through his nose, which was now nearly five feet long, "This is too butch for me!". "Some people", said the Snake to him, "do not know what is good for them".

Peer Gynt is certain to get a broken neck from his curiosity. "We told you so". Shoemaker, stick to your last! The world is malicious; otherwise there would be no Peer Gynts. And the world sees to it that he does break his neck. He starts off impetuously, but is dragged back like a dog on a leash who wants to go after a passing bitch. He leaves his mother and the girl he is supposed to marry. He is emotionally bound to both of them and is unable to cut loose. He has a bad conscience, is tempted by the devil. He turns into an animal, grows a tail. He tears himself loose once more, and escapes the danger. He holds on to his ideals. But the world knows nothing but business. Everything else is considered just a curious caprice. He wants to win the world, but it will not let itself be won. It has to be taken by storm. But it is too complicated, too brutal. Ideals are maintained only for the stupid. To take the world by storm requires knowledge, thorough knowledge, and a lot of it. But Peer Gynt is a dreamer, he has not learned anything worth while. He wants to change the world, and he does not realize that he has the world inside himself. He dreams of a great love for *his* woman, his girl, who to him is mother, lover and companion, and bears his children. But Solveig is untouchable as a woman, and his mother reprimands him, even though kindly. To her, he is too much like his crazy father. And the other one, Anitra, is nothing but a common slut! Where is the woman one can really love, the woman of one's dreams? One has to be like Brand to achieve what Peer Gynt wants. But then, Brand does not have enough imagination. Brand has strength, but Peer Gynt feels life itself. Too bad things are broken up this way! He lands among the capitalists. He loses his money in the accepted fashion; the others are practical capitalists, and not dreamers. They know their business; they are not as stupid at it as Peer Gynt. Broken and worn out he returns, in his old age, to the peasant hut, to Solveig, who for him takes the place of his mother. He is cured of his illusion; he has learned what life gives to the one who dares to feel it. That is the fate of most of those who do not keep quiet. The others don't even take a chance of making fools of themselves. They are clever and superior to begin with.

That was Ibsen, and his Peer Gynt. It is a drama that is not going to be out of date until the Peer Gynts are shown to be right *after all*. Until that time, the "upright" and the "well-behaved" will have the last laugh.

I wrote a long and learned paper on "The libido conflict and delusion of Peer Gynt", and in the summer of 1920 I became a guest member of the Vienna Psychoanalytic Society. Soon afterward, the International Congress at The Hague took place. Freud presided. The papers were mostly on clinical subjects, the discussion was good and objective. Freud would, as always, give a summary which was brief and to the point, and then give, in a few sentences, his own opinion. It was a great treat to hear him. He was an excellent speaker, unemotional but clever and often bitingly ironical.

He was finally enjoying the success that followed many lean years. At that time, there were as yet no orthodox psychiatrists in the society. The only active psychiatrist, Tausk, a highly gifted person, had committed suicide shortly before. His article, "*Ueber den Beeinflussungsapparat bei der Schizophrenie*", was highly significant. He showed that the "influencing apparatus" was a projection of the patient's own body, particularly of the genitals. I did not rightly understand this until I discovered that vegetative sensations are based on bio-electric currents. Tausk was right: what the schizophrenic patient experiences as the persecutor is really he himself. I can add now: because he cannot cope with his vegetative currents that are breaking through. He must feel them as alien, to be part of the outer world, and as having malicious purpose. Schizophrenia only shows, in a grotesque degree, a condition which characterizes man of today quite generally; the average human being of today has lost contact with his real nature, with his biological core, and experiences it as hostile and alien. He must of necessity hate anybody who tries to bring him into contact with it.

The psychoanalytic society was like a community of people forced to present a united front against a world of enemies. One had to feel respect for such a science. I was the only young medical man among all the "grown-ups", people ten to twenty years my senior. On October 13, 1920, I read my paper as candidate for membership in the psychoanalytic society. Freud did not like to have papers read from manuscript. He said it made the listener feel like somebody running behind a fast car in which the speaker comfortably rides along. He was right. So I prepared myself thoroughly to speak without the manuscript, but wisely kept the manuscript at hand. I had hardly spoken three sentences when I completely lost the thread. Fortunately, I immediately found the place in the manuscript. It went well. True, I had not complied with Freud's wishes. Such details are important.

Many more people would have something intelligent to say, and much less nonsense would be presented, if the authoritarian fear of speaking without manuscript did not put the brakes on. It should be possible for anybody with good command over his material to speak extemporaneously. But one wants to be particularly impressive, wants to be sure not to make a fool of oneself, one feels every eye fixed upon one—and prefers to look at the manuscript. Later on, I made hundreds of extemporaneous speeches and had a reputation as a speaker. That, I owe to my early resolution never again to take a manuscript with me, but rather to "swim". My paper was very well received, and at the next meeting I was admitted to membership.

Freud knew very well how to keep distance and to make himself respected. But he was not overbearing; on the contrary, very kind. Behind this, however, one felt a certain coldness. Only rarely did he thaw out. He was great when he bitingly took to task some half-baked know-it-all, or when he took a stand against the psychiatrists, who treated him abominably. When he touched upon some burning question of psychoanalytic theory, he was adamant. There were hardly any discussions of psychoanalytic technique, a lack which I felt very keenly in my work with patients. There was neither a training institute nor an organized curriculum. The counsel to be had from older colleagues was meager. "Just go on analyzing patiently," they would say, "It'll come." What would come, and how, one did not quite know. One of the most difficult points was the handling of patients who were severely inhibited or even remained silent. The later psychoanalysts have never experienced this desolate being at sea in matters of technique. When a patient failed to produce associations, if he did not "want to have" dreams, or did not have anything to say about them, one would sit there, helpless, for hours. The technique of *analysis of resistances,* although theoretically formulated, was not practised. One knew, of course, that the inhibitions were resistances against the uncovering of unconscious sexual contents; one also knew that they had to be eliminated; but how? If one told the patient, "You have a resistance", he would look at one uncomprehendingly. If one told him that he "was defending himself against his unconscious", one was not any better off. Trying to convince him that his silence or resistance was senseless, that it really was distrust or fear, was somewhat more intelligent, but no more fruitful. Yet, the older colleagues kept saying: "Just keep on analyzing."

This "Just-go-on-analyzing" was the beginning of my whole concept and technique of character-analysis. But of that I had then, in 1920, no idea. I went to Freud. He had a marvellous capacity for solving complicated situations theoretically. But from a technical point of view, these solutions were unsatisfactory. Analyzing, he said, meant, first of all, to be patient. The unconscious was timeless. One should not be too ambitious therapeutically. On other occasions he advised a more active procedure. I finally came to the conclusion that therapeutic endeavor could be genuine only if and when one had the patience to learn to *understand* the process of cure itself. One still knew all too little about the nature of mental illness. These details may seem unimportant when one is in the process of presenting the "functioning of living matter". On the contrary: they are very important. The question as to the *how* and *whence* of the incrustations and rigidities in human emotional life was the guiding light leading to the investigation of bio-energy.

In one of the later meetings, Freud modified the original therapeutic formula. Originally it said that the symptom *had* to disappear once its unconscious meaning had been brought into consciousness. Now Freud said: "We have to make a correction. The symptom *may,* but it must not of necessity, disappear when its unconscious meaning is uncovered." This modification seemed very important. What were the conditions that led from the "may" to the "must"? If the process of making the unconscious conscious did not of necessity eliminate the symptom, what else was necessary? Nobody knew the answer. Freud's modification of his therapeutic formula did not even make much of an impression. One continued to interpret dreams, slips and associations, without troubling to find out what were the mechanisms of cure. The question, "Why is it we do *not* cure?" did not arise. This fact is easily understood if one remembers the stage psychotherapy was in at that time. The customary neurological therapeutic methods such as bromides or "There is nothing wrong with you, you're just nervous", were such a bore to the patients that it was a relief to them if, for a change, they could just lie on the couch and let their minds wander. More than that, they were told to "tell everything that went through their heads". It was not until many years later that Ferenczi openly stated that nobody ever followed that rule, and that nobody could. Today this is so much of a matter-of-course that we do not even expect it.

Around 1920, the belief was that one could "cure" the average neurosis in about three to six months, at the most. Freud referred several patients to me with the notation, "for psychoanalysis, impotence, three months". I tried hard. On the outside, the suggestion psychotherapists and the psychiatrists inveighed against the "depravity" of psychoanalysis. But we were deeply convinced of its correctness; every case showed how unbelievably right Freud was. And the older colleagues kept on saying, "Just keep on analyzing".

My first articles dealt with clinical and theoretical matters, and not with technique. There could be no doubt that one would have to understand many more things before results could improve. That really inspired one to work hard in the effort to understand. One belonged to an elite of scientific fighters and formed a front against quackery in the therapy of neuroses. These historic details may make vegetotherapists of the present day feel more patient if "orgastic potency" does not come easily and quickly.

Chapter III

GAPS IN THE THEORY OF SEX AND IN PSYCHOLOGY

1. "PLEASURE" AND "INSTINCT"

On the basis of my biological studies, and against the background of Freud's definition of instinct, I tackled a certain difficulty in the theory of the pleasure principle. According to Freud, there existed the peculiar phenomenon that *sexual* tension—in contrast to the general nature of tension—was of a pleasurable nature. According to customary concepts, tension could be *only unpleasurable,* and only release of tension could bring pleasure. My interpretation of this phenomenon was as follows: During sexual preliminaries a tension is created which would be experienced as unpleasurable *if* it were not followed by gratification. However, the anticipation of the pleasure of gratification produces not only tension, but also discharges a *small* quantity of sexual energy. This partial satisfaction, plus the anticipation of the great end-pleasure, outweighs the unpleasure of the initial tension. This interpretation was the beginning of my later functional theory of sexual activity. I came to see in the instinct nothing but the "*motor aspect of pleasure*". Modern psychological science had given up the concept that our perceptions are nothing but passive experiences, and had replaced it by the more correct concept that each perception is based on an *active* attitude of the ego toward the sensation or the stimulus ("Wahrnehmungs*intention*", "Wahrnehmungs*akt*"). This was an important step ahead, for now one could understand how the same stimulus which in one case produces a sensation of pleasure, may, in another case —with a different inner attitude—not be perceived at all. The sexological significance of this is that a gentle stroking at an erogenous zone may result in a pleasurable sensation in one individual, whereas this may be absent in another individual who feels only a touching or rubbing. This was the beginning of the differentiation between full orgastic pleasure and pure tactile sensations, or, fundamentally, the differentiation of *orgastic potency* from *orgastic impotence.* Those who are acquainted with my electro-biological research will realize that the "active attitude of the ego toward perception" is identical with the flowing of the electric charge of the organism toward the periphery.

Thus, pleasure had an active motor and a passive sensory component, both of which are fused into one. The motor component of pleasure is experienced passively at the same time as the sensory component is actively perceived. At that time, scientific thinking was rather complicated, but good. Later I learned to formulate it more simply: A drive is no longer something that exists *here* and seeks pleasure *there,* but *it is motor pleasure itself.*

Here was a gap: How was one to explain the urge for repetition of pleasure that had once been experienced? I remembered Semon's theory of the engrams and made the following formulation: *The sexual drive is nothing but the motor memory of previously experienced pleasure.* The concept of drives became thus *reduced to the concept of pleasure.*

There remained the question as to the *nature* of pleasure. With the false modesty in vogue at that time I pronounced a "semper ignorabimus". Nevertheless, I continued to struggle with the problem of the relationship between the quantitative concept of "drive" and the qualitative concept of "pleasure". According to Freud, the drive was determined by the quantity of excitation, i.e., the *amount* of libido. Yet I had found pleasure to be the nature of drives, and it was a psychic *quality*. And, according to the theories I was then familiar with, quantity and quality were incompatible, were absolutely separated fields. There seemed no way out. Yet, although unaware of it, I had found the beginning of my later functional unification of the quantitative concept of excitation and the qualitative concept of pleasure. Thus, with my clinical-theoretical explanation of drive, I had come right up to the limits of mechanistic thinking which said: opposites are opposites and nothing else; they are incompatible. Later, I had the same experience with such concepts as "science" and "everyday life", or the alleged incompatibility of fact-finding and evaluation.

Today, this review of the past proves to me the fact that correct clinical observation never can lead one astray. Even if philosophy is wrong! Correct observation leads of necessity to functional formulations in terms of energy concepts, unless one reaches some premature conclusion. Why so many good scientists are afraid of functional thinking is in itself a riddle.

I presented these views in the Vienna Psychoanalytic Society in 1921 in a paper entitled *"Zur Triebenergetik"*. I remember that they were not understood. From then on I abstained from theoretical discussions and presented only clinical material.

2. GENITAL SEXUALITY AND NON-GENITAL SEXUALITY

The following diagrams illustrate the identity of drive and pleasure:

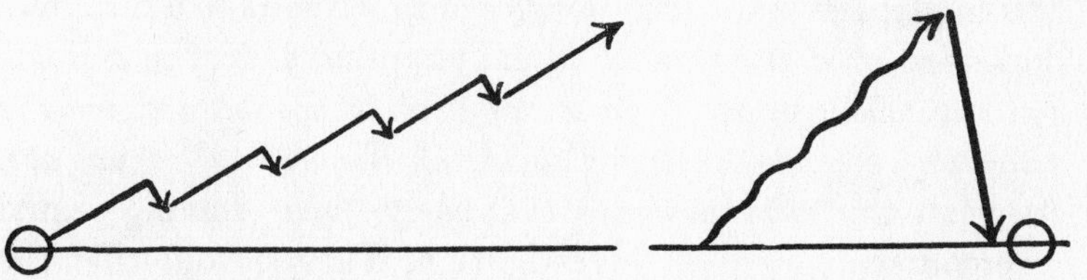

Fig. 1. Forepleasure mechanism. Fig. 2. End-pleasure mechanism.

Fig. 1 shows that in forepleasure, gratification is always less than the tension; more than that, it increases the tension. *Only in end-pleasure* (fig. 2) *does the energy discharge equal the tension.*

This concept kept guiding me in all my sex-economic considerations and publications. Fig. 1 depicts also the *sexual stasis* which results from lack of gratification and which causes all kinds of disturbances of psychic and vegetative equilibrium. In Fig. 2 we see a diagram illustrating orgastic potency, which guarantees energy *equilibrium.*

The theoretical considerations just set forth were guided by definite clinical findings. For instance, I had treated a young waiter who suffered from total incapacity for erection; that is, he never had had an erection in his life. Physical examination was negative. At that time, a strict distinction was made between psychic and physical disease. Where physical findings were present, psychotherapy was automatically ruled out. Of course, from the point of view of our present knowledge that was wrong, but it was correct on the basis of the assumption that *psychic* illnesses have *psychic* causes. There were a great many misconceptions regarding the interrelations of psychic and somatic functioning.

I had treated this patient unsuccessfully from January, 1921 to October, 1923, six hours a week. The absence of any kind of genital phantasy in this patient directed my attention to the diverse masturbatory activities in other patients.

Strikingly, the manner in which many patients masturbated, depended on certain pathological phantasies. *Not in a single patient was the act of masturbation accompanied by the phantasy of experiencing pleasure in the normal sexual act.* At best, the phantasy was that they "were having sexual intercourse". On closer investigation, it turned out that the patients neither visualized nor felt anything concrete in this phantasy. This expression of "having sexual intercourse" was used mechanically; in most cases, it covered the desire to "prove oneself a man", to rest in the arms of a woman (usually of an older woman), or to "penetrate a woman". In brief, it might mean anything, except genital sexual pleasure. That was new to me. I could not have guessed the existence of such a disturbance. Although psychoanalytic literature contained much data on the disturbances of potency, this was nowhere mentioned. From then on I made it a point to investigate thoroughly the phantasies accompanying masturbation as well as the type of the masturbatory act. An infinite variety of peculiarities presented themselves. Such general, meaningless expressions as "I masturbated yesterday" or "I slept with so-and-so" covered the most extraordinary practices.

Soon, two major groups became distinguishable. In the first group, the penis functioned as such in the phantasy. There was ejaculation; but it did not serve the purpose of providing genital pleasure. The penis was a murderous weapon, or it was a means of "proving" potency. The patients achieved ejaculation by pressing the genital against the mattress, the body remaining "as if dead". Or, the penis would be squeezed with a towel, pressed between the legs, or rubbed against the thigh. Only a phantasy of rape would bring about ejaculation. In a great many cases, ejaculation would not be permitted to occur at all or only after one or several interruptions. But, at any rate, in this group the penis became erect and active.

In the second group, however, there was neither behavior nor phantasies that could be called genital. The patients in this group would squeeze their *flaccid* penis; they would stimulate their anus with their fingers; they would try to get their penis into their own mouths; or they would tickle the penis from behind between the thighs. There were phantasies of being beaten, bound or tortured, or of eating feces. Or phantasies of having the genital sucked, in which case it would represent a nipple. In brief, although these phantasies made some use of the genital organ, they were, nevertheless, phantasies having a *non-genital* goal.

These observations showed that the *form* of the act, in the phantasy and the actual manipulation, proved a simple avenue of approach to the unconscious conflicts. They also pointed to the role of genitality in the therapy of the neuroses.

At the same time, I was occupied with the question as to the *limits of the patients' memory* during analysis. The recalling of repressed infantile experiences was considered the chief task of therapy. However, Freud himself had come to consider the possibility of the appearance of infantile ideas—together with a feeling of their having been experienced at one time—as quite limited. One had to be content, he said, with the fact that early memories appear in the form of phantasies, from which the original situation could be "reconstructed". The reconstruction of early infantile situations was rightly considered highly important. If one had not done this painstaking work for years, one could have no conception of the multitude of unconscious attitudes of the infant. In the long run, this was much more important than quick superficial results. None of my present concepts of the biological functions in psychic life could have developed without the background of many years' investigation of unconscious phantasy life. The goal of my work today is the same as it was twenty years ago: *Re-awakening of the earliest infantile experiences.* The *method* of reaching this goal, however, has changed so considerably that it no longer can be called psychoanalysis.

These observations concerning the patients' genital manipulations decisively influenced my clinical outlook and made me perceive new connections in psychic life. However, my work was entirely within the framework of general psychoanalytic experience, even as regards the function of memory. After some three years of clinical work, I found that the memories of my patients were very meager and unsatisfactory. It was as if an essential barrier stood between the patient and his memories. In September, 1922, I gave a talk on the subject in the psychoanalytic society. My colleagues were more interested in my theoretical considerations of *déjà vu,* which I took as a starting point, than in the technical therapeutic questions involved. I really had nothing much to offer in the way of practical suggestions, and it is always easier to raise questions than to answer them.

Founding of the "Vienna Seminar for Psychoanalytic Therapy". In September, 1922, an International Psychoanalytic Congress took place in Berlin. The German analysts under Karl Abraham did their best to make it a success. Some Americans were there. The scars of the war were beginning to heal. The International Psychoanalytical Association was the only organization which had maintained, so far as was possible, international connections during the war. Freud spoke on "The Ego and the Id". After *"Jenseits des Lustprinzips",* which had appeared a short time previously (1921), it was a clinical treat. The basic idea was as follows: Thus far we have been paying attention only to the repressed instincts. They were more easily accessible than the ego; peculiarly enough, because the ego, one should think, is closer to consciousness. Paradoxically, however, it is much less accessible than the repressed sexuality. The only possible explanation lies in the fact that essential parts of the *ego* itself are unconscious, i.e., *repressed.* Not only the prohibited sexual desire, but also the defensive forces of the ego are unconscious. From this, Freud postulated the existence of an "unconscious guilt feeling". He did not equate it as yet with an *unconscious need for punishment;* that remained for Alexander, and, especially, Reik, to do. Freud also discussed a peculiar phenomenon called the "negative therapeutic reaction". Peculiarly enough, a great many patients, instead of reacting to an interpretation with an improvement, unexpectedly reacted by getting worse. There was, concluded Freud, a force in the unconscious ego which opposed the patient's getting well. Not until about eight years later did this force reveal itself to me as a *fear of pleasurable excitation* (pleasure-anxiety) and as an *organic incapacity for pleasure* (*"Lustunfähigkeit"*).

At the same congress, Freud suggested as the subject for a prize essay the question of the mutual relationship of theory and therapy: *In how far does theory further therapy; and, conversely, in how far does an improved technique lead to better theoretical formulations?* As one can see, Freud's mind was occupied at that time with the unfortunate situation of therapy. He was searching earnestly for a solution. In his talk there were already indications of the later theory of the death instinct as a central clinical fact; the all-important theory of the repressed defensive functions of the ego; and the unity of theory and practice.

This formulation of theoretical-technical problems by Freud determined my clinical work of the next five years; it was simple, clear, and in keeping with clinical needs. As early as the next congress, in Salzburg in 1924, three well-known psychoanalysts gave papers which attempted to solve the question for the solution of which Freud had offered a prize. They did not take into account any practical every-day question and lost themselves in metapsychological speculations. The question was *not* solved, and the contestants did not receive a prize. Although exceedingly interested, I had not entered the contest. But I had set in motion several undertakings for the purpose of reaching a definitive solution of this decisive question. *Character-analytic vegetotherapy* of 1940 is *the* answer to the problem stated by Freud in 1922. It took systematic effort over a decade to arrive at a solution. It accomplished much more than I dreamed of then. The fact that it finally cost me my membership in the Psychoanalytic Association was annoying, but the scientific reward was substantial.

On the way back from Berlin to Vienna, I suggested to some younger colleagues, who were not yet members but who were already practising psychoanalysis, the founding of a "technical seminar". Its purpose was to be the improvement of technique through systematic case studies. I also suggested a "seminar of youngsters", i.e., regular meetings of the "youngsters" without the "oldsters", where everybody could vent his theoretical doubts and troubles, and, above all, could learn to speak freely. Both suggestions were carried out. When I officially suggested to the Association the founding of a seminar, Freud gave his enthusiastic approval. Hitschmann, the director of the psychoanalytic dispensary, which had been founded on May 22, 1922, took over the leadership. Not feeling sufficiently experienced, I did not have the ambition to assume this role. A year later, Nunberg took it over, and from 1924 until I moved to Berlin in 1930, it was under my direction. It became the birthplace of systematic psychoanalytic therapy. Later, the Berlin group founded a technical seminar patterned after that in Vienna. From the Vienna seminar came that young generation of analysts who took part in the early development of character-analysis and used parts of it in their practice, without, however, participating in its later development. Toward this later development, they had an indifferent and often a hostile attitude. I shall have to describe the many clinical sources from which the technical seminar, at a later date highly celebrated, derived its strength. In this seminar, those psychological convictions took shape which finally gave access to the sphere of biological functioning.

3. PSYCHIATRIC AND PSYCHOANALYTIC DIFFICULTIES IN THE UNDERSTANDING OF MENTAL DISEASE

In the summer of 1922 I was graduated from the University of Vienna. I had already been doing psychoanalysis for over three years, was a member of the Psychoanalytic Society, and was engaged in several clinical investigations. I soon became especially interested in schizophrenia. Psychiatry then consisted in nothing but describing and classifying patients. There was no therapy. Patients either got well spontaneously, or they were transferred to Steinhof, an institution for chronic cases. In Vienna they did not even use the more modern methods which Bleuler was introducing at Burghölzli.[1] Discipline was severe. Attendants had their hands full, particularly on the "disturbed wards". Wagner-Jauregg, my chief, was just working out his famous malaria therapy for general paresis, for which he later received the Nobel prize. He was good to the patients, a remarkable neurological diagnostician, but he did not know anything about psychology, and made no bones about it. There was something very appealing in his rough peasant candor. The chief of the psychotherapeutic clinic, where patients were treated with bromides and suggestion, claimed "cures" in over 90 per cent of the patients. As I knew that he did not really cure *any* of them, and that his results were of the "Better-everyday-in-every-way" variety, I became inter-

[1] Psychiatrische Universitäts-Klinik, Zürich.

ested in the question as to what the suggestion psychotherapists meant by "cure".

Thus, the problem of a *theory of psychotherapy* introduced itself into the psychoanalytic technical seminar. It fitted in well with my own technical difficulties. A patient used to be considered "cured" when he said he was feeling better, or when the individual symptom of which he had complained, disappeared. The psychoanalytic concept of cure was not defined.

Of the impressions gained at the psychiatric hospital I shall mention only those which had a lasting effect in the direction of sex-economy. At that time I did not know how to organize them; but later they fitted in well with the basic concepts of my psychosomatic theory. I was working in the psychiatric hospital at the time when Bleuler's modern theory of schizophrenia, based on Freud, began to influence psychiatric thought; when Economo published his great work on post-encephalitis; and when Schilder made his brilliant contributions to the knowledge of depersonalization, the posture reflexes, and the psychology of general paresis. At that time, Schilder was collecting material for his work on the body image. He showed that the body has a psychic representation in certain unitary sensations of form, and that this body image corresponds roughly to the actual functions of the organs. He also attempted to establish a correlation between the various ego-ideals and organic disturbances such as aphasias and general paresis. Pötzl had done similar work with brain tumors. Schilder expressed the belief that the Freudian unconscious was indeed perceptible in some vague form, "in the background of consciousness", as it were. The psychoanalysts disagreed. Physicians with a philosophical orientation, like Fröschels, also doubted the existence of completely unconscious ideas. These controversies were meant to do away with the theory of the unconscious. It was necessary to take a stand against them, particularly in the face of the difficult situation that was created by the sex-negating attitude of scientific workers. These divergencies of opinion are important. For sex-economic research later succeeded in demonstrating that *the Freudian "unconscious" is actually tangible in the form of vegetative impulses and bodily sensations.*

My present concept of the antithetical-functional identity of psychic and somatic impulses was at that time foreshadowed in the following manner: A girl was admitted to the hospital with a complete paralysis and muscular atrophy of both arms. Neurological examination gave no clue to the etiology; to do a psychological examination was not customary. I learned from the patient that the paralysis had set in after a shock. Her fiancé had tried to embrace her; she had become frightened and had stretched out her arms "as if paralyzed". After that, she had been unable to move her arms, and gradually atrophy had set in. If I remember correctly, I did not put down this episode in the chart. That would have aroused the ridicule or the anger of the chiefs; Wagner-Jauregg himself missed no opportunity to poke fun at sexual symbolism. This case impressed on me the fact that *a psychic experience may produce a lasting alteration in an organ.* Later, I termed this phenomenon *physiological anchoring* of a psychic experience. It differs from hysterical conversion in that it cannot be influenced psychologically. In my later clinical work, this concept proved applicable in such diseases as gastric ulcer, bronchial asthma, pylorospasm, rheumatism and various skin diseases. Sex-economic cancer research also took its start from this concept of physiological anchoring of libidinous conflicts.

I was much impressed one day by a catatonic patient who suddenly shifted from stupor into excitement. It was one great discharge of rage and aggression. After the seizure had subsided, he was clear and accessible. He assured me that his explosion had been a pleasurable experience, a state of happiness. He did not remember the previous stuporous phase. It is a well-known fact that stuporous catatonics in whom the onset of the disease is sudden, and who are capable of outbursts of rage, have a good chance of recovery; in contrast, slowly developing forms of schizophrenia, like hebephrenia, tend to deteriorate slowly but surely. The textbooks of psychiatry offered no explanation for these phenomena, but later on I began to understand them. For, when I learned to help emotionally blocked and muscularly hypertonic neurotics to have outbursts of anger, a considerable improvement in the general condition always took place. *In stuporous catatonia, the muscular armoring process involves the whole system; the discharge of energy becomes more and more restricted. In the seizure, a strong impulse breaks through the armor from the vegetative center, and thus liberates muscular energy which had been previously bound.* This liberation must in itself be pleasurable. It was very impressive, and could not be explained on the basis of the psychoanalytic theory of catatonia. The *physical* reaction here was so powerful that the explanation of the catatonic's "complete regression to the womb and to autoeroticism" did not seem sufficient. The psychic *content* of the catatonic phantasy *could not be the cause* of the somatic process. It might be that the content was only activated by a peculiar general process and that it then in turn perpetuated the condition.

There was a serious contradiction in psychoanalytic theory. Freud postulated for his psychology of the unconscious a physiological foundation which still had to be established. His theory of the instincts was a beginning. One also looked for connections with established medical pathology. More and more there became perceptible a tendency in the psychoanalytic literature which, about ten years later, I came to criticize as the "psychologizing of the somatic". It culminated in unscientific psychologistic *interpretations* of bodily processes with the aid of the theory of the unconscious. If, e.g., a woman skipped her menstrual period without being pregnant, this was taken as expressing her aversion for husband or child. According to this concept, practically all physical diseases were due to unconscious wishes or fears. Thus, one acquired cancer, "in order to . . ."; one perished from tuberculosis because one unconsciously wished to, etc. Peculiarly enough, psychoanalytic experience provided a multitude of observations which seemed to confirm this view. The observations were undeniable; but critical consideration warned against such conclusions. How could an unconscious wish produce cancer? Little was known about cancer, and even less was known about the real nature of this peculiar though doubtless existing unconscious! Groddeck's *"Buch vom Es"* is full of such examples. It was metaphysics; but even mysticism is "right in some way". It was only mystical as long as one could not correctly state in what way it was right, or where correct things were expressed incorrectly. Certainly, no "wish" in the then current sense could conceivably produce deep organic changes. The "wish" had to be comprehended on a deeper level than it could be by psychoanalytic psychology. Everything pointed to deep-lying biological processes of which the "unconscious wish" could be no more than an expression.

The conflict between the psychoanalytic explanation of psychic disturbances on the one hand, and the neurological and physiological on the other hand, was equally violent. "Psychogenic" and "somatogenic" stood as absolute antitheses. This was the labyrinth in which the young psychoanalyst, working with psychotics, had to find his way. One way of evading the difficulty was the assumption of a "multiple" causation of psychic illness.

In the same sphere of problems were post-encephalitis and epilepsy. In 1918 Vienna was afflicted by a serious epidemic of the grippe. Many of those who came through the acute disease gradually developed a syndrome characterized by a general paralysis of vital activity. Motions became slow, the face stiff and mask-like, the speech deteriorated; every impulse seemed to be held as if by a brake. At the same time, inner psychic activity seemed to be intact. The disease was called post-encephalitis lethargica, and was incurable. Our wards were full of it. The patients were a depressing sight. In my helplessness I hit upon the idea of muscular exercises, hoping to overcome the marked extrapyramidal rigidity. Though the spinal cord was assumed to be damaged, as well as the vegetative centers in the brain, and Economo even assumed a participation of the "sleep center", Wagner-Jauregg thought my plan was sensible. I acquired various apparatuses and had the patients exercise on them according to their individual condition. Watching them, I was struck by the specific facial expression in each individual patient. One patient, e.g., would show the exaggerated features of the "criminal" *facies*. His behavior with the apparatus corresponded with that impression. A high school teacher would show a strict "teacher's face"; in the performance of the exercises he was somehow "professorial". Noticeably, adolescents tended to show hypermotility. In general, the disease took a more elated form in puberty, and at an advanced age more lethargic forms. I did not publish anything on the subject, but these impressions lasted. At that time, disturbances of vegetative functioning were viewed entirely in terms of the pattern of those occurring in the voluntary nervous system. Certain nerve centers were assumed to be affected; impulses were assumed to be disturbed or newly created; mechanical lesions of the nerves were considered to be the cause of the disturbance. Nobody thought of the possibility of a *generalized* disturbance of vegetative functioning. As far as I know, the question has remained unsolved. The post-encephalitic disturbance is most likely a disturbance of the function of the total body impulses, in which the nerve pathways play only a mediating role. The connection between specific character structure and the individual kind of vegetative inhibition cannot be doubted. There is no question that the disease originates from an infection. "*Total body impulse*" and "*general inhibition of vegetative functioning*", then, were the two lasting impressions which were to exert a decisive influence on my later work. Nothing was known about the nature of vegetative impulses.

My absolute conviction of the correctness of Freud's statements concerning the sexual etiology of neuroses and psychoses was confirmed by the obviousness of the sexual disturbance in schizophrenia and related disturbances. What had to be laboriously unravelled by interpretation in a compulsion neurotic was plainly expressed by the psychotic patient. All the more peculiar was the attitude of the psychiatrists, who took no cognizance of this and outdid each other in deriding Freud. There is no case of schizophrenia that would not unmistakably present sexual conflicts after the establishment of a merely superficial contact. The content may vary considerably, but the undiluted sexual element is always in the foreground. Official psychiatry only classifies, and the contents of conflicts are only a disturbing complication. What it finds important is whether a patient is disoriented only in space or also in time. What it is that brought about one or the other kind of disorientation is a matter of indifference. What happens is that *the consciousness of the psychotic patient is overrun with all those sexual ideas which under ordinary circumstances are carefully kept secret and unconscious or only become very vaguely conscious.* Ideas of sexual intercourse, even with father or mother, all kinds of perverse behavior, like having feces smeared over the genitals, phantasies of sucking, etc., flood consciousness. No wonder that the patient reacts to these experiences with an inner disorientation; the strange inner situation produces intense anxiety.

If an individual has admitted his repressed sexuality to consciousness, at the same time retaining his defenses against it, he must begin to experience the outer world as strange. After all, the world does put such a specimen outside its pale, considering him an outcast. To the psychotic individual, the world of sexual feelings becomes so immediately close that he must depart from the usual thinking and living. He is likely to see straight through the sexual hypocrisy of his environment. He will ascribe to the physician or relative the very thing he immediately experiences. He experiences realities, *not phantasies* concerning realities. People *are* "polymorphously perverse", and so are their morals and institutions. They have erected powerful dams against this flood of dirt and the antisocial: internally, their moralistic attitudes and inhibitions; and externally, the vice squad and public opinion. In order to exist, man must deny himself, must adopt artificial attitudes and forms of living of his own creation. The very thing that is really alien to him and a constant burden, he now considers as innate, as the "eternal moral essence of the human being", as the "truly human" as contrasted with the "animal". This contradiction explains many psychotic phantasies about the reversal of the actual situation; psychotic patients want to lock up nurses and doctors as being the real patients, considering themselves right and the others wrong. This idea is not as far from the truth as one might think. Great and sensible people have thought and written about it, as, e.g., Ibsen in his "Peer Gynt". Everyone is right in some way. The psychotics, also, must be right in some definite way. But how? Certainly not in the way they say. But if one is able to establish contact with psychotics, they show themselves capable of conversing very seriously and sensibly on the many peculiarities of life.

At this point, the careful reader will be aware of a misgiving. He will ask whether the bizarre, perverse sexual manifestations of the psychotic really represent a breaking through of the "natural". Are coprophagia, homosexual phantasies, sadism, etc., natural manifestations of life? This objection is well justified. What breaks through to the surface in the schizophrenic are *perverse* tendencies. But in the background of the schizophrenic world are other things which are only obscured by the perverse. The schizophrenic patient experiences his body sensations, his vegetative currents, in the form of ideas and concepts which are partly borrowed from the environment, partly acquired in the *defense* against his *natural* sexuality. The average "normal", also, thinks of sexuality in terms of unnatural, perverse concepts, as evidenced by such expressions as "screwing", "laying a woman", "making a man", "doing a little business after dinner", "I'll show you some tricks", etc., etc. Together with his natural sexual sensations, the human has also lost the corresponding words and concepts. If what breaks through in the schizophrenic were nothing but perversions, he would not have cosmic phantasies of the world coming to an end, but only of perversions. *What characterizes schizophrenia is the experience of the vital element, the vegetative, in the body;* only, the organism is not prepared for it, and so the experience is confusing and takes place in the form of the everyday ideology of perverse sexuality. The neurotic and the perverse are to the schizophrenic, as far as their feeling of life is concerned, as the miserly shopkeeper is to the big-scale safe-cracker.

Thus, to the impressions gained from post-encephalitis lethargica were added those from schizophrenia. The concepts of a (gradual or rapid) "*vegetative desiccation*" (*Verödung*) and of a "*splitting up of unitary, organized vegetative functioning*" came to be essential points of departure for my later investigations. Schizophrenic "scattering" and helplessness, confusion and disorientation, catatonic blocking and hebephrenic deterioration, all appeared as nothing but different manifestations of one and the same process, i.e., *progressive splitting up of the normally unitary function of the vital apparatus*. It was not until twelve years later that this unitary quality of the vital function became clinically tangible in the form of the orgasm reflex.

If one begins to question the absolute reasonableness of this respectable world, the access to the nature of the psychotic becomes easier. I observed a young girl who had spent years in a hospital bed, doing nothing except making certain pelvic movements and rubbing her genital parts with her fingers. She was completely shut in. Sometimes she would smile quietly. Only occasionally could one establish contact with her. She did not reply to any questions, but occasionally her face would manage an expression that one could understand. When one *really knows* the incredible suffering of infants who are subjected to the prohibition of masturbation, one can understand such an attitude in psychotics. They give up the world and obtain in a world of their own what was once denied them by an irrational world. They do not take revenge, they do not punish, they do no harm. They just go to bed and obtain for themselves the last remnant of pathologically distorted pleasure.

All this was beyond the comprehension of psychiatry. Psychiatry did not dare to comprehend it, or it would have had to reorganize itself radically. Freud had opened an avenue of approach to the problem, but his "interpretations" were laughed at. As I understood psychotics somewhat better, thanks to the theory of infantile sexuality and of the repression of instincts, I became completely a disciple of Freud and began to understand that the sole function of official psychiatry was that of *diverting* attention from a real elucidation of sexuality and its significance. It had to "prove", with *every possible* means, that psychoses are caused by heredity, by disturbances of brain function or the glands of inner secretion. The psychiatrists gloated over the fact that general paresis showed symptoms similar to schizophrenia or melancholia. "You see, that's what comes from immorality", was and still is more or less their attitude. Nobody thought that the disturbed bodily functions might equally well be the *result* of a general disturbance of vegetative functioning.

Concerning the interrelation of psyche and soma there were three basic concepts:

1. Every psychic disturbance or manifestation has a physical cause. This is the formula of *mechanistic materialism.*
2. Every psychic disturbance or manifestation has an exclusively psychic cause. (To the religious way of thinking, this applies also to physical disease.) This is the formula of *metaphysical idealism.* It is identical with the concept that "spirit creates matter" and not the reverse.
3. Psychic and somatic are two parallel processes in mutual interaction: *psychophysical parallelism.*

There was at that time no *unitary* concept of *functional* psychosomatic interrelation. In my clinical work, philosophical questions did not play any role. I had not come to therapy from philosophy, but from therapy to the development of the method which at first I employed unconsciously. This method required clarity about the interrelationships of psyche and soma.

Many different people made similar, correct observations. Yet, in their scientific work, they opposed each other, as, e.g., Adler, with his theory of the nervous character, opposed Freud's theory of the sexual etiology of the neuroses. It is hard to believe, and yet true: "character" and "sexuality" were two opposite, incompatible, poles in psychoanalytic thinking. In the psychoanalytic society, "character" was an unwelcome subject for discussion. Understandably enough, for there were few things about which there was so much loose talk as about "character". But hardly anybody made a clear distinction between *moral evaluation* of character (as "good" or "bad") and scientific *investigation* of character. Characterology and ethics were—and are to this day—practically identical. Even in psychoanalysis, the concept of character was not divorced from such evaluation; to be an "anal" character was unpleasant; less so, an "oral character", although that meant being considered an infant.

Freud had shown how certain character traits derive from early infantile drives, and Abraham contributed brilliant investigations of character traits in melancholia and manic-depressives. All the more confusing, then, was this intermingling of moral evaluation and factual description. True, it was said that science had to proceed "objectively" and without making "judgments"; nevertheless, practically every sentence on character attitudes contained a judgment. Not by any means—which would have been correct—a judgment in the sense of "healthy" or "sick", but in the sense of "good" or "bad". There was the view that there were certain "bad characters" which were unsuitable for psychoanalytic therapy. Psychoanalytic therapy was assumed to require a certain definite degree of psychic organization in the patient, and many patients were not worth the trouble. In addition, many patients were considered so "narcissistic" that psychoanalytic therapy could not break through such a barrier. Low mentality also was considered an obstacle to psychoanalytic treatment. Thus, analytic therapy was limited to circumscribed neurotic symptoms in intelligent people with "correctly developed" character and the ability to give free associations.

This feudal concept of an extremely individualistic psychotherapy could not fail to come immediately into conflict with practical demands of medical work when in May, 1922 the Vienna psychoanalytic dispensary was opened. At the Budapest congress in 1918, Freud had pointed out the necessity of free clinics. However, he said, mass treatment would make necessary the mingling of the "copper of suggestive therapy" with the pure gold of psychoanalysis.

In Berlin, a psychoanalytic clinic had been functioning since 1920 under Abraham. In Vienna, the medical chiefs as well as the state health authorities made the greatest difficulties. The psychiatrists opposed the founding of the clinic with all kinds of subterfuges, and the members of the official medical organization feared an encroachment on their earnings. In brief, the general opinion was that the clinic was quite unnecessary. Finally it came about nevertheless, and we moved into some rooms on the cardiac ward. Six months later, we were not allowed to go on. Thus it went back and forth, because the representatives of official medicine did not know what to make of it. It simply did not fit the framework of their thinking. Hitschmann, the chief of the psychoanalytic clinic, described these difficulties in a pamphlet issued on the occasion of the tenth anniversary of the clinic. But to go back to the main subject.

The eight years of work as first assistant and assistant chief of the psychoanalytic clinic provided a multitude of insights into the neuroses of people in poor circumstances. The clinic was always crowded. The patients were industrial laborers, employees, homeworkers, students and farmers. Every psychoanalyst agreed to give one hour a day without compensation. But that was not sufficient. Soon, we had to separate the more suitable cases from the less suitable ones. Thus, we were forced to search for *prognostic criteria.* Analytic therapy was assumed to require a daily hour for at least six months. It became immediately evident: *Psychoanalysis is not a therapy for large-scale application.* The problem of the *prevention* of the neuroses did not exist, and if it had been brought up, one would not have had anything to offer. Soon, the work in the clinic confronted me with the following facts:

Neuroses are widely prevalent, like an epidemic; they are not a fad of pampered women, as was later claimed in the fight against psychoanalysis.

Disturbances of genital function far outnumbered any other forms of disturbance as the reason for seeking help in the clinic.

If one was to make any headway, the *establishment of prognostic criteria* in the treatment of diverse cases was indispensable. Previously, no attention had been paid to this important question.

Equally decisive was a clarification of the question as to why one achieved a cure in one case and not in another. This would give a means of better selection of patients. At the time, no *theory of therapy* had been formulated.

Neither in psychiatry nor in psychoanalysis was it customary to ask patients about their *social conditions.* That there was poverty and need, one knew; but somehow that did not seem to be relevant. In the clinic, however, one was constantly confronted by these factors. Often enough, social help was the first thing necessary. Suddenly, the fundamental *difference between private practice and clinic practice* was evident.

After some two years of clinic work it was clear that *individual psychotherapy has a very limited scope.* Only a small fraction of the psychically sick could receive any treatment. Working with this fraction, one lost hundreds of hours' work because of failure due to unsolved technical problems. There remained a small group which repaid the efforts made. Psychoanalysis has never made a secret of this unfortunate state of affairs in therapy.

There was, in addition, a group of cases which one never saw in private practice, whose psychic disturbance made them incapable of social adjustment. In psychiatry, they used to be diagnosed as "psychopathy", "moral insanity" or "schizoid degeneration". "Poor heredity" was considered the only etiological factor. Their symptoms did not fit any of the customary categories. Compulsive behavior, hysterical twilight states, phantasies of murder, and murderous impulses made an orderly working life impossible for them. But in these poor patients, these symptoms which in the well-to-do appeared to be no more than harmless symptoms without social significance, had a sinister character. Their moral inhibitions were—as a result of their economic misery—reduced to such a minimum that their perverse and criminal impulses came near forcing their way into behavior. (This type of individual is described in some detail in my book, "*Der triebhafte Charakter*", 1925). For three years, I had predominantly cases of this type under my care at the clinic. When sent for psychiatric observation, they were given short shrift. They were put on the disturbed ward until they calmed down. After that they were discharged, or, if they developed a psychosis, they were transferred to a mental hospital. They came almost exclusively from the wage-earning class.

One day a young, pretty woman of the working class came to the clinic with two little boys and an infant. She was unable to talk. She wrote on a piece of paper that a few days previously she had suddenly lost her speech. Analysis was out of the question; so I attempted to eliminate the speech disturbance by suggestion. After a few hypnotic sessions, she began to talk in a low, hoarse and apprehensive voice. For years she had been suffering from the compulsion to kill her children. The father of the children had deserted her, and she and the children were on the verge of starvation. She tried to make a living by sewing at home. Then she began to think of murder. She was about to push her children into the water when she was gripped by terrible anxiety. From then on she was tormented by the impulse to confess to the police, in order to protect the children from herself. This intention also aroused violent anxiety. She was afraid of being *hanged. The mere thought of it constricted her throat.* Being afraid of her own impulse, she protected herself against its realization by way of her mutism. The mutism was really an *extreme spasm of her throat* (vocal cords). It was not difficult to find out what infantile situation was expressed in it. In her early life an orphan, she had been brought up by strangers. They had lived six or more in one room. As a little girl, she was exposed to sexual attacks on the part of adult men. She was tormented by the longing for a protective mother. In her phantasies she was a protected infant at the breast. *Her throat had always been the seat of her choking anxiety and of her longing.* Now she was a mother and saw her children in a situation similar to her own, and felt that they should not go on living. In addition, she had transferred her hatred of her husband to his children. In brief, an unbelievably complicated situation which nobody could understand. She was totally frigid, but in spite of severe genital anxiety she slept with a number of men. I helped her to the extent that she became able to master some of her difficulties. The boys were taken to a good institution. She managed to resume work. We collected money for her. But in reality the misery continued, only somewhat alleviated. The helplessness of such people drives them to unpredictable actions. She would come to my house at night and threaten suicide or murder of her infant unless I did this or the other thing. I looked her up in her home. There I had before me not the lofty problems of the etiology of the neuroses, but the question as to how a human organism could possibly tolerate such a life year in, year out. There was nothing, absolutely nothing, to brighten this life; nothing but misery, loneliness, gossip of the neighbors, worry about her daily bread, and, in addition, criminal chicaneries on the part of landlord and employer. Her working capacity was exploited in the extreme. Ten hours of daily toil brought in about thirty cents. In other words, she and three children were supposed to live on a monthly income of about ten dollars. The remarkable thing was: she did live on it! How she managed I never was able to find out. At the same time, she was not at all physically neglected. She even read books, some of which she asked to borrow from me.

When later on Marxists again and again argued that the sexual etiology of the neuroses was a bourgeois fancy idea, that only "material want" caused neuroses, I was reminded of such cases. As if the sexual want were not a "material" one! It was not the "material want" in the sense of the Marxian theorists that caused the neuroses, but the neuroses of these people robbed them of their ability to do anything sensible about their needs, actually to do something constructive about their situation, to stand the competition on the labor market, to get together with others in similar social circumstances, to keep a cool head to think things out. If anyone should try at this point to interject the argument that such cases are the exception, he can be contradicted by facts, particularly if he is one of those who try to do away with the neuroses by calling them a "disease of bourgeois ladies".

The neuroses of the working population are different only in that they lack the cultural refinement of the others. They are a crude, undisguised rebellion against the psychic massacre to which they are all subjected. The well-to-do citizen carries his neurosis with dignity, or he lives it out in one or another way. In the people of the working population it shows itself as the grotesque tragedy which it really is.

Another patient suffered from so-called *nymphomania.* She was never able to achieve satisfaction. So she slept with all available men, without gratification. Finally she masturbated with a knife handle, or even with the blade, until she bled from the vagina. If a person knows the tortures to which an insatiable, highstrung sexual excitation can drive one, then he will stop talking about such things as the "transcendental quality of phenomenal spirituality". This patient, too, revealed the devastating role played by the poor, care-burdened worker's family with lots of children. In such families, the mothers have no time to bring up their children carefully. When the mother notices the child masturbating, well, she throws a knife at the child. The child associates the knife with the fear of punishment for sexual behavior and the guilt feeling about it, does not dare to satisfy herself, and later on, with unconscious guilt feelings, tries to achieve an orgasm with the same knife.[1]

Cases like these differed fundamentally from the common neuroses and psychoses. These impulsive characters seemed to represent *a transitional stage from neurosis to psychosis.*

---

[1]This case is described in detail in my book, "*Der triebhafte Charakter*".

The ego was still in good order, but it was torn between instinct and morals; torn between the affirmation and denial of instincts and morality. The ego seemed to rage against its own conscience, to try to rid itself of it by exaggerating the impulsive acts. The conscience revealed itself clearly as the result of a brutal upbringing full of inconsistencies. Compulsion neurotics and hysterics were brought up from an early age in a consistently antisexual atmosphere. These patients, on the other hand, had had an early youth with little sexual restriction, often with sexual seduction. But then they had suffered a sudden and brutal punishment which continued as a sexual guilt feeling. The ego defended itself by means of repression against the exaggerated conscience as, in other cases, it defended itself against the sexual wishes.

In these impulsive characters, the stasis of sexual energy was much more pronounced and its effects much more evident than in the neuroses with inhibited drives. I had to struggle most with the *character* of these patients. The difficulties they presented *fluctuated exactly with the degree of sexual tension or gratification.* Every release of sexual tensions through genital satisfaction immediately reduced the breaking through of pathological drives. Those readers who are familiar with sex-economic concepts will notice that these patients showed all the elements which later on went to form my basic theory: the character resistance, the therapeutic role of genital gratification, and the role of sexual stasis in increasing antisocial and perverse sexual impulses. The impressions gained from these patients could be organized only after similar experiences with neuroses with inhibited drives. I wrote a monograph in which I formulated for the first time the necessity of "character-analysis". Freud read the manuscript within three days and wrote me an approving letter. It was possible, he thought, that from now on similar mechanisms would be found operating between ego and superego as had been previously found between ego and id.

The increase of perverse and antisocial impulses through a disturbance of normal sexual function was a new finding. In psychoanalysis, such cases were explained on the basis of "the constitutional intensity of a drive". The anal sexuality of compulsion neurotics was considered to be caused by a "strong erogenous '*Anlage*' of the anal zone". According to Abraham, melancholics had a "strong oral disposition" which predisposed them to depressive moods. The masochistic phantasy of being beaten was assumed to be the result of a "strong skin eroticism"; exhibitionism was thought to be due to an especially strong erogenicity of the eye; sadism was supposed to be caused by an "increased muscle eroticism". These conceptions are decisive for an understanding of the extent of clarification required before I could organize my clinical experiences concerning the role of genitality. What was beyond all explanation was the lack of understanding I met.

The connection between the intensity of antisocial and perverse behavior and disturbed genital function could not be doubted. However, this was at variance with the psychoanalytic conception of isolated "partial impulses". Freud had assumed a development of the sexual instinct from pregenital to genital levels. But this view got lost in mechanistic concepts, somewhat in the following manner: Every erogenous zone is determined by heredity. Every erogenous zone (mouth, anus, eye, skin, etc.) has a corresponding partial impulse: sucking, defecating, looking, being beaten, etc. Ferenczi even believed that genital sexuality resulted from a combination of pregenital qualities. Freud maintained that the little girl has only a clitoris sexuality and *no vaginal* eroticism.

My observations showed again and again that *impotence increased the pregenital impulses and that potency decreased them.* In my attempts to adapt these facts to psychoanalytic theory, I began to think that a full-fledged sexual child-parent fixation was possible *on any of* the levels of infantile sexual development. The boy could very well desire his mother orally only, even at the age of five; the girl's desire for her father could be exclusively anal or oral. The relationship of the infant to the adult of either sex could be very complex. Freud's formula: "I love my father or mother and hate my mother or father" was only a beginning. I began to distinguish *pregenital* from *genital* child-parent relationships. Patients with the former showed far deeper regressions and more serious psychic disturbances than the latter. The genital relationships had to be considered as a normal phase of development, the pregenital ones as pathological. If a boy loved his mother on an anal, i.e., perverse level, the later establishment of a genital relationship with women was much more difficult for him than if he had had a strong genital attachment to his mother. In the latter case, therapy had only to undo the fixation, whereas in the former case the whole character had developed in the direction of the passive and the feminine. Similarly, prospects for a cure were better when a girl had a vaginal or anal attachment to her father than when she had herself assumed the sadistic masculine role. For that reason, hysterics with their genital incest fixation were an easier therapeutic task than compulsion neurotics with their pregenital structure.

The question remained as to *why* it was easier to accomplish the resolution of the genital fixation than of the pregenital. I knew as yet nothing about the fundamental difference between genital and pregenital sexuality. Psychoanalysis did not—and still does not—make such a distinction. Genitality was assumed to be capable of being sublimated just as anality or orality. The gratification of either was considered "gratification". "Cultural suppression" and "rejection" applied in either case.

I shall have to go into greater detail. The contention of the psychoanalysts that they have included the theory of genitality in their theory of the neuroses is erroneous. Precise definition is therefore imperative. It is true that my publications on the subject since 1922 have—to some extent—been absorbed by psychoanalytic thought; without, however, having brought about an understanding of their essential meaning. This differentiation of pregenital from genital pleasure was the point of departure for the independent development of sex-economy. Without it, no sentence of my theory holds water. Its correct investigation leads automatically, step by step, over the path which I had inevitably to take, if I did not want to sacrifice my work.

CHAPTER IV

THE DEVELOPMENT OF THE ORGASM THEORY

1. FIRST EXPERIENCES

In December, 1920, Freud referred a young student to me who was suffering from compulsive rumination, compulsive counting, compulsive anal phantasies, excessive masturbation and severe neurasthenic symptoms, such as headaches and pains in the back, lack of concentration, and nausea. The compulsive rumination immediately turned into compulsive associating. It looked pretty hopeless. After some time, an incest phantasy broke through, and for the first time the patient masturbated *with satisfaction.* With that, all the symptoms disappeared suddenly. In the course of a week they gradually returned. When he masturbated a second time, the symptoms disappeared again, only to return again after a short time. This was repeated for several weeks. Finally it was possible to analyze his guilt feelings about masturbation and to correct some practices and attitudes which interfered with complete gratification. After that, his condition improved visibly. After nine months of treatment, he was discharged, considerably improved, and able to work. He kept in touch with me for over six years; he married and remained well.

At the same time, I treated the waiter mentioned above, who suffered from complete lack of erection. The treatment ran smoothly. In the third year, the unequivocal reconstruction of the "primal scene" was possible. When he was about two years old, his mother had another child, and he was able to watch the delivery from the next room. He received the vivid impression of a big bloody hole between his mother's legs. All that remained in his consciousness of this impression was a feeling of *"emptiness"* in his own genitals. According to psychoanalytic knowledge of that time, I connected the lack of erection merely with the traumatic impression of the "castrated" female genital. That was doubtless correct. But not until a few years ago did I begin to give closer attention to and to understand the genital "feeling of emptiness" in my patients. It corresponds to the *withdrawal of biological energy from the genital.* At that time, I misjudged the general attitude of this patient. He was quiet, placid, "good", doing everything that was asked of him. He never got upset. In the course of three years' treatment, he *never* got angry or critical. That is, according to the concepts of that time, he was a "well integrated", thoroughly "adjusted" character, with only one serious symptom ("monosymptomatic neurosis"). I reported the case in the technical seminar, and earned praise for the correct elucidation of the traumatic primal scene. His symptom, lack of erection, was fully explained—theoretically. As the patient was industrious and "adjusted to reality", none of us was struck by the fact that just his lack of emotionality, his complete imperturbability, was *the* pathological characterological soil on which his erective impotence could persist. My older colleagues considered my analytic work complete and correct. But on leaving the meeting I felt dissatisfied. If everything was as it should be, why did the impotence fail to budge? Obviously, here was a gap that none of us understood. A few months later I discharged the patient, uncured. He took it as stoically as he had taken everything else all this time. The consideration of this patient impressed on me the important character-analytic concept of "*emotional block*" ("*Affektsperre*"). I had thus hit upon the highly important connection between the prevalent rigid character structure of today and genital "deadness".

This was the period when psychoanalytic treatment was beginning to take more and more time. When I started out, an analysis of six months was considered long. In 1923, a year was considered a matter of course. The view even gained ground that two and more years would not be bad, considering the fact that neuroses were very complicated and serious disturbances. Freud had written his famous "History of an infantile neurosis" on the basis of a case analyzed for five years; true, he had obtained from it the knowledge of a whole infantile world. But the psychoanalysts were making a virtue out of necessity. Abraham contended that for an understanding of a chronic depression years were needed; that the "passive technique" was the only correct one. Among themselves, colleagues joked about the temptation to sleep during analytic hours; if a patient did not produce any associations for hours on end, one had to smoke a lot to keep awake. Some analysts even derived high-sounding theories from this: If the patient kept silent, "perfect technique" required equal silence on the part of the analyst, for hours and weeks. I tried myself to follow this "technique". But nothing came of it; patients only developed a profound helplessness, a bad conscience, and thus became stubborn. Jokes, like that of the analyst who, in the course of a session, awoke out of a deep sleep and found the couch empty, did not improve matters; nor did profound explanations to the effect that there was no harm in the analyst falling asleep, inasmuch as his unconscious dutifully kept watch over the patient. In short, the situation was depressing and looked hopeless. On the other hand, Freud warned against therapeutic ambitiousness. Years later I understood what he meant. After having discovered the mechanisms of the unconscious,

Freud himself originally had entertained the definite hope of being now on the way to a dependable causal therapy. He was wrong. His disillusionment must have been enormous. His conclusion, that one must, above all, keep investigating, was correct. Premature therapeutic ambitiousness is not conducive to the discovery of new facts. I had no more of an idea than anybody else as to the field into which this necessary research would lead. Neither did I know that it was the psychoanalysts' fear of the social consequences of psychoanalysis that made them arrive at such bizarre attitudes in the question of therapy. It boiled down to the following questions:

1. Is Freud's theory of the etiology of the neurosis complete?
2. Is a scientific theory of technique and theory possible?
3. Is Freud's theory of instinct correct and complete? If not, in what respects?
4. What makes sexual repression necessary, and with it, the neurosis?

These questions contained, in embryo, everything that later came to be called *sex-economy*. If these retrospective questions had been consciously formulated at that time, they would have kept me forever from any further investigation. It is my good fortune not to have had at that time any idea of the consequences of these questions, and thus to have been able to go on quite naively with my clinical work and my work toward the elaboration of the theoretical edifice of psychoanalysis. I did it with the conviction of working for Freud and *his* life work. In connection with my own life work, I do not regret for a moment the suffering which this not very self-confident attitude brought me later on. This attitude was the very prerequisite for my later discoveries.

2. SUPPLEMENTATION OF FREUD'S THEORY OF THE ANXIETY NEUROSIS

As mentioned before, I came to Freud through the field of sexology. It is thus not surprising that his theory of the *actual neuroses* (*Aktualneurosen*) which I later termed *stasis neuroses* (*Stauungsneurosen*) struck me as much more in keeping with natural science than the "interpretation" of the "meaning" of symptoms in the "psychoneuroses". Freud applied the name of actual neuroses to neuroses which resulted from present-day ("*aktuelle*") disturbances of sex life. According to this concept, anxiety neurosis and neurasthenia were disturbances which lacked a "psychic etiology". Instead, they were the *immediate* result of dammed-up sexuality. They were like toxic disturbances. Freud assumed the existence of "*chemical sexual substances*" which, if not correctly "metabolized", caused such symptoms as palpitation, cardiac irregularity, acute anxiety attacks, sweating and other vegetative symptoms. He did not establish a connection between anxiety neurosis and the vegetative system. Anxiety neurosis, so his clinical experience showed, was caused by sexual abstinence or coitus interruptus. It had to be distinguished from neurasthenia, which, in contradistinction, was caused by "sexual abuse", such as excessive masturbation, and which was characterized by pain in the back, headaches, general irritability, disturbances of memory and concentration, etc. That is, Freud classified *according to their etiology* syndromes which official neurology and psychiatry did not understand. For this, he was attacked by the psychiatrist Löwenfeld, who, like hundreds of other psychiatrists, denied completely the sexual etiology of the neuroses. Freud was trying to adapt his concepts to clinical terminology. As he put it, the symptoms of the actual neuroses, in contrast to those of the *psychoneuroses,* especially hysteria and compulsion neurosis, betrayed no psychic content whatsoever. The symptoms of the latter always had a tangible content, *also always of a sexual nature*. Only, the concept of sexuality had to be taken in a broad sense. At the bottom of every psychoneurosis was the incest phantasy and the fear of injury to the genital. They were, indeed, *infantile* and *unconscious* sexual ideas which expressed themselves in the psychoneurotic symptom. Freud made a very sharp distinction between actual neuroses and psychoneuroses. The psychoneuroses, understandably, occupied the center of the clinical interest of the psychoanalyst. According to Freud, the treatment of the actual neuroses consisted in the elimination of the harmful sexual practices, such as sexual abstinence or coitus interruptus in anxiety neurosis, excessive masturbation in neurasthenia. The psychoneuroses, on the other hand, called for psychoanalytic treatment. In spite of this sharp distinction, Freud admitted a connection between the two. He thought it likely that every psychoneurosis centered around an "actual-neurotic core". This illuminating statement, which Freud never followed up, was the starting point of my own investigations of stasis anxiety.

In the actual neurosis in Freud's sense, biological energy is misdirected; it is blocked from access to consciousness and motility. The anxiety ("*Aktualangst*") and the immediate vegetative symptoms are, as it were, malignant growths which are nourished by the undischarged sexual energy. But on the other hand, the peculiar psychic manifestations of hysterias and compulsion neuroses also looked like biologically meaningless malignant growths. Where did *they* derive their energy from? Undoubtedly from the "actual-neurotic core" of the dammed-up sexual energy. This, and nothing else, could be the *source of energy* in the psychoneurosis. No other interpretation would fit Freud's suggestion. However, the majority of psychoanalysts opposed Freud's theory of the actual neuroses. They contended *that actual neuroses did not exist at all;* that these disturbances, also, were "psychically determined"; that even in the so-called "free-floating anxiety" unconscious psychic contents could be demonstrated. The chief exponent of this view was Stekel. He, like others, failed to see the fundamental difference between psychosomatic affect and psychic content of a symptom. In other words, it was quite generally contended that every kind of anxiety and nervous disturbance was of *psychic* origin, and *not of somatic* origin, as Freud had assumed for the actual neuroses. Freud never resolved this contradiction, but he continued to adhere to his distinction between the two groups of neuroses. Notwithstanding the general assertions as to the non-existence of anxiety neurosis, I saw such cases in great numbers in the psychoanalytic clinic.[1] However, the symptoms of the actual neuroses had undeniably a psychic *superstructure. Pure* actual neuroses are rare. The distinction was not as sharp as Freud had assumed. Such specialized questions may seem unimportant to the layman.

---

[1] *Translator's note:* The same situation still exists in this country. A leading American psychoanalyst wrote me some three years ago: "I personally don't believe that there is a word of truth in that notion that so-called actual neuroses have somatic symptoms which have no psychic meaning . . . . I think, as a matter of fact, that a good many analysts are in doubt about this, although with customary over-solicitude about the old man's feelings, don't argue about it very much in the open. . . . One sees intense anxiety so frequently in patients who have no orgastic impotence that I cannot believe in the reality of the whole notion. I think that Freud must have been over-impressed by a couple of early experiences, or possibly by some element in his own personal struggle with masturbation". Similarly, one of the most widely read psychoanalytic writers in America referred in a recent paper to Freud's theory of the actual neuroses as "the now generally discarded theory of anxiety".

From my own experience over some eight years here, I can confirm the fact that one does not see cases of actual neurosis in private psychoanalytic practice, or only extremely rarely. Due to their predominantly somatic—not psychic—symptomatology, anxiety-neurotic patients, as a rule, do not seek the help of the psychiatrist or psychoanalyst. They go to the cardiologist, gynecologist, gastroenterologist or other specialist, according to what their symptoms happen to be. In the psychiatric clinic of a general hospital, however, these patients are seen every day. They are referred there from the medical, surgical, gynecological and other clinics, usually after attempts of treatment without recognition of the real cause have failed. In a pyschiatric clinic, the psychiatrist who is able to recognize an anxiety neurosis soon finds himself with an imposing record of patients who—after many years of futile treatment—improved rapidly and considerably once their condition was diagnosed correctly.

But it will be shown that they contained decisive problems of human health.

There could be no doubt: *The psychoneuroses had an actual-neurotic core and the actual neuroses had a psychoneurotic superstructure.* Was there any sense in making the distinction? Was it not just a matter of a quantitative difference?

While most analysts ascribed everything to the psychic content of the neurotic symptoms, leading psychopathologists, like Jaspers, contended that psychological interpretation of meaning, and thus, psychoanalysis, were not within the realm of natural science at all. The "meaning" of a psychic attitude or action, they said, could be comprehended only in terms of philosophy, and not of natural science. Natural science dealt only with *quantities* and energies, philosophy with psychic *qualities;* and there was no bridge between the quantitative and the qualitative. It was plainly a matter of the question as to whether or not psychoanalysis and its method belonged to natural science. In other words: *Is a scientific psychology in the strict sense of the word at all possible?* Can psychoanalysis claim to be such a psychology? Or is it only one of the many philosophical schools? Freud himself paid no attention to these methodological questions and quietly continued to publish his clinical observations; he disliked philosophical discussions. But I had to fight such arguments on the part of un-understanding antagonists. They tried to classify us as mystics and thus to settle the question. But we knew that—for the first time in the history of psychology—we were engaging in *natural science.* We wanted to be taken seriously. It was only in the hard-fought controversies over these questions that the sharp weapons were forged with which I later was able to defend Freud's cause. If it were true that only experimental psychology in the sense of Wundt was "natural science", because it measured human reactions quantitatively, then, I thought, something was wrong with natural science. For, Wundt and his pupils knew nothing of the human in his living reality. They evaluated him according to the number of seconds he needed to react to the word "dog". They still do. We, on the other hand, evaluated a person according to the manner in which he handled his conflicts in life, and the motives which activated him. To me, there loomed behind this argument the more important question as to whether it might be possible to arrive at a concrete formulation of Freud's concept of "*psychic energy*", or whether it might be possible even to subsume it under the general concept of energy.

Philosophical arguments cannot be countered with facts. The Viennese philosopher and physiologist Allers refused to enter upon the question of the existence of an unconscious psychic life, on the grounds that the assumption of an "unconscious" was "*a priori* erroneous from a philosophical point of view". I hear similar objections today. When I assert that highly sterilized substances produce life, it is argued that the slide was dirty, or that, if there seems to be life, it is "only a matter of Brownian movement". The fact that it is very easy to distinguish dirt on the slide from the bions, and equally easy to distinguish Brownian movement from vegetative movement, is not taken into consideration. In brief, "objective science" is a problem in itself.

In this confusion, I was unexpectedly aided by such everyday clinical observations as the ones provided by the two patients mentioned above. Gradually it became clear that *the intensity of an idea depends upon the quantity of the somatic excitation* with which it is connected. Emotions originate from the instincts, consequently from the *somatic* sphere. Ideas, on the other hand, certainly are a definitely "psychic", "non-somatic" thing. *What, then, is the connection between the "non-somatic" idea and the "somatic" excitation?* For example, the idea of sexual intercourse is vivid and forceful if one is in a state of full sexual excitation. For some other time after sexual gratification, however, it cannot be vividly reproduced; it is dim, colorless and vague. Just here must the secret of the interrelation between the "*physiogenic*" anxiety neurosis and the "psychogenic" psychoneurosis be hidden. The first patient temporarily lost all his psychic compulsion symptoms after he had experienced sexual gratification; with the return of sexual excitation, they recurred and lasted until the next occasion of gratification. The second patient, on the other hand, had meticulously worked through everything in the psychic realm, but in him, sexual excitation remained absent; the unconscious ideas at the root of his erective impotence had not been touched by the treatment.

Things began to take shape. I began to understand that an idea, endowed with a very small amount of energy, was capable of provoking an *increase* of excitation. The excitation thus provoked, in turn made the idea vivid and forceful. If the excitation subsided, the idea would collapse also. If, as is the case in the stasis neurosis, the idea of sexual intercourse does not arise in consciousness, due to moral inhibition, the excitation attaches itself to other ideas which are less subject to censorship. From this, I concluded: the stasis neurosis is a *somatic* disturbance, caused by sexual excitation which is misdirected because it is frustrated. However, *without a psychic inhibition, sexual energy can never become misdirected.* I was surprised that Freud had overlooked this fact. Once an inhibition has created the sexual stasis, this in turn may easily increase the inhibition and reactivate infantile ideas which then take the place of normal ones. That is, infantile experiences which in themselves are in no way pathological, may, due to a present-day inhibition, become endowed with an excess of sexual energy. Once that has happened, they become urgent; being in conflict with adult psychic organization, they have to be kept down by repression. Thus, the chronic psychoneurosis with its infantile sexual content, develops on the basis of a sexual inhibition which is conditioned by present-day circumstances and is apparently "harmless" at the outset. This is the nature of Freud's "regression to infantile mechanisms". All cases that I have treated showed this mechanism. If the neurosis had developed not in childhood, but at a later age, it was shown regularly that some "normal" inhibition or difficulty of the sexual life had created a stasis, and this in turn had reactivated infantile incestuous desires and sexual anxieties.

The next question was: Are the customary antisexual attitude and sexual inhibition which initiate every chronic neurosis "neurotic" or "normal"? Nobody discussed this question. The sexual inhibition, e.g., of a well brought up middle class girl seemed to be considered as entirely a matter-of-course. I thought so myself, or rather, I just did not give any thought to the question. If a young, vivacious girl developed a neurosis in the course of her unsatisfying marriage, with cardiac anxiety, etc., nobody asked to know the reason for the inhibition which kept her from achieving sexual gratification *in spite of all.* As time went on, she would develop a full-fledged hysteria or compulsion neurosis. The first cause of the neurosis was the moral *inhibition,* its driving force the *unsatisfied sexual energy.*

The solution of many problems ramify from this point. There were, however, serious obstacles to the immediate and vigorous undertaking of such solutions. For seven years, I believed that I was working altogether as a Freudian. Nobody had any idea that these questions were the beginning of a dangerous mingling of basically incompatible scientific views.

3. ORGASTIC POTENCY

The case of the waiter who was not cured threw into doubt the correctness of Freud's formula of therapy. The other case revealed unmistakably the actual mechanism of cure. For a long time, I tried to harmonize these antitheses. Freud, in his "History of the Psychoanalytic Movement", relates how he overheard Charcot tell a colleague the story of a young woman suffering from severe symptoms, whose husband was impotent or very clumsy in the sexual act. The colleague apparently not understanding the connection, Charcot suddenly exclaimed with great vivacity: "*Mais, dans des cas pareils, c'est toujours la chose génitale, toujours! toujours! toujours!*" "I know", says Freud, "that for a moment I was almost paralyzed with amazement, and I asked myself, 'But, if he knows that, why does he never say so'?" A year after this experience with Charcot, the Viennese physician Chrobak referred a patient to Freud. She was suffering from severe anxiety attacks and, having been married for eighteen years to an impotent man, was still a virgin. Chrobak commented, "We know only too well what the only prescription for such cases is, but we cannot prescribe it. It is 'Rx. Penis normalis, dosim. Repetatur'." Which means, the hysterical patient's trouble is that she has no genital satisfaction. Thus, Freud's attention was called to the sexual etiology of hysteria, but he avoided the full implication of these statements. They seem banal and sound like folklore. My contention is that every individual who has managed to preserve a bit of naturalness knows that there is only one thing wrong with neurotic patients: the *lack of full and repeated sexual satisfaction.*

Instead of simply investigating and confirming this fact and to take up the fight for its recognition, I was for years entangled in the psychoanalytic theories which *distract* one from this. Most of the theories evolved by the psychoanalysts since the publication of Freud's "The Ego and the Id" have had only *one* function: that of making the world forget the implication of Charcot's statement, "In these cases, it is always a matter of genitality, always, always, always". Such facts as that the genital organs of the human do not function normally, and therefore real satisfaction is impossible for both sexes; that this is the basis of most of the existing psychic misery; that it even leads to relevant conclusions with regard to cancer; all this was too simple to be recognized. Let us see whether I am indulging in monomanic exaggeration.

The following facts were confirmed again and again in my private practice as well as at the psychoanalytic clinic and the psychiatric-neurological hospital:

The severity of any kind of psychic disturbance is in direct relation to the severity of the disturbance of genitality.

The prognosis depends directly on the possibility of establishing the capacity for full genital satisfaction.

Among the hundreds of patients I observed and treated within a few years, there was *not one woman* who did not suffer from a complete absence of vaginal orgasm. Among the men, roughly 60 to 70 per cent showed gross genital disturbances, either in the form of erective impotence or premature ejaculation. This inability to obtain genital gratification —which should be the most natural thing in the world—thus proved a symptom which was never absent in female patients, and rarely absent among the males. To the rest of the men, who were seemingly genitally healthy, but otherwise neurotic, I gave no further thought at first. Such loose clinical thinking was entirely in line with the psychoanalytic concept of that time, that impotence or frigidity was "*only one symptom among many others*".

In November, 1922, I had given a paper before the Psychoanalytic Society on the "Limitations of memory during analysis". It aroused much interest, because all therapists tortured themselves about the fundamental rule (of free association) which patients did not follow, and about the recollections which patients ought to have brought and did not. All too frequently the "primal scene" was an arbitrary reconstruction which carried little conviction. I wish to emphasize here that Freud's formulation regarding the existence of traumatic experiences between the ages of one and four cannot be doubted. All the more important was a study of the shortcomings in the method of reaching them.

In January 1923, I reported the case of an elderly woman with a tic of the diaphragm, whose condition improved after genital masturbation had become possible to her. My report met with approval and general concurrence.

In October 1923, I gave a paper on "Introspection in a case of schizophrenia". This patient had particularly good insight into the mechanism of her delusions of persecution, and confirmed the finding of Tausk concerning the role of the genital influencing apparatus.

After three years' study of the subject, I gave my first comprehensive paper on "Genitality from the point of view of psychoanalytic prognosis and therapy" in November 1923. While I was talking, I became increasingly aware of a chilling of the atmosphere of the meeting. I used to speak well, and thus far had always found my audience attentive. When I finished, there was an icy stillness in the room. After a pause, the discussion began. My assertion that the genital disturbance was an important, and perhaps the most important symptom of the neurosis, was erroneous, they said. Even worse, they said, was my contention that an evaluation of genitality provided prognostic and therapeutic criteria. Two analysts bluntly asserted that they knew any number of female patients with a completely healthy sex life! They seemed to me more excited than their usual scientific reserve would have led one to expect.

In this controversy, I started out by being at a disadvantage. I had had to admit myself that among the male patients there were many with an apparently undisturbed genitality, though the same was not true of the female patients. I was searching for the *source of energy* of the neurosis, for its somatic core. This core could be nothing but dammed-up sexual energy. But I could not imagine what should cause the stasis if potency was present.

Two misleading concepts dominated psychoanalysis at that time. First, a man was called "potent" when he was able to carry out the sexual act. He was considered "very potent" when he was capable of carrying out the sexual act several times during one night. The question as to how many times a night a man "can do it" is a favorite topic of conversation among men in all walks of life. Roheim, a psychoanalyst, even went so far as to state that "with a slight exaggeration, one could say that the woman obtains real gratification only if after the sexual act she suffers from an inflammation (of the genital)".

The second misleading concept was the belief that a partial impulse—such as the impulse to suck the maternal breast—could be dammed up by itself, isolated from other impulses. This concept was used to explain the existence of neurotic symptoms in the presence of "complete potency"; it corresponded to the concept of mutually independent erogenous zones.

In addition, the psychoanalysts denied my assertion that genitally healthy female patients were not to be found. A woman was considered genitally healthy when she was capable of a clitoris orgasm. The sex-economic differentiation of clitoris excitation and vaginal excitaton was unknown. In brief, nobody had any idea of the *natural function of the orgasm.* There remained a doubtful group of genitally healthy men who seemed to invalidate all my assumptions regarding the prognostic and therapeutic role of genitality. For, there was no doubt: *If my assumption was correct* that the disturbance of genitality formed the source of energy of the neurotic symptoms, *then not a single case of neurosis with undisturbed genitality would be found.*

In this case, I had the same experience that I later often

had in making scientific discoveries. A series of clinical observations had led to a general assumption. This assumption had gaps here and there, and was vulnerable to what seemed to be valid objections. And one's opponents rarely miss an opportunity to detect such gaps and to take them as a basis for rejecting the whole. As du Teil once said, "Scientific objectivity is not of this world, and perhaps of none". Objective collaboration on a problem is scarcely to be hoped for. But, unintentionally, my critics often helped me along, just by their objections "on fundamental grounds". So it was at this time. The objection that genitally healthy neurotics existed in great numbers, made me scrutinize "genital health". It is unbelievable yet true that an exact analysis of genital behavior beyond such vague statements as "I have slept with a man, or a woman" was strictly taboo in psychoanalysis of that time.

The more exactly I had my patients describe their behavior and sensations in the sexual act, the firmer became my clinical conviction that all of them, *without exception,* suffered from a *severe* disturbance of genitality. This was especially true of those men who bragged the loudest about their sexual conquests and about how many times a night they "could do it". There was no doubt: they were erectively very potent, but ejaculation was accompanied by little or no pleasure, or even the opposite, by disgust and unpleasant sensations. An exact analysis of the phantasies accompanying the act revealed mostly sadistic or self-satisfied attitudes in the men, anxiety, reserve or masculinity in women. To the so-called potent man, the act had the significance of conquering, piercing or raping the woman. They wanted to give proof of their potency, or to be admired for their erective endurance. This "potency" could easily be destroyed by laying bare its motives. It served to cover up serious disturbances of erection or ejaculation. In *none* of these cases was there as much as a trace of *involuntary behavior* or *loss of alertness* during the act.

Slowly groping ahead, I thus learned, bit by bit, to recognize the signs of *orgastic impotence.* It took another ten years before I understood the disturbance well enough to be able to describe it and to develop a technique for its elimination.

The study of this disturbance remained the central clinical problem of sex-economy and is far from being concluded. It plays a similar role in sex-economy to that played by the Oedipus complex in psychoanalysis. One who does not thoroughly understand it cannot be regarded as a sex-economist. He will not comprehend its implications and consequences. He will not understand the distinction between healthy and sick, nor will he understand the nature of pleasure anxiety; he will understand neither the pathological nature of the child-parent conflict, nor the basis of marital unhappiness. He may become a sex-reformer, but he will never really alter sex misery. He may admire the bion-experiments, may even imitate them, but he will never do sex-economic research upon life-processes. He will never comprehend religious ecstasy and certainly not Fascist irrationalism. He will continue to believe in the antithesis of nature and culture, instinct and morals, sexuality and achievement. He will not be able to solve in any real sense one single question of pedagogy. He will never comprehend the identity of the sexual process and the life process, and, therefore, also the sex-economic theory of cancer. He will consider healthy what is sick, and sick what is healthy. He will, finally, misinterpret the human longing for happiness and overlook the human *fear* of happiness. In brief, he may be anything but a sex-economist, one who knows that man is the only biological species which has destroyed its own natural sex function, and that that is what ails him.

I shall present the orgasm theory in the way in which it

developed, i.e., not systematically. Thus, its inner logic will more readily become evident. It will be seen that no human brain could possibly invent these interconnections.

Up until 1923, the year when the orgasm theory was born, sexology and psychoanalysis knew only of an *ejaculative* and an *erective* potency. But, without the inclusion of the economic, experiential and energy aspects, the concept of sexual potency has no meaning at all. Erective and ejaculative potency are nothing but indispensable prerequisites for *orgastic potency*. Orgastic potency is the *capacity for surrender to the flow of biological energy without any inhibition*, the capacity for *complete discharge of all dammed-up sexual excitation* through *involuntary pleasurable contractions of the body*. Not a single neurotic individual possesses orgastic potency; the correlary of this fact is the fact that the vast majority of humans suffer from a character-neurosis.

The intensity of pleasure in the orgasm (in the sexual act which is free of anxiety and unpleasure, and unaccompanied by phantasies) *depends on the amount of sexual tension concentrated in the genital;* the pleasure is all the more intense the greater in amount and the steeper the "drop" in the excitation.

The following description of the orgastically satisfying sexual act covers only some typical, biologically determined phases and modes of behavior. It does not take into account the preliminaries which present no general regularity. Furthermore, the fact should be borne in mind that the bioelectric processes of orgasm are as yet unexplored; for this reason, this description is of necessity incomplete.

A. Phase of voluntary control of the excitation.

1.* Erection is pleasurable, and not painful as it is in the

*The arabic figures (1-10) in the text correspond to the arabic figures in the legend to the diagram.

case of priapism ("cold erection"), spasm of the pelvic floor or of the spermatic duct. The genital is not over-excited, as it is after prolonged periods of abstinence or in the case of premature ejaculation. The genital of the woman becomes hyperemic and, through ample secretion of the genital glands, moist in a specific way; that is, in the case of undis-

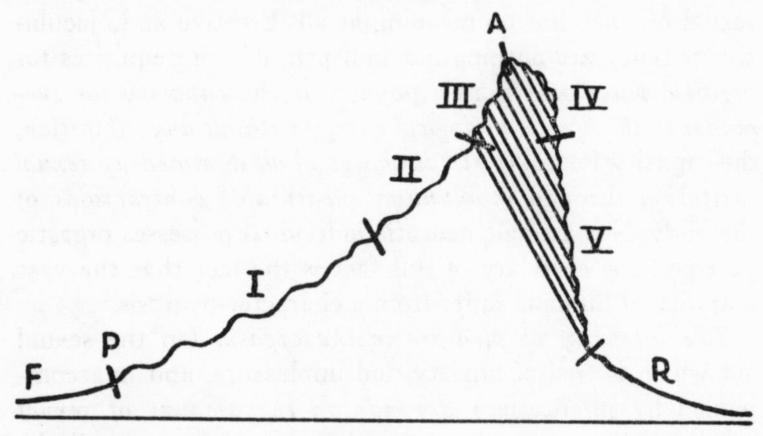

Diagram of the typical phases of the sexual act with orgastic potency, in both sexes.

F = forepleasure (1, 2). P = penetration (3). I (4, 5) = phase of voluntary control of increase in excitation in which voluntary prolongation is as yet harmless. II (6 a-d) = phase of involuntary muscle contractions and automatic increase in excitation. III (7) = sudden and steep ascent to the acme (A). IV (8) = orgasm. The *shaded* part represents the phase of *involuntary body contractions.* V (9, 10) = steep "drop" of the excitation. R = relaxation. Duration, about five to twenty minutes.

turbed genital functioning, the secretion has specific chemical and physical properties which are lacking when the genital function is disturbed. An important criterion of orgastic potency in the male is the *urge* to penetrate. For, there may be erections without this urge, as is the case, e.g., in many erectively potent narcissistic characters, and in satyriasis.

2. The man is spontaneously gentle, that is, without having to cover up opposite tendencies, such as sadistic impulses,

by a forced kind of gentleness. Pathological deviations are: aggressiveness based on sadistic impulses, as in many compulsion neurotics with erective potency; inactivity of the passive-feminine character. In the "onanistic coitus" with an unloved object the gentleness is absent. The activity of the woman normally differs in no way from that of the man. The widely prevalent passivity of the woman is pathological and mostly due to masochistic phantasies of being raped.

3. The pleasurable excitation, which during the preliminaries has maintained about the same level, suddenly increases—both in the man and in the woman—with the penetration of the penis. The man's sensation of "being sucked in" corresponds to the woman's sensation that she is "sucking the penis in".

4. In the man, the urge to penetrate very deeply increases; without, however, taking the sadistic form of wanting to "pierce through" the woman, as is the case in compulsive characters. As a result of *mutual, slow, spontaneous and effortless* frictions the excitation is concentrated on the surface and the glans of the penis, and the posterior parts of the vaginal mucous membrane. The characteristic sensation which precedes ejaculation is still completely absent, in contradistinction to cases of premature ejaculation. The body is as yet less excited than the genital. Consciousness is completely concentrated on the perception of the pleasure sensations; the ego participates in this activity in so far as it attempts to exhaust all possibilities of pleasure and to attain a maximum of tension before orgasm occurs. Needless to say, this is not done by way of conscious intention, but quite spontaneously and differently for each individual, on the basis of previous experience, by a change in position, the manner of friction and rhythm, etc. According to the consensus of potent men and women, the pleasure sensations are all the more intense the slower and more gentle the frictions are, and the better they harmonize with each other.

This presupposes a considerable ability to identify oneself with one's partner. Pathological counterparts are, e.g., the urge to produce violent frictions, as occurring in sadistic compulsive characters with penis anesthesia and inability to have an ejaculation; or the nervous haste of those suffering from premature ejaculation. Orgastically potent individuals never talk or laugh during the sexual act—with the exception of words of tenderness. Both talking and laughing indicate a serious lack of the capacity for surrender, which requires an undivided absorption in the sensations of pleasure. Men to whom surrender means being "feminine" are always orgastically disturbed.

5. In this phase, interruption of friction is in itself pleasurable, due to the particular sensations of pleasure which appear when one is at rest; the interruption can be accomplished without mental effort; it prolongs the sexual act. When one is at rest, the excitation decreases a little, without, however, completely subsiding, as it does in pathological cases. The interruption of the sexual act through retraction of the penis is not unpleasurable, provided it occurs after a period of rest. With continued friction, the excitation keeps increasing above the level previous to the interruption, and begins to spread more and more to *the whole body,* while the excitation of the genital remains more or less at the same level. Finally, as a result of another, usually sudden, increase of genital excitation, there sets in the second phase:

B. Phase of involuntary muscle contractions.

6. In this phase, a *voluntary* control of the course of excitation is *no longer possible.* It shows the following characteristics:

a. The increase in excitation can no longer be controlled voluntarily; rather, it takes hold of the whole personality and produces tachycardia and deep expirations.

b. Bodily excitation becomes more and more concentrated

upon the genital, a "melting" kind of sensation sets in, which may best be described as a radiation of excitation from the genital to other parts of the body.

c. This excitation results first in involuntary contractions of the total musculature of the genital and of the pelvic floor. These contractions occur in waves: the crests of the waves occur with the complete penetration of the penis, the troughs with the retraction of the penis. However, as soon as the retraction goes beyond a certain limit, there occur immediately spasmodic contractions which expedite ejaculation. In the woman, there occurs in this case a contraction of the smooth musculature of the vagina.

d. In this stage, interruption of the sexual act is absolutely unpleasurable, for both man and woman; instead of occurring rhythmically, the muscular contractions which lead to the orgasm as well as to the ejaculation, occur, in the case of interruption, in the form of spasms. This results in intensely unpleasant sensations and occasionally in pain in the pelvic floor and the lower back; in addition, as a result of the spasm, ejaculation occurs earlier than in the case of an undisturbed rhythm.

The voluntary prolongation of the first phase of the sexual act (1 to 5 in the diagram) to a moderate degree is harmless, and rather serves to intensify pleasure. On the other hand, interruption or voluntary modification of the course of excitation in the second phase is harmful, because here the process takes place in reflex form.

7. Through further intensification and an increase in the frequency of the involuntary muscular contractions, the excitation increases rapidly and steeply up to the acme (III to A in the diagram); normally, the acme coincides with the first ejaculatory muscular contraction in the man.

8. Now occurs a more or less intense clouding of consciousness; the frictions become *spontaneously more intensive,* after having subsided momentarily at the point of the

acme; the urge to "penetrate completely" becomes more intense with each ejaculatory muscle contraction. In the woman, the muscle contractions take the same course as in the man; experientially, the difference is only that during and immediately after the acme the healthy woman wants to "receive completely".

9. The orgastic excitation takes hold of the whole body and results in *lively contractions of the whole body musculature.* Self-observations of healthy individuals of both sexes, as well as the analysis of certain disturbances of orgasm, show that what we call the release of tension and experience as a motor discharge (descending portion of the orgasm curve) is predominantly the result of a *flowing back of the excitation from the genital to the body.* This flowing back is experienced as a *sudden decrease* of the tension.

The acme thus represents the point at which the excitation changes its direction: up to the point of the acme, the direction is toward the genital, and at the point of the acme it turns into the opposite direction, i.e., toward the whole body. *The complete flowing back of the excitation toward the whole body is what constitutes gratification.* Gratification means two things: shift of the direction of flow of excitation in the body, and unburdening of the genital apparatus.

10. Before the zero point is reached, the excitation tapers off in a gentle curve and is immediately replaced by a *pleasant bodily and psychic relaxation;* usually, there is a strong desire for sleep. The sensual relations have subsided; what continues is a grateful tender attitude toward the partner.

In contradistinction, the orgastically impotent individual experiences a leaden exhaustion, disgust, repulsion, or indifference, and occasionally, hatred toward the partner. In the case of satyriasis and nymphomania, sexual excitation does not subside. Insomnia is one of the most important indications of lack of gratification; on the other hand, it would be erroneous to assume necessarily the existence of satisfaction if the patient reports that he or she goes to sleep immediately after the sexual act.

Looking back over the two main phases of the sexual act, we see that the first phase (F and I in the diagram) is characterized mainly by the *sensory*, the second phase (II to V) by the *motor* experience of pleasure.

The involuntary contractions of the organism and the complete discharge of the excitation are the most important criteria of orgastic potency. The part of the curve drawn in shaded lines (diagram, p. 80) represents the *involuntary* vegetative release of tension. There are partial releases of tension which are *similar* to an orgasm; they used to be taken for the actual release of tension. Clinical experience shows that man—as a result of the general sexual repression—has lost the capacity for *ultimate vegetatively involuntary surrender*. What I mean by "orgastic potency" is exactly this ultimate, hitherto unrecognized portion of the capacity for excitation and release of tension. Orgastic potency is the biological primal and basic function which man has in common with all living organisms. All feelings about nature derive from this function or from the longing for it.

Normally, that is, in the absence of inhibitions, the course of the sexual process in the woman is in no way different from that in the man. In both sexes, the orgasm is more intense if the peaks of genital excitation coincide. This occurs frequently in individuals who are able to concentrate their tender as well as their sensual feelings on a partner; it is the rule when the relationship is undisturbed by either internal or external factors. In such cases, at least *conscious* phantasies are completely absent; the ego is undividedly absorbed in the perception of pleasure. The *ability to concentrate oneself with one's whole personality on the orgastic experience, in spite of possible conflicts, is a further criterion of orgastic potency.*

Whether *un*conscious phantasies are also absent, is difficult to say. Certain indications make this probable. Phantasies which cannot be permitted to become conscious, can only be disturbing. Among the phantasies which may accompany the sexual act one has to distinguish phantasies which are in harmony with the actual sexual experience from those that contradict it. If the partner is able to draw upon himself all sexual interests at least for the time being, unconscious phantasy activity becomes unnecessary; the latter, by its very nature, stands in opposition to the actual experience because one phantasies only that which one cannot obtain in reality. There is such a thing as a *genuine transference* from an original object to the partner. If the partner corresponds in his essential traits to the object of the phantasy, he can replace the object of the phantasy. The situation is different, however, when the transference of sexual interests takes place *in spite of the fact* that the partner does *not* correspond in his fundamental traits to the object of the phantasy; when it takes place only on the basis of a neurotic searching for the original object, without the inner ability to establish a *genuine* transference; in that case, no illusion can eradicate a vague feeling of insincerity in the relationship. Whereas in the case of genuine transference there is no reaction of disillusionment after the sexual act, it is inevitable here; here, we can assume, unconscious phantasy activity during the act was not absent, but served the purpose of maintaining the illusion. In the former case, the original object—its place having been taken by the partner—lost its interest and, with it, its power of creating phantasies. In the case of genuine transference there is none of the overestimation of the partner; those characteristics which are at variance with the original object are correctly evaluated and well tolerated. Conversely, in the case of false neurotic transference, there is excessive idealization, and illusions predominate; the negative qualities are not perceived and phantasy activity is not allowed to rest, lest the illusion be lost.

The harder the imagination has to work in order to bring about an equivalence of the partner with the ideal, the more does the sexual experience lose in intensity and sex-economic value. Whether and to what extent incompatibilities—which occur in any relationship of some duration—diminish the intensity of the sexual experience, depends entirely on the nature of these incompatibilities. They will be the more likely to lead to a pathological disturbance, the stronger the fixation upon the original object is and the greater the incapacity for a genuine transference, and the greater the effort that has to be made to overcome the aversion toward the partner.

4. SEXUAL STASIS: THE SOURCE OF ENERGY OF THE NEUROSIS

In the psychoanalytic clinic, I had—ever since clinical experience had called my attention to it in 1920—carefully observed and taken notes on the disturbances of genitality. In the course of some two years, I had collected sufficient material to warrant the conclusion: *The disturbance of genitality is not,* as was previously assumed, *one* symptom among others, *but it is* the *symptom of the neurosis.* Gradually, everything began to point in one direction: the neurosis is not merely the result of a *sexual* disturbance in the broader sense of Freud; it is rather, the result of a *genital* disturbance, in the strict sense of *orgastic impotence.*

If I had again restricted sexuality to mean exclusively genital sexuality, I would have reverted to the old, erroneous concept of sexuality before Freud: sexual is only what is genital. Instead of this, in amplifying the concept of genital function by that of orgastic potency, and by defining it in terms of energy, I extended the psychoanalytic theories of sex and of libido further along their proper lines of development. I argued as follows:

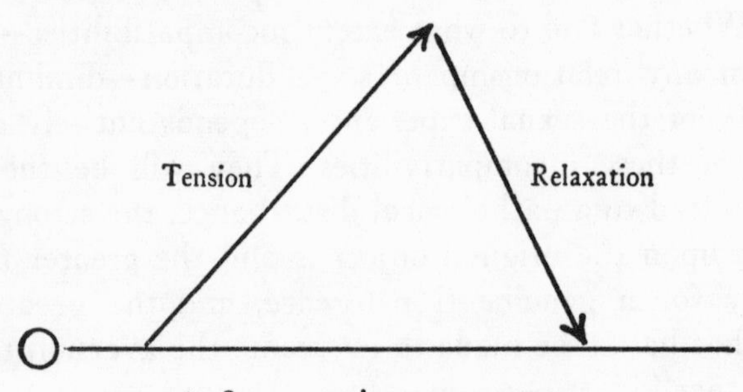

1. Sex-economic energy process.

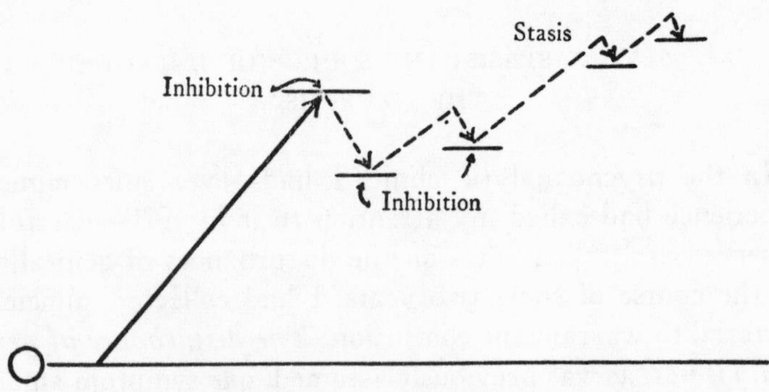

2. Inhibition. Disturbed sex-economy (stasis).

1. If every psychic disturbance has a core of dammed-up sexual energy, then it can be caused only by a disturbance of orgastic satisfaction. *Impotence and frigidity thus are the key to an understanding of the economy of the neuroses.*

2. *The energy source of the neurosis lies in the differential between accumulation and discharge of sexual energy.* The neurotic psychic apparatus is distinguished from the healthy

one by the constant presence of undischarged sexual energy. This is true not only of the stasis neuroses (actual neuroses of Freud) but for all psychic disturbances, with or without symptom formation.

3. Freud's therapeutic formula is correct but incomplete. The first prerequisite of cure is, indeed, to make the repressed sexuality conscious. However, though this alone *may* effect the cure, it *need not* of necessity do so. It does so only if at the same time the *source of energy, the sexual stasis,* is eliminated; in other words, *only if the awareness of instinctual demands goes hand in hand with the capacity for full orgastic gratification.* In that case, the pathological psychic growths are deprived of their energy at the source (*principle of energy-withdrawal*).

4. The supreme goal of a causal analytic therapy, therefore, is the establishment of orgastic potency, of the ability to discharge an amount of sexual energy equal to that accumulated.

5. Sexual excitation is definitely a *somatic* process; neurotic conflicts are of a *psychic* nature. A slight conflict, in itself normal, will produce a *slight* disturbance of the sexual energy equilibrium. This slight stasis will re-enforce the conflict, and this in turn the stasis. In this way, psychic conflict and somatic stasis mutually increase each other. The central psychic conflict is the sexual child-parent relationship. It is present in every neurosis. It is the *historical* experiential *material* that furnishes the *content* of the neurosis. All neurotic phantasies stem from the infantile sexual attachment to the parents. But the child-parent conflict could not produce an enduring disturbance of the psychic equilibrium if it were not continually nourished by the actual stasis which this conflict itself originally produced. Sexual stasis is, therefore, the etiological factor which—constantly present in the immediate situation—affords to the neurosis, not its content,

but its *energy*. The historical pathological incestuous attachment to parents and siblings loses its strength when the energy stasis in the immediate situation is eliminated; in other words, when full orgastic gratification takes place in the immediate present. *The pathogenicity of the Oedipus complex,* therefore, depends on *whether or not there is a physiologically adequate discharge of sexual energy.* Thus, actual neurosis (stasis neurosis) and psychoneurosis are interwoven, and cannot be thought of as independent of each other.

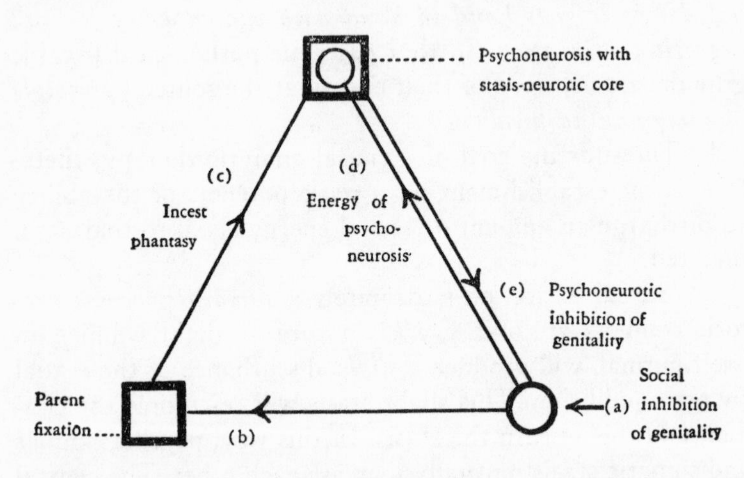

Diagram: Interrelation of infantile psychic content of the neurotic conflict on the one hand and sexual stasis on the other.

a. Social inhibition of genitality, resulting in stasis (○).
b. Stasis results in fixation to parents (historical content, □).
c. Incest phantasy.
d. Energy source of the neurosis.
e. Psychoneurosis maintains stasis (*present-day stasis of energy*).

6. *Pregenital* (oral, anal, muscular, etc.) sexuality differs in its dynamics basically from *genital* sexuality. If nongenital sexual behavior is continued, the genital function becomes disturbed. The resulting sexual stasis, in turn,

activates pregenital phantasies and behavior. These, as found in the neuroses and perversions, are not only the cause of the genital disturbance, but at least as much its result. (This is the beginning of the distinction between *natural* [*primary*] and *secondary* drives which I formulated in 1936.) This finding, *general sexual disturbance is* a result *of genital* disturbance, i.e., simply, of orgastic impotence, was the most important finding with regard to the theory of instinct and the theory of culture: Genital sexuality, as I understood it, was a function which was unknown and not in keeping with the usual concepts of human sexual activity; no more than "sexual" and "genital" are the same, or "genital" in sex-economy and "genital" in common parlance.

7. Furthermore, a question which had been on Freud's mind a good deal found a simple solution. Psychic disturbances present only "qualities". And yet, one senses everywhere the so-called "quantitative" factor, i.e., the *strength* and *force*, the *energy cathexis* of psychic experiences and activities. In a meeting of the inner circle, Freud counselled foresight. We had to be prepared, he said, that one of these days the psychotherapy of the neuroses would meet a dangerous competitor, a future *organotherapy*. Nobody could as yet have an idea as to what it would be like, but one could already hear the footsteps of its exponents behind one, he said. Psychoanalysis would have to be placed upon an organic foundation. A true Freudian intuition! When Freud said this, I knew immediately that the solution of the problem of quantity in the neurosis also included the solution of the problem of organotherapy. The avenue of approach to the problem could only be the treatment of the physiological sexual stasis. I had already started on this road. Not until five years ago did the efforts to solve the problem bear fruit in the form of the basic principles of the *character-analytic technique of vegetotherapy*. In between lay fifteen years of hard work and difficult struggles.

Between 1922 and 1926 the orgasm theory was formulated and consolidated, bit by bit, followed by the technique of character-analysis. Every bit of further experience, therapeutic successes as well as failures, confirmed the theory which had taken form by itself from those first decisive observations. The ways in which the work was to branch out soon became clear:

The clinical work with patients led in *one* direction to *experimental* work in sex-economy, in *another* direction to the question: *Whence does social suppression of sexuality originate, and what is its function?*

Much later, i.e., only after 1933, the first line of problems resulted in a biological side-branch of sex-economy, namely, bion research, sex-economic cancer research, and the investigation of the orgone radiation. The second line, about seven years later, split up into sexual sociology and sex policy on the one hand, and political psychology and mass psychology on the other.[1]

The orgasm theory determined the psychological, psychotherapeutic, physiological-biological and the sociological sectors of sex-economy. I am far from claiming that this structure of sex-economy could replace such specialized disciplines as the above. The claim which sex-economy can make today, however, is that of being an inwardly consistent, scientific theory of sex, from which a variety of aspects of human life may expect stimulating revivification. This claim makes imperative a detailed presentation of this structure in all its ramifications. Since the life process is identical with the sexual process—an experimentally proven fact—the wide ramification of sex-economy is a logical necessity. *In everything living, sexual vegetative energy is at work.* This statement is dangerous, just because it is simple and absolutely correct. If it is to be applied correctly, it must be kept from

---

[1] Cf. my books, *"Die Sexualität im Kulturkampf"*, *"Der Einbruch der Sexualmoral"*, and *"Die Massenpsychologie des Faschismus"*.

becoming a platitude or a catch phrase. One's followers are in the habit of making things easy for themselves. They take over all that has been acquired through hard toil, and work with it with as little disturbance to themselves as possible. They do not take the pains of applying again and again all methodological subtleties. They become stultified, and the problem with them. I hope I shall succeed in saving sex-economy from this fate.

Chapter V

THE DEVELOPMENT OF THE CHARACTER-ANALYTIC TECHNIQUE

1. DIFFICULTIES AND CONTRADICTIONS

Psychoanalysis was making use of the method of free association as a means of eliciting and interpreting unconscious phantasies. The therapeutic effect of interpretation turned out to be limited. There were hardly any patients who were capable of giving their associations free rein. Improvements which were achieved in spite of this limitation were the result of a breaking-through of genital energy. As a rule, this came about in the train of free associations, but, it must be said in truth, *accidentally*. It was easy to see that the setting free of genital energies had great therapeutic effect, but one did not seem to possess the power to direct them and set them in operation. One did not know to what processes this accidental breaking-through of genitality was to be ascribed. It was necessary, therefore, to gain an orientation in the laws that governed psychoanalytic technique.

I have already described the hopelessness of the technical situation at that time. When, in the fall of 1924, I took over the technical seminar, I already had an idea of the work lying ahead. In the previous two years, the *lack of system* in the case reports had interfered with the work. I therefore designed an outline for a systematic report. As the cases always presented a bewildering mass of material, I suggested reporting only as much as was necessary for a clarification of the technical problems; the remainder would come out in the discussion anyhow. The usual presentation was to describe the case history without any reference to the technical problems, and then to give some rather irrelevant suggestions. This seemed futile. If psychoanalysis was a causal, scientific therapy, then the proper technical procedure had to become evident from the structure of the case itself. And the structure of the neurosis was determined by fixations in infantile situations. Experience showed, furthermore, that resistances were, as a rule, being evaded; partly because one failed to recognize them, partly due to the belief that resistances were a hindrance to psychoanalytic work, and had better be avoided. Consequently, during the first year of my work as a leader of the seminar, we discussed exclusively situations of resistance. Completely helpless at first, we soon began to learn a great deal.

The most important result of the first year of seminar work was the decisive realization of the fact that to most analysts, "transference" meant only positive and not also negative transference; this in spite of the fact that a theoretical distinction of this kind had been made by Freud long ago. Analysts shied away from bringing out, listening to, confirming or denying opposing opinions and embarrassing criticism from the patient. In short, one felt personally insecure, largely because of the sexual material and the lack of understanding of human nature.

It was further shown that it was the unconscious hostile attitudes of the patient which formed the basis of the whole neurotic structure. Every interpretation of unconscious material bounced back upon the analyst as a result of this *latent hostility*. Consequently, it was a mistake to interpret any unconscious contents before these latent hostile attitudes were elicited and eliminated. True, this was in line with well-known technical principles; but it required to be put in practice.

The discussion of practical technical problems in the seminar did away with many mistaken and convenient attitudes cherished by therapists. For example, the "waiting". This "waiting" attitude was in most cases nothing but helplessness. We soon came to condemn the common habit of simply blaming the patient when he showed resistance. What was more in accord with psychoanalytic principles was to attempt to understand the resistance and to eliminate it by *analytic* means. On the other hand, it was customary, when an analysis seemed to be petering out, to set a date of termination. By a certain date, the patient had to make up his mind "to give up his resistance to getting well". If he could not, he was said to have "insuperable resistances". Of the physiological anchoring of such resistances nobody had an idea at that time.

There was a series of faulty technical procedures to be done away with. As I had been committing these mistakes myself for some five years, paying for them with serious failures, I knew them well and recognized them in others. One of these mistakes was the lack of system in dealing with the associative material presented by the patient. The material was interpreted in the order in which "it came up", with complete disregard of the depth from which it came, and of the resistances which stood in the way of a real understanding of the material. Often enough, this led to grotesque situations. The patients were quick to find out the analyst's theoretical expectations and presented associations accordingly. They produced material for the analyst's benefit. If they were sly characters they would lead the analyst astray more or less consciously, e.g., by producing such confusing dreams that no one could possibly understand them. The fact was overlooked that the actual problem was just this constant confusion of the dreams, and not their content. Or else, patients would produce symbol upon symbol. They were quick to find out their sexual significance, and soon they were able to operate with *concepts*. They would, for example, talk of the "Oedipus complex", without a trace of affect. Secretly, they did not believe in the interpretations of the material, whereas the analyst, as a rule, took the material at its face value. Most treatment situations were chaotic. There was no order in the material, no structure in the treatment, and, consequently, no evolving of a process. Most cases petered out after two or three years' treatment. Occasionally, there were improvements, but nobody knew why. Thus, we arrived at the concepts of *orderly and systematic work on the resistances.*

During treatment, the neurosis breaks up, as it were, into individual resistances, each of which has to be kept apart and eliminated separately, proceeding always from the most superficial, from that which is closest to the patient's conscious experience. This technical procedure was nothing new, was indeed nothing but a consistent putting into practice of Freud's concepts. I warned against trying to "convince" a patient of the correctness of an interpretation. If the specific resistance toward an unconscious impulse is comprehended and eliminated, the patient grasps it spontaneously. The resistance, it should be remembered, contains the very impulse against which it is directed. If the patient recognizes the meaning of the defense, he is already on the point of grasping that against which he defends himself. However, that requires exact and consistent eliciting of every trace of distrust and rejection of the analyst in the patient. There was not a patient to be found without a deep mistrust of the treatment. The difference lay only in their way of concealing it. I once reported a case which concealed his mistrust most cleverly by being overly polite and by agreeing with everything. Behind this mistrust lay the real source of anxiety. Thus, he offered up everything, without, however, betraying his aggressions. In this situation it was necessary to let his clear-cut dreams of incest with his mother go without interpretation as long as he had not expressed his aggressions toward me. Such procedure was in strict contradiction to the customary practice of interpreting every dream detail or association. However, it was in accord with the principles of resistance-analysis.

Soon, I found myself getting into a conflict. As practice and theory were at variance, many analysts were bound to become upset. They found themselves confronted with the necessity of adapting their practice to theory, i.e., of relearning technique. For, quite unawares, we had discovered that characteristic of the human of today to ward off *genuine* sexual and destructive impulses with insincere, forced and misleading attitudes. The adaptation of the technique to this hypocritical character in the patient led to consequences of which nobody had any idea, and which everybody unconsciously dreaded: It was a matter of *really freeing the patients' aggression and sexuality*. It was a matter of the personal structure of the therapist who had to tolerate and direct these forces. However, we analysts were children of our times. We were dealing with material which theoretically we acknowledged but practically evaded and did not want to experience. We were held tight in formal academic conventions. The analytic situation, however, required freedom from conventionality and a highly liberal attitude toward sexuality. The actual goal of therapy, that of making the patient capable of orgasm, was not mentioned in these first years of the seminar. I avoided the subject instinctively. It was not liked and aroused animosity. Furthermore, I was not too sure about it myself. In fact, it was not easy to understand correctly the bathroom habits and sexual peculiarities of one's patients and at the same time to maintain one's social or professional dignity. Thus, one preferred to talk of "anal fixation" or "oral wishes", and the animal was and remained untouched.

The situation was not an easy one, anyhow. A series of clinical observations had resulted in a hypothesis concerning the therapy of the neuroses. To realize the therapeutic goal in practice required great technical skill. The more frequently clinical experience confirmed the fact that realization of genital satisfaction leads to a speedy cure of a neurosis, the more difficulties were presented by the other cases, in which this realization was not possible, or only partially so. The concern with these cases was the incentive to a thorough study of the obstacles lying in the path of genital satisfaction. It is not easy to present this phase of the work systematically. I shall attempt to give as vivid a picture as possible of how the genital theory of the therapy of the neuroses gradually became more and more interwoven with the development of the character-analytic technique. In the course of a few years, they became an inseparable unity. The clearer and the more solid the basis of the work became, the greater grew the divergences with the psychoanalysts of the old school. During the first two years, things went smoothly. But after that, opposition on the part of the older colleagues began to make itself felt. They simply could not follow; they feared for their reputation as "experienced authorities". Confronted with our new findings, they could say one of two things. Either, "that's old stuff, you'll find that in Freud", or else, "that's all wrong". Indeed, in the long run, the role played by genital satisfaction in the therapy of the neuroses could not possibly be denied; it forced itself upon one in the discussion of every single case. This strengthened my position, but it also made enemies for me. The goal of "capability for orgastic genital satisfaction" determined the technique in the following manner: "All patients are genitally disturbed. They must become genitally healthy. That means, we must find and destroy all pathological attitudes which prevent the establishment of orgastic potency". To work out such a technique meant a task for a generation of analytic therapists. For, the obstacles to genitality were innumerable and infinitely manifold; they were anchored socially no less than psychically and, more importantly, as was shown only much later, physiologically.

The primary emphasis was on the study of the pregenital fixations, the abnormal modes of sexual satisfaction, and of the *social* obstacles to a satisfying sex life. Without my intending it, questions relating to marriage, puberty and the social inhibitions of sexuality gradually came into the foreground of the discussions. All this seemed still to fit entirely into the framework of psychoanalytic investigation. My young colleagues showed great industry and made no secret of their enthusiasm for the seminar. Their later conduct, unworthy of physicians and scientists, when it came to a break (1934), still does not permit one to overlook their achievements in this seminar.

In 1923, Freud's "The Ego and the Id" was published. Its immediate effect on practice, which constantly had to deal with the patients' sexual difficulties, was confusing. In practice, one did not know what to do with the "superego" or "unconscious guilt feelings"; they were theoretical formulations concerning very obscure facts. There was no technical procedure for dealing with these. One preferred to deal with fear of masturbation or sexual guilt feelings. In 1920, "Beyond the Pleasure Principle" had appeared, in which Freud, at first hypothetically, placed the death instinct on an even footing with the sexual instinct; more than that, he ascribed to it instinctual energy from an even deeper level. Those analysts who did not practise and those who were unable to comprehend the sexual theory, began to apply the new "ego theory". It was a sad state of affairs. Instead of sexuality, one now talked of "Eros". The superego, which was introduced as an auxiliary theoretical concept of psychic structure, was made use of by inept practitioners as if it were a clinical fact. The Id was "wicked"; the Superego sat there with a long beard and was "strict"; and the poor Ego tried to be a "go-between". Living, fluent description of facts came to be replaced by a mechanical blueprint which made all further thinking unnecessary. Clinical discussions were fewer and fewer, and speculation took their place. Soon there appeared outsiders who had never done an analysis and gave highsounding talks on the ego and superego, or on schizophrenias they had never seen. Sexuality became an empty shell, the concept of "libido" became devoid of any sexual content and turned into an empty phrase. Psychoanalytic communications lost their serious quality and showed more and more of a pathos reminiscent of the ethical philosophers. Some psychoanalytic writers began to translate the theory of the neuroses into the lingo of "ego psychology". The atmosphere was "clearing".

Slowly but surely it became cleared of the very achievements which characterized Freud's work. The adaptation to a world which shortly before had threatened the psychoanalysts and their science with annihilation, took place unobtrusively at first. They still spoke of sexuality, but no longer meant it. As they had at the same time retained some of the old pioneer pride, they developed a bad conscience and began to usurp my new findings as old parts of psychoanalysis, in order to annihilate them. The formal element crowded out the content; the organization became more important than its task. It was the beginning of that process of disintegration which has thus far destroyed all great social movements in history: just as the primitive Christianity of Jesus was transformed into the Church, and Marxian science into Fascist dictatorship, so, many psychoanalysts changed into the worst enemies of their own cause.

The cleavage within the movement had become irreparable. Today, after fifteen years, this fact has become evident to everyone. I did not comprehend it clearly until 1934. Too late. Up to that time, I had, against my inner conviction, struggled for *my own* theories within the framework of the International Psychoanalytical Association, outwardly and really with complete sincerity, in the name of *psychoanalysis.*

Around 1925, there began a parting of the ways in psychoanalytic theory, of which their exponents were at first unaware, but which has become quite obvious by now. To the extent to which the advocacy of a cause loses ground, *personal* intrigue gains ground. What is pretended to be scientific interest, begins to be really behind-the-scenes politics, tactics and diplomacy. It is to the painful experience of this development within the International Psychoanalytical Association that I owe what is perhaps the most important result of my labors: the knowledge of the mechanism of any kind of politics. The presentation of these facts is by no means irrelevant. It will show that the critical evaluation of these manifestations of deterioration within the psychoanalytic movement (such as the theory of the death instinct) was an indispensable prerequisite for the break into the realm of vegetative life which a few years later I succeeded in making.

Reik had published a book on "*Geständniszwang und Strafbedürfnis*" in which the whole original concept of the neurosis was made upside down. That the book was well received was so much the worse. Reduced to the simplest terms, his innovation consisted in the elimination of the concept that the child *fears* punishment for sexual behavior. Freud, in "Beyond the Pleasure Principle" and in "The Ego and the Id" had assumed the existence of an unconscious need for punishment; this was supposed to account for the resistance against getting well. At the same time, the concept of the "death instinct" was introduced. Freud assumed the living substance to be governed by two opposing instinctual forces; the life forces, which he equated with the sexual instinct ("Eros"), and the "death instinct" ("Thanatos"). According to him, "eros" would rouse the living substance out of its equilibrium, which is like the passivity of inorganic matter; it would create tension, would unite life into ever larger units. It was vigorous, turbulent and the cause of life's tumult. But behind it acted the mute, yet "much more momentous" death instinct; the tendency to reduce the living to the lifeless, to nothingness, to Nirvana. According to this concept, life really was nothing but a disturbance of eternal silence, of nothingness. In the neurosis, accordingly, these positive life or sexual forces were opposed by the death instinct. Though the death instinct itself could not be perceived, it was argued, its manifestations were too obvious to be overlooked. Humans constantly showed *self-destructive tendencies;* the death instinct manifested itself in masochistic tendencies. These tendencies were at the bottom of the unconscious guilt feeling, which one might also call *need* for punishment. Patients simply did not want to get well because of this need for punishment which was satisfied in the neurosis.

It was only through Reik that I really found out where Freud began to err. Reik exaggerated and generalized many correct findings, such as the fact that criminals tend to give themselves away, or that to many people it is a relief to be able to confess a crime. Up to that time, a neurosis was considered to be the result of a conflict between sexuality and *fear* of punishment. Now, the formulation came to be that the neurosis was a conflict between sexuality and *need* for punishment, i.e., the direct opposite of the fear of punishment for sexual behavior. Such formulation meant a complete liquidation of the psychoanalytic theory of the neuroses. It was in complete contradiction to all clinical insight. Clinical observation left no doubt of the correctness of Freud's original formulation: the patients had come to grief as a result of *their fear of punishment for sexual behavior,* and *not* as a result of any *desire* to be punished for it. True enough, many patients developed *secondarily* a masochistic attitude of wanting to be punished, of harming themselves or of clinging to their neurosis. But that was a secondary result—or a way out—of the complications into which they were driven by the inhibition of their sexuality. It was undoubtedly the task of the therapist to eliminate these desires for punishment as what they were, namely, *neurotic* formations, and to free the patient's sexuality; *not* to confirm these tendencies to self-injury as manifestations of deeper biological strivings. The adherents of the death instinct—who grew in numbers as well as dignity, because now they could talk of "Thanatos" instead of sexuality—ascribed the neurotic self-damaging tendency of a sick organism to a biological primary instinct of the living substance. From this, psychoanalysis has never recovered.

Reik was followed by Alexander. He examined some criminals and stated that quite generally crime is motivated by an unconscious need for punishment. He did not ask what was the origin of such unnatural behavior. He failed to mention the sociological basis of crime. Such formulations made any further thinking unnecessary. If one was not able to cure, the death instinct could be blamed. When people committed murder, it was in order to go to prison; when children stole, it was to obtain relief from a conscience that troubled them. I marvel today at the energy that was expended at that time on the discussion of such opinions. And yet, Freud had had something in mind which merited considerable effort in evaluating it; this I shall show later. However, inertia prevailed, and the labors of decades were lost. The patients' "*negative therapeutic reaction*" was later shown to be nothing but the result of theoretical and technical inability to establish orgastic potency in the patient, in other words, to handle their *pleasure anxiety.*

One day, I took my troubles to Freud. I asked him whether it had been his purpose to introduce the death instinct as a clinical theory. (He himself had indicated that one could not grasp the death instinct in one's daily work with patients). Freud reassured me, saying that "it was only a hypothesis". It might as well be left out; it would not alter the foundations of psychoanalysis in the least. Well, he had engaged in speculation for a change, he said, and he knew very well that his speculation was being misused. I should not let myself be bothered by that, and just continue my clinical work. I was relieved, but also determined to take a decided stand against this talk of the death instinct in the various aspects of my work.

My critical review of Reik's book and the article criticizing Alexander's theory appeared in 1927. In my technical seminar little was heard of the death instinct as an explanation for therapeutic failures. One had no use for such explanations if painstakingly exact clinical presentations were made. Occasionally, one or the other death instinct theorist would try to make his opinion felt. I carefully abstained from any direct attack on this erroneous doctrine; clinical work itself would make it no longer viable. The more carefully the mechanisms of the neuroses were studied, the more certain we were to win. In the Psychoanalytic Association at large, however, the mistaken interpretation of the ego-theory flourished more and more. The tension kept growing. Suddenly it was discovered that I was "very aggressive", or that I was "only riding my hobby" and was overemphasizing the significance of genitality.

At the Psychoanalytic Congress in Salzburg in 1924, I had amplified my first formulations concerning the therapeutic significance of genitality by the introduction of the concept of "orgastic potency". My paper dealt with two fundamental facts:

1. *The neurosis is the expression of a disturbance in genitality,* and not only of sexuality in general.

2. *Relapse into neurosis after psychoanalytic cure may be averted to the extent to which orgastic satisfaction in the sexual act is assured.*

The paper was a success. Abraham congratulated me on the successful formulation of *the economic factor in the neurosis.*

In order to establish orgastic potency in the patient, it was not sufficient to liberate the existing genital excitations from inhibitions and repressions. Sexual energy is *bound up* in the symptoms. Consequently, each dissolution of a symptom *liberates* a certain amount of psychic energy. At that time, the concepts of "psychic energy" and "sexual energy" were not by any means identical. The amount of energy thus liberated transferred itself spontaneously to the genital system: *potency improved.* The patients dared to approach a partner, they relinquished abstinence, or the sexual embrace was a richer experience for them. However, the expectation that the liberation of energy from the symptoms would also lead to the establishment of the orgastic function was fulfilled only in a few cases. Careful consideration led one to the conclusion that apparently an insufficient amount of energy was liberated from neurotic fixation points. True enough, the patients discarded symptoms and were capable of doing work of a sort, but on the whole they remained blocked. Thus the question suggested itself: *Where else, besides the neurotic symptoms, is sexual energy bound up?* This question was new, but not outside the framework of psychoanalysis; on the contrary, it was only a consistent applicaton of analytic methodology over and above the symptom. At first I could find no answer to it. Clinical and therapeutic problems cannot be solved by cogitation; the answer to them is found in the course of the handling of everyday tasks. This would seem to be true of any kind of scientific work. A correct formulation of the problems originating in practice consistently leads to other questions which gradually condense to a unified picture of the whole problem.

The psychoanalytic theory of the neuroses made it appear plausible to look for the energy that was lacking for the establishment of orgastic potency in the *non*-genital, i.e., infantile pregenital activities and phantasies. If sexual interest is directed to a high degree toward sucking, biting, being petted, anal habits, etc., then the capacity for genital experience suffers. This confirms the view that the sexual partial impulses do not function independently of each other, but form a *unity*—like a liquid in communicating pipes. There can be *only one uniform sexual energy, seeking satisfaction at various erogenous zones, and attached to different ideas.* This concept was at variance with certain views which just at that time began to flourish. Ferenczi published a theory of genitality according to which the genital function was composed of pregenital excitations, anal, oral and aggressive. These views contradicted my clinical experience. I found, on the contrary, that any admixture of non-genital excitations in the sexual act or in masturbation *reduced* orgastic potency. A woman, for instance, who unconsciously equates her vagina with her anus, may be afraid of passing a flatus in sexual excitation and of being embarrassed by it. Such an attitude is capable of paralyzing all normal vital activity. A man to whom his penis has the unconscious meaning of a knife, or to whom it is something with which to prove his potency, is incapable of complete surrender to the act. Helene Deutsch published a book on female sex functions in which she contended that the culmination of sexual satisfaction for the woman lay in the act of childbirth. According to her, there was no primary vaginal excitability, but only one that is composed of excitations which were displaced from mouth and anus to the vagina. Otto Rank, at about the same time, published his "Trauma of Birth", in which he asserted that the sexual act corresponded to a "return to the womb".

I was on very good terms with these analysts and valued their opinions, but my experience and concepts came into sharp conflict with theirs. Gradually it became clear that it is a *fundamental error to try to give the sexual act a psychological interpretation,* to attribute to it a psychic meaning as if it were a neurotic symptom. But this is what the psychoanalysts did. On the contrary: any idea occurring in the course of the sexual act only has the effect of hindering one's absorption in the excitation. Furthermore, such psychological interpretations of genitality constitute a denial of genitality as a biological function. By composing it of non-genital excitations, one denies the existence of genitality. The function of the orgasm, however, had revealed the *qualitative* difference between genitality and pregenitality. *Only the genital apparatus can provide orgasm and can discharge sexual energy completely. Pregenitality,* on the other hand, can *only increase vegetative tensions.* One readily sees the deep rift which formed here in psychoanalytic concepts.

The therapeutic conclusions to be drawn from these opposing concepts were incompatible. If, on the one hand, genital excitation is nothing but a mixture of non-genital excitations, the therapeutic task would be that of shifting anal or oral eroticism upon the genital apparatus. If, on the other hand, my views were correct, then genital excitation had to be liberated from its admixture with pregenital excitations, had to be "crystallized out", as it were.

Freud's writings gave no clue to the solution of the problem. He believed that the libidinal development in the child progressed from the oral to the anal and from there to the *phallic* level. The phallic level was ascribed to both sexes, the phallic eroticism in the girl manifesting itself in the clitoris, just as in the boy it manifests itself in the penis. Only at puberty, Freud said, were all infantile sexual excitations subsumed under the "primacy of the genital". This genital now "*entered the service of procreation*". During the first years, I had overlooked the fact that this formulation contained the old identification of genitality and procreation, according to which sexual pleasure was considered a function of procreation. This oversight was called to my attention by a psychoanalyst in Berlin at a time when the rift was already obvious. My connection with the International Psychoanalytical Association in spite of my theory of genitality had been made possible by the fact that I kept referring to Freud. In doing so, I did injustice to my theory and made the separation from the organization of the psychoanalysts difficult for my co-workers.

Today, such views seem impossible. I can but marvel at the earnestness with which one then discussed the question as to whether or not there was a primary genital function. Nobody had any idea of the social basis of such scientific naiveté. The further development of the theory of genitality made it obvious enough.

2. SEX-ECONOMY OF ANXIETY

The sharp discrepancies apparent in psychoanalytic theory after 1922 can also be presented in terms of the central problem of anxiety. Freud's original concept was this: *If somatic sexual excitation is barred from perception and discharge, it is converted into anxiety. How* this "conversion" took place, nobody knew. As my therapeutic problem was always that of liberating sexual energy from its neurotic fixations, this question clamored for clarification. Stasis anxiety (*Stauungsangst*) was undischarged sexual excitation. In order to change it back into sexual excitation, one had to know how this *first* conversion into anxiety took place.

In 1924, I treated two women with cardiac neurosis in

the psychoanalytic clinic. With them, whenever genital excitation appeared, cardiac anxiety subsided. In one case the alternation of cardiac anxiety and genital excitation could be observed for weeks. Every inhibition of vaginal excitation would immediately result in oppression and anxiety "in the region of the heart". This observation beautifully confirmed Freud's original concept of the relationship between libido and anxiety. But it showed more than that: it was now possible to *localize the seat of the sensation of anxiety:* it was the *cardiac and diaphragmatic region.* The other patient showed a similar interrelationship, but, in addition, she showed an urticaria. When the patient did not dare to permit her vaginal excitation to make itself felt, there occurred *either* cardiac anxiety *or* large itching wheals in various places. Obviously, sexual excitation and anxiety had something to do with the functions of the vegetative nervous system.

Freud's original formulation thus underwent the following correction. *There is no conversion* of sexual excitation into anxiety. *The same excitation which appears in the genital as pleasure, manifests itself as anxiety if it stimulates the cardiovascular system.* That is, in the latter case it appears as the *exact opposite of pleasure.* The vasovegetative system will function at one time in the direction of sexual excitation, and again, when the latter is inhibited, in the direction of anxiety. This proved to be a happy thought. It led in a straight line to my present concept: *sexuality and anxiety present two opposite directions of vegetative excitation.* It took about another ten years to establish the bio-electrical character of these processes.

Freud had made no mention of the vegetative nervous system in connection with his theory of anxiety. I did not doubt for a moment that he would accept this amplification of his theory with approval. However, when, late in 1926, I presented my concept at a meeting at his house, he rejected the connection between anxiety and the vasovegetative system. I have never understood why.

It became increasingly clear that the overburdening of the vasovegetative system with undischarged sexual energy is the fundamental mechanism of anxiety, and thus, of the neurosis. Each new case amplified earlier observations. Anxiety always develops, I reasoned, when the vegetative system is over-stimulated in a *specific* way. Cardiac anxiety is present in such diverse conditions as angina pectoris, bronchial asthma, nicotine poisoning, and hyperthyroidism. In other words, anxiety always develops when some abnormal stimulus acts on the cardiac system. In this way, stasis anxiety on a sexual basis fits entirely into the general problem of anxiety. As in other cases the heart is stimulated by nicotine or other toxic substances, so it is in this case stimulated by undischarged sexual energy. The question as to the nature of this overstimulation remained open. I did not know then of the opposite role played here by the sympathetic and the parasympathetic.

To my clinical thinking, there was a difference between *anxiety* on the one hand and *fear* (*Befürchtung*) or *anxious anticipation* (*Erwartungsangst*) on the other. "I am afraid of being beaten, punished or castrated" is something different from the "anxiety" experienced in the moment of actual danger. Fear or anxious anticipation becomes affective anxiety only if accompanied by a stasis of excitation in the autonomic system. There were a great many patients who showed castration "anxiety" without any *affect* of anxiety. And on the other hand there were affects of anxiety in the absence of any idea of danger, as, e.g., in people living in sexual abstinence.

One had to distinguish anxiety as a *result* of dammed-up excitation ("stasis anxiety") on the one hand, and anxiety as the *cause* of sexual repression. The former dominated the stasis neuroses (actual neuroses, Freud), the latter the psychoneuroses. But, both kinds of anxiety were operative *simultaneously* in either case. First, fear of punishment or social ostracism causes the damming-up of excitation. This excitation becomes displaced from the genital-sensory system to the cardiac system and there produces stasis anxiety. The anxiety experienced in fright also can be nothing but sexual energy which becomes suddenly dammed up in the cardiac system. In order to produce anxious anticipation, a *small* amount of stasis anxiety is sufficient. It appears with nothing more than the vivid imagination of a possibly dangerous situation. One anticipates somatically, as it were, the danger situation by imagining it. This was in accord with the earlier consideration that the strength of an idea, be it pleasure or anxiety, is determined by the actual amount of excitation at work in the body. With the idea or anticipation of a danger situation, the organism behaves as if the danger situation were already present. Possibly, the process of imagination, quite generally, is based upon such reactions of the organism. During these years, I was working on my book, "*Die Funktion des Orgasmus*", where these things are discussed in special sections on "Vasomotor neurosis" and "Anxiety and vasovegetative system".

In the fall of 1926, Freud's book, "*Hemmung, Symptom und Angst*" appeared. In this book, many of the original formulations concerning actual anxiety ("*Aktualangst*") were withdrawn. Neurotic anxiety now was defined as a "signal of the ego", the ego reacting to a danger threatening from a repressed impulse in the same way as it reacts to a real, external danger. A relationship between actual anxiety and neurotic anxiety, Freud now said, could *not* be established. That was a bad state of affairs, but—he concludes his considerations on the subject with a "*non liquet*". Anxiety was no longer to be considered a *result* of sexual repression, but as its *cause*. The question as to the stuff of which anxiety was made "had lost its interest" and the concept of the conversion of libido into anxiety "was no longer important". Freud overlooked the fact that anxiety—a biological phenomenon—cannot make its appearance in the ego without a preparatory process having taken place somewhere in the deep biological layers.

This was a hard blow to my work on the anxiety problem, for I had succeeded in solving, to a considerable extent, the problem of anxiety by recognizing it as a result of repression on the one hand, and as a cause of repression on the other. From now on it became even more difficult to defend the concept of anxiety as resulting from sexual stasis. Naturally, Freud's formulations carried great weight, and it was not exactly easy to maintain a different opinion from his, certainly not on central problems. In the "*Funktion des Orgasmus*" I had passed over this difficulty in an insignificant footnote. There was a consensus of opinion that anxiety was the *cause* of sexual repression. I maintained that anxiety was also a *result* of sexual stasis. This, Freud now refuted.

The rift deepened rapidly and disturbingly. I was convinced that the antisexual attitude of the psychoanalysts would make capital of Freud's new formulations and would exaggerate into grotesque positive formulations what in Freud had been merely an error. Unfortunately, I was right. Since the publication of "*Hemmung, Symptom und Angst*", there is no longer any psychoanalytic theory of anxiety that would be in accord with clinical facts. I was also thoroughly convinced of the correctness of my extension of Freud's original concept of anxiety. The fact that I kept coming closer and closer to its *physiological basis* was gratifying on the one hand, but on the other it meant further accentuation of the conflict.

In my clinical work, the process of conversion of stasis anxiety into genital excitation became steadily more important. Where it was possible to bring it about, there were good and lasting therapeutic results. However, I did not succeed in all cases in liberating cardiac anxiety and in producing its alternation with genital excitation. This raised the question: *What is it that keeps the biological excitation, once genital excitation is inhibited, from manifesting itself as cardiac anxiety? Why does stasis anxiety not make its appearance in all cases of psychoneurosis?*

Here, too, early psychoanalytic formulations came to my aid. Freud had shown that in the neurosis, anxiety becomes *bound* in a certain way. The patient escapes anxiety, e.g., by producing a compulsive symptom. If one disturbs this functioning of the compulsion, anxiety immediately appears. Not always, however. A great many cases of compulsion neurosis of long standing, or cases of chronic depression could not be disturbed in this way. Somehow, they were inaccessible. Especially difficult were the emotionally blocked ("*affektgesperrt*") compulsive characters. They gave associations in great numbers freely, but there never was a trace of affect. All therapeutic efforts bounced back, as it were, from a "thick, hard wall". The patients were "*armored*" against any attack. There was no technique known in the literature that would shake this hardened surface. It was the *whole character* that resisted. With this, I was at the beginning of *character-analysis*. Apparently, *the character armor was the mechanism which was binding all energy.* It was also the mechanism that made so many psychoanalysts contend that there was no such thing as stasis anxiety.

3. CHARACTER ARMOR AND DYNAMIC LAYERS OF THE DEFENSE MECHANISMS

The theory of the "character armor" was the result of a method of working which attempted—gropingly at first—to crystallize out clearly the resistances of the patient. Between 1922, when the therapeutic role of genitality was recognized, and 1927, when the "*Funktion des Orgasmus*" was published, innumerable experiences pointed in one and the same direction: *The obstacle to getting well lies in the patient's "whole being", the "character"*. In the treatment, the character armor makes itself felt in the form of "*character resistance*".

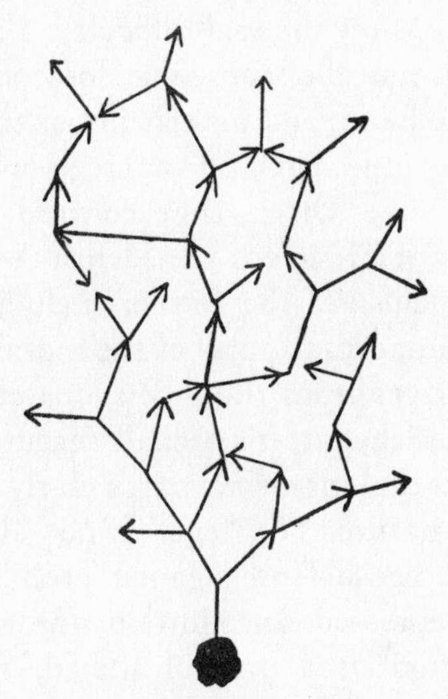

Diagram: Structure of the armor as a result of the interplay of dynamic forces.

A description of the preceding groundwork may make an understanding of the sex-economic theory of character and structure easier than the systematic presentation in my book, "*Charakter-Analyse*". There, my analytic theory of character may still appear as an amplification of Freud's theory of the neuroses. However, it soon came into opposition with it. It grew out of the struggle against the mechanistic concepts of psychoanalysis.

The task of psychoanalytic therapy was that of uncovering and eliminating resistances, not that of interpreting the unconscious directly. In principle, one had to proceed, therefore, from the ego-defense against unconscious impulses. However, it turned out that there was not only *one* layer of ego-defense to be broken through in order to get at the vast realm of the unconscious. *In reality, instinctual desires and defensive functions of the ego, closely interwoven, permeate the whole psychic structure* (cf. diagram, p. 115).

This fact constitutes the real difficulty. Freud's schema of the interrelationships of unconscious, foreconscious, and conscious on the one hand, and his schema of the psychic structure as consisting of id, ego and superego on the other hand, were not coextensive. Often, they contradicted each other. The unconscious of Freud's is not identical with the id. The latter is more inclusive; the former includes the repressed desires and also important parts of the moral superego. Since the superego derives from the incestuous child-parent relationship, it carries the latter's archaic features; it is invested with great instinctual intensity, particularly of an aggressive and destructive nature. The "ego" is not identical with the "conscious"; the ego-defense against prohibited sexual impulses is itself repressed. In addition, the ego itself is only a specially differentiated part of the id, though later on, under the influence of the superego, it comes into opposition with its own source, the id. Also, if one understands Freud correctly, "early infantile" is not the same as id or unconscious, and adult not the same as ego or superego. I only want to point out some difficulties of psychoanalytic theory, without wanting to discuss or settle them. That I leave to the psychoanalytic theorists. At any rate, sex-economic character research has clarified some important relevant issues. The sex-economic concept of the psychic apparatus is not psychological, but *biological.*

For the clinical work, the differentiation of "*repressed*" and "*capable of becoming conscious*" was of primary importance. Also, the differentiation of the various developmental stages of infantile sexuality. With these one could operate. One could not operate with the id, which was not tangible, nor with the superego, which was only a construction. Nor with the unconscious in the narrow sense, because, as Freud correctly pointed out, it was tangible only in its conscious derivatives. (To Freud, the unconscious was never more than an "indispensable assumption"). Tangible in practical terms were the pregenital manifestations and the various forms of moral or anxious defense. Much of the confusion was due to the fact that psychoanalysts failed to differentiate between theory, hypothetical construction and practically visible and alterable facts, and to their belief that they were working directly with the unconscious. These errors blocked the way to an exploration of the vegetative nature of the id, and consequently, the access to the biological basis of psychic functioning.

The layering of the psychic apparatus confronted me for the first time in the above-mentioned case of a passive-feminine young man with hysterical symptoms, inability to work, and ascetic impotence. He was overly polite and, because of fear, extremely sly. He yielded in every situation. His politeness represented the outermost, visible layer of his structure. He produced abundant material concerning his sexual attachment to his mother. He "offered up" this material without any inner conviction. Instead of discussing this material, I only kept pointing out his politeness as a defense against me and any really affective insight. As time went on, his hidden aggression appeared increasingly in his dreams. As the politeness decreased, he became offensive. In other words, *the politeness had been warding off the hatred.* I let the hatred come out fully by destroying every defense mechanism against it. The hatred up to that time had been unconscious. Hatred and politeness were antitheses, and at the same time the over-politeness was a disguised manifestation of hatred. Over-polite people are among the most dangerous and ruthless.

The liberated hatred in turn was warding off a severe fear of his father. That means, it was at one and the same time a repressed impulse and an unconscious ego defense against anxiety. The more clearly the hatred came out, the clearer became the manifestations of anxiety. Finally the hatred gave way to new anxiety. This hatred by no means represented the original infantile aggression, but was of a later date. The newly released anxiety was a defense against a *deeper* layer of destructive hatred. The former had gained satisfaction in depreciation and ridicule; the deeper destructive attitude was composed of murderous impulses against his father. It found expression in feelings and phantasies, when the fear of it (*"Destruktionsangst"*) was eliminated. This destructive attitude thus was the repressed element, kept down by the anxiety. *But at the same time it was identical with this fear of destruction.* For, it could not show itself without creating fear, and the fear of destruction could not appear without simultaneously betraying the destructive aggression. In this way the *antithetical-functional identity of defense and the repressed* revealed itself. As published some eight years later, it is represented in the diagram on the following page.

The destructive tendency towards the father was in turn a protection against the destruction by the father. When I uncovered its protective function, genital anxiety appeared. That is, the destructive tendencies against the father served the function of protecting the patient against castration by the father. The fear of being castrated, which was covered up by the destructive hatred of the father, was in itself a defense against a still deeper layer of destructive aggression; of the tendency, namely, to castrate the father and thus to get rid of him as a rival for the mother. The second layer of destructiveness was *destructive only;* the third was destructive with a *sexual* connotation. It was itself checked by the fear of castration, but it also warded off a very deep and intense layer of passive, loving, feminine attitude toward the father. To be feminine toward the father meant to be castrated, to have no penis. For this reason, the little boy had to protect himself against this love by means of a strong destructive aggression *against* the father. It was the healthy little *man* who thus defended himself. And this little man desired his mother very strongly. When his femininity—which had been superficially recognizable in his character—was dissolved, his genital incest desire came to the fore, and with that, his full genital excitability. For the first time, he was erectively potent, though still not orgastically potent.

This was the first time that a systematic and orderly, layer-by-layer resistance- and character-analysis had succeeded.[1] The concept of "layering" or "stratification of the

[1]For a detailed presentation of this case, cf. my book *"Charakter-Analyse"*.

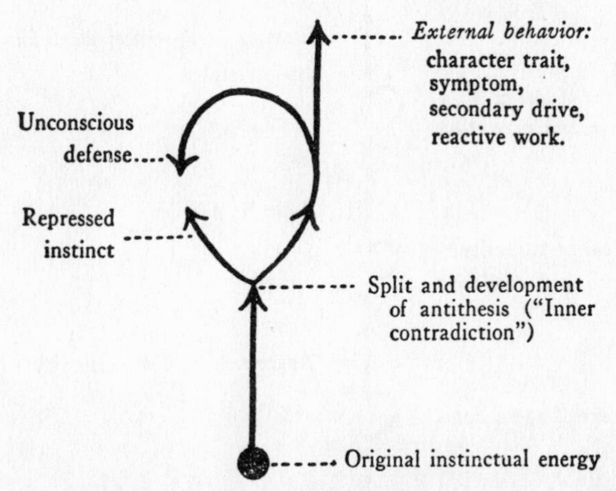

Diagram of the antithetical-functional unity of instinct and defense. Due to the present-day human character structure, an "inner contradiction" is always interposed between biological impulse and action: man acts "reactively" and with an inner conflict.

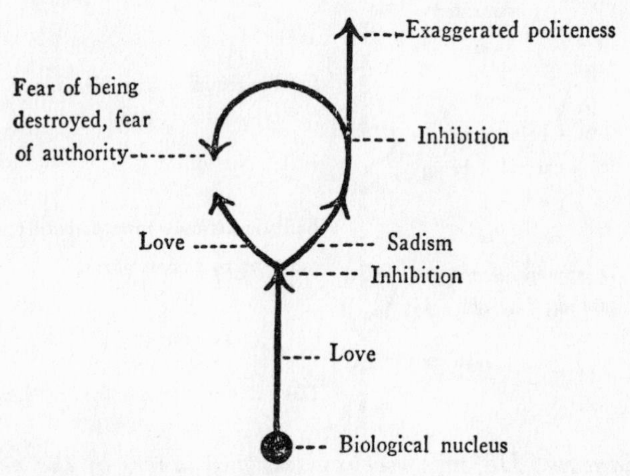

The same diagram, in terms of specific impulses, by way of illustration.

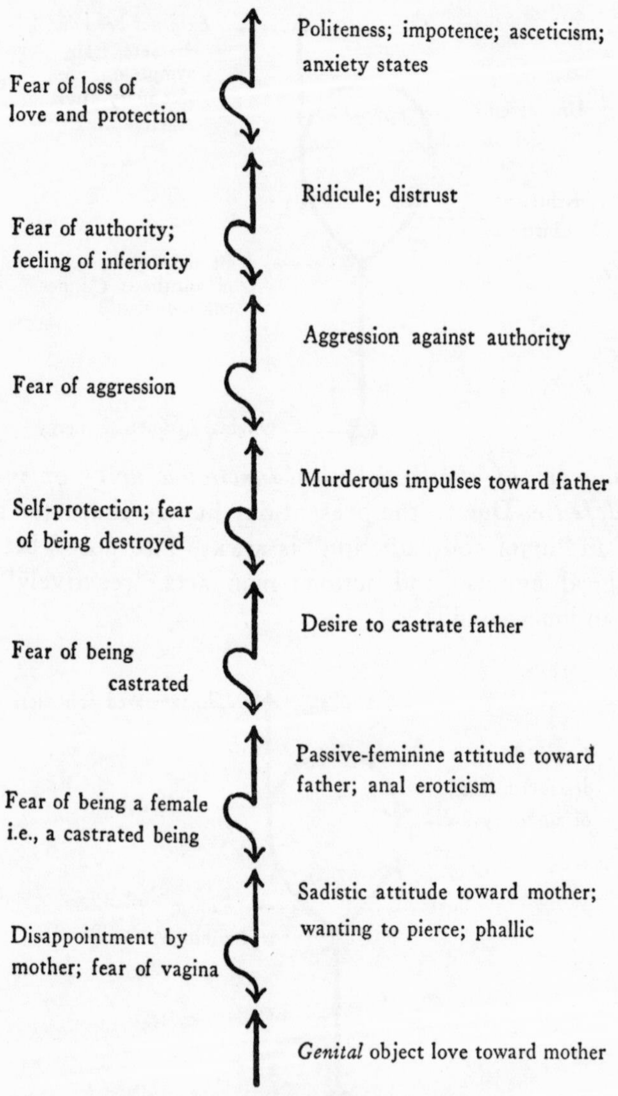

Diagram: Defense mechanisms and layers of the neurotic structure.

armor" (*Panzerschichtung*) opened many possibilities in clinical work. The psychic forces and contradictions no longer presented a chaos, but a historically and structurally understandable entity. The neurosis of each individual patient revealed a specific structure. The structure of the neurosis corresponded to the development. That which had been repressed latest in childhood was found to lie nearest the surface. However, early infantile fixations, if they covered later conflicts, could be dynamically deep and superficial. For example, the oral fixation of a woman to her husband, deriving from a deep fixation to her mother's breast, may belong to the most superficial layer of character when she has to ward off genital anxiety toward her husband. The ego defense —seen from the point of view of energy—is itself nothing but a repressed impulse in a defensive function. This is true of all moral attitudes of the human of today.

As a rule, the structure of the neurosis corresponded to the development, but in reverse order. The "antithetical-functional unity of instinct and defense" made it possible to comprehend the present-day and the infantile experience *simultaneously*. There was no longer an antithesis between the historical and the contemporaneous. *The whole experiential world of the past was alive in the present in the form of character attitudes. The make-up of a person is the functional sum total of all his past experiences.* These statements may sound academic, but they are absolutely decisive for an understanding of the alteration of individual structure.

This structure was not a schema which I imposed upon patients. The logic with which a correct analysis of the resistances revealed and eliminated layer after layer of the defense mechanisms, showed me that this stratification is present objectively and independently of me. The layers in the character may be compared to geological or archeological strata which, similarly, are solidified history. A conflict which has been active at a certain period of life always leaves its traces in the character, in the form of a rigidity. It functions automatically and is difficult to eliminate. The patient does not feel it as something alien to him, but often feels it as something rigid and unyielding or as a loss or diminution of spontaneity. Each of these layers in the character structure is a piece of life history which is preserved *in another form* and is still active. It was shown that by loosening up these layers, the old conflicts could—more or less easily—be revived. If the layers were particularly numerous and functioning automatically, if they formed a compact unit which was difficult to penetrate, they seemed like an "*armor*" surrounding the living organism. This armor may be superficial or deep-lying, soft as a sponge or hard as nails. In each case its function was to protect against unpleasure. However, the organism paid for this protection by losing a great deal of its capacity for pleasure. The latent content of this armor were the conflicts of the past. The energy that held the armor together consisted mostly in destructiveness which had become bound. This was shown by the fact that destructiveness would be set free as soon as the armor began to crack. Whence came this destructive and hateful aggression? What was its function? Was it primary, i.e., *biological* destructiveness? It has taken many years to solve such questions.

I found that people reacted with intense hatred to any attempt to disturb the neurotic equilibrium which was maintained by their armor. This inevitable reaction proved a major obstacle in the path of the investigation of character structure. Destructiveness itself was indeed never free. It was always covered up by opposing character attitudes. Where life situations really called for aggression, action, decision, for taking a stand, there was, instead, consideration, politeness, restraint, false modesty; in short, all kinds of character traits which enjoy high esteem as human virtues. But there was no doubt: *they paralyzed every rational action, every living, active impulse* in the individual.

And if it happened that there appeared some aggression, it was confused, aimless, and seemed to cover up a deep feeling of insecurity or a pathological egotism. In other words, it was *pathological,* not healthy, rationally directed aggression.

Gradually, I began to comprehend the *latent hatred* which is never lacking in patients. If one did not let oneself be deceived by the patient giving associations without any affect, if one was not content with dream interpretation, if, instead, one approached the patient's character defense, he would inevitably get *angry.* At first this was puzzling. He would complain about the emptiness in his emotional life. If, however, one showed him the same emptiness in the manner of his communications, his coldness, his bombastic or artificial behavior, then he would get angry. A symptom such as a headache or a tic he felt as alien to himself. But his fundamental personality,—that was himself. He felt disturbed and angry when it was pointed out to him.

Why can a person not perceive his own innermost self? Since it is he himself! Gradually I began to see that it is just this "he himself", this character make-up, which forms the compact tough mass that stands in the way of analytic endeavors. The total personality, the *character,* the whole individuality resisted. But why? Obviously, because it *served a secret function of defense and protection.* I was well acquainted with Adler's characterology. Had I perhaps gone astray on his path? There were the self-assertion, the inferiority feeling, the will to power, the vanity and the overcompensations for weakness. So, Adler seemed to be right after all! But his contention was that character, and *not sexuality,* caused the neurosis. Where, then, was the connection between *character* mechanisms and *sexual mechanisms?* For, I did not doubt for a moment that Freud's, and not Adler's, theory of the neuroses was the correct one.

It took years before it became clear: *the destructiveness*

which is bound up in the character is nothing but anger about frustration in general and denial of sexual gratification in particular. If the analysis penetrated to a sufficient depth, every destructive tendency gave way to a sexual one. Destructive tendencies were shown to be nothing but *reactions;* reactions to disappointment in love or to loss of love. If the desire for love or for satisfaction of the sex urge meets insuperable obstacles, one begins to hate. However, the hatred cannot be expressed, it must be bound in order to avoid the anxiety it causes. That is, frustrated love causes anxiety. So does inhibited aggression; and anxiety inhibits the expression of both hatred and love.

I now understood how to formulate theoretically what I had learned analytically. It was the same thing in reversed order, and I reached a most important conclusion: *The orgastically unsatisfied individual develops an insincere character and a fear of* any behavior which he has not thought out beforehand—in other words, *behavior which is spontaneous and truly alive,—as well as a fear of becoming aware of sensations of a vegetative origin.*

About this time, the theories about the destructive instincts became prominent in psychoanalysis. In his article on primary masochism, Freud had introduced an important modification of his earlier concepts. Originally, hatred was considered a primary, biological tendency, like love. Destructiveness being at first directed against the world, was later, under the influence of this world, turned back against the person himself; it thus became masochism, i.e., the *desire to suffer.* Now, this view was reversed: "primary masochism" or "death instinct" was considered primary, a biological force already inherent in the cells. Destructive aggression now came to be considered as masochism directed outwards, and by being turned back against the ego it appeared as "secondary masochism".

It was assumed that latent negative attitudes in the patient stemmed from his masochism. Freud also ascribed the "negative therapeutic reaction" and the "unconscious guilt feeling" to it. For many years, I paid special attention to the various kinds of destructiveness which caused guilt feelings and depressions, and began to realize their significance for the character armor as well as their relation to sexual stasis.

With Freud's consent, I was planning to summarize in a book what was known at that time of psychoanalytic technique. In this, I had to take a definite stand on the question of destructiveness. I had as yet no definite views of my own. Ferenczi, in a paper on "Further development of 'active technique'," disagreed with Adler. "The exploration of character", he wrote, "never takes a prominent place in our therapy. . . . It is touched upon only when certain abnormal, psychosis-like, traits disturb the normal continuation of the analysis". This was a correct formulation of the attitude of psychoanalysis at that time towards the role of character. This was at the time when I was engrossed in characterological studies, working on the development of psychoanalysis toward "character-analysis". Real cure could be achieved only through elimination of the *characterological basis* of the symptoms. The difficulty of this task lay in understanding those analytic situations which required not symptom-analysis, but character-analysis. The difference between my technique and Adler's characterological attempts was that it consisted in *character-analysis through analysis of the sexual behavior*. Adler, however, had said: "Analysis *not* of the libido, *but* of the character." My conception of the character armor has nothing in common with Adler's formulation of individual character traits. Any such comparison of the sex-economic theory of structure with Adler's characterology would betray a fundamental misconception. Character traits such as "inferiority feeling" or "will to power" are only superficial manifestations of the *armoring* process in the *biological* sense, i.e., in the sense of vegetative inhibition of vital functioning.

In my book "*Der triebhafte Charakter*" (1925) I had, based on my experience with impulsive characters, arrived at the necessity of extending symptom-analysis to character-analysis. That was logical, but the necessary clinical and technical foundation was lacking. I knew as yet no way of providing it and adhered to Freud's theory of the ego and superego. But a character-analytic technique could not be worked out with these psychoanalytic auxiliary concepts. What was needed was a *functional theory of psychic structure,* based on biological facts.

At the same time, clinical experience had shown the goal of therapy to be orgastic potency. I knew the goal, and with a few patients I succeeded in reaching it, but about a technique with which one could be sure to reach it I knew nothing. More than that: the surer I became of the therapeutic goal, the more I had to admit the inadequacy of my technical skill. Instead of diminishing, the discrepancy between goal and achievement grew.

The therapeutic usefulness of Freud's schemata of psychic functioning proved limited. The making conscious of unconscious desires and conflicts had no considerable effect unless genitality was established. As to the concept of the unconscious need for punishment, nothing could be accomplished with it. For, if there were such a thing as a biological instinct to remain ill and to suffer, any therapeutic endeavor would be hopeless!

This sad state of affairs in the matter of therapy was the undoing of many. Stekel gave up working on the resistance against the uncovering of unconscious material and "shot at the unconscious with interpretations", as is still the habit of "wild psychoanalysts". A hopeless situation. He denied the existence of the actual neuroses and of the castration complex. He was after quick cures. So he separated himself from the tedious, but fundamentally productive yoke of Freud.

Adler rejected the sexual etiology of the neuroses when he became aware of guilt feelings and aggression. He ended up as a finalistic philosopher and social moralist.

Jung had generalized the concept of libido to such an extent as to make it completely lose its meaning of *sexual* energy. He ended up with the "collective unconscious" and, with that, in mysticism, which he later, as a National Socialist, officially represented.[1]

Ferenczi, that talented and outstanding person, was perfectly aware of the sad state of affairs in therapy. He looked for a solution in the *somatic* sphere, and developed an "active technique" directed at the somatic tension states. But he did not know the stasis neurosis and failed to take the orgasm theory seriously.

Rank also was aware of the inadequacies of technique. He recognized the longing for peace, for return to the womb. He misunderstood the fear of living in this terrible world and misinterpreted it in a biological sense as the trauma of birth, which he supposed to be *the* nucleus of the neurosis. He failed to ask himself why people long to get away from real life and back into the protective womb. He came into conflict with Freud, who continued to adhere to the libido theory, and became an outsider.

---

[1] *Translator's note:* In 1933, Jung took over the presidency of the *Allgemeine Aerztliche Gesellschaft für Psychotherapie* and the editorship of its organ, the *Zentralblatt für Psychotherapie.* Speaking about the major goal of the Zentralblatt, Jung stated in the first number edited by him: "That there are actual differences between Germanic and Semitic psychology has long been known to intelligent people. These differences are no longer going to be obliterated, which can be only to the advantage of science." This was completely in line with the simultaneous statement of the *Reichsführer* of the *Deutsche Allgemeine Aerztliche Gesellschaft für Psychotherapie,* Prof. Dr. M. H. Göring, that "the society (for psychotherapy) assumes of all members who are active as writers or speakers that they have worked through in all scientific earnest Adolf Hitler's fundamental work *'Mein Kampf'* and that they acknowledge it as the basis of their work. The society wants to cooperate in the work of the Volkskanzler, to educate the German people *to a heroic, self-sacrificing attitude*" (italics the translator's).

All of them came to grief upon the *one* question which determines *every* psychotherapeutic situation: *What shall the patient do with his natural sexuality, once it is liberated from repression?* Freud neither hinted at this question, nor, as it turned out later, even tolerated it. Finally, Freud himself—due to the avoidance of this central question—created gigantic difficulties by postulating a biological instinct to suffer and die.

Such questions did not lend themselves to a theoretical solution. The example of Rank, Jung, Adler and others warned against making contentions which were not in every detail substantiated by clinical observation. I was exposed to the danger of oversimplifying the whole problem and of saying: "Just let patients have sexual intercourse if they live in abstinence, just let them masturbate, and everything will be all right". In this way, analysts tried to misinterpret my theory of genitality, and, in fact, that is what many physicians and even psychiatrists were telling their patients. They had heard that lack of sexual satisfaction was the cause of neuroses, and so they let their patients "satisfy themselves". They attempted quick cures.

What was overlooked was the fact that the essence of a neurosis is the *inability of the patient to obtain gratification.* The focal point of this seemingly simple but actually very complicated problem is *"orgastic impotence"*. My first relevant observation was the fact that genital satisfaction relieved symptoms. However, clinical observation showed also that only very rarely is genital energy available in the necessary amount. It was necessary to look for the places and mechanisms in which this energy was bound up or misdirected. Pathological destructiveness—or, simply, human malice quite generally—proved to be one of these misdirections of genital energy. It took extensive, theoretically correct work to arrive at this conclusion. The patients' aggression proved to be misdirected, burdened with guilt feelings, shunted off from reality, and usually itself severely repressed. Freud's new theory of a primary biological destructiveness made a solution more difficult. For, if the everyday manifestations of sadism and brutality, free and repressed, were the expression of a *biological, i.e., natural,* instinctual force, psychotherapy had little chance indeed, as did our highly valued cultural ideals. If even the drive for self-destruction were an unchangeable biological fact, there would seem to be no other prospect left than mutual slaughter among human beings. If that were so, neuroses would be *biological* manifestations.

What, then, did we practise psychotherapy for? I did not want to speculate on this question; I wanted to have an unequivocal answer. Behind such statements as the above there were affective hindrances to learning the truth. Furthermore, my experience pointed to a certain path leading to a practical goal: *Sexual stasis is the result of a disturbed orgastic function. Neuroses are curable by the elimination of their source of energy, i.e., the sexual stasis.* This path was leading over secret and dangerous ground; genital energy was bound, covered up, and disguised in many places and various ways. The subject was banished by the official world. The techniques of research and therapy had to be recovered from the unfortunate condition in which they were. Only a practical dynamic method of psychotherapy could safeguard one from following dangerous by-paths. In this way, character-analysis became, in the course of the succeeding ten years, the technique which helped to disclose the stopped-up sources of genital energy. As a therapeutic method, it had four tasks:

1. Detailed investigation of *human behavior, including that in the sexual act.*
2. An understanding of *human sadism* and a method of handling it.
3. Exploration of the most important psychopathological

manifestations having their roots in the periods *preceding* the infantile genital phase. The ways *in which non-genital sexuality impedes* the genital function had to be discovered.

4. Exploration of the *social* causation of genital disturbances.

4. DESTRUCTION, AGGRESSION AND SADISM

The psychoanalytic use of the terms "aggression", "sadism", "destruction" and "death instinct" was confusing. "Aggression" seemed to be synonymous with "destruction". This, in turn, was "death instinct turned toward the outer world". "Sadism" remained the *primary* partial impulse which, at a certain stage of sexual development, began to become active. I made it a point to study the origin and purpose of all human actions which came under the heading "hatred". What I *never* could find in my clinical work was a will to die, a death instinct as a primary impulse, corresponding to the sexual instinct or to the need for food. All psychic manifestations which might be interpreted as "death instinct" proved to be *products of the neurosis.* Suicide, for example, proved to be either an unconscious revenge upon another person with whom the patient identified himself, or a way of escaping the pressure of an all too complicated life situation.

Clinically, the patients' fear of death reduced itself regularly to a *fear of catastrophe,* and this in turn to *genital anxiety.* Furthermore, the death instinct analysts frequently confused anxiety and instinct. The fact that *fear of death and dying is identical with unconscious orgasm anxiety, and that the alleged death instinct, the longing for dissolution, for nothingness, is unconscious longing for orgastic release of tension,* that did not become clear to me until about eight years later. Thus, I could hardly be accused of "premature and schematic generalization of the orgasm theory".

A living being develops a *destructive* impulse when it

wants to destroy a source of danger. In that case, destruction or killing of the object is the biologically rational goal. The motive is not any primary pleasure in destruction, but the interest of the "life instinct" (to use the then current term) *to escape anxiety and to preserve the total ego. We destroy in a danger situation because we want to live and because we do not want to suffer anxiety.* The destructive instinct, then, makes its appearance in the service of a primary biological will to live. It carries, in itself, no sexual connotation. Its aim is not pleasure, although liberation from pain always is a pleasurable experience.

These things are important for many basic concepts of sex-economy. Sex-economic theory denies the *primary* biological character of destructiveness. An animal does not kill another animal for the pleasure of killing; that would be sadistic murder for pleasure's sake. It kills because it is hungry or feels its life threatened. Here, too, destruction appears as a function of the living in the service of the "life instinct". What the latter is, we still do not know.

"Aggression" in the strict sense of the word has nothing to do with either sadism or destruction. Its literal meaning is "approaching". *Every positive manifestation of life is aggressive;* pleasurable sexual activity as well as destructive hateful activity; sadistic activity as well as the securing of food. Aggression is the living manifestation of the *musculature,* the system of motion and locomotion. Much of the pernicious inhibition of aggression which our children have to suffer is due to the equation of "aggressive" with "wicked" or "sexual." *The goal of aggression is always that of making possible the gratification of a vital need.* Aggression is, therefore, *not* an instinct in the proper sense, *but the indispensable means* of gratifying any instinct. The instinct in itself is aggressive because the tension calls for gratification. Thus, we have to distinguish a *destructive,* a *sadistic,* a *locomotor,* and a *sexual aggressiveness.*

If aggressive sexuality is barred from gratification, the urge to obtain gratification remains, nevertheless. The impulse arises to obtain it by *all possible means.* The aggressive tone begins to drown out the tone of love. If the pleasure aim has been completely eliminated, if it has become unconscious or beset with anxiety, then aggression—originally only a means to an end—becomes itself the behavior which will release tension. Aggression then becomes pleasurable *as such.* In this way, sadism arises. The loss of the real love aim results in hatred. One hates most when one is prevented from loving or being loved. Thus, aggression assumes the character of destructiveness *with sexual aims,* as, e.g., in sex murder. Its prerequisite is the complete inability to experience sexual pleasure in a natural way. The perversion "sadism" (the impulse to satisfy oneself by hurting or destroying the object) is, therefore, a mixture of primary sexual and secondary destructive impulses. It does not exist in the animal kingdom and is a recent acquisition of man, a *secondary drive.* Every kind of *destructive action by itself is the reaction of the organism to the denial of the gratification of a vital need, especially the sexual.*

During the years of 1924 to 1927, when these things became clear to me, I nevertheless retained in my publications the term "death instinct", in order not to be "out of step". In my clinical work, however, I denied the existence of the death instinct. Its biological interpretation I did not discuss, because I had nothing to say about it. In practical work it always appeared as destructive instinct. However, I had already formulated the *relationship between the destructive instinct and sexual stasis,* at first according to its intensity. The question as to the biological nature of destructiveness I left open. Lack of facts warned me to be cautious. But even at that time there was no doubt that every suppression of sexual urges produces hatred, aggression as such, i.e., motor unrest without a rational goal, and destructive tendencies. Soon, numerous examples appeared in clinical practice, everyday life and the life of animals.

It was impossible to overlook the decrease of hatred in patients at the time when they acquired the ability to obtain natural sexual pleasure. Every transformation from a compulsion neurosis to hysteria was accompanied by a diminution of hatred. Sadistic perversions or sadistic phantasies during the sexual act decreased to the same extent to which satisfaction increased. These observations explained, among other things, the increase of marital conflicts commonly occurring with a decrease of sexual attraction and satisfaction, as well as the decrease of marital brutality when another, satisfactory partner was found. I made inquiries about the behavior of wild animals and learned that they are harmless when their hunger and their sexual needs are satisfied. Bulls are only dangerous when being led to the cow, not on being led away. Dogs are dangerous when kept on the chain, because exercise and sexual satisfaction are made impossible. The cruel character traits of people with chronic lack of sexual satisfaction thus became understandable. They are well known, e.g., in sharp-tongued spinsters and ascetic moralists. The mildness and kindness of individuals capable of genital satisfaction was striking in contrast. I have never seen individuals capable of genital satisfaction who had sadistic character traits. If such people showed sadistic tendencies, it could safely be assumed that they had met with a sudden obstacle to their accustomed gratification. The behavior of women at the menopause shows the same thing. There are women at the menopause without any trace of acrimony or irrational hatred, and there are others who during these years develop a malicious character. It can easily be demonstrated that they differ in their sexual past. The latter type are women who never had a satisfactory love relationship and now regret it and—consciously or unconsciously—suffer from the results of their abstinence or lack of gratification. Motivated by hatred and envy, they become the bitterest enemies of any progress. The general sadistic destructiveness of our times is the result of the prevalent inhibition of natural love life.

An important source of genital energy had become evident: By the elimination of destructive aggression, of sadism, energies are liberated which can be transferred to the genital system. It soon became clear that orgastic potency and strong destructive or sadistic impulses are incompatible. One cannot want to give the partner sexual happiness and simultaneously want to destroy him or her. The slogans of "sadistic masculine and masochistic feminine sexuality" were therefore wrong. So was the concept that phantasies of rape are part of normal sexuality. If psychoanalysts make such assumptions, they simply fail to think in terms beyond the prevalent human sexual structure.

Just as genital energies, when they meet frustration, are transferred into destructive ones, so can they be *transferred back into genital energies if there is freedom and gratification.* The theory of the primary biological nature of sadism was untenable clinically and hopeless from a cultural point of view. But even realizing this did not solve the problem of how to achieve the therapeutic aim of orgastic potency. For, the destructive energies, too, were bound in many places and in various ways. If the energy was to be liberated, the technical task was, therefore, that of finding the mechanisms inhibiting the reactions of hatred. The most fruitful object of investigation in this connection proved to be the character armor in the form of the emotional block ("*Affektsperre*").

The development of systematic resistance-analysis into character-analysis did not take place until after 1926. Up to that time, the work in the technical seminar was concentrated on the study of latent resistances and on pregenital disturbances. Patients would show certain typical behavior when liberated sexual energy made itself felt in the genital system. As genital excitation increased, most patients responded with a flight into non-genital attitudes. The sexual energy seemed to *"oscillate"* between the genital and pre-genital loci of excitation.

About 1925 I treated a young American woman who had suffered from severe bronchial asthma since early childhood. Every situation involving sexual excitation would produce an attack. Thus, she would have an attack when she was about to have sexual intercourse with her husband, or when she flirted and started to become aroused. She would become severely dyspneic and could get relief only from special antispasmodic drugs. She suffered from vaginal hypesthesia; her throat, however, was highly irritable. There were strong unconscious impulses—directed against her mother—to suck and bite. She suffered from choking sensations. The phantasy of having a penis sticking in her throat was clearly manifested in dreams and actions. When these phantasies became conscious, the asthma disappeared for the first time. However, it was replaced by severe attacks of vagotonic diarrhea, alternating with sympatheticotonic constipation. The phantasy of having a penis in her throat was superseded by that of "having a baby in her stomach and having to expel it". With the appearance of diarrhea, the genital disturbance became more severe; she lost vaginal sensations completely and refused to have sexual intercourse. She was afraid of an attack of diarrhea during sexual intercourse. When the intestinal symptoms subsided, she experienced for the first time pre-orgastic vaginal excitation. However, it did not exceed a certain limit. Any *increase* in excitation produced either anxiety or an attack of asthma. For some time, asthma, and with it the oral excitations and phantasies, were present again as if they had never been treated. With each relapse they reappeared, and again and again the excitation progressed to the genital system. Every time, there was an increased capacity for tolerating vaginal excitation. The intervals between relapses became longer. This continued for some months. *The asthma disappeared with each progress in vaginal excitation and returned with each shift of excitation from the genital to the respiratory organs.* This oscillation of sexual excitation between respiratory organs on the one hand and pelvis on the other, was accompanied by the corresponding oral and genital infantile phantasies: when the excitation was above, the patient became demanding in the infantile way, and depressive; when the excitation became genital again, the patient was feminine and desirous of the man. The genital anxiety which made her retreat again and again appeared at first as the fear of being injured in the sexual act. When this was resolved, there appeared a *fear of bursting or dissolution with excitation.* Gradually, the patient became accustomed to vaginal excitation and finally experienced orgasm. This time, the spasm in the throat failed to recur, and with it the asthma. When last heard from seven years later, the patient was still well.

This case confirmed my concept of the therapeutic function of the orgasm; but in addition it revealed some important mechanisms. I understood now that *non-genital excitations and modes of gratification are retained for fear of the intense orgastic sensations in the genital;* they are retained because they cause the occurrence of much milder sensations. Here was an important part of the enigma of instinctual anxiety.

If sexual excitation is checked, there arises a vicious circle: *the checking increases the stasis of excitation, and the increased stasis diminishes the ability of the organism to decrease it. Thus, the organism acquires a fear of excitation, in other words, sexual anxiety.* This sexual anxiety, therefore, is caused by an external frustration of instinctual gratification, and is anchored internally by the fear of the dammed-up sexual excitation. This is the mechanism of *orgasm anxiety.* It is the fear of the organism—which has become unwilling to experience pleasure—of the *overpowering* excitation of the genital system. *Orgasm anxiety forms the basis of the general pleasure anxiety,* which is an integral part of the prevailing human structure. It usually shows itself as a generalized fear of any kind of vegetative sensation or excitation or the perception of these. Since joy of living and orgastic pleasure are identical, general fear of life is the ultimate expression of orgasm anxiety.

The manifestations and mechanisms of orgasm anxiety are manifold. They all have in common the fear of the overpowering orgastic genital excitation. The mechanisms of checking this show great variation. Their elaboration took some eight years. Up to 1926 only a few typical mechanisms had been disclosed. They were most easily studied in female patients. In the male, orgasm anxiety is often covered up by the sensation of ejaculation. In women, however, it appears in undisguised form. Their most frequent fear is that of soiling themselves during excitation, of passing wind or of urinating involuntarily. The more drastically vaginal excitation is inhibited, the more non-genital phantasies have taken possession of the genital, the stronger is the inhibition, and, consequently, orgasm anxiety. Orgastic excitation, if curbed, is experienced as a threat of *physical destruction.* Women fear "falling into the power of the man", being injured or exploded from within by him. Under these circumstances, the vagina becomes in phantasy a biting organ which is going to render harmless the menacing penis. Every case of vaginismus has this origin. If it appears before the act, its significance is that of refusing penetration to the penis. If it appears during the act, it reveals the unconscious desire to retain the penis or to bite it off. In the presence of strong destructive impulses, the organism is afraid of "letting go" for fear that destructive fury might break through.

Women's reactions to orgasm anxiety are individually different. Most of them keep their bodies still, with a semiconscious vigilance. Others make violent, forced movements, because gentle motions result in too much excitation. The legs are pressed together, the pelvis is pulled back. In order to curb the orgastic sensation, the breath is always held. This latter phenomenon, peculiarly enough, escaped my attention until 1935.

One of my female patients with masochistic phantasies of being beaten had the unconscious fear of soiling herself with feces during sexual excitation. At the age of four, she had developed the masturbation phantasy that her bed contained a piece of apparatus that would automatically eliminate the dirt. Keeping the body still, for fear of soiling oneself, is a very common symptom of holding back.

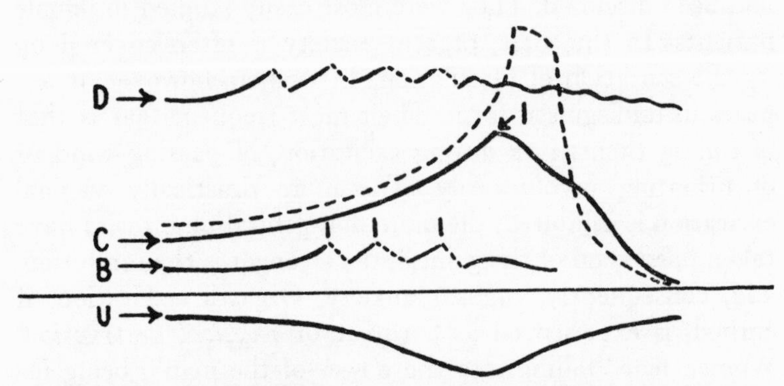

Diagram: Typical disturbances of genitality in both sexes.

U = Unpleasure and disgust in the case of ***total anesthesia*** in the sexual act.

B = ***Genital hypesthesia;*** limited pre-orgastic pleasure, intermittent inhibitions (I) with subsiding of sensations.

C = Normal pre-orgastic genital excitation, decrease of excitation without orgasm: ***isolated orgastic impotence.***

D = Orgasm disturbance in *nymphomania and satyriasis:* strong pre-orgastic excitation, no subsiding of excitation, no orgasm.

I = Inhibition; - - - - - - - - = Normal orgasm curve, for comparison.

Orgasm anxiety is often experienced as *fear of dying.* If there is present at the same time a hypochondriacal fear of catastrophe, every strong excitation has to be inhibited. The clouding of consciousness (a part of normal orgasm) becomes an anxiety-laden instead of a pleasurable experience. As a defense, one has to be always "on one's guard", "not to lose one's head"; one is "vigilant". This expresses itself in the forehead and eyebrows as an attitude of vigilance.

Every form of neurosis has its characteristic form of genital disturbance. Hysterical women show a localized lack of vaginal excitability with generalized hypersexuality. Their typical genital disturbance is *abstinence* as a result of genital anxiety. Hysterical men suffer either from erective impotence or premature ejaculation.

Compulsion neuroses show rigid, ascetic, well rationalized abstinence. Women are frigid and generally unexcitable. Men are often erectively potent, but always orgastically impotent.

Among the neurasthenias, there is a chronic form characterized by spermatorrhea and a pregenital structure. Here, the penis has completely lost the role of a penetrating pleasure organ. It represents a breast being given to the child, a piece of feces being expelled, etc.

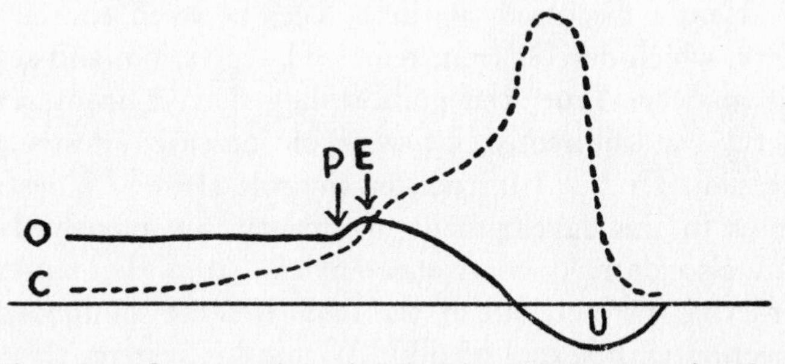

Diagram: Course of excitation in premature ejaculation.
O = overexcitation of genital; P = penetration; E = ejaculation; U = unpleasure after ejaculation; C = curve of normal orgasm for comparison.

A fourth group is formed by the men who show excessive erective potency, for fear of the woman and in defense against unconscious homosexual phantasies. The sexual act serves the purpose of proving their "potency", the penis serves as a piercing instrument with sadistic phantasies. These are the phallic-narcissistic males, as they are always found among army officers of the Prussian type, Don Juans and other *compulsively* self-confident individuals. They all suffer from a severe orgastic disturbance. To them, the sexual act is nothing but an evacuation, followed by a reaction of disgust. They do not embrace a woman, they "make" her. Their sexual behavior creates among women an intense disgust for the sexual act.

Some of these clinical findings I reported at the International Psychoanalytic Congress in Homburg, 1925, in a paper *"Ueber die chronische hypochondrische Neurasthenie"*. In this paper I discussed in particular what I had called *"genital asthenia"*, a disturbance in which the individual does not permit genital excitation to occur with ideas of genital activity, but only with ideas of a pregenital nature (such as sucking, piercing, etc.). Another part of the subject appeared under the title *"Quellen der neurotischen Angst"*, in the *Festschrift* to Freud's seventieth birthday in May, 1926. Here I discussed the differences between conscience-anxiety, which derives from repressed aggression, and sexual stasis anxiety. True, the guilt feeling derives from sexual anxiety, but indirectly, by way of increased destructive aggression. That is, I introduced the role played by destructiveness in the development of anxiety. Six months later, Freud also derived conscience-anxiety from the repressed destructive instinct, but at the same time he minimized its connection with sexual anxiety. Within his system, this was logical; for, he considered the destructive instinct a *primary* biological instinct, on a par with sexuality. In the meantime, I had shown that *the intensity of the destructive impulse depends on the degree of sexual stasis,* and had differentiated "aggression" from "destruction". Theoretical and specialized as these differentiations may sound, they are, nevertheless, of fundamental significance. They led in an entirely different direction from Freud's concept of destruction.

The major part of the clinical findings were brought together in my book, *"Die Funktion des Orgasmus"*. I presented the manuscript, with a dedication, to Freud on May 6, 1926. His reaction on reading the title was not gratifying. He looked at the manuscript, hesitated for a moment, and said, as if disturbed: "That thick"? I felt uneasy. That was not a rational reaction. He was always very polite and would not have made such a cutting remark without a basis.

It had always been Freud's habit to read a manuscript in a few days and then to give his opinion in writing. This time, more than two months elapsed before I received his letter. It ran:

"Dear Dr. Reich: I took plenty of time, but finally I did read the manuscript which you dedicated to me for my anniversary. I find the book valuable, rich in observation and thought. As you know, I am in no way opposed to your attempt to solve the problem of neurasthenia by explaining it on the basis of the absence of genital primacy".

With regard to an earlier paper concerning the problem of neurasthenia, Freud had written me:

"I have known for a long time that my formulation of the *Aktualneurosen* was superficial and in need of thoroughgoing correction. . . . Clarification was to be expected from further, intelligent investigation. Your efforts seem to point a new and hopeful way. . . . Whether your assumption really solves the problem, I do not know. I still have certain doubts. You, yourself, leave unexplained some of the most characteristic symptoms, and *your whole concept of the displacement of the genital libido is not yet satisfying to me ("ist mir noch nicht mundgerecht")*.[1] However, I trust you will keep the problem in mind and will arrive at a satisfactory solution".

These latter comments referred to some partial solution of the problem of neurasthenia in 1925, the first-quoted letter to a detailed presentation of the orgasm problem and the role of somatic stasis in the neurosis. One can notice an increased coolness. At first I did not understand. Why should Freud reject the "orgasm theory" which was enthusiastically welcomed by most of the younger analysts? I had no idea that the deterrent factor here lay in the consequences of the orgasm theory for the whole theory of the neuroses.

On his seventieth birthday, Freud had told us that we should not trust the world. All these celebrations, he said, meant nothing. Psychoanalysis was being accepted only in

[1] Italics mine. W. R.

order to be destroyed all the more easily. Saying "psychoanalysis", he meant the theory of sex. But I had made a decisive contribution exactly to the *confirmation* of the theory of sex—and Freud rejected it? For this reason, I withheld the book on the function of the orgasm for a few months to think it over; it did not go to the printer until January, 1927.

In December, 1926, in Freud's inner circle, I gave a talk on character-analytic technique. As the central problem I presented the question as to whether, in the presence of a latent negative attitude, one should interpret the patient's incestuous desires, or whether one would have to wait until the patient's distrust was eliminated. Freud interrupted me: "Why would you *not* interpret the material in the order in which it appears? *Of course* one has to analyze and interpret incest dreams as soon as they appear". This I had not expected. I kept on substantiating my point of view. The whole idea was foreign to Freud. He did not see why one should follow the line of the resistances instead of that of the material. In private conversations about technique he seemed to have thought differently. The atmosphere of the meeting was unpleasant. My opponents in the seminar gloated and pitied me. I remained calm.

In the seminar, the problems of a "theory of therapy" stood in the foreground in the years after 1926. As the official report of the psychoanalytic clinic stated: "The causes of psychoanalytic successes and failures, the criteria of cure, an attempted typology of the neuroses according to the resistances and to prognosis, the questions of character resistance and character-analysis, of the 'narcissistic resistances' and the 'emotional block' were studied from the clinical and theoretical standpoint, always on the basis of concrete cases. Also, a number of publications dealing with technical problems were reviewed".

The repute of our seminar became greater. Freud, in a

letter, acknowledged the originality of my work with reference to psychoanalytic theory in general (*"gegenüber dem Gemeingut"*). However, this *"Gemeingut"* was not sufficient for the training of practising analysts. My contention was that I simply applied psychoanalytic principles consistently to the study of character. I did not know that I was interpreting Freud's theory in a way which he himself was soon to reject. I had as yet no idea of the incompatibility of the orgasm theory and its consequences with the principles of the later psychoanalytic theory of the neuroses.

5. THE GENITAL CHARACTER AND THE NEUROTIC CHARACTER. THE PRINCIPLE OF SELF-REGULATION

My physiological intuitions—for that was all it amounted to at that time—did not lend themselves to practical or theoretical application. So I proceeded to develop my character-analytic technique. The orgasm theory was sufficiently substantiated clinically to provide a solid basis for this.

In 1928, I published an article, *"Zur Technik der Deutung und der Widerstandsanalyse"*, in the Internationale Zeitschrift für Psychoanalyse. It was the first of a number of articles which, in the course of the next five years, came to make up the book *"Charakter-Analyse"* (1933). It was to appear in the Internationaler Psychoanalytischer Verlag. It was in type and I was already reading the second proof, when the Executive Committee of the International Psychoanalytical Association decided that the Verlag should publish the book only "on commission", i.e., without the imprint of the Verlag: Hitler had just assumed power.

With typical technical errors of the usual, so-called "orthodox" psychoanalysis as a starting point, the principle of *consistency* was developed in the seminar. Psychoanalysis followed the rule of interpreting the material offered by the patient as it appeared, without any consideration of stratification and depth. I suggested a systematic working through from a central point of the psychic surface which was important in the immediate situation. The neurosis was to be undermined from one point of which one could be sure. Every bit of psychic energy which was liberated through the dissolution of defensive functions would reinforce the unconscious instinctual demands and thus increase their accessibility. The stratification of the neurotic mechanisms had to be taken into account by way of a systematic peeling off of the strata in the character armor. Direct interpretations of unconscious instinctual material could only impede this procedure, and was therefore to be avoided. First the patient had to gain contact with himself before he could comprehend the connections between his conscious and his unconscious. As long as the armor was operative, the best a patient could achieve was an intellectual understanding, from which, as experience taught us, little therapeutic effect could be expected.

A further rule developed in the seminar was to start consistently *from the defense mechanisms*, and not to touch upon repressed sexual impulses so long as the defense mechanisms were not eliminated. In the analysis of resistances I suggested rigid consistency, i.e., lingering at that part of the defense mechanisms which at the moment proved the main hindrance. As every patient had a character armor constructed according to his individual history, the technique of destroying the armor had to fit the individual case and had to be newly developed step by step in each case. This requirement excluded the possibility of a schematic technique. The bulk of the responsibility for success rested with the therapist. As the armor *restricts* the patient, his inability to be honest is part of his illness, and not malicious intention, as many believed at that time. Correct dissolution of the rigid armor must finally lead to the liberation of anxiety.

Once the stasis anxiety is liberated, there is every possibility for the establishment of free-flowing energy, and with it, of genital potency. It remained only a question whether by the handling of the character armor the ultimate sources of energy were being tapped. I had my doubts, which later proved justified. However, there was no question that the character-analytic technique represented a considerable step forward in the handling of severe, inveterate neuroses. The emphasis was no longer on the content of the neurotic phantasy, but on the energy function. As the so-called fundamental psychoanalytic rule, "to say everything that comes to mind", was impracticable in most patients, I made myself independent of it by taking as the point of attack not only what the patient said, but *everything* he presented, particularly the *manner* of his communications or of his silence. Patients who kept silent were also communicating, were expressing something that gradually could be understood and handled. In my case presentations, I still put the *how* beside the *what* of the old Freudian technique. However, I already knew that the how, the *form* of behavior and communications, was much more essential than what the patient related. Words can lie. The *mode of expression never lies.* It is the immediate, unconscious manifestation of the character. In the course of time, I learned to comprehend the very form of the communications itself as an immediate manifestation of the unconscious. Attempts to convince or persuade patients became less important and soon superfluous. What the patient did not comprehend spontaneously and automatically, was of no therapeutic value. Character attitudes had to be understood spontaneously. The intellectual understanding of the unconscious gave way to the patient's becoming aware of his own mode of expression. For years, patients had not heard any psychoanalytic technical terms from me. They were thus deprived of the possibility of covering up an instinctual desire behind a word.

The patient no longer talked about his hatred, he felt it; he could not escape it, as long as his armor was being correctly taken apart.

Narcissistic types were considered unsuitable subjects for psychoanalytic treatment. Through the destruction of the armor, these cases became accessible. Thus I was able to record cures of severe character disturbances such as were considered inaccessible to the usual method.[1]

The transference of love and hatred to the analyst lost its more or less academic character. It is one thing to talk about infantile anal eroticism, to remember that such things were felt at one time; it is quite another thing to feel them actually during the session as an urge to pass wind or even to have to give in to it. In this case, there is no need for persuading or convincing the patient. I finally had to free myself of the academic attitude toward the patient and had to say to myself that as a sexologist I could not treat sexuality any differently than the internist treats various bodily organs. Thus I discovered the serious hindrance caused by the rule—imposed by most analysts—that, for the duration of the treatment, the patient had to observe sexual abstinence. If that rule was imposed, how could the patient's genital disturbances be understood and eliminated?

---

[1]Herold, like others, underestimates the differences between character-analysis and the usual psychoanalytic technique, when he presents them as mere technical refinements instead of fundamental theoretical differences. (Carl M. Herold, "A Controversy about Technique", Psychoanalytic Quarterly, 8, 1939). However, the following argument of his is correct: "We often hear raised at this point in the controversy the objection that all this is not new and is practised by every good analyst. This is a very elegant way of suggesting modestly that one is a really good analyst but it leaves unanswered the question why these really good analysts did not trouble themselves to state these things with such clarity, especially as they should have known that among the younger analysts there was a keen desire for such technical advice. This desire must indeed have been very strong, judging from the eagerness with which Reich's book and ideas were absorbed by the younger German analysts. They had been stuffed with complicated theories but given very few clues as to how to use them in practice. Reich offered a clear summing up of the theoretical aspects of the practical situation in which a young analyst finds himself, not elaborate enough perhaps to include all the intricate details, but simple enough to be readily usable in practical work".

These details of technique, which are presented at some length in my book, *"Charakter-Analyse"*, are mentioned here not for reasons of technique. They serve to illustrate the change in basic orientation which enabled me to recognize in my patients who were on their way to health the principle of sexual self-regulation (*"sexuelle Selbststeuerung"*), and to formulate it and to make it of use for later work.

Many psychoanalytic rules had the definite character of taboos, and thus only reinforced the neurotic taboos of the patient. Thus, for example, the rule that the analyst should not be seen, that he should be a blank screen, as it were, upon which the patient would project his transferences. This, instead of eliminating, confirmed in the patient the feeling of dealing with an "invisible", unapproachable, superhuman, that is, according to infantile thinking, a sexless being. How could the patient overcome his fear of sex which made him ill? Treated thus, sexuality remained forever something diabolical and forbidden, something which was under all circumstances to be "condemned" or "sublimated". It was forbidden to look at the analyst as a sexual being. How could the patient dare to come out with critical remarks? Patients know a great deal about their analysts, anyhow, though they seldom come out into the open with this knowledge when treated with this kind of technique. With me, they learned first of all to overcome any fear of criticizing me. According to the usual technique, the patient was supposed "only to recall and in no case to do anything". In rejecting this method, I found myself in agreement with Ferenczi. Of course, the patient should be "allowed to do". Ferenczi had difficulties with the Psychoanalytic Association because—with good intuition—he let his patients play, like children. I attempted in every possible way to free them of their characterological rigidity. They should look at me in an un-authoritative, *human* way.

Another important factor of my success in handling patients was that I freed them of their genital inhibitions with every means at my disposal compatible with professional medical work. No patient was claimed to be cured unless he was able at least to masturbate without guilt feelings. I considered it most important to keep track of the patients' genital life during the treatment. (I think the fact has been understood that this has nothing to do with a superficial "masturbation therapy" such as is practised by many "wild analysts"). In following this rule, I learned to distinguish pseudo-genitality from the natural genital attitude. Thus, in the course of years, the traits of the "*genital character*", as opposed to the neurotic character, gradually took shape.

I learned to overcome the fear of patients' behavior and discovered an undreamed-of world. *Beneath these neurotic mechanisms, behind all these dangerous, grotesque, irrational phantasies and impulses, I found a bit of simple, matter-of-fact, decent nature.* I found this in every single patient in whom it was possible to penetrate sufficiently deeply; this fact gave me courage. I gave the patients more and more freedom of action, and was not disappointed. True enough, dangerous situations would occur. But it may be significant that in my extensive and varied practice I did not have a single suicide. The cases of suicide that happened during psychoanalytic treatment I came to understand only much later: patients committed suicide when their sexual energies had been stirred up without being allowed proper discharge. The fear of the evil instincts which dominates the whole world had severely blocked the work of the psychoanalytic therapists. They had taken for granted *the absolute antithesis of nature* (instinct, sexuality) *and culture* (morality, work, duty) and had thus arrived at the thesis that the "living out of impulses" was contradictory to the cure. Finally, I learned to overcome my fear of these impulses. For it became clear *that these antisocial impulses which fill the unconscious are evil and dangerous only as long as the discharge of energy by way of a natural love life is blocked.*

If it is blocked, there are, basically, three pathological ways out: unbridled, self-destructive *impulsiveness* (addictions, alcoholism, crime as a result of guilt feeling, psychopathic impulsiveness, sex murder, rape of children, etc.); the *instinct-inhibited character-neuroses* (compulsion neurosis, anxiety hysteria, conversion hysteria); and the *functional psychoses* (schizophrenia, melancholia or manic-depressive disease); not to mention the neurotic mechanisms which dominate politics, war, marital life, education, etc., all of which are results of genital frustration.

With the attainment of the capacity for full genital surrender, the whole being of the patients changed so rapidly and so basically that at first I could not understand it. It was difficult to see how the tenacious neurotic process could admit of such a sudden change. Not only did the symptoms of neurotic anxiety disappear, but the whole being changed. The disappearance of symptoms could be understood on the basis of the withdrawal of the sexual energy that had previously nourished the symptoms. The genital character, however, seemed to follow different, as yet unknown laws. A few examples may be mentioned here.

Quite spontaneously, patients began to feel the moralistic attitudes of the environment as something alien and queer. However strictly they might have previously defended the principle of premarital chastity, now they felt such a demand as grotesque. They no longer had any contact with it, they became indifferent to it.

As far as work was concerned, their reactions changed noticeably. If previously they had worked mechanically, without any inward relationship to the work, if they had looked upon work as a necessary evil which one takes upon oneself without giving it much thought, now they began to discriminate. If, due to neurotic disturbances, they had not been working, they began to feel a strong need for some vital work in which they could have a personal interest. If the work in which they were engaged lent itself to the absorption of real interest, they blossomed out. If, however, their work was mechanical as e.g., that of an employee, a merchant or a clerk, it became an almost unbearable burden. The difficulty which now made its appearance in such cases was hard to overcome. For, the world was not geared to a consideration of the human interest in work. Teachers who, though liberal, had not been particularly critical of present-day education, began to feel the usual manner of handling children as painful and intolerable. In short, the utilization of instinctual forces in work differed according to the work itself and according to social conditions. Gradually, two trends could be distinguished. One was a growing absorption in some social activity; the other was a sharp protest of the organism against empty, *mechanical* work.

In other cases, establishment of genital satisfaction resulted in a complete breakdown of work. This seemed to confirm the warnings of the world that sexuality and work are contradictory. Examined more closely, this state of affairs became less disturbing. It turned out that these were patients who in their work had always been driven by a compulsive sense of duty, which was in sharp contrast to their inner wishes which they had renounced. These wishes were by no means antisocial. On the contrary. An individual, e.g., who felt best suited to be a free-lance writer and who worked as a law clerk, had to muster all his forces to master his rebellion and to keep his healthy impulses repressed. Thus I recognized the important rule that not all that is unconscious is also antisocial, or that not all that is conscious is also social. On the contrary, there are highly valuable, even culturally important traits and impulses which have to be repressed for considerations of material survival. On the other hand, there are highly antisocial activities which society rewards with fame and honor. Divinity students were very difficult to deal with in this respect; there was always a serious conflict between sexuality and the practice of their vocation. I decided, therefore, not to accept any more clergymen for treatment.

The change in the sexual sphere was equally striking. Patients who up to the attainment of orgastic potency had no conflicts about going to prostitutes, now felt incapable of doing so. Women who previously had patiently endured living with an unloved man, who had suffered the sexual act as a "marital duty", were no longer able to do so. They went on strike, would have no more of it. What could I say against it? It was at variance with all accepted views, such as the one that a wife, as a matter of course, has to grant her husband sexual satisfaction as long as the marriage lasts; whether she wants to or not, whether she loves him or not, whether she is aroused or not. The ocean of lies in this world is deep!

From the point of view of my official position it was embarrassing when a woman, freed of her neurotic mechanisms, frankly began to demand of life the gratification of her need for love, and no longer troubled herself about official morals. After a few timid attempts, I no longer dared to present such facts in the seminar or in the psychoanalytic society. I would have had to meet the empty objection that I was imposing my views on my patients. I would have had to come out bluntly and to make it quite clear that the moralistic and authoritarian prejudice was not on my side, but that of my opponents. It also would have been useless to alleviate this impression by means of presenting that side of the picture which was more in keeping with official morality. For example, some of my female patients, married and unmarried, had been in the habit, up to time of cure, of going to bed with every Tom, Dick and Harry. Orgasmotherapy made it impossible for them to continue such behavior. Their previous behavior had been the result of the fact that they experienced no sensations in the sexual act whatsoever; whereas now, they experienced full sensation in the act and therefore regarded it as an important part of their lives, not to be dealt with as lightly as their former behavior would indicate. That, in other words, they became "moral", in the sense of wanting only one partner, but one who loved and satisfied them.[1] It would have been of no use. Where scientific work is bound by moralistic concepts it is not guided by facts.

The painful thing about all of this is the bragging about "scientific objectivity". The more one is caught in the toils of dependency, the louder one claims to be an "objective scientist". A psychoanalyst, in sending me a woman for treatment who suffered from melancholia, suicidal impulses and acute anxiety, went so far as to stipulate explicitly "not to destroy the marriage". As I learned during the first hour, the patient had been married for four years. Her husband had not deflowered her, but, instead, had engaged in various perverse practices with her. These, in her sexual ignorance, she had endured as part of the "natural marital duties". This marriage, said the referring analyst, should not be destroyed under any circumstances! After three hours, the patient

---

[1] *Translator's note:* The idea of a natural (as distinct from a compulsive) morality is so alien to most people that in talking or writing about it one is always in danger of being misunderstood. In going over the manuscript, Dr. Silverberg pointed out a possible misunderstanding at this point; with his permission I am quoting his comment: "I would suggest some emendation here in order to avert the impression that orgasmotherapy makes people monogamous. As I gather the meaning, the orgastically potent woman takes her sexual life seriously enough not to want to fritter her energies away indiscriminately, but is apt to let each relationship develop and run its own course, one at a time. This does not mean that she remains 'true' to one man all her life, but only so long as the relationship with him 'lasts', a period determined by certain inner laws within the relationship itself and usually of considerably longer duration than is implied in the case of the woman who sleeps with every Tom, Dick and Harry. I think Dr. Reich should make it clear that he is not referring here to 'monogamy' in its present-day usage of 'true to one man until death (or divorce) do us part'."—This comment makes the point quite clear. The subject is discussed extensively in Dr. Reich's book, *"Die Sexualität im Kulturkampf"*.

broke off because of severe acute anxiety, and because she felt the analytic situation to be one of seduction. I knew this, but there was nothing I could do. A few months later I learned that she had committed suicide. This kind of "objective science" is a millstone around the neck of a drowning humanity.

My concepts of the relation of psychic structure to the existing social order became confused. The changes occurring in my patients were both positively and negatively ambiguous. Their new structure seemed to follow laws which had nothing in common with the usual moral concepts and demands, laws which were new to me, of whose existence I had previously had no idea. The picture presented at the end by all of them was that of a *different kind of sociality*. It contained the best principles of official morality, such as, for example, that one does not rape women or seduce children. However, there appeared at the same time, moral attitudes which, although entirely valid from a social point of view, were, nevertheless, in striking contradiction to the usual concepts. Thus, for example, they evolved the attitude that it was the sign of an inferior nature to lead a chaste life under pressure of external compulsion, or to remain faithful out of duty. The attitude, e.g., that it is unsatisfactory and ugly to embrace a partner against his or her will, would seem to be unassailable, even from the point of view of the strictest morality: yet, it was at variance with the concept of "marital duty" which enjoyed the protection of the law.

These few examples may suffice for many. This different kind of morality was not governed by a "Thou shalt" and "Thou shalt not", but resulted spontaneously from the demands of genital desire and satisfaction. An unsatisfactory act was abstained from not because of fear, but because it failed to provide sexual happiness. These people abstained from a sexual act, even when they felt the desire for it, if and when external or internal circumstances failed to guarantee full satisfaction. It was as if the moral agencies disappeared completely and were replaced by better and more tenable safeguards against antisociality; safeguards which were not at variance with natural needs, but were, on the contrary, based on the principle that *life is to be enjoyed.* The deep chasm between "I want to" and "I dare not" disappeared. It was replaced, as it were, by a *vegetative consideration:* "I would like to very much, but I would not get much out of it, it would not give me pleasure". Without question a basically different thing. Behavior became organized according to a self-regulatory principle. This self-regulation brought with it a certain harmony, because it made unnecessary and eliminated the struggle against an instinct which, though repressed, constantly kept pressing forward. The interest simply was shifted to another aim or love object which offered fewer obstacles to satisfaction. The prerequisite was that the interest—which in itself was natural and social—was subject neither to repression nor to moral condemnation. It merely became satisfied at a different place and under different circumstances.

If for example, a young man loved a "nice" girl from a so-called "good family", that was natural enough. If he wanted to embrace her sexually, that was not "well adjusted" according to current social standards, but it was healthy. If the girl proved herself healthy enough to overcome all internal and external difficulties, everything went well. It was against official morality, but it was entirely sensible, healthy behavior. If, on the other hand, the girl proved weak, apprehensive, emotionally dependent on parental opinion, in brief, neurotic, the sexual embrace could only result in difficulties. The young man could make a *rational* choice *unless* he were morally inhibited himself and considered the thought of sexually embracing the girl as a kind of insult: He would either be able to help the girl to gain her own independence, or else he would withdraw from the situation. In the second case—which is as rational as the first—he would in time turn to another girl, one who would not present these difficulties.

On the other hand, a neurotic young man, one who is "moral" in the old sense, would have acted entirely differently in the same situation. He would have simultaneously desired the girl and renounced the fulfillment of his desire. He would thus have created a lasting conflict. The desire would have been kept under the pressure of moral denial, until the *conscious* conflict had been terminated by repression of the desire, and had thus become an unconscious conflict. The young man would have found himself in an increasingly difficult situation. He would have renounced the possibility of instinctual gratification with this girl, and would not have turned to another. The inevitable result would be a neurosis, for both partners. *The chasm between morals and instincts would continue to exist.* Or else, the instinct would manifest itself secretly in other places or in dangerous ways. The young man might equally well develop compulsive phantasies of rape, actual impulses to rape, or the traits of the double standard of morality. He would go to prostitutes and expose himself to venereal disease. There would be no possibility of inner harmony. From a purely social point of view, only damage would have been done. Not even compulsive morality would have been served in any way. This example permits infinite variations. It applies to the marital situation as well as to any other phase of love-life.

Let us compare *moral regulation* and *sex-economic self-regulation:*

Moral regulation operates as *duty.* It is incompatible with natural instinctual gratification. Self-regulation follows the natural laws of pleasure; it is not only compatible with *natural* instincts, but, rather, functionally identical with them. Moral regulation creates a sharp, insoluble conflict, that of *nature* versus *morals.* Thus it increases instinctual pressure, which in turn necessitates increased moral defense. It makes a natural circulation of energy in the organism impossible. Self-regulation withdraws the energy from a desire which cannot be satisfied by transferring the energy to other goals or partners. It consists in a steady alternation of tension and release of tension, as do all natural functions. The individual with a moral character structure performs his work without inward participation, as a result of the demands of a "Thou shalt" which is alien to the ego. The individual with a sex-economic character structure performs his work in unison with his sexual interests, out of the large reservoir of vital energy. The individual with a moral structure appears to follow the rigid laws of the moral world; in fact, he only adjusts outwardly and rebels inwardly. Thus he is exposed in the highest degree to an unconscious compulsive and impulsive antisociality. The healthy, self-regulated individual does not adjust himself to the irrational part of the world and insists on his natural rights. To the neurotic moralist, he appears sick and antisocial; in reality he is incapable of antisocial actions. He develops a *natural* self-assurance, based on sexual potency. The individual with a moral structure, without exception, is genitally weak and therefore under the constant necessity of compensating, i.e., of developing a false, rigid self-assurance. He tolerates sexual happiness in others poorly, because this arouses him, while he is at the same time incapable of enjoying it also. To him, the sexual act is essentially a demonstration of "potency". To the individual with a genital structure, sexuality is a pleasurable experience and nothing but that; work is joyous vital activity and achievement. To the morally structured individual, work is burdensome duty or only a means of making a living.

The character armor is also different in the two types. The individual with a moral structure has to develop an armor which is restrictive, dominating every action, functioning

Neurotic character *Genital character*

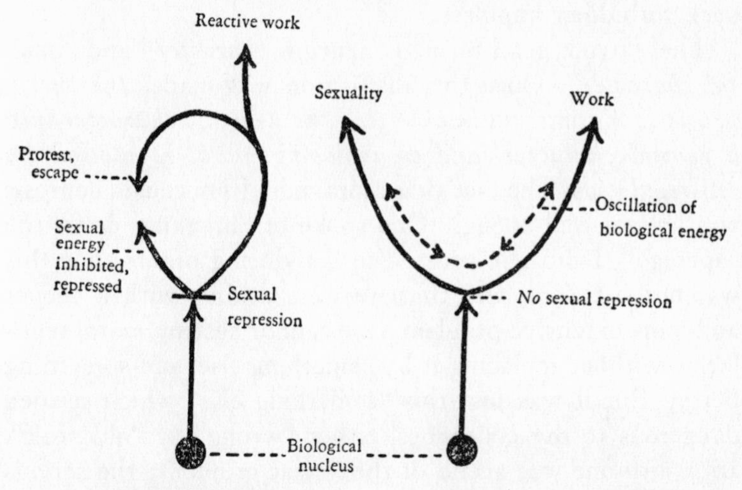

Reactive work

The achievement is mechanical, forced, devoid of vitality; it serves the purpose of deadening the sexual urge and is in acute conflict with it. Only small amounts of biological energy can be discharged in an interest in work. Work is essentially unpleasurable. Sexual phantasies are intense and interfere with work; thus, they have to be repressed, thereby creating neurotic mechanisms which in turn decrease the working capacity still further. The reduced achievement in work charges every sexual impulse with guilt feelings. Self-confidence is reduced; this leads to compensatory neurotic phantasies of grandeur.

Sex-economic work

Here, the biological energy oscillates between work and sexual activity. Work and sexual activity are not opposites; that is, work does not serve to suppress the sexual urge, nor are there any sexual phantasies to interfere with work. Rather, work and sexuality support each other on the basis of a sound self-confidence. The interest is concentrated, fully and without conflict, either in work or in sexual activity, borne by the feeling of potency and the capacity to give oneself.

Diagram: Reactive and sex-economic way of working.

automatically regardless of what the external situation may be. The attitude cannot be changed, even though he may try to change it. The moralistic bureaucrat remains so even in bed. The healthy character type, on the other hand, is able to close up in one place and to open up in another. He is in command of his armor, because it does not have to keep back forbidden impulses.

These two types I termed *"neurotic character"* and *"genital character"*. Once this distinction was made, *the therapeutic task consisted in changing the neurotic character into a genital character, and in replacing moral regulation by self-regulation.* The fact that moral inhibition causes neurosis was known well enough. One spoke of "breaking down the superego". I did not succeed in convincing others that this was not sufficient, and that we were dealing with a deeper and more extensive problem. One cannot destroy moral regulation without replacing it by something else, and something better. But it was just this "something else" which seemed dangerous to my colleagues, either "wrong" or "old stuff". In reality one was afraid of the "meat grinder": the serious encounter with the world of today which arranges and judges everything in existence according to the principles of moral compulsion. I myself did at that time not realize the extremely far-reaching social consequences of these findings. I simply followed the path of my clinical work; that, however, I did with great determination. There is a certain kind of logic which one cannot escape, even though one would like to.

It was not until a few years ago that I began to comprehend why free, self-regulated behavior is exhilarating, but nevertheless causes severe anxiety. The basically different attitude toward the world, toward people, toward one's own experiences which characterizes the genital character, is simple and matter-of-course. It is immediately self-evident, even to people who are structurally far different. It is a secret ideal of everyone, and is always the same even though given various names. Nobody would deny the desirability of the capacity to love, or of sexual potency. Nobody would dare to postulate incapacity for love, or impotence, as they result from authoritarian education, as reasonable goals for human striving. To be spontaneously social is natural; and it is not exactly ideal to force oneself to be social, against criminal impulses. It is evident to anyone that it is better and healthier not to have an impulse to rape in the first place, than to have to curb it morally.

Nevertheless, no other part of my theory has endangered my work and existence as much as the contention that self-regulation is possible, that it does exist naturally, and that it might conceivably become universal. Of course, had I only formulated a hypothesis about it, in mincing words and pseudoscientific phraseology, I would have reaped only fame and fortune. But my therapeutic work required continuous improvements in the technique of changing people, and thus, deeper and deeper probing of the question: *If the traits of the genital character are so matter-of-course and so desirable, how is it possible continuously to overlook the close connection between sociality and complete sexuality?* Why is everything that governs life today dominated by the exactly opposite concept? *Why has the concept of a sharp antithesis of nature and culture, instinct and morals, body and mind, devil and God, love and work, become one of the outstanding features of our culture and Weltanschauung?* Why is this concept safeguarded against transgression with legal prosecution? Why did one follow the development of my scientific work with such great interest, only to turn in horror to defame it when it became a question of taking it seriously in practical terms? At first I believed the reason to be malice, treachery or scientific cowardice. Only after many years of bitter disappointment was the answer disclosed.

Most of my uneasy and bewildered reactions toward my opponents—who at that time were becoming increasingly numerous—were the result of the erroneous assumption that that which is correct *in principle* can also be accepted by people in a simple and matter-of-fact fashion, and be carried out. Since I had been able to comprehend and formulate these obvious facts, since they fitted so marvelously the purposes of therapeutic work, why should not my colleagues comprehend them just as well? On the one hand, they greeted my concepts with great enthusiasm; on the other hand, they seemed to shrink from coming into closer contact with them. I had touched upon their simple human ideals and ideas. I should soon learn that ideals are smoke and that ideas may change rapidly. What was at work here? In the first place, the thought of making a living and the fact of being part of an organization; further, a dependent attitude toward authority, and . . . ? Something was lacking.

The very thing that was desired as an ideal, aroused anxiety and dread in reality. It was alien to the individual with the prevalent structure. The whole official world fought it. The mechanisms of self-regulation lay slumbering deep down in the organism, covered up and permeated by compulsive mechanisms. Money-making as the content and goal of life contradicts every natural feeling. The world required it and molded humans accordingly, by bringing them up in certain ways and by placing them in certain life situations. The chasm, then, which was so obvious in social ideology between morals and reality, between the demands of nature and culture, was present, in a different form, *within* people. In order to be able to exist in this world, they had to fight and destroy in themselves that which was most true, most beautiful, most their own; they had to surround it with the thick walls of their character armor. In so doing, they came to grief inwardly, and, for the most part, also externally; but they spared themselves the struggle with this impossible order of things. A dim reflection of the deepest and most natural feelings for life, of *natural* decency, of *spontaneous* honesty, of real love, could be seen in a certain "sentiment" which seemed the more false the thicker the armor which was built up against naturalness. The falsest pathos still contains a bit of real life. Thus I arrived at the conclusion that human mendacity and meanness are still a reflection of the deep biological nucleus. Only thus can we understand the fact that the ideology of human morality and integrity could survive and be defended by masses of people for so long, in spite of the actual ugliness of life. Since people cannot and dare not live their real lives, they hang on to that last glimmer of it which comes out in their hypocrisy.

Such considerations led to the concept of the *unity of social structure and character structure.* Society molds the human character. The character, in turn, reproduces social ideology *en masse,* and thus reproduces its own suppression in the negation of life. This is the basic mechanism of so-called "tradition". I had no idea of the significance this was to have some five years later for the understanding of Fascist ideology. I was not speculating in the interest of political movements, nor was I constructing a *Weltanschauung.* Every clinical problem led to these conclusions. Thus it was not surprising to find that the absolute contradictions in the moral ideology of society were photographically identical with the contradictions in human structure.

According to Freud, the very existence of culture is based on the "cultural" repression of instinct. I had to agree with him—conditionally: the culture *of today* is indeed based on sexual repression. But, came the next question: *Is cultural development* as such *based on sexual repression?* And: Could it not be that this culture is based only on the repression of *unnatural, secondary impulses?* Nobody had ever spoken of that which I had found deep down in the human being, and which I now was able to bring forth through my technique. Nobody had any opinion about it.

Soon I came to realize that, in discussing "sexuality", people meant something different from what I meant. Pregenital sexuality was generally considered antisocial and unnatural. But this condemnation extended to the sexual act. Why did a father feel the sexual behavior of his daughter to be something dirty? Not just because of unconscious jealousy. That would not explain the violence of his reaction, which might go as far as murder. No: Genital sexuality, in our culture, is, in fact, debased, degraded. To the average man, the sexual act is an act of evacuation or a proof of mastery. Against this, the woman rebels instinctively, and rightly so; similarly, the father in the case of his daughter. Under such circumstances, being sexual means nothing pleasant. This evaluation of sexuality explains how so much can be written nowadays about the debasing qualities and the danger of sex. But, *this "sexuality" is a pathological caricature of natural love.* This caricature has entirely crowded out that genuine happiness in love which everybody most deeply longs for. People have lost the feeling for natural sexual experience. The usual evaluation of sexuality refers to its caricature, and *its* condemnation *is justified.*

Thus, any controversy in the sense of fighting for or against sexuality is senseless and leads nowhere. In such a controversy, the moralists would, and should, win. The caricature of sexuality should not be tolerated. The sexuality exercised in brothels *is* disgusting.

This is the point which always blocks discussion and makes the struggle for a healthy life so difficult. This makes my opponents argue beside the point. What I have in mind in speaking of sexuality is not neurotic mechanical coition but the loving embrace; not the urinating-into-the-woman, but making her happy. In other words, *unless we differentiate the secondary unnatural aspects of sexuality from the natural sexual needs deeply hidden in every person, we cannot get anywhere.*

Thus arose the problem: How can one make this accessible to masses of people, to pass over from theory to reality, to make what is a matter of natural laws for some people a matter of actual experience for all? There is no doubt: *an individual solution of the problem is unsatisfactory and misses the point.*

The question as to the social problem in psychotherapy was new at that time. There were three avenues of approach to the social problem: First, the *prophylaxis of the neuroses;* second—obviously related to it—*sexual reform*[1]; and finally, the *general problem of culture.*

[1]The problem of sexual reform is treated extensively in my book, *Die Sexualität im Kulturkampf,* and therefore not dealt with here.

Chapter VI

A BIOLOGICAL REVOLUTION THAT MISCARRIED

1. THE PREVENTION OF THE NEUROSES AND THE PROBLEM OF CULTURE

The innumerable questions arising from my work in the sex hygiene clinics[1] made me want to hear Freud's ideas about these problems. In spite of his encouraging words at the time we talked about my plans of starting these clinics, I was not sure of his approval. There was a latent tension in the psychoanalytic society, and I determined to find out just where my colleagues stood. The first personal defamations of my character on sexual grounds had come to my ears. After the publication in the Zeitschr. f. Psychoanal. Pädagogik of my articles dealing with the sexual enlightenment of children, rumors were being circulated to the effect that I had my children watch sexual intercourse, that, abusing the transference situation, I cohabited with my patients during analytic sessions, and such. They were the typical reactions of sexually unhealthy individuals to the fight for sexual happiness on the part of healthy individuals. I knew that nothing could compare in hatred and bitterness to this reaction, nothing in this world could match this reaction in

---

[1] *Translator's note:* In the original: *Sexualberatungsstellen.* Inasmuch as we have no such centers in this country, we lack the corresponding expression. The literal translation would be "sex counselling centers".

its silent, murderous instigation of human suffering. Murder in war gives the victims the feeling of heroism in their suffering. But individuals with a healthy feeling for life have to carry in silence the stigma of depravity with which individuals with perverse, guilt- and anxiety-laden phantasies brand them. There was not a single organization in society which would have championed the natural feeling for life. I tried my best to force the discussion from the personal to an objective basis. For it was clear what these defamatory rumors were intended to accomplish: just the opposite, to shift the discussion from a factual to a personal basis.

On December 12, 1929, I gave my talk on the *prophylaxis of the neuroses,* in Freud's inner circle. These monthly sessions at Freud's home were open only to the officers of the psychoanalytic society and a few guests. Everybody knew that the discussions at these meetings were of far-reaching importance. Psychoanalysis had become a world-embracing movement. One had to consider one's statements very carefully. I was fully aware of the responsibility involved. It would have been impossible for me to evade this by uttering half-truths. It was a matter of either presenting the problem as it was, or keeping quiet. To keep quiet was no longer possible. Many thousands of people crowded into my meetings to hear what psychoanalysis had to say about social and sexual misery.

The following questions, culled from thousands of similar questions asked again and again in such meetings, speak their own language:

What does one do when the woman has a dry vagina, though emotionally she wants to have intercourse?

How often should one have sexual intercourse?

Should one have sexual intercourse during the menstrual period?

What should one do when one's wife goes with another man?

What should one do when the man does not satisfy one? When he is too quick?

May one have intercourse from behind?

Why is homosexuality punished?

What is the woman to do when the man wants to have intercourse and she doesn't?

What can one do about insomnia?

Why do men like so much to talk about their sexual relations with women?

In Soviet Russia, do they punish sexual intercourse between brother and sister?

What is one to do if one wants to have sexual intercourse, and several other people sleep in the same room?

Why don't doctors help a woman when she gets pregnant and doesn't want the child or isn't able to have it?

My daughter is only seventeen and already has a boy friend. Is that bad? He isn't going to marry her anyhow.

Is it very bad to have relations with several people?

The girls make such a fuss, what shall I do?

I am terribly lonesome and want a boy friend badly, but when a boy does come around I get scared.

My husband goes with another woman. What should I do? I would like to do likewise. Should one do that?

I have been living with my wife for eight years. We love each other, but sexually we can't make a go of it. I long for another woman. What should I do?

My boy is three years old and keeps playing with himself. I try to punish him, but it does no good. Is that bad?

I masturbate every day, sometimes three times a day. Is that harmful to health?

Zimmermann (a Swiss reformer) says that, in order to avoid pregnancy, one should avoid ejaculation, by not moving inside the woman. Is that correct? Why, it hurts!

I read in a book for mothers that one should have intercourse only when one wants a child. That's nonsense, isn't it?

Why is everything sexual forbidden?

If sexual freedom were established, wouldn't there be chaos? I'm afraid I'd lose my husband!

The woman is by nature different from the man. The man is polygamous, the woman monogamous. Bearing children is a duty. Would you let your wife go with other men?

You talk about sexual health. Do you mean to say you let *your* children masturbate?

In the meetings, our husbands behave quite differently from at home. At home they behave like tyrants. What can one do about it?

Are you married? Do you have children?

Doesn't sexual freedom mean the complete destruction of the family?

I suffer from bleedings from the womb. The clinic doctor doesn't give a damn, and I have no money for a private doctor. What should I do?

My period always lasts ten days and it hurts terribly. What should I do?

At what age can one start having intercourse?

Is masturbation harmful? They say it makes you go crazy!

Why are our parents so strict with us? I am never allowed to come home any later than eight o'clock, and I'm already sixteen.

My husband always demands sexual intercourse and I don't feel like it. What should I do?

I am engaged and it often happens that when we have intercourse my fiancé can't find the right place, so we don't get any satisfaction. I may add that my fiancé is twenty-nine years old but has never had intercourse before.

Can impotent people get married?

What should ugly people do who can't find a boy friend or girl friend?

What should an elderly spinster do? After all, she can't throw herself at some man!

Is it possible for a man to do without sexual intercourse, by daily showers, athletics, etc.?

Does continued withdrawal lead to impotence?

What should be the relationship between boys and girls in a summer camp?

Does sexual intercourse at an early age lead to mental disease?

Is withdrawal harmful?

Is it harmful to interrupt masturbation just before ejaculation?

Does leukorrhea come from masturbation?

In the course of these evenings at Freud's home, devoted to a discussion of the prophylaxis of the neuroses and the problem of culture, Freud for the first time clearly stated those views which in 1931 were published in "*Das Unbehagen in der Kultur*" and which were often strictly contradictory to his views as expressed in "*Die Zukunft einer Illusion*". I had not "provoked" Freud, as some accusingly said. Neither were my arguments "dictated from Moscow", as was contended by others; in fact, at that very time I was using these arguments against the economic theorists in the socialist movement who, with their slogans of the "inevitable course of history" and of "economic factors" were destroying the very people whom they professed to liberate. All I had tried to do was to make the issues clear, and I do not regret it today. The fight was against the increasing attempts to do away with the psychoanalytic theory of sex, and to evade its social consequences.

By way of introduction, I pointed out that I wished what I had to say to be considered as a private and personal communication. Four questions needed clarification:

1. *What are the inevitable conclusions of psychoanalytic theory and therapy?* That is, if one continued to adhere to the central significance of the sexual causation of the neuroses!

2. *Is it possible to continue to limit oneself to the neuroses of the individual,* as they present themselves in private practice? The neurosis is an epidemic of the masses that works through subterranean channels. All of humanity is psychically ill.

3. *What is the proper place of psychoanalytic theory in the social system?* That it has to take a definite place in it cannot be doubted. It is a matter of the all-important social question of *psychic economy;* this is identical with *sexual economy,* if the theory of sex is to be carried to its conclusion rather than to be restricted in its scope.

4. *Why does society produce the neuroses en masse?*

I proceeded to answer these questions against the background of statistics gathered in mass meetings and youth groups. According to the information provided by these people of diverse vocations, *60 to 80 per cent of them were suffering from severe neurotic ailments.* In evaluating these figures, the fact should be kept in mind that their statements pertained only to such common neurotic symptoms as they were *conscious* of, and thus did not cover the character-neuroses of which they were unaware. In meetings which were for the purpose of discussing mental hygiene, the percentage went above 80 per cent because, as was to be expected, neurotics came to these meetings in particularly great numbers. The argument that only neurotics came to such meetings anyhow, is contradicted by the fact that in closed meetings of certain organizations (such as freethinkers, workers, groups of adolescent school children, political youth groups of any kind), i.e., in meetings without a selective attraction to neurotics, the percentage of definite neuroses (symptom neuroses) was only about 10 per cent below that of open meetings. In the six sex hygiene clinics of Vienna that I conducted, about 70 per cent of all clients proved in need of treatment. Only about 30 per cent, composed of stasis neuroses of a milder sort, could be improved by counsel or social work. That meant, that in the case of an organization for sex hygiene embracing the whole population, at best 30 per cent of the people could be helped by simple measures. The rest of the population, i.e., about 70 per cent (more in women, less in men), needed intensive therapy, requiring in each case—with a doubtful outcome—an average of two to three years. To set oneself such a goal for one's practical social endeavor was senseless. Mental hygiene on such an individualistic basis was nothing but a dangerous utopia.

The situation clearly called for *extensive social measures for the prevention of the neuroses.* True, the principles of these measures could be derived from the experiences with the individual patient, just as one tries to fight an epidemic according to the experience gained from an infected individual. The difference, however, is tremendous. Smallpox can be prevented by one quick vaccination. The measures necessary for the prevention of the neuroses, however, present a dark and terrifying picture. Nevertheless, they cannot be escaped. Success can lie only in the destruction of the sources from which neurotic misery stems.

Where are the sources of the neurotic plague?

First of all, in the authoritarian, sex-suppressing *family upbringing* with its inevitable sexual child-parent conflict and sexual anxiety. Just because Freud's clinical observations were correct, it was inevitable to draw the consequences which I drew. Furthermore, I had solved a problem which previously had remained obscure: the relationship between the sexual child-parent attachment and the general social suppression of sexuality. The realization that sex repression is a fact characteristic of *education as a whole* made the problem appear in a different light.

It was easy to see that the majority of people became neurotic. The question was rather how people—under present conditions of education—could remain *healthy!* This much more interesting question called for an examination of the relationship between authoritarian family upbringing and sex repression.

Parents—unconsciously at the behest of authoritarian, mechanized society—repress the sexuality of infants and adolescents. Since the children find their way to vital activity blocked by asceticism and in part by unemployment, they develop a sticky kind of parent fixation characterized by helplessness and guilt feelings. This in turn prevents their growing out of the infantile situation with all its sexual anxieties and inhibitions. Children thus brought up become character-neurotic adults and re-create their illness in their own children. And so it goes on from generation to generation. In this way, conservative tradition, a tradition which is afraid of life, is perpetuated. How can humans grow up to be healthy, and remain healthy, in spite of this?

The orgasm theory provided the answer: accidental or socially conditioned circumstances sometimes make possible the attainment of genital gratification; this in turn eliminates the energy source of the neurosis and alleviates the fixation in the infantile situation. Thus there can be healthy individuals in spite of the family situation. The sexual life of the youth of 1940 is, fundamentally, freer than that of the youth of 1900, but it is also more burdened with conflicts. The difference between the healthy and the sick individual is not that the former did not experience the typical family conflicts or sex repression. Rather, a peculiar and, in this society, unusual combination of circumstances, particularly the industrial collectivation of work, makes it possible for him to escape the clutches of both with the aid of a sex-economic way of living. There remains the question as to the later fate of such individuals. Certainly, they do not have an easy life. At any rate, the *"spontaneous organo-therapy of the neurosis"*, as I termed the orgastic release of tension, enables them to overcome the pathological family ties as well as the effects of social sex repression. There are human beings of a certain kind, living and working here and there, unobtrusively, who are equipped with *natural* sexuality; they are the *genital characters*. They are found frequently among the industrial workers.

The plague of the neuroses is bred during three principal phases of life: in *early infancy* through the atmosphere of the neurotic parental home; in *puberty;* and finally, in *compulsive marriage* based on strictly moralistic standards.

In the first phase, much harm is done by strict and premature training for excremental cleanliness, and the demand to be "good", to show absolute self-restraint and quiet good behavior. These measures prepare the ground for the most important prohibition of the following period, the *prohibition of masturbation*. Other restrictions of infantile development may vary, but these are typical. The inhibition of infantile sexuality is the basis for the fixation to the parental home and its atmosphere, the "family". This is the origin of the typical lack of independence in thought and action. Psychic mobility and strength go with sexual mobility and cannot exist without it. Conversely, psychic inhibition and awkwardness presupposes sexual inhibition.

In *puberty,* the same harmful educational principle that leads to psychic impoverishment and character armoring is repeated. This repetition takes place on the solid basis of the previously established inhibition of infantile impulses. *The basis of the puberty problem is sociological, not biological.* Nor does it lie in the child-parent conflict, as is assumed by psychoanalysis. For, those adolescents who find their way into a real sexual and working life, outgrow their infantile fixation to their parents. The others, hard hit by the actual sex suppression, are pushed back all the more into the infantile situation. This is the reason why most neuroses and psychoses develop at puberty. Barasch's statistics regarding the relationship of the duration of marriages to the age at which genital sexual life is taken up, confirms the close connection between the demands of abstinence and those of marriage: the earlier an adolescent takes up satisfactory sexual intercourse, the less capable does he become of conforming to the strict demand of "only *one* partner, and that one for life". Whatsoever attitude one may take toward this finding, the fact remains and cannot be denied. It means: the purpose of the demand for sexual abstinence is that of *making the adolescent submissive and capable of marriage.* That it does do. But in doing so it creates the very sexual impotence which in turn destroys marriage and accentuates the problem of marriage.

It is sheer hypocrisy to give a youth the legal right to marry, say, on the eve of his sixteenth birthday, thus inferring that in this case sexual intercourse does *no* harm, if at the same time one demands "continence until marriage", even if such marriage cannot take place until the age of, say, thirty. In the latter case, one finds all of a sudden that "sexual intercourse at an early age is harmful or immoral". No thinking person could tolerate such reasoning any more than he could tolerate the resulting neuroses and perversions. To mitigate the severity with which masturbation is penalized is merely a convenient subterfuge. *What is at stake is the gratification of the physical needs of ripening youth. Puberty signifies coming into sexual maturity,* and primarily nothing else. What esthetic philosophies call "cultural puberty", is, to put it mildly, just so much talk. *Sexual happiness of maturing youth is a central issue in the prevention of the neuroses.*

The function of youth at any given time is that of representing the *next* step of civilization. The parent generation at any given time tries to restrain youth to their own cultural level. Their motives for doing so are predominantly of an irrational nature: they have had to yield, and become irritated when youth reminds them of what they have been unable to achieve. The typical rebellion of adolescent youth against the parental home is, therefore, not a neurotic manifestation of puberty; it is, rather, the preparation for the social function which this youth will have to fulfill as adults. Youth has to *fight for* its capability for progress. Whatever the cultural tasks confronting any new generation may be, the inhibiting factor is always the older generation's fear of youth's sexuality and fighting spirit.

I have been accused of harboring the Utopian idea of a world in which I would eliminate unpleasure and have nothing but pleasure. This is contradicted by my repeated statement that education, as it is, makes the human incapable of pleasure, *by armoring him against unpleasure. Pleasure and joie de vivre are inconceivable without fight, without painful experiences and without unpleasurable struggling with oneself.* Not the Yogies' and Buddhists' theories of

Nirvana, not the hedonistic philosophy of Epicurus,[1] not the renunciation of monasticism—are what characterizes psychic health, but the alternation of painful struggle and happiness, of error and truth, of mistake and reflection upon it, of rational hatred and rational love, in brief, full vitality in all possible situations of life. The capacity of tolerating unpleasure and pain without fleeing disillusioned into a state of rigidity goes hand in hand with the capacity to take happiness and to give love. To use Nietzsche's words: he who wants to learn to "jubilate to high heaven" must be prepared to be "dejected unto death". In contrast to this, our European social concepts and education have turned the young — depending on their social position — either into dolls wrapped in cotton wool or into dried-up, chronically morose machines of industry or "business", incapable of pleasure.

The *problem of marriage* calls for clear thinking. Marriage is neither merely a matter of love, as claimed by some, nor merely an economic institution, as claimed by others. It is the form into which sexual needs were forced by socio-economic processes.[2] Sexual and economic needs, especially on the part of the woman, merge into the desire for marriage, apart from the ideology acquired in early childhood, and the moral pressure of society. Every marriage sickens as a result of an ever increasing conflict between *sexual* and *economic* needs. The sexual needs can be satisfied with one and the same partner only for a limited period of time. Economic dependence, moral demands and habituation, on the other hand, work towards permanence of the relationship. This

---

[1] This term is used here in the sense of everyday parlance. In reality, Epicurus and his school have nothing in common with the so-called "Epicurean philosophy of life" but the name. The earnest natural philosophy of Epicurus was interpreted by the half-educated and uneducated masses of people in a specific way: it came to mean the gratification of the *secondary* impulses. There are no means of defending oneself against such corruption of correct thoughts. Sex-economy is threatened by the same fate at the hands of human beings who suffer from pleasure anxiety and of science which is afraid of the subject of sexuality.

[2] Cf. L. Morgan, "Ancient Society."

conflict is the basis of marital misery. *Premarital* continence is supposed to prepare for marriage. But the very same continence creates sexual disturbances and thus undermines marriage. Full sexual capacity can make a marriage happy. But the same capacity is at variance with every aspect of the moralistic demand for a life-long monogamous marriage. This is a fact, and nothing but a fact. Again, we may take whatever attitude we care to toward this. But we should not be hypocritical about it. These contradictions—under unfavorable external and internal circumstances—lead to resignation. This requires far-reaching inhibition of the vegetative impulses. This in turn brings forth all possible neurotic mechanisms. Sexual partnership and human companionship in marriage then become replaced by a child-parent relationship and mutual slavery, in brief, by masked incest. These things have been described so often and are so well known today as almost to be platitudinous; they remain unknown only to a great many clergymen, psychiatrists, social reformers and politicians.

Such inner obstacles to mass mental hygiene, serious enough in themselves, are made far more serious by the *external* social conditions which produce them. Psychic misery is not purposed by the sexual chaos of today: it is rather an inseparable part of it. For, *compulsive marriage and the compulsive family go on re-creating the human structure of this economically and psychically mechanized age.* From the sexual hygiene point of view, simply everything is wrong in this order. Biologically speaking, the healthy human organism calls for three to four thousand sexual acts in the course of a genital life of, say, 30 to 40 years. The wish for offspring is satisfied with two to four children. Moralistic and ascetic ideologies condone sexual pleasure even in marriage only for the purpose of procreation; carried to its logical conclusion, that would mean at the most *four* sexual acts in a life-time. And with such a principle, medical authorities agree; and people suffer in silence, or they cheat on it and become hypocrites. But nobody makes any forceful attempt to do away with such an absurdity. This absurdity expresses itself in the official or moral prohibition of the use of contraceptives or information about them. This results in sexual disturbances and fear of pregnancy, which in turn arouses infantile sexual anxieties and undermines marriage. In an inevitable manner, the elements of the chaos combine in their effect. The prohibition of masturbation encountered in childhood creates a fear of any manipulation of the vagina. Thus, women come to be afraid of using contraceptives, and resort to "criminal abortion", which in turn is a starting point for innumerable neurotic manifestations. Fear of pregnancy precludes satisfaction in both man and woman. About 60 per cent of the adult male population practise withdrawal. This practice produces sexual stasis and nervousness *en masse*.

About all this, science and the medical profession say nothing. More than that, they impede, with evasions, academisms, erroneous theories and direct obstruction, every serious scientific, social or medical attempt to remedy the situation. When one hears all the talk about the "moral necessity" and the "harmlessness" of abstinence and withdrawal, propounded in the most dignified and authoritative manner, one has every reason for indignation. I did not say this in the meeting at Freud's, but the facts themselves did of necessity evoke this feeling of indignation.

Another, largely overlooked problem is the *housing problem*. According to statistics of Vienna in 1927, more than 80 per cent of the population lived four or more in one room. That means, that in over 80 per cent of the population a physiological sexual gratification is impossible, even under the best inner conditions. Neither medicine nor sociology even mention this fact.

Mental and sexual hygiene presuppose a regulated, economically secure existence. An individual who worries about where the next meal is coming from cannot enjoy pleasure and easily becomes a sexual psychopath. That is, if we hope for the prevention of the neuroses, we must count on a radical change in *everything* that causes the neuroses. This is why the question of the prevention of the neuroses never came up for discussion, why it was not even thought of. My statements could not help being provocative, whether I wanted it or not. The facts alone contained a good deal of provocativeness. I did not even mention such legal concepts as "marital duty" or "obedience to parents even to the extent of tolerating being beaten". Mention of such things was not customary in academic circles and was considered "unscientific". Yet, although nobody was inclined to listen to the facts presented, nobody could deny them either. For, everyone knew that individual therapy was socially unimportant, that education was in a hopeless state, and that ideas and lectures about sexual enlightenment were not sufficient. This situation led with inescapable logic to the *problem of culture* in general.

Up to 1929, the relationship of psychoanalysis and "culture" had not been discussed. Not only did the psychoanalysts see no contradiction between the two, but, quite generally, they considered Freud's theory to be "promoting culture" and not at all as critical of it. Between 1905 and 1925, the opponents of psychoanalysis had continually pointed to the "cultural danger" which was to be expected from psychoanalysis. The opponents and a listening world had imputed to psychoanalytic theory more than psychoanalysis had intended. This was due to the deep need felt by everybody for clarity in sexual matters, and to the fear of sexual chaos felt by the "bearers of culture". Freud believed that his theory of sublimation and renunciation of the instinct had abolished the danger. Gradually, the rumblings subsided, particularly with the flourishing of the theory of the death instinct and after the repudiation of the theory of stasis anxiety. The theory of a biological will to suffer saved embarrassment. These theories proved that psychoanalysis was not in conflict with culture. This equanimity was now threatened by my publications. In order not to be compromised by them, one called my views either "old stuff", or erroneous. But I had not made things easy for myself by any means. I had not simply come out with the contention that psychoanalysis was at variance with culture, and that it was "revolutionary". Things were much more complicated than many think today.

My views could not simply be disregarded. More and more clinicians were working with the genital theory of therapy. These views could not be denied either, only minimized at best. They confirmed the revolutionary character of a scientific theory of sex. Had it not been proclaimed that Freud had opened a new cultural era? But neither could they be openly concurred in. That would have conflicted with the material security of the psychoanalysts as well as with their contention that psychoanalysis was *only* "promoting culture". *Nobody asked what it was in this "culture" that was being promoted and what it was that was being endangered.* It was overlooked that, by its very development, that which is "new" criticizes and negates that which is old.

The leading circles in social science in Austria and Germany rejected psychoanalysis and tried to compete with it in the attempt to understand human nature. It was far from easy to find the right way through this difficulty. It is surprising how I was able to keep from making some really big blunders at that time. The temptation was great to take some short-cut, to make some compromise, to try to find a quick practical solution. One might have said, for example, that sociology and psychoanalysis could be united without any difficulty; or, that psychoanalysis, though correct as a psychology of the individual, was culturally unimportant.

This is, in fact, what was said by Marxists with psychoanalytic leanings. But that was no solution. I was too much of a psychoanalyst to be superficial, and too much interested in a development of the world toward freedom to be content with a banal answer. For the moment I was content with having been able to coordinate psychoanalysis and sociology, even if only methodologically for the time being.[1] My friends' and enemies' unceasing accusations that I was jumping to conclusions did not disquiet me, though they often annoyed me. I knew that none of them was making as much of a theoretical or practical effort, and my finished manuscripts were kept in the desk drawer for years before I would decide to publish them. I was willing to leave being "smart" to others.

The relationship of psychoanalysis and culture began to clarify itself when a young psychiatrist read a paper on "*Psychoanalyse und Weltanschauung*" at Freud's. Only a very few know that Freud's "*Unbehagen in der Kultur*" originated from these discussions on culture, which took place in order to refute my maturing work and the "danger" which was supposed to arise from it. The book contains sentences which Freud used in our discussion to oppose my views.

In this book, which did not appear until 1931, Freud, though acknowledging natural sexual pleasure to be the goal of human striving, at the same time attempted to demonstrate the untenability of this principle. His theoretical and practical basic formula was always: The human—normally and of necessity—progresses from the "pleasure principle" to the "reality principle". *He must renounce pleasure and adjust himself.* Freud neither questioned the irrational in this "reality", nor did he ask *which kind of pleasure is compatible with sociality and which kind is not.* Today I con-

[1] Cf. Wilhelm Reich, Dialektischer Materialismus und Psychoanalyse, 1929.

sider it a fortunate thing for real mental hygiene that this problem was brought to light. It made for clarity and made it impossible to consider psychoanalysis any longer a force for reshaping culture, without a *practical criticism* of the conditions of education and without any attempt to *change* them. Otherwise, what is the meaning of that often abused word "progress"?

The following concept corresponded to the academic attitude at that time. Science, they said, has to do with problems of what *is*, social pragmatism with problems of what *should be*. "What is" (*science*) and "what should be" (*social pragmatism*) are two different things which have no common ground. The finding of a fact does not involve a "should be", that is, the indication of a goal which should be striven toward. With a scientific finding, every ideological or political group could do what it pleased. I took issue with these ethical logicians who took refuge from reality in an abstract formula. If I find that an adolescent is made neurotic and incapable of work by the sexual abstinence which is demanded of him, that is "science". From the point of view of "abstract logic", one may conclude that he should continue to live in abstinence, as well as that he should give it up. Such a conclusion is "Weltanschauung" and its realization social pragmatism. But, I said, *there are scientific findings from which, in practice, only one thing follows, and never the other.* What is logically correct may be practically wrong. If today somebody would come out with the finding that abstinence is harmful to the adolescent, without drawing the conclusion that abstinence should be given up, he would be simply laughed at. This is why it is so important to formulate problems in terms of practice. A physician cannot allow himself to take an abstract point of view. Whoever refuses to draw the practical conclusions from the above finding must of necessity make erroneous statements of a "purely scientific" nature. He will have to contend with "scientific authority" that abstinence is *not* harmful to the adolescent; in short, he will have to camouflage the truth and play the hypocrite, in order to defend his demand for abstinence. *Every scientific finding has a basis in Weltanschauung and a practical consequence in social life.*

For the first time, I saw clearly the abyss between abstract logical thinking and functional thinking in terms of natural science. Abstract logic has often the function of admitting scientific facts without letting them have any practical consequences. Thus, practical functionalism, which postulates unity of theory and practice, appealed more to me.

Freud's point of view was this: the attitude of the average man toward religion is understandable. A famous poet once said,

> Wer Wissenschaft und Kunst besitzt,
> *hat* auch Religion,
> Wer jene beiden nicht besitzt,
> der *habe* Religion![1]

This statement is correct for our times, like everything that is contended by a conservative ideology. The right of the conservatives is identical with the right to attack it with scientific and medical knowledge so deeply that the source of conservative arrogance, ignorance, is destroyed. The fact that the question is unanswered as to the pathological spirit of toleration on the part of the working multitudes, as to their pathological renunciation of the knowledge and the cultural fruits of this world of "science and art", as to their helplessness, fear of responsibility and their craving for authority—the fact that this question is unanswered is bringing the world towards an abyss in the form of the pestilence of Fascism. What is the sense of science anyhow, if it taboos such questions? What kind of a conscience can a scientist

[1]He who has Science and has Art, Religion, too, has he;
Who has not Science, has not Art, Let him religious be!
(From the translation of *"Das Unbehagen in der Kultur"* by Joan Riviere).

have who is, or might be, able to work out an answer and who wilfully fails to fight against this psychic plague? Today, in the face of danger to life, that becomes clear to all the world which twelve years ago could scarcely be mentioned. Social life has placed in sharp focus problems which at that time were considered to be merely the concern of individual physicians.

Freud was able to justify the renunciation of happiness on the part of humanity as splendidly as he had defended the fact of infantile sexuality. A few years later, a pathological genius—making the best of human ignorance and fear of happiness—brought Europe to the verge of destruction *with the slogan of "heroic renunciation"*.

"Life as it is imposed on us", writes Freud, "is too hard for us, too full of pain, disillusionments and impossible tasks. In order to bear it, we cannot do without palliatives. . . . There are perhaps three of these; powerful diversions of interest which makes us think little of our own misery; substitute gratifications which lessen it; and narcotics which make us insensitive to it. Something of this kind is indispensable".

At the same time (in *"Die Zukunft einer Illusion"*) Freud rejected the most dangerous of the illusions, religion.

"The ordinary man cannot imagine this Providence otherwise than in the person of a greatly exalted father. Only such a one could understand man's needs, could be softened by his prayers and placated by the signs of his remorse. The whole thing is so obviously infantile, so incongruous with reality that to one whose attitude to humanity is friendly it is painful to think that the great majority of mortals will never be able to rise above this view of life".

Thus, Freud's correct findings concerning religious mysticism ended in resignation. And on the outside, life was seething with the struggle for *a rational Weltanschauung and a scientifically regulated social order*. In principle, there was no disagreement. Freud did not declare himself as having no Weltanschauung. He refuted the pragmatic Weltanschauung in favor of the scientific. He felt himself in opposition to social pragmatism as represented by the European political parties. I tried to show that the striving for a democratization of the work process is and must be *scientifically rational.* At that time, the destruction of Lenin's social democracy and the development of dictatorship in the Soviet Union, and the relinquishing of all principles of truth in sociological thinking had already begun. There was no denying that. I rejected the unpragmatic standpoint of Freud which evaded the social consequences of scientific discoveries. I had only a faint inkling of the fact that Freud's point of view as well as the dogmatic attitude of the Soviet government, each in its own way, had their good reasons: *Scientific, rational regulation of humanity is the supreme goal. However, the acquired irrational structure of the masses of people, that is, those who participate in the making of history, makes dictatorship through utilization of the irrational possible.* It depends on *who* exerts power, to what *purpose,* and *against what.* At any rate, the original social democracy in Russia was at the outset the most human solution possible under existing conditions of history and human structure. That, Freud had explicitly admitted. The degeneration of Lenin's social democracy into the dictatorial Stalinism of today is an undeniable fact and is grist in the mill of the opponents of democracy. Freud's pessimism seemed to be cruelly justified during the ensuing years: "there is nothing that can be done". After what had happened in Russia, the development of true democracy appeared to be a Utopia. It really looked now as if "he who does not have art and science, had better have" the "socialist religion" to which an enormous world of scientific thought had degenerated. The fact has to be stressed that Freud's attitude was only an expression of the general fundamental attitude of academic scientists: they had no confidence in democratic self-education and the intellectual productivity of the masses of people; for that reason, they did nothing to stem the tide of dictatorship.

Ever since the beginning of my activity in the field of sexual hygiene I had been convinced that cultural happiness in general and sexual happiness in particular are the very content of life and should be the goal of practical social endeavor. I was contradicted on all sides, but my findings were more important than all objections and difficulties. The whole of literature, from the dime novel to the best of poetry, proved me correct. All cultural interest (movies, the novel, poetry, etc.) revolves around sexuality, thrives on the affirmation of the ideal and the negation of the actual. Cosmetic industries, fashion trades and business advertising make their living by this. If all humanity dreams and writes of happiness in love, why could not this dream of life be realized? The goal was clear. The facts found in the biological depths called for medical action. Why did the striving for happiness continue to remain a phantastic something, at war with hard reality? Freud gave up hope, in the following manner.

What does human behavior itself disclose as the goal of life? What do humans expect of life, what do they want to get out of it? Such were the questions in Freud's mind in 1930 after those discussions which had brought the sexual demands of the masses right into the scientist's peaceful study and had brought about a sharp clash of opinions.

Freud had to admit: *"The answer can hardly be missed. They strive for happiness; they want to become happy and remain so"*. They want to experience strong sensations of pleasure. It is simply the pleasure principle which sets up the goal of life. This principle governs the operation of the psychic apparatus from the very beginning.

"There can be no doubt about its purpose, and yet its program is in conflict with the whole world, with the macrocosm as well as with the microcosm. It simply cannot be put into execution; the whole constitution of things runs counter to it. One might say that the intention that man should be 'happy' is not included in the scheme of 'Creation'. What is called happiness in its narrowest sense comes from the gratification—most often instantaneous—of highly pent-up needs, and by its very nature can only be a transitory experience".

In saying so, Freud expressed a feeling which is part of the human *incapacity* for happiness. The argument sounds well, but it is erroneous. According to this argument, it would seem as if asceticism were a necessary prerequisite for happiness. In so arguing, the fact is overlooked that the damming-up of a need is itself experienced as pleasure, *provided it has a prospect of gratification and does not last too long.* Also the fact that this damming-up makes the organism rigid and incapable of pleasure if this prospect does not exist or if pleasure is constantly threatened with punishment. The supreme experience of happiness, the sexual orgasm, characteristically presupposes a damming-up of energy. From that, one cannot draw Freud's conclusion that the pleasure principle "simply cannot be put into execution". Today I have experimental proof of the incorrectness of this contention. At that time I only felt that Freud was hiding a reality behind a phrase. To admit the possibility of human happiness would have meant scrapping the theories of the repetition-compulsion and of the death instinct. It would have meant a criticism of the social institutions which destroy happiness in life. To maintain his position of resignation, Freud adduced arguments which he borrowed from the existing situation, without asking, however, whether this situation was of its nature inevitable and unchangeable. I could not see how Freud could believe that the discovery of infantile sexuality could have no effect whatsoever in bringing about changes in the world. He seemed to be doing a cruel injustice to his own work, and to feel the tragedy of this contradiction. For, when I set forth my arguments against him, he said that I was either totally wrong or "I would have one day to carry the heavy lot of psychoanalysis all alone". Since I was not wrong, his prophecy proved correct.

Freud, in the discussion as well as in his book, escaped into the theory of biological *suffering*. He was looking for a way out of the cultural catastrophe in an "effort of the Eros". In a private conversation in 1926, Freud had expressed the hope that the revolutionary "experiment" in Soviet Russia might succeed. Nobody had as yet any idea of the catastrophic failure of Lenin's attempt for a social democracy. Freud knew, and he said so in writing, that humanity is sick. The connection between this general illness and the catastrophe that took place in Russia and later in Germany was as alien to the thinking of the psychiatrist as to that of the statesman or political scientist. Three years later, conditions in Germany and Austria were already so disturbed as to affect any professional activity. Irrationalism in political life became plainly evident; analytical psychology penetrated more and more into sociological problems. In my work, "man" as patient and "man" as social being merged more and more into one. I saw that neurotic and hungry masses were falling prey to political pirates. Freud, in spite of his knowledge of the psychic plague, was afraid of the inclusion of psychoanalysis in the political chaos. His conflict made him seem all the more human to me, for it was so intense. Today I also understand the necessity of his resignation. For fifteen years, he had been fighting for the recognition of simple facts. The world of his colleagues had besmeared him, called him a charlatan, had even called the sincerity of his motives into question. He was not a social pragmatist, only a "pure scientist", but as such strict and honest. The world could no longer deny the facts of unconscious psychic life. So it began anew its old accustomed game of debasing what it cannot otherwise destroy. It gave him a great many pupils, who came to a table all set for them and who did not have to work hard for what they got. They had only *one* interest: to make psychoanalysis socially acceptable as quickly as possible. They carried the conservative traditions of this world into their organization, and without an organization, Freud's work could not exist. One after the other, they sacrificed the libido theory or diluted it. Freud knew how difficult it is to continue to advocate the libido theory. But the interest of self-preservation and of safeguarding the psychoanalytic movement prevented him from saying what in a more honest world he certainly would have fought for. He had with his science far transcended the narrow intellectual horizon of his contemporaries. His school pulled him back into it. He knew in 1929 that in my youthful scientific enthusiasm I was right. But to admit this would have meant to sacrifice half of the organization.

That psychic disturbances are the result of sexual repression was an established fact. Analytic pedagogy and therapy attempted to eliminate the repression of the sexual instincts. *What happens,* was the question, *to the instincts once they are liberated from repression?* The answer of psychoanalysis was: the instincts are *rejected* or *sublimated.* Of actual satisfaction there was no mention; there could not be, because the unconscious was thought of as the inferno of antisocial and perverse impulses alone.

For a long time, I tried to obtain an answer to the question as to *what happens to the natural genitality of children and adolescents after it is liberated from repression.* Should it, too, be "rejected or sublimated"? It was never answered by the psychoanalysts. And yet, it constitutes the central problem of character formation.

The whole process of education suffers from the fact that social adjustment demands repression of natural sexuality, and that this repression makes people ill and antisocial. What had to be questioned, therefore, was whether the demands of education were justified. They were based on a fundamental misconception of sexuality.

Freud's great tragedy was that he escaped into biologistic theories; he might have kept silent or let people do as they pleased. And so he came to contradict himself:

Happiness, he said, is an illusion; for, suffering threatens inexorably from three sides. "From one's *own body* which is destined to disintegration and decay". *Why then,* one must ask, *does science keep dreaming of the prolongation of life?* "From the *outer world* which is capable of attacking us with overpowering inexorable destructive forces". *Why then,* one must ask, *did great thinkers spend their lives thinking about liberty? Why then, did millions of fighters for liberty shed their blood in the struggle against this threatening outer world?* Had not pestilence been finally vanquished? And had not physical and social slavery been at least diminished? Should it not be possible to vanquish the disease of cancer? Or possible to vanquish wars as it had been possible to vanquish pestilence? Should it never be possible to vanquish the moralistic hypocrisy which makes cripples out of our children and adolescents?

More serious and difficult was the *third* argument against the human longing for happiness: the suffering which springs from relations with other people, said Freud, is more painful than any other. One might be inclined to consider it as some superficial and accidental intrusion, but at the same time it is no less fatefully inescapable than the suffering from other sources. Here spoke Freud's own bitter experiences with the human species. Here he touched upon our problem of structure, in other words, the irrationalism which determines people's behavior. Some of this I had come to feel painfully in the psychoanalytic society; an organization the very task of which consisted in the medical mastery of irrational behavior. Now Freud said that this was fateful and inescapable.

But how? Why then did one assume the lofty viewpoint of rational science? Why then did one proclaim the education of the human towards rational, realistic behavior? For a reason which I could not understand, Freud did not see the contradiction in his attitude. On the one hand, he had—correctly—reduced human thinking and behavior to unconscious irrational motives. On the other hand, there could exist for him a Weltanschauung in which the very law he had found should *not* be valid. A science beyond its own principles! Freud's resignation was nothing but a shunning of the gigantic difficulties presented by the pathological in human behavior, the malicious. *He was disillusioned.* Originally he believed that he had discovered the radical therapy of the neuroses. In reality, he had made no more than a beginning. Things were much more complicated than the formula of the making conscious of the unconscious would lead one to believe. He had claimed that psychoanalysis could comprehend general problems of human existence, not merely medical problems. But he did not find his way into sociology. In "*Jenseits des Lustprinzips*" he had touched upon important biological questions in a hypothetical way, and thus arrived at the theory of the death instinct. It proved a misleading theory. Freud himself viewed it very skeptically at first. But the psychologizing of sociology as well as of biology took away every prospect for a practical solution of these enormous problems.

In addition, Freud had, in his practice as well as from their reactions to his teachings, come to know his fellow humans as highly unreliable, malicious beings. For decades he had now been living in seclusion from the world, for the protection of his own peace of mind. Had he entered upon all the irrational objections that were raised, he would have lost himself in petty destructive struggles. In order to seclude himself, he needed a skeptical attitude toward human "values"; more than that, a certain contempt for the human of his day. Knowledge came to mean more to him than human happiness. This all the more as the humans did not seem able to manage their happiness if ever it presented itself. This attitude corresponded completely to the academic superiority of the time, and had its substantiation in facts. But it did not seem admissible to judge general problems of human existence from the point of view of a scientific pioneer.

Although I understood Freud's motives, two important facts kept me from following him here. One was the steadily increasing demand on the part of uneducated, mistreated, psychically ruined people for a revision of the social order in terms of earthly happiness. Not to see this, or to fail to take it into account, would have been a ridiculous ostrich policy. I had come to know this mass awakening too well to be able to deny it or to underestimate it as a social force. Freud's motives were correct. But so were those of the awakening masses of people. To disregard them meant inescapably to take the side of the non-working parasites of society.

The other fact was that I had learned to see people *in two ways.* They were often corrupt, incapable of thinking, faithless, full of meaningless slogans, treacherous, or simply empty. *But that was not natural. They had been made that way by the existing conditions of life.* In principle, then, they could also be made *different:* decent, straightforward, capable of love, sociable, cooperative, truly and without compulsion social. More and more I had to realize that what is called "bad" or "antisocial" is really neurotic. For example, a child plays in a natural fashion. The environment puts on the brakes. At first the child fights back, then it succumbs; it loses its capacity for pleasure while keeping up the fight against the inhibition of pleasure in the form of pathological, aimless, irrational spite reactions. In the same way, human behavior in general was only a reflection of the affirmation and the negation of life in the social process. Was it conceivable that the conflict between the striving for pleasure and its social frustration could some day be solved? Psychoanalytic investigation of sexuality seemed to be the first step in the direction of such a change. But this first beginning did not make good the promise it seemed to hold out. It turned first into an abstract, then into a conservative doctrine of "cultural adaptation" with a great many insoluble contradictions.

The conclusion was irrefutable: *The human longing for life and pleasure cannot be banished. But the social regulation of sexual life can be changed.*

At this point, Freud began to create justifications for an ascetic ideology. "Unrestricted gratification" of all needs, he said, would seem to be the most tempting mode of life, but that would mean putting enjoyment before caution, and would bring swift punishment. To that I could reply even at that time that we have to distinguish the *natural* strivings for happiness from the secondary, *antisocial* strivings which are the result of compulsive education. The secondary, unnatural drives can be kept in bounds only by moral inhibition; that will always be so. To the natural pleasure needs, on the other hand, the principle of freedom applies, if you will, the "living out". One only has to know what the word "drive" means in each case.

"The efficiency of narcotics in the struggle for happiness and in warding off misery ranks so highly as a benefit that both individuals and races have given them an established position in their libido economy", writes Freud. But he does not add one word of medical opposition to this substitute gratification which ruins the organism! Not a word about the cause of narcotic addiction, namely the denial of sexual happiness! Not a word about the connection between addiction and lack of genital satisfaction in the whole psychoanalytic literature!

Freud's proposition was hopeless. True, he said, the striving for pleasure could not be eradicated. But what should be changed was not the social chaos, but the striving for pleasure itself. The complicated structure of the psychic apparatus admitted of a number of modes of influence. Just as instinctual gratification is happiness, so it becomes the source of grave suffering if the outer world denies gratification. It was to be hoped, therefore, that by influencing the instinctual impulses (*i.e., not by influencing the frustrating world!*) we would be able to free ourselves from part of the suffering. This influencing would seek to master the inner sources of the needs. To an extreme degree this is done by killing the instincts, as taught by oriental philosophy and put into practice by Yoga. This from Freud, the same man who had presented to the world the incontrovertible facts of infantile sexuality and of sexual repression!

Here, one no longer could and should follow Freud. More than that, one had to muster all forces to fight against the consequences of such concepts, coming, as they did, from such an authority. It was to be foreseen that in the days to come all the evil spirits representing the fear of living would call Freud to witness. This was no way of dealing with a human problem of the first order. One could not defend the resignation of the Chinese coolie or the infant mortality of a cruel East Indian patriarchy which was just suffering its first defeats. The most burning problem of the misery of childhood and adolescence was the killing of spontaneous vital impulses by the process of education in the interest of a dubious refinement. This, science should not condone; it could not take such a convenient way out. The less so, as Freud himself did not question the role of the human striving for happiness and its basic correctness.

As he admitted, the striving for a positive fulfillment of happiness, that orientation of life which revolves around love and expects all satisfaction from loving and being loved, would seem to be the most natural to everyone; sexual love provided the most intense sensations of pleasure and thus became the prototype of all striving for happiness. But, he said, this concept had a weak point, or else it would not have occurred to anybody to abandon this way of living for another. One is never more unprotected against suffering, he said, than when one loves, never more helpless and unhappy than upon the loss of love or a love object. The program of the pleasure principle, the attainment of happiness, he concluded, could not be put into practice. Again and again Freud maintained the unchangeability of human structure as well as of the conditions of human existence. Freud had in mind here attitudes like the neurotic reactions of disappointment of emotionally and economically dependent women.

The overcoming of these points of view of Freud, and the working out of the sex-economic solution of this problem took place in two parts. First, the striving for happiness had to be clearly comprehended in its *biological* nature. Thus it could be separated from the secondary distortions of human nature. Secondly, there was the great question as to the social practicability of that which humans most deeply long for and at the same time are so much afraid of.

Life, and with it, the striving for pleasure, does not take place in a vacuum, but under definite natural and social conditions. The first part was *biological* uncharted territory. Nobody had as yet investigated the pleasure mechanism from the point of view of biology. The second part was *sociological,* or rather, uncharted territory of social sexual policy. If it is generally recognized that people have a natural striving, and social conditions prevent them from attaining their goal, then the question naturally arises as to what ways and means might make this goal attainable. This applies to sexual happiness no less than to economic goals. It takes a particular mentality characterized by the use of cliché, to deny for sexuality what otherwise (e.g. with regard to making money or preparing for war) one would not hesitate to admit. The safeguarding of the distribution of goods requires a rational economic policy. A rational sexual policy is not different if the same obvious principles are applied to the sexual instead of the economic needs. It did not take much to recognize sexual hygiene as the focal point of mental hygiene in general, to differentiate it from the shallow attempts at sexual reform and from the pornographic mentality, and to advocate its basic scientific principles.

The entire cultural production, as expressed in literature, poetry, art, dance, movies, folklore, etc., is characterized by its interest in sex.

There is no interest with a stronger influence on man than the sexual interest.

Patriarchal laws pertaining to culture, religion and marriage are essentially laws *against* sex.

Freud's psychology had found the libido, the energy of the sexual instinct, to be the central motor of psychic activity.

Human pre-history and mythology are—in the strict sense of the word—reproductions of the sexual economy of humanity.

There was no escaping the question: *Is sexual repression an indispensable part of the cultural process in general?* If scientific investigation could answer this question unequivocally in the affirmative, then any attempt at a positive social program was hopeless. Then, also, any psychotherapeutic endeavor was hopeless.

This *could not* be correct. It ran counter to all human endeavor, all scientific findings and intellectual productions. As my clinical work had given me the unshakeable conviction that the sexually complete person is also culturally the more productive one, the acceptance of Freud's solution was out of the question. The question as to whether sexual repression is necessary or not was replaced by a much more important question: What are the human motives for evading a clear answer to this question consistently and

—so far—so successfully? I searched for the motives of a man like Freud, who placed his authority at the disposal of a conservative ideology, who, through his theory of culture, threw overboard what he had elaborated as a scientist and physician. Surely, he did it neither because of intellectual cowardice nor for conservative political motives. He did it in the framework of a science which, like all others, was dependent on society. The social barrier made itself felt not only in the therapy of the neuroses, but also in the investigation of the origin of sexual repression.

In my sex hygiene clinics, the fact became clear to me that *the function of the suppression of infantile and adolescent sexuality is that of facilitating for the parents the authoritarian submissiveness of the children.*

In the very beginnings of the economic patriarchy, the sexuality of children and adolescents used to be fought by direct castration or genital mutilation of one kind or another. Later, psychic castration by way of implanting sexual anxiety and guilt feeling became the accepted method. Sex repression serves the function of keeping humans more easily in a state of submissiveness, just as the castration of stallions and bulls serves that of securing willing beasts of burden. However, nobody had thought of the devastating results of this *psychic castration,* and nobody can predict how human society will be able to cope with them. Later, after I had forced the issue in print,[1] Freud confirmed the connection between sexual repression and submissiveness:

"Fear of revolt among the oppressed", he writes, "then becomes a motive for ever stricter regulations. A high-water mark in this type of development has been reached in our Western European civilization. Psychologically, it is fully justified in beginning by censoring any manifestations of the sexual life of children, for there would be no prospect of curbing the sexual desires of adults if the ground had not been prepared for it in childhood. Nevertheless there is no sort

[1] Wilhelm Reich, *"Geschlechtsreife, Enthaltsamkeit, Ehemoral"*, 1930.

of justification for the lengths beyond this to which civilized society goes in actually denying the existence of these manifestations".

The formation of the sex-negative character structure, then, was the real, though unconscious, goal of education. Consequently, psychoanalytic pedagogy could no longer be discussed without discussing the problem of structure; neither could the latter be discussed without defining the *goal* of education. Education serves the purposes of the social order of any given time. If this social order contradicts the interest of the child, then education must leave the child out of consideration, and must do one of two things: either openly relinquish its set goal, "the welfare of the child", or else *pretend* to advocate it. This kind of education failed to distinguish between the *compulsive family* which suppresses the children, from the *family* which is built upon the deep natural love relationship between parents and children, and which is constantly being destroyed by the compulsive family relationships. Education, furthermore, failed to take cognizance of the gigantic revolution which had been taking place since the turn of the century in human sex life as well as in family life. With its "ideas" and "reforms" it was—and still is—hobbling far behind the actual changes. In short, it was caught in its own irrational motives of which it did not know nor dared to know.

Nevertheless, the plague of the neuroses is comparable to a pestilence. It disintegrates everything that human effort, thinking and work creates. Pestilence was attacked without hindrance, because such attack did not encroach either on profit or on mystical emotional interests. To fight against the plague of the neuroses is far more difficult. Everything that thrives on human mysticism clings to it and possesses power. Who would accept the argument that the psychic plague should not be attacked because the necessary measures of mental hygiene would be asking too much of the people?

Blaming it on lack of funds is a poor excuse. The sums that go up in smoke in one week of the war would be enough to provide for the hygienic needs of millions and millions. We are also apt to underestimate the gigantic forces that lie fallow in people and press towards expression and action.

Sex-economy had comprehended the biological goal of human striving, which was at variance with human *structure* and certain institutions of our social order. Freud sacrificed the goal of happiness to the existing human structure and the existing sexual chaos. There was nothing left for me to do but to retain the goal and to study the laws according to which this human structure *develops* and can be *altered*. I had no idea of the extent of the problem, let alone of the fact that neurotic psychic structure becomes *somatic innervation*, a "second nature", as it were.

For all his pessimism, Freud could not let matters rest in such a state of hopelessness. His final statement was:

> "The fateful question of the human species seems to me to be whether and to what extent its cultural development will succeed in mastering the derangements of communal life caused by the human instinct of aggression and self-destruction. . . . And now it may be expected that the other of the two 'heavenly forces', eternal Eros, will put forth his strength so as to maintain himself against his equally immortal adversary".

This statement was much more than the turn of phrase for which it was taken by the psychoanalysts, certainly more than just a brilliant remark. *"Eros" presupposes full sexual capacity*. Full sexual capacity, in turn, presupposes a general affirmation of life, and a fostering of it on the part of society. Freud seemed secretly to wish me luck in my undertaking. He expressed himself obscurely, but the very material ways had indeed been found which would one day fulfill his hope: *Only the liberation of the natural capacity for love in human beings can master their sadistic destructiveness.*

2. THE SOCIAL ORIGIN OF SEXUAL REPRESSION

Of course, the question as to the practicability of general human happiness could not be answered in a *practical* sense at that time. At this point, the unsophisticated person will ask whether science upon its heights has nothing better to do than to ask such stupid questions as to whether the earthly happiness of human beings is "desirable" or "practicable". That, he might say, is a *matter of course.* Nevertheless, things are not as simple as they might appear to the buoyant, enthusiastic adolescent or the cheerful happy-go-lucky individual. In the centers that had a decisive influence upon public opinion in Europe around 1930, the demand of the masses of people for happiness was neither considered a matter of course, nor was its absence regarded as a matter for question. There was at that time literally no political organization which would have considered it important enough to concern itself with such "banal, personal", "unscientific" or "unpolitical" questions.

However, the social events around 1930 raised just *this* question in all its significance. It was the tide of Fascism which swept across Germany like a hurricane and made people ask in utter bewilderment how such a thing was possible. Economists, sociologists, cultural reformers, diplomats and statesmen alike, tried to find an answer in old books. The answer could not be found in old books. There was not a single political pattern that would have fitted this eruption of irrational human emotions which Fascism represented. Never before had politics itself been questioned as an irrational thing.

In this volume, I shall discuss only those social events which threw into sharp focus the clash of opinions as it had taken place in Freud's study. I have to neglect here the broad social-economic background.[1]

---

[1]Cf. my books, Massenpsychologie des Faschismus, 1933; Der Einbruch der Sexualmoral, 1935; Die Sexualität im Kulturkampf, 1936.

Freud's discovery of infantile sexuality and of the process of sexual repression was, sociologically speaking, the first beginning of an awareness of the denial of sex which had been existing for thousands of years. This awareness was still clothed in highly academic forms and did not trust its own ability to walk. Human sexuality claimed the right to be moved from the backstairs of social life, where for thousands of years it had been leading a filthy, unhealthy, purulent existence, to the front of the shiny edifice which was so grandly called "culture" and "civilization". Sex murders, criminal abortions, sexual agony of adolescents, killing of the vital forces in children, perversions galore, pornography and the vice squad, exploitation of human longing for love by greedy and vulgar business enterprises and advertising, millions of diseases, psychic and somatic, loneliness and crippling everywhere, and on top of all this, the neurotic swash-buckling of the would-be saviors of humanity—all these things could hardly be considered as ornaments of civilization. The moral and social evaluation of the most important biological human function was in the hands of sexually frustrated ladies and vegetatively dead professors. There was, after all, no objection to the societies of sexually frustrated ladies and vegetative mummies; but one had to protest against the fact that it was exactly these mummies who not only tried to foist their attitudes upon healthy and flourishing organisms, but were actually able to do so. The disappointed and the mummies appealed to the general sexual guilt feeling and called to witness the *sexual chaos* and the "decline of civilization and culture". The masses of human beings knew, indeed, what was going on, but they kept silent because they were not quite sure whether their natural vital feelings might not be criminal after all. They had never heard anything different. Thus, the findings of Malinowski's research in the South Sea islands had an extraordinarily fruitful effect. Their effect was not that of arousing the lascivious curiosity with which sexually disturbed traders reacted to the South Sea girls or raved about Hawaiian hula dances; it was serious.

As early as 1926, Malinowski, in one of his publications, rejected the concept of the biological nature of the sexual child-parent conflict discovered by Freud (i.e., the Oedipus conflict). He pointed out, correctly, that the child-parent relationship changes with social processes; that, in other words, it is of a *sociological* and not of a biological nature. Specifically, the family in which a child grows up is itself the *result* of sociological development. With the Trobriand islanders, for example, not the father, but the mother's brother determines the upbringing of the children. This is an important characteristic of the matriarchate. The father plays only the role of a friend to his children. The Oedipus complex of the European does not exist among the Trobriand islanders. Of course, the child in the Trobriand islands also develops a family conflict with its taboos and precepts, but the laws governing behavior are fundamentally different from those of the Europeans. Apart from an incest taboo for brother and sister, they contain no sexual restrictions. The English psychoanalyst Jones raised a sharp protest against this contention, with the counter assertion that the Oedipus complex, as found in the European, was the "*fons et origo*" of all culture; and that, therefore, the family of today was an unalterable *biological* institution. In this controversy, it was simply a matter of the decisive question as to *whether sexual repression is biologically determined and unalterable, or sociologically determined and alterable.*

In 1929, Malinowski's main work, "The Sexual Life of Savages" appeared. It contains a wealth of material which confronted the world with the fact that sexual repression is of sociological and not of biological origin. Malinowski himself did not discuss this question in his book. All the more telling was the language of his material. In my book, "*Der*

Einbruch der Sexualmoral" I attempted to show *the sociological origin of sex denial* on the basis of the available ethnological material. I shall summarize the points which are relevant here:

Children in the Trobriand islands know no sex repression and no sexual secrecy. Their sex life is allowed to develop naturally, freely and unhampered *through every stage of life, with full satisfaction.* The children engage freely in the sexual activities which correspond to their age. Nonetheless, or rather, just for this reason, the society of the Trobrianders knew, in the third decade of our century, no sexual perversions, no functional psychoses, no psychoneuroses, no sex murder; they have no word for theft; homosexuality and masturbation, to them, mean nothing but an unnatural and imperfect means of sexual gratification, a sign of a disturbed capacity to reach normal satisfaction. To the children of the Trobrianders, the strict, obsessional training for excremental control which undermines the civilization of the white race, is unknown. The Trobrianders, therefore, are *spontaneously* clean, orderly, social without compulsion, intelligent and industrious. The socially accepted form of sexual life is spontaneous monogamy without compulsion, a relationship which can be dissolved without difficulties; thus, there is no promiscuity.

At the time when Malinowski made his studies of the Trobriand islanders, there was living a few miles away, on the Amphlett Islands, a tribe with patriarchal authoritarian family organization. The people inhabiting these islands were already showing all the traits of the European neurotic, such as distrust, anxiety, neuroses, perversion, suicide, etc.

Our science, permeated by sex-negation as it is, has thus far succeeded in reducing the significance of decisive facts to zero by the simple method of presenting side by side the important and unimportant, the banal and the great, in neat coordination. The difference just mentioned, between the matriarchal, free organization of the Trobriand islanders, and the patriarchal, authoritarian one on the Amphlett Islands, has more weight from a mental hygiene point of view than the most intricate and seemingly exact graphs of our academic world. This difference signifies: *The determining factor of the mental health of a population is the condition of its natural love life.*

Freud had contended that the sexual latency period of our children, between the ages of about six to twelve, was a biological phenomenon. My observations of adolescents from diverse strata of the population had shown that, given a natural development of sexuality, a latency period did not exist. Where a latency period occurs, it is an unnatural product of culture. For this statement I had been attacked by the psychoanalysts. Now it was confirmed by Malinowski: the sexual activities of the children in the Trobriand islands take place *without interruption* according to their respective age, without a latency period. Sexual intercourse is taken up when puberty demands it. The sexual life of the adolescents is monogamous; a change of partners takes place quietly and in an orderly manner, without violent jealousy. In strict contradistinction to our civilization, the society of the Trobrianders bestows care upon and facilitates adolescent sex life, particularly with regard to huts where they can be by themselves, and in other respects to the extent of their knowledge of natural processes.

There is only *one group* of children that is excluded from this natural course of events. These are the children who are predestined for a certain type of economically advantageous marriage. This kind of marriage brings economic advantages to the chief, and is the nucleus from which a patriarchal social order develops. This cross-cousin marriage is found wherever ethnological research has revealed actual or historical matriarchy (cf. e.g., Morgan, Bachofen, Engels). The children destined for this kind of marriage are, just like ours, brought up in sexual abstinence; they show neuroses and those character traits with which we are familiar in our character-neurotics. Their sexual abstinence has the function of making them submissive. *Sexual suppression is an essential instrument in the production of economic enslavement.*

Thus, sexual suppression in the infant and the adolescent is not, as psychoanalysis—in agreement with traditional and erroneous concepts of education—contends, the prerequisite of cultural development, sociality, diligence and cleanliness; *it is the exact opposite.* The Trobriand islanders, with full freedom of natural sexuality, have not only attained a high degree of agriculture, but, due to the absence of secondary drives, they have maintained a general state of affairs which to any European nation of 1930 or 1940 must appear like a dream.

Healthy children show a natural spontaneous sexuality. Sick children show an unnatural, that is, perverse sexuality. The alternative with which we are confronted in the matter of sexual education is thus not: *sexuality* or *abstinence;* but: *natural and healthy,* or *perverse and neurotic sexual life.*

Sexual repression is of social-economic and not of biological origin. Its function is that of laying the foundation for authoritarian patriarchal culture and economic slavery, as we see it most clearly in Japan, China, India, etc. In the early beginnings, human sex life followed natural laws which laid the basis for a natural sociality. Since then, the period of the authoritarian patriarchy of the last four to six thousand years has, with the energy of the suppressed natural sexuality, created the secondary, perverse sexuality of the human of today.

3. FASCIST IRRATIONALISM

It would not be too much to say that the cultural revolutions of our century are determined by the struggle of humanity for a re-establishment of the *natural* laws of love life. This struggle for naturalness, for unity of nature and culture, reveals itself in the diverse forms of mystical longing, cosmic phantasies, "oceanic" feelings, religious ecstasis, and particularly in the progressive development of sexual freedom; it is unconscious, full of neurotic conflicts and anxiety and is apt to take the forms which characterize the secondary, perverse drives. A humanity which has been forced for millennia to act contrary to its fundamental biological law and has, therefore, acquired a second nature which is actually a *counter*-nature, must needs get into an irrational frenzy when it tries to restore the fundamental biological function *and at the same time is afraid of it.*

The patriarchal, authoritarian era in human history has attempted to keep the secondary antisocial drives in check with the aid of compulsive moral restrictions. Thus, what is called the cultured human came to be a living structure *composed of three layers.* On the surface he carries the artificial mask of self-control, of compulsive, insincere politeness and of artificial sociality. With this layer, he covers up the second one, the Freudian "unconscious", in which sadism, greediness, lasciviousness, envy, perversions of all kinds, etc., are kept in check, without however, having in the least lost any of their power. This second layer is the artifact of a sex-negating culture; consciously, it is mostly experienced only as a gaping inner emptiness. Behind it, in the depths, live and work *natural* sociality and sexuality, *spontaneous* enjoyment of work, *capacity for love.* This third and deepest layer, representing the *biological nucleus* of the human structure, is unconscious and dreaded. It is at variance with every aspect of authoritarian education and régime. It is, at the same time, man's only real hope of ever mastering social misery.

All discussions of the question whether man is good or bad, a social or antisocial being, are philosophical pastimes.

Whether man is a social being or an irrationally reacting mass of protoplasm, depends on whether his fundamental biological needs are in harmony or in conflict with the institutions which he has created. For this reason, it is impossible to relieve the working individual from his responsibility for the order or disorder, that is, for the *economy, individual and social, of the biological energy.* Passing this responsibility enthusiastically from himself to some Führer or politician has become one of his essential characteristics, since he is no longer able to understand either himself or his institutions, of which he is only afraid. Fundamentally, he is helpless, incapable of freedom, and craving for authority, for he cannot react spontaneously; he is armored and expects commands, for he is full of contradictions and cannot rely on himself.

The cultivated European bourgeoisie of the 19th and early 20th century had taken over the compulsive moral forms of behavior of feudalism and made them the ideal of human behavior. Since the age of rationalism, people had begun to search for the truth and to clamor for freedom. As long as the compulsive moral institutions were in force—outside the individual as compulsive law and public opinion, inside him as compulsive conscience—there was a kind of surface calm, with occasional eruptions from the volcanic underworld of the secondary drives. So long as that was so, the secondary drives remained nothing but curiosities, of interest only to the psychiatrist. They manifested themselves as symptom neuroses, neurotic criminal acts, or as perversions. But when the social upheavals began to arouse in the Europeans the longing for freedom, independence, equality and self-determination, they were naturally impelled towards liberation of the vital forces within them. Social enlightenment and legislation, pioneer work in the social sciences, and liberal organizations, they all attempted to put "freedom" into this world. After the first world war had destroyed many of the compulsive authoritarian institutions, the European democracies tried to "lead mankind toward freedom".

But this European world, in its striving for freedom, made a grave miscalculation. It overlooked what the destruction of the living function in the human over thousands of years had cultivated into a monstrosity; it overlooked the deep-seated, general defect of the *character-neurosis*. And then, the great catastrophe of the psychic plague, that is, the catastrophe of the irrational human character, broke out in the form of the victory of the dictatorships. The forces which had been kept in check for so long by the superficial veneer of good breeding and artificial self-control, now, borne by the very multitudes that were striving for freedom, broke through into action:

In the concentration camps; in the persecution of the Jews; in the destruction of all human decency; in the mowing down of civilian populations by sadistic monsters to whom machine-gunning civilians is a delightful sport and who get a feeling of life only when parading in goose-step; in the gigantic mass deceit in which the state claims to be representing the interest of the people; in the engulfment of tens of thousands of young people who, helplessly and loyally, believed that they were serving an idea; in the destruction of billions' worth of human work, a fraction of which would suffice to do away with poverty all over the world; in brief, in a St. Vitus dance which will continue to recur as long as the bearers of knowledge and work do not succeed in eradicating, within themselves and outside of themselves, that mass neurosis which calls itself "politics" and which thrives on the characterological helplessness of human beings.

Between 1928 and 1930, at the time of the controversies with Freud above described, I had little idea of Fascism, about as little as the average Norwegian in 1939 or the average American in 1940. Only between 1930 and 1933 did I become acquainted with it in Germany. I felt perplexed when I was confronted with it and when I recognized in it, bit by bit, the subject of the controversy with Freud. Gradually I began to understand the logic in this. The controversies had dealt with an evaluation of human structure, with the role played by the human longing for happiness, and with the irrationalism in social life. In Fascism, the psychic mass disease revealed itself in an *undisguised* form.

The enemies of Fascism, liberal democrats, socialists, communists, Marxist and non-Marxist economists, etc., looked for an answer to the problem either in the personality of Hitler or in formal political blunders on the part of Germany's diverse democratic parties. The one as well as the other meant to trace the psychic plague back to individual shortsightedness or to the brutality of one single man. In reality, Hitler was only the expression of a tragic conflict in the human masses, the *conflict between longing for freedom and actual fear of freedom.*

German Fascism said in so many words that it was operating not with the thinking and the knowledge of people, but with their infantile emotional reactions. What carried Fascism to power and subsequently secured its place, was neither its political program nor any of its innumerable and confused economic promises; it was *essentially its appeal to an obscure mystical feeling, to an undefined, nebulous but nevertheless extremely powerful longing*. Not to understand this, means not to understand Fascism, which is an international phenomenon.

The irrationality in the political strivings of the German masses can be illustrated in terms of the following contradictions.

The German masses wanted "freedom". Hitler promised them absolute, authoritarian leadership with the explicit exclusion of any expression of opinion. Out of thirty-one million voters, seventeen million jubilantly carried Hitler to power in March, 1933. Those who looked at things with open eyes knew: The masses of people *felt helpless and incapable of taking the responsibility for the solution of the chaotic social problems within the old political system and frame of thinking*. The Führer should and would do it *for them.*

Hitler promised the abolition of democratic discussion of opinion. The masses of people came running to him. They had long since grown tired of these discussions, because they had always evaded their personal everyday concerns, that is, that which was *subjectively* important. They did not want discussions of "the budget" or of "high diplomacy"; they wanted actual, true knowledge about their own lives. When they did not get that, they gave themselves over to authoritarian leadership and the illusionary protection which was promised to them.

Hitler promised the abolition of the freedom of the individual and the establishment of the *"freedom of the nation"*. Enthusiastically, the masses of people exchanged their potentialities for individual freedom for *illusionary* freedom, that is, freedom through identification with an idea; they did so because this illusionary freedom relieved them of any individual *responsibility*. They craved *a "freedom" which the Führer should conquer for them and guarantee to them:* the freedom to howl, to escape from the truth into a fundamental falsehood, to be sadistic, to brag—though one was in actuality a cipher—about one's superior race, to impress girls with uniforms instead of strong human qualities, to sacrifice oneself for imperialistic goals instead of the actual struggles of everyday life, etc., etc.

The previous education of the masses of people towards the recognition of a formal, political authority instead of an authority based on *factual* knowledge formed the soil in which the Fascist demand for authority could readily strike roots. Fascism, therefore, was not a new kind of philosophy, as its friends and many of its enemies wanted us to believe; much less even does it have anything to do with a rational revolution against intolerable social conditions; Fascism is nothing but *the extreme reactionary consequence of all undemocratic types of leadership of the past.* Neither is the *race theory* anything new; it is nothing but the consistently and brutally applied *continuation of the old theories of heredity and degeneration.* It is for this reason that the psychiatrists of the hereditarian school and the eugenicists of the old school were particularly accessible to Fascism.

What is new in the Fascist movement is the fact that the extreme political reaction succeeded in making use of the deep longings of the masses of people for freedom. *Intense longing for freedom plus fear of the responsibility of freedom results in Fascist mentality,* no matter whether it is found in a Fascist or a Democrat.

What is new in Fascism is that *the masses of people themselves assented to their own subjugation and actively brought it about.* The craving for authority proved stronger than the wish for independence.

Hitler promised the subjugation of woman to man, the abolition of her economic independence, her exclusion from the process of determining social life, and her relegation to the home and hearth. The women, whose individual freedom had been suppressed for centuries and who had developed the fear of an independent way of living in a particularly high degree, were the first to hail him.

Hitler promised the abolition of socialist and democratic organizations. The socialist and democratic masses hastened to him because their organizations, though they had done a great deal of talking about freedom, had not as much as mentioned the difficult problem of human craving for authority and their helplessness in matters of practical politics. The masses of people were disillusioned by the irresolute attitude of the old democratic institutions. *Disillusionment in the liberal organizations plus economic crisis plus tremendous urge for freedom result in Fascist mentality,* that is, in the willingness of the people to surrender to an authoritarian father figure.

Hitler promised the sharpest measures against contraception and the sexual reform movement. In the Germany of 1932, there were about 500,000 people in organizations which struggled for a rational sex reform. Yet, these organizations never dared to touch upon the core of the problem, namely, the longing for sexual happiness. I know from many years' work among the masses that this is exactly what they were looking for. They were disappointed when one gave them learned talks about eugenics, instead of telling them how they could bring up their children to be lively and uninhibited, how adolescents could cope with their sexual and economic problems, and how married people could deal with their typical conflicts. The masses of people seemed to feel that the advice about the "technique of love-making", such as given by Van de Velde, might be profitable to the publisher, but that it did not really touch their problems, nor did they feel that it was in any way a response to their problems. Thus it happened that the disappointed masses hastened to Hitler who, though in a mystical way, appealed to deeply vital forces. *Sermonizing about freedom, without the constant, resolute struggle to set the responsibility involved in freedom into operation in the occurrences of everyday life, together with the social prerequisites of such freedom, leads to Fascism.*

For decades, German science had been struggling to achieve the separation of the concept of sexuality from that of procreation. Of this struggle, the working masses of people knew nothing, for it was stored away in academic volumes and therefore had no social effect. Now Hitler promised to make procreation, and *not happiness in love,* the basic principle of his cultural program. Brought up not to call a spade a spade and to say "eugenic improvement of the racial stock" when they meant "happiness in love", the masses of people hastened to Hitler, because he attached to the old concept a strong, though irrational, emotion. *Reactionary concepts plus revolutionary emotion result in Fascist mentality.*

The church had preached "happiness in the hereafter", and had, with the aid of the concept of sin, deeply implanted in the human structure the helpless dependence on an omnipotent supernatural figure. But the economic crisis of 1929 to 1933 had confronted the masses of people with the most acute *earthly* want. They were unable to master this want *themselves,* either socially or individually. Hitler came along, declaring himself a God-sent *earthly* Führer, omnipotent and omniscient, who would be able to eradicate the *earthly* misery. The stage was prepared for new masses of people to acclaim him, people who were hemmed in between their own individual helplessness and the small gratification provided by the idea of happiness in the hereafter. An earthly God who made them shout "Heil" at the top of their lungs meant more to them emotionally than a God whom they never could see and who no longer helped them even emotionally. *Sadistic brutality plus mysticism results in Fascist mentality.*

Germany, in its schools and universities, had been struggling for decades for the principle of the "*freie Schulgemeinde*", for modern spontaneous achievement and self-government of the student. The democratic authorities responsible for education were unable to outgrow those authoritarian principles which instilled in the student a fear of authority and at the same time a rebelliousness which took on every possible irrational form. Liberal educational organizations not only lacked the protection of society, but they were, instead, constantly threatened in their existence by all kinds of reactionary bodies, and were dependent on private subsidies. So it was not surprising that these *beginnings* in the direction of a new *structural formation* of the mass of people remained nothing but a drop in the bucket. Youth ran to Hitler in masses. He did not impose any responsibility on them, but he built upon their structure as it had been evolved by means of the authoritarian family. Hitler obtained a firm grip on the youth movement because democratic society had failed to do everything in its power to educate youth towards a way of living in which they took responsibility for their freedom.

In the place of voluntary achievement, Hitler promised the principle of *compulsive discipline* and *work as duty*. Several millions of German workers and employees cast their vote for Hitler. The democratic institutions had not only failed to cope with unemployment; they had shown themselves definitely afraid of actually leading the working masses of people towards actual responsibility for their achievement in work. They had been brought up not to understand anything of the process of work or the totality of the process of production, and simply to receive their pay envelopes. Thus, these millions of workers and employees did not find it difficult to submit to Hitler's principle; it was nothing but the old principle in an *accentuated* form. Now they were able to identify themselves with "the state" or "the nation" which was—*in their place*—"great and strong". Hitler, in his writings and speeches, declared openly that the masses of people only give back what is being poured into them, because they are, basically, infantile and feminine. The masses of people hailed him; for here was one who was going to *protect* them.

Hitler decreed the subordination of all science under the concept of "race". Major sections of German science submitted, for the theory of race had its roots in the metaphysical theory of heredity; a theory which, with the aid of the concepts of "inherited substances" and "Anlagen" had again and again enabled science *to evade the duty of trying to understand the development of living functions and of comprehending in its actuality the social origin of human be-*

havior. There used to be a general belief that when one stated that cancer, or neuroses or psychoses, were of hereditary origin, one had really said something. *The Fascist theory of race is only a continuation of the convenient theories of heredity.*

There is hardly any other slogan of German Fascism that fired the masses of people as much as the slogan of the "throbbing of German blood" and its "purity". The purity of the German blood means freedom from syphilis, from "Jewish contamination". The fear of venereal disease, as a continuation of infantile genital anxiety, is deeply rooted in every single mortal. Thus it is understandable that the masses of people acclaimed Hitler, for he promised them "purity of blood". Every human being feels in himself what is called "cosmic" or "oceanic" feelings. Dry academic science felt itself too superior to concern itself with such "mysticisms". But, this cosmic or oceanic yearning in people is nothing but the expression of their orgastic longing for life. Hitler appealed to this longing. Therefore, the masses acclaimed him and not the dry rationalists who tried to stifle these obscure feelings for life with economic statistics.

In Europe, the "preservation of the family" had always been an abstract slogan behind which were hidden the most reactionary mentality and behavior. He who dared to distinguish between authoritarian compulsive family and natural love relationship between children and parents, was considered an "enemy of the fatherland", a "destroyer of the sacred institution of the family", an outlaw. There was no official agency which would have dared to point out what was pathological in the family, or would have dared to do something about the suppression of the children through the parents, about family hatreds, etc. The typical authoritarian German family, particularly in the country and small town, bred Fascist mentality by the million. This family created in the children a structure characterized by compulsive duty, renunciation and absolute obedience to authority which Hitler knew so splendidly how to exploit. By advocating the "preservation of the family" and *at the same time* taking youth out of the family and putting them in its own youth groups, Fascism took into account *the fixation to the family as well as the rebellion against the family*. Because Fascism emphatically impressed on the people the emotional identity of "family", "state", and "nation", the familial structure of the people could easily be continued in the Fascist, national one. True, this did not solve one single problem of the *actual* family or the *actual* needs of the nation, but it made it possible for the masses of people to transfer their family ties from the compulsive family to the larger "family" called "nation". "Mother Germany" and "Father-God-Hitler" became the symbols of deeply rooted infantile emotions. Now, in his identification with the "strong and unique German nation", every ordinary mortal, with all his misery and inferiority feelings, could be *"something big"*, even if it was in an *illusionary* manner. Finally, the ideology of the "race" succeeded in harnessing the sexual energies and in diverting them. *The adolescents were now able to have sexual intercourse, if they believed—or pretended to believe—that they were begetting children in the interest of improving the race.*

The natural vital forces not only continued to be kept from developing, but, in addition, to the extent to which they could manifest themselves, had to do so now in much more disguised forms than ever before. As a result of this "revolution of the irrational", there were in Germany more suicides and more social misery than ever before. The mass death in the war for the glory of the German race is the apotheosis of this witches' dance.

Hand in hand with the longing for "purity of blood", i.e., liberation from sin, goes the persecution of the Jews. The Jews tried to explain or to prove that *they too* were moral, that *they too* belonged to the nation, or that *they too* were

"German". Anti-Fascist anthropologists attempted by way of skull measurements to prove that the Jews were *not* an inferior race. Christians and historians tried to point out that Jesus was of Jewish origin. But—it was not a matter of rational problems at all; that is, it was not a question of whether the Jews *too* were decent people, whether they were *not* inferior or whether they had *proper* skull sizes. The problem lay somewhere else entirely. It was just at this point that the consistency and correctness of sex-economic thinking proved itself.

When the Fascist says "Jew", he means a certain irrational feeling. As one can convince oneself in every treatment, of Jews and Non-Jews, which penetrates deeply enough, the "Jew" has the irrational significance of the "money-maker", the "usurer", the "capitalist". On a deeper level, "Jew" means "filthy", "sensual", "brutally lustful", but also "Shylock", "castrator", "slaughterer". The fear of natural sexuality is as deeply rooted in all humans as is the horror of perverse sexuality. Thus we can easily understand that the persecution of the Jews, so cleverly executed, stirred up the deepest antisexual defense functions of the antisexually brought up individual. Thus, the ideology of the "Jews" made it possible to harness the *anticapitalist* as well as the *antisexual* attitudes of the masses and put them completely at the service of the Fascist machinery.

Unconscious longing for sexual happiness and sexual purity, plus simultaneous fear of normal sexuality and abhorrence of perverse sexuality, results in Fascist sadistic anti-semitism. "The Frenchman" has the same meaning to the German as "the Jew" and "the negro" to the unconsciously Fascist Englishman. "Jew", "Frenchman", "negro" have the meaning of "sexually sensual".

And so it happened that the modern "sex reformer", sexual psychopath and criminal pervert Julius Streicher was able to put his paper, "Der Stürmer", into the hands of millions of German adolescents and adults. Nothing could demonstrate more clearly than the "Stürmer" the fact that sexual hygiene has long ceased to be a problem restricted to medical circles; that, rather, it has become a problem of decisive social significance. The following samples of Streicher's imagination, quoted from the "Stürmer", may illustrate the above:

"Helmut Daube, 20, had just graduated from college. He went home around 2 AM, and at 5 AM his parents found his dead body in front of the house. The throat was cut straight through to the spinal column, *the genitals were removed.* There was no blood. The hands were cut up. The lower abdomen showed several knife blows".

"One day, the old Jew attacked the unsuspecting Non-Jewess, raped and desecrated her. As time went on, he would sneak into her room whenever he pleased; the door could not be locked".

"A young couple, taking a walk outside of Paderborn, came upon *a hunk of flesh* right in the middle of the road. On closer examination, they found to their horror that it was *a female genital which had been anatomically dissected from the body".*

"The Jew had cut up the woman *into pieces weighing about a pound.* Together with his father, he had scattered the pieces all over the neighborhood. They were found in a little woods, in the meadows, on tree stumps, in a pool, in a brook, in a sewer, and in the cesspool. *The cut-off breasts were lying in the hay loft".*

"While Moses throttled with a handkerchief the child which Samuel put on his knees, the latter *took a knife and cut a piece off the child's jaw.* The others collected the blood in a bowl, at the same time stabbing the naked victim with pins".

"The woman's resisting did not check his lust, on the contrary. He tried to shut the window so that the neighbors could not look in. But then he touched the woman again in a vile, typically Jewish manner. . . . He talked to her urgently, saying she should not be so prudish. He locked windows and doors. His words and his behavior became more and more shameless. More and more he cornered his victim. When she threatened to cry for help, he only laughed, and more and more he pushed her toward the couch. From his mouth came the lewdest and vilest expressions. *Then, like a tiger, he leaped upon the female body, to finish his devilish work".*

Up to this point in this book, many readers undoubtedly thought that I was exaggerating when I spoke of the psychic plague. I can only assure them that I did not introduce this term frivolously nor as a neat figure of speech. I mean it very seriously. In millions and millions of people, German and otherwise, the "Stürmer", during the past seven years, has not only confirmed their genital castration anxiety, but, in addition, has stimulated to a tremendous degree the perverse phantasies which lie dormant in everybody. After the downfall of the principal standard bearers of the psychic plague in Europe, it will remain to be seen how one can cope with this problem. It is not a German but *an international problem, because genital anxiety and longing for love are international facts.* Fascist youths, who had maintained a bit of natural feeling for life, came to see me in Scandinavia and asked me what attitude they should take toward Streicher, the theory of race and all the other outcroppings of the time. There was something wrong there, they said. I summarized the most necessary measures in the following outline:

"What is to be done?

Generally: This reactionary obscenity must be counteracted by a well organized and factually correct enlightenment concerning the difference between *healthy* and *pathological* sexuality. Every average individual will understand the difference, because he has felt it in himself. Every average individual is ashamed of his perverse, pathological ideas of sex and longs for clarity, help and natural sexual gratification.

Specifically: We must enlighten and help. This can be done in the following ways:

1. Collection of all the material which makes the pornographic character of Streicherism self-evident to any thinking person. Distribution of it in hand-bills. The *healthy* sexual interest of the masses of people must be aroused, made conscious and be supported.

2. Collection and distribution of all the material that will show the population that Streicher and his accomplices are psychopaths

themselves, and are jeopardizing the health of the people. There are Streichers everywhere in the world.

3. Uncovering of the secret of Streicher's influence on the people: he stimulates their pathological phantasies. The population will be grateful for good explanatory material and will read it.

4. *The only way of combatting that pathological sexuality* which forms the fertile soil for Hitler's theory of race and for Streicher's criminal activity *is to contrast it to the natural sexual processes and attitudes.* The people will immediately grasp the difference and will show burning interest in it, once they are shown what it is that they really want and only do not dare to express. For example:

a. An absolute prerequisite for a healthy, satisfactory sex life is the possibility of being alone with one's partner, without being disturbed. That means: adequate housing for all those who are in need of it, including youth.

b. Sexual gratification is not identical with procreation. The healthy individual has sexual intercourse some three to four thousand times during his life, but an average of only two or three children. Contraceptives are an absolute necessity for sexual health.

c. The vast majority of men as well as women are sexually disturbed as a result of a training which inhibits their sexuality; that is, they are not satisfied in sexual intercourse. What is necessary, therefore, is the establishment of a sufficient number of clinics for the treatment of sexual disturbances. What is necessary, is *a rational sex education which will affirm the validity of love.*

d. Youth is made ill by its conflicts about masturbation. Masturbation is harmless to health only when it is not accompanied by guilt feelings. *Youth has a right to a happy sex life under the best of conditions. Chronic sexual abstinence is definitely harmful.* Pathological phantasies disappear only with a satisfactory sex life. Fight for this right!"

I know that hand-bills and enlightenment alone will not do. What is necessary is *work on the human structure, on a broad basis and with the protection of society;* work on this structure which produces the psychic plague, which makes it possible for psychopaths to function as dictators and modern "sex reformers". In one word, what is necessary is *the liberation of natural sexuality in the masses of people and its underwriting by society.*

In 1930, human sexuality was a Cinderella of society, no more than an object of dubious reform bodies. By 1940, it has become a cornerstone of social problems. If it is correct that Fascism, in an irrational manner but successfully, utilized the sexual longings of the masses of people and thus created chaos, then it must be correct that the perversions which it allowed to erupt can be banished by a universal *rational solution of the problem of sexuality.*

The events in Europe between 1930 and 1940 in all their profusion of mental hygiene problems confirmed my point of view in the controversy with Freud. The painful thing about this confirmation is the feeling of powerlessness, and the knowledge that natural science is still far from comprehending what in this book I termed the "biological nucleus" of character structure.

By and large, we, as humans as well as physicians and teachers, are as helpless in the face of the biological aberrations of life, as, say, the humans of the middle ages were in the face of infectious diseases. At the same time we feel in ourselves that the experiencing of the Fascist plague will mobilize those forces in the world which are needed to solve this problem of civilization.

The Fascists make the claim of carrying out the "*biological revolution*". What is correct is that *Fascism has put before us in unmistakable form the fact that the vital functions of the human have become thoroughly neurotic.* In Fascism there operates, at least from the point of view of the masses of its adherents, a tremendous will to life. However, the forms in which this will to life has manifested itself has shown only too clearly the results of an ancient psychic enslavement. *For the time being, only the perverse drives have broken through. The post-Fascist world will carry out the biological revolution which Fascism did not create but which it made necessary.*

The ensuing chapters of this volume discuss the functions

of the "biological nucleus". Its scientific comprehension and the social mastery of the problem presented by it, will be an achievement of rational work, militant science and natural love function, of *truly* democratic, courageous and collective efforts. Their goal is the earthly happiness, material and sexual, of the masses of people.

Chapter VII

THE BREAK-THROUGH INTO THE VEGETATIVE REALM

The orgasm theory had confronted me with the question: What was to become of the sexual energy that was *liberated* in the therapeutic process? The world strictly opposes all requirements of sexual hygiene. The natural instincts are *biological* facts which can neither be effaced from the earth nor be basically altered. Like everything living, man needs first of all satisfaction of his hunger and gratification of his sexual instinct. Society as it is today, impedes the first and denies the second. That is, there is *a sharp conflict between natural demands* and certain *social institutions*. Caught as he is in this conflict, man gives in more or less to one side or the other; he makes compromises which are bound to fail; he escapes into illness or death; or he rebels—senselessly and fruitlessly—against the existing order. In this struggle, human structure is molded.

Human structure contains the biological as well as the sociological demands. Everything that is signified by position, fame and authority, defends the sociological demands against the natural demands. I was amazed to see how one could so thoroughly overlook the enormous importance of the natural demands. Even Freud, though he himself had discovered quite a considerable part of it, became inconsistent. To him, instincts soon became nothing but "mythical entities"; they were "undeterminable", though "rooted in chemical processes".

The contradictions were enormous. In clinical therapeutic work, everything was determined by the instinctual demands, and practically nothing by society. On the other hand, there were "society and culture" with their "reality demands". True, man was fundamentally determined by his instincts, but at the same time the instincts had to adapt themselves to a sex-negating reality. True, the instincts sprang from physiological sources, but at the same time the individual had an "eros" and a "death instinct", fighting each other. There was, with Freud, an absolute dualism of instincts. There was no connection between sexuality and its alleged biological counterpart, the death instinct; there was only antithesis. Freud psychologized biology when he assumed biological "tendencies", i.e., forces with this or that "intention". Such views were metaphysical. Their criticism was justified by later experimental proof of the simple functional nature of instinctual life. It was impossible to understand neurotic anxiety in terms of the theory of eros and death instinct. Finally, Freud gave up the libido-anxiety theory.

The biological "repetition-compulsion" beyond the pleasure principle was supposed to explain masochistic behavior. A will to suffer was assumed. This was in keeping with the theory of the death instinct. In brief, Freud transferred laws which he had discovered in the functioning of the psyche to its biological foundation. As society was considered to be constructed like an individual, there arose a methodological overburdening of psychology which could not hold water, and which, in addition, paved the way for speculations on "society and Thanatos". Psychoanalysis began to claim increasingly that it could explain all existence; at the same time it was shying away more and more from a correct sociological and physiological, as well as a purely psychological, comprehension of the single object, Man. Yet, there could be no doubt that what made man different from the other animals was *a specific interlacing of biophysiological, sociological and psychological processes.* The correctness of this *structural principle* of my theory was proven by the solution of the problem of masochism. From there on, psychic structure revealed itself, bit by bit, as a dynamic unification of biophysiological and sociological factors.

1. THE PROBLEM OF MASOCHISM AND ITS SOLUTION

According to psychoanalysis, the pleasure in suffering pain was simply the result of a biological need; "masochism" was considered an instinct like any other, except that it had a peculiar goal. In therapy, nothing could be done with such a concept. For, if one told a patient that "for biological reasons" he *wanted* to suffer, everything remained as it was. Orgasmotherapy confronted me with the question as to why the masochist turned the otherwise easily understandable demand for pleasure into a demand for pain. A drastic occurrence in my practice cured me from an erroneous formulation by which psychology and sexology had been misled. In 1928 I treated a man who suffered from a masochistic perversion. His lamentations and his demands to be beaten blocked any progress. After some months of conventional psychoanalytic work my patience wore thin. One day, when he asked me again to beat him, I asked him what he would say if I actually did. He beamed with happy anticipation. I took a ruler and gave him two hard slaps on the buttocks. He yelled loud; there was no sign of pleasure whatsoever, and from that time on such demands were never repeated. However, his lamentations and passive reproaches persisted.

My colleagues would have been horrified had they learned of this happening; but I had no regrets. All of a sudden I realized that—contrary to general belief—pain is far from being the instinctual goal of the masochist. When beaten, the masochist, like any other mortal—experiences *pain.* A whole industry (procuring instruments of torture, pictures and descriptions of masochistic perversions, and prostitutes to satisfy them) flourishes on the basis of that mistaken concept of masochism which it helps to create.

But the question remained: *If the masochist does not strive for pain,* if he does not experience it as pleasure, *why, then, does he ask to be tortured?* After much effort, I discovered what is at the basis of this perverse behavior—at first glance a truly fantastic idea: The masochist *wishes to burst and imagines that the torture will bring this about. In this manner alone does he hope to obtain relief.*

The masochistic lamentations revealed themselves as the expression of a painful *inner tension* which could not be discharged. They were open or disguised entreaties for *liberation* from the instinctual tension. As the masochist—due to his pleasure anxiety—is unable actively to bring about gratification, he expects the orgastic release, the very thing he is most deeply afraid of, in the form of a *liberation from the outside,* provided by somebody else. The desire to burst is opposed by an equally deep fear of the very same thing. The masochistic tendency to *self-depreciation* began to appear in an entirely new light. *Self-aggrandizement* is, as it were, a biopsychic erection, a fantastic expansion of the psychic apparatus. A few years later I learned that it is based upon the perception of electrical charges. The opposite is self-depreciation. The masochist shrivels up because of his fear that he may expand to the point of *bursting.* Behind the masochistic self-depreciation works impotent ambition and an inhibited wish to be great. The masochist's provoking to punishment became clear as an expression of the deep *wish to be brought to gratification against his own will.* Women with a masochistic character never have sexual intercourse without the phantasy of being seduced or raped. The man is to force them—*against their own will*—to the very thing they anxiously long for. They cannot do it themselves because they feel that it is prohibited or charged with intense guilt feelings. The well-known vindictiveness of the masochist, whose self-confidence is seriously impaired, finds an outlet in placing the other person in a bad light or in provoking him into cruel behavior.

Masochists frequently have the peculiar idea that their skin, particularly that of the buttocks, gets "warm" or "burning". The desire to be scratched with hard brushes or to be beaten until the skin breaks, is nothing but the desire to end a tension by bursting. That is, the attendant pain is by no means the goal; it is only an unpleasant accompaniment of the liberation from a doubtless actual tension. Masochism is the prototype of a *secondary* drive, and an emphatic demonstration of what results from the repression of natural drives.

In the masochist, orgasm anxiety is present in a *specific form.* Other patients either do not permit any sexual excitation to occur in the genital itself, as in the case of compulsion neurotics; or they escape into anxiety, as in the case of hysterics. The masochist, however, persists in pregenital stimulation; he does not elaborate it into neurotic symptoms. This increases the tension, and consequently, along with simultaneously increasing incapacity for discharge, the orgasm anxiety, also. Thus, the masochist finds himself in a vicious circle of the worst kind. The more he tries to work himself out of the tension, the more he gets entangled in it. At the moment when orgasm should occur, the masochistic phantasies undergo an acute intensification; often they do not become conscious until this very moment. The man may imagine that he is being pulled through a fire, the woman, that her abdomen is being slashed or her vagina burst. To many, this is the only way of reaching a modicum of gratification. To be *forced* to burst means to resort to external help in attaining relief from tension.

Since the fear of orgastic excitation is part of every neurosis, masochistic phantasies and attitudes are to be found in every case of neurosis. The attempt to explain masochism as a perception of an internal death instinct, as a result of a fear of death, was in strict contradiction with clinical experience. As a matter of fact, masochists develop very little anxiety—as long as they can engage in masochistic phantasies. They do develop anxiety if and when hysterical or compulsion-neurotic mechanisms take the place of the masochistic phantasies. On the contrary, full-fledged masochism is an excellent means of avoiding anxiety, since it is always *the other person* who does the bad things or causes them to be done. In addition, the double significance of the idea of *bursting* (desire for and fear of orgastic release) satisfactorily explains every detail of the masochistic attitude.

The desire to burst (or the fear of it) which I soon found in all patients, was puzzling. It did not fit into customary psychological concepts. An idea must have a certain origin and a certain function. We are used to derive ideas from concrete impressions; the idea originates in the outer world and is relayed to the organism by the sense organs in the form of a perception; its energy derives from inner, instinctual sources. Such an external origin could not be found for the idea of bursting, which made it difficult to coordinate. At any rate, I was able to record some important findings:

Masochism is not a biological instinct. It is the result of a disturbance in gratification, and an ever unsuccessful attempt to overcome this disturbance. *It is a result, and not the cause, of the neurosis.*

Masochism is the expression of a sexual tension which cannot be discharged. Its immediate cause is pleasure anxiety, that is, fear of orgastic discharge.

It consists in an attempt to bring about the very thing that is most deeply dreaded: the pleasurable relief from tension, which relief is being experienced and feared as a process of bursting.

The understanding of the mechanism of masochism opened an avenue of approach into biology. Human pleasure anxiety became understandable as the result of a fundamental alteration of the *physiological* pleasure function. Suffering and wanting to suffer are the results of having lost the organic capacity for pleasure.

With this, I had hit upon the dynamics of all religions and philosophies of suffering. When, as sex counselor, I had to deal with a great many Christian people, I began to see the connection. Religious ecstasy follows exactly the model of the masochistic mechanism: the religious individual expects from God, an omnipotent figure, the relief from an inner sin, that is, an inner sexual tension; a relief which the individual is unable to bring about himself. The relief is desired with *biological* energy. But at the same time, it is experienced as "sin", and so the individual does not dare to bring it about himself. Somebody else has to do it—in the form of a punishment, an absolution, a deliverance, etc. About this, more will be said in another place. The masochistic orgies of the middle ages, the inquisition, the religious castigations, tortures and acts of expiation betrayed their function: they were *unsuccessful, masochistic attempts at sexual gratification.*

The masochist differs in his disturbance of the orgasm in that he inhibits pleasure at the moment of highest excitation and keeps on inhibiting it. In so doing, he creates a contradiction between the tremendous expansion which is about to occur and the reverse direction. In all other forms of orgastic impotence, the inhibition sets in *before* the acme of excitation. This fine detail, though seemingly only of academic interest, decided the fate of my later scientific work. My notes of the years between 1928 and about 1934 show that my biological experimental work up to the bion research had this finding as a starting point. I cannot possibly present the whole story. I will have to simplify, or, rather, impart those first phantasies of mine which I never would have dared to publish, had they not been confirmed by the experimental and clinical work of the ensuing ten years.

2. THE FUNCTIONING OF A LIVING BLADDER

The fear of bursting and the desire to be made to burst had been discovered in one specific case of masochism. Later on I found it in all masochists, and—without exception—in all patients to the extent to which they had masochistic tendencies. The refutation of the concept of masochism as a biological instinct went far beyond a criticism of Freud's theory of the death instinct. I kept asking myself: what is the origin of this idea of bursting, which, in all patients, makes its appearance shortly before the establishment of orgastic potency?

I soon found that in most cases this idea appears in the form of a kinesthetic perception of the state of the body. In outspoken cases there is regularly the idea of the body as a *taut bladder*. The patients complain about being taut, filled up, as if they were going to burst, to explode. They feel "blown up", "like a balloon". They dread any loosening of their armor because it makes them feel as if they were being "pricked open". Some patients express a fear of "melting away", of "dissolving", of losing their "hold on themselves", their "contour". They cling to the rigid armoring of their movements and attitudes as a drowning person clings to a board. Others have the strongest desire to "burst". Many a case of suicide occurs on this basis. The more acute the sexual tension becomes, the more distinct become these sensations. They promptly disappear when the orgasm anxiety is overcome and sexual relaxation can take place. Then the hard features of the character disappear, the person becomes "soft" and yielding and at the same time develops an elastic sort of strength.

The crisis in a successful character analysis occurs just at this point; when intense preorgastic sensations are prevented from taking their normal course by spasms of the musculature which are caused by anxiety. At a time when the excitation has reached its peak and calls for unhampered discharge, pelvic spasm has an effect similar to that of pulling the emergency brake when going at 100 miles an hour; everything goes helter-skelter. Something like that happens to the patient in the genuine process of getting well. He has to make his choice: either to let go entirely of his bodily inhibitory mechanisms, or, to fall back into his neurosis. *The neurosis is but one thing: the sum total of all the inhibitions of the natural sexual pleasure which in the course of time have become mechanical.* All other manifestations of the neurosis are the result of this *original* disturbance. Around 1929 I began to grasp the fact that the original pathogenic conflict of mental disease (the conflict between striving for pleasure and moral frustration) is structurally anchored in a physiological way in the muscular disturbance. *The psychic conflict between sexuality and morality works in the biological depths of the organism as a conflict between pleasurable excitation and muscular spasm.*

Masochistic attitudes attained great significance for the sex-economic theory of the neuroses: they represent this conflict in pure culture. Compulsion neurotics and hysterics —who avoid the orgastic sensation by way of developing anxiety or neurotic symptoms—regularly go through a phase of masochistic suffering in the process of getting well. This occurs at a time when the fear of sexual excitation has been eliminated to a sufficient extent so that they allow preorgastic genital excitation to occur, without, however, as yet allowing the *acme* of excitation *without inhibition, i.e., without anxiety*.

Masochism, furthermore, became a central problem in *mass psychology*. The question as to how this problem may be practically solved in the future seemed of decisive significance. The working millions suffer the most severe deprivations of all kinds. They are being dominated and exploited by a few people in power. Masochism flourishes like a weed in the form of the diverse patriarchal religions, as ideology and practice, smothering every natural claim of life. It keeps people in a profound state of humble resignation. It frustrates their attempts to cooperative rational action and makes them forever afraid of taking the responsibility for their existence. This is the stumbling block of even the best intentions for a democratization of society.

Freud explained the chaotic and catastrophic social conditions as the result of the death instinct at work in the society. The psychoanalysts contended that the masses were *biologically* masochistic. The need for a police force, so some said, was a natural expression of the biological masochism of the masses; people are indeed submissive to authoritarian governments as is the individual to the powerful father.

Since, however, rebellion against the dictatorial authority, the father, was considered as neurotic, the adjustment to his demands and institutions, on the other hand, as normal, the refutation of this theory required the demonstration of two facts: *First,* the fact that there exists no *biological* masochism; and *second,* that the adjustment to contemporaneous reality (in the form, e.g., of irrational education or irrational politics) is in itself neurotic.

I had no preconceived idea in this direction. The demonstration of these facts resulted from the interplay of many observations—far from the furious mêlée of ideologies. They resulted from the simple answer to an almost stupid question: *How would a bladder behave if it were blown up with air from the inside, and could not burst?* Let us assume that its membrane would be tensile, but could not be torn. This picture of the human character as an armor around the living nucleus was highly relevant. The bladder, if it could express itself in its state of insoluble tension, would complain. In its helplessness, it would look for the causes of its suffering on *the outside,* and would be reproachful. It would ask to be pricked open. It would provoke its surroundings until it had achieved its aim as it conceives this. *What it could not bring about spontaneously from the inside, it would passively, helplessly, expect from the outside.*

Let us think of the biopsychic organism, whose energy discharge is disturbed, in terms of an *armored* bladder. The membrane would be the character armor. The stretching takes place as the result of continuous production of inner energy (sexual energy, biological excitation). The biological energy presses towards the outside, be it to pleasurable discharge, be it towards contact with people and objects. The urge for expansion is synonymous with a *direction from within outward.* It is opposed by the force of the surrounding armor. This armor not only prevents the bursting, but, in addition, exerts a pressure *from without towards the inside.* It results in a rigidity of the organism.

This picture was in accord with the physical processes of *internal pressure* and *surface tension.* With these concepts I had come into contact when, in 1926, I reviewed for the psychoanalytic journal a most significant book by Fr. Kraus,[1] the famous Berlin internist.

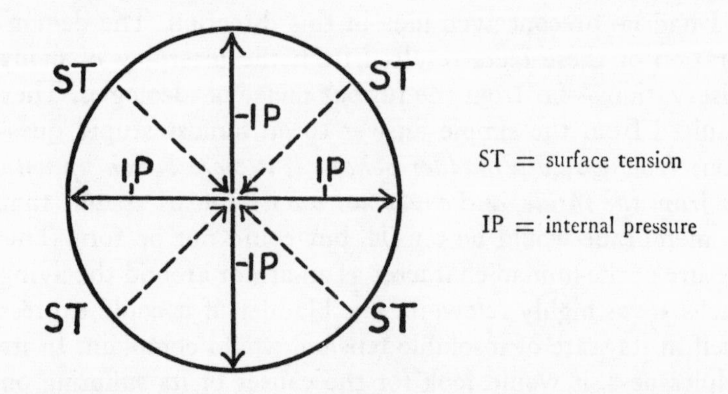

The neurotic organism lent itself exceedingly well to the comparison with a taut, peripherally armored bladder. This peculiar analogy between a physical phenomenon and the characterological situation stood the test of clinical observation. The neurotic patient has become rigid at the body periphery, at the same time having retained his "central" vitality with its demands. He is not at ease "within his own skin", he is "inhibited", "unable to realize himself", "hemmed in" as if by a wall; he "lacks contact", he feels "tight enough to burst". He strives with all his might 'towards the world", but he is "tied down". More than that: he is so little able to stand the difficulties and disappointments in life, and the efforts to establish contact with life are so painful, that he prefers to "withdraw into himself". That is, the functional

[1] Kraus, Fr., Allgemeine und spezielle Pathologie der Person. I. Teil: Tiefenperson. Leipzig, Thieme, 1926. Pp. 252. *Translator's note:* The findings and concepts of Kraus, at the time of their publication, were revolutionary, i.e., at variance with the usual mechanistic thinking in medicine. Consequently, they met with little understanding. G. R. Heyer, in one of his books on psychosomatic medicine, states frankly that the book was too difficult for him to understand. Most critics, however, simply declare that Kraus is "all wrong", without, however, going to the trouble of really studying his works or of proving or disproving his findings.

direction of "towards the world, out of the self", is opposed by another direction, that of "away from the world, back into the self".

This equation of something highly complicated with something simple seemed fascinating. The neurotically armored organism cannot burst like an ordinary bladder in order to get rid of its tension. It has only two ways out: either to become "masochistic", or else "healthy", that is, *able to admit the orgastic discharge of the dammed-up energy*. This orgastic discharge consists in a decrease of tension by way of a "discharge to the outside" in the form of contractions of the total body. The question still remained as to *what it was* that was discharged to the outside. I was far from the present knowledge of the functioning of biological energy. I thought of orgasm with its discharge of substances from the body also in terms of proliferations from a highly tensed bladder; after the detachment of the proliferating body, the surface tension and the internal pressure decrease. Plainly, the ejaculation of the semen alone could not account for this; for, ejaculation, if not accompanied by pleasure, does *not* reduce the tension.

I had no reason to regret this bit of speculation. It was to lead to very concrete facts. In this connection, a little occurrence at the Berlin Psychoanalytic Congress in 1922 may be worth mentioning. As a result of studying Semon and Bergson, I had engaged in a scientific phantasy. One should, I said to some of my friends, take Freud's picture of the "sending out of libido" literally and seriously. Freud had likened the sending out and retracting of psychic interest to the putting out and retracting of pseudopodia in the ameba. The putting forth of sexual energy is plainly visible in the erection of the penis. I thought that erection was functionally identical with the putting out of pseudopodia in the ameba, whereas, conversely, erective impotence, due to anxiety and accompanied by shrinking of the penis, was functionally identical with the retraction of the pseudopodia. My friends were horrified at such muddled thinking. They laughed at me, and I was offended. But thirteen years later, I was able to establish experimental proof for this assumption. I will have to show how the facts led to this proof.

3. THE FUNCTIONAL ANTITHESIS OF SEXUALITY AND ANXIETY

The comparison of erection with protrusion of pseudopodia on the one hand, and the shrinking of the penis with their retraction on the other, led to the assumption of a functional antithesis between sexuality and anxiety. This antithesis was expressed in the *direction* of biological functioning. I could not rid myself of that idea. Since, through my experiences, everything I had learned from Freud about the psychology of instincts had come into a state of flux, the picture just mentioned linked itself with the very important question as to the biological basis of psychic functioning. Freud had postulated a physiological foundation for psychoanalysis. His "unconscious" was deeply rooted in the biophysiological realm. In the depths of the psyche the clear-cut psychic tendencies gave way to mysterious workings which could not be fathomed by psychological thinking alone. Freud had attempted to apply to the sources of life the psychological concepts derived from psychoanalytic investigation. This led inevitably to a personification of the biological processes and to the re-instatement of such metaphysical concepts as had previously been eliminated from psychology. In studying the function of the orgasm, I had learned that, in the somatic realm, it is not admissible to think in terms derived from the psychic realm. Every psychic occurrence has, in addition to its causal determination, a *meaning* in terms of a relation to the environment. To this corresponded the psychoanalytic *interpretation.* However, in the physiological realm, there is no such "meaning", and its existence cannot be assumed without re-introducing a supernatural power. *The living simply functions,* it has no "meaning".

Natural science attempts to exclude metaphysical assumptions. Yet, if unable to explain the why and how of biological functioning, one is apt to look for a "purpose" or a "meaning" to put into the function. I found myself right back in the problems of the early period of my work, in the problems of mechanism and vitalism. I avoided a speculative answer, but I had as yet no method for the correct solution of the problem. I was acquainted with dialectic materialism, but did not know how to apply it to investigation in the natural sciences. True, I had given Freud's discoveries a functional interpretation, but the inclusion of the physiological foundation of psychic life raised the new question as to the *correct method.* To say that the soma influences the psyche, is correct, but one-sided. That, conversely, the psyche influences the soma, is an everyday observation. But it is inadmissible to enlarge the concept of the psyche to the extent of applying its laws to the soma. The concept that psychic and somatic processes are mutually independent, and only in "interaction", is contradicted by daily experience. I had no solution to the problem. Only one thing was clear: *the experience of pleasure, that is of expansion, is inseparably linked up with living functioning.*

It was at this point that my recently developed concept of the masochistic function came to the rescue. I reasoned: The psyche is determined by *quality,* the soma by *quantity.* In the psyche, the determining factor is the *kind* of an idea or wish; in the soma, however, it is the *amount* of energy at work. Insofar, psyche and soma were different. But the study of the orgasm showed that the *quality of a psychic attitude depended on the amount of the underlying somatic excitation.* The idea of sexual intercourse and its pleasure is intense, colorful and vivid in a state of intense somatic excitation. After gratification, however, the idea can be reproduced only with difficulty. I had in mind the picture of an ocean wave which, rising and falling, influences the movements of a piece of wood floating on its surface. It was no more than a vague idea that psychic life emerges and submerges from the underlying biophysiological process, depending on what stage of this process happens to be current. This wave-like process seemed to be represented in the appearance and disappearance of consciousness at the time of waking up or falling asleep. It was all rather obscure and intangible. What was clear was only that the biological energy dominates the psychic as well as the somatic. *There is functional unity.* True, biological laws can apply in the psychic realm, but the converse is not true. This necessitated a critical evaluation of Freud's concepts of the instincts.

Visual imagination is doubtless a psychic process. There are unconscious ideas which can be deduced from their outward manifestations. The unconscious itself, according to Freud, cannot be grasped. But if it "dips into" the biophysiological realm, it must be possible to grasp it by way of a method which grasps the *common factor* which dominates the *whole* biopsychic apparatus. This common factor cannot be the "meaning"; nor can it be the "purpose"; these are *secondary* functions. From a consistent functional point of view, there is, in the biological realm, no purpose, no aim; only *function* and *development,* following certain laws. There remained the *dynamic structure,* the *balance of forces.* This is valid in all realms; this was something one could hold on to. What psychology calls "tension" and "relaxation" is an antithesis of forces. My idea of the bladder, as simple as it was, was entirely in accord with the concept of *unity of the psychic and the somatic.* Along with unity, there is, at the same time, antithesis. This concept was the germ of my theory of sex.

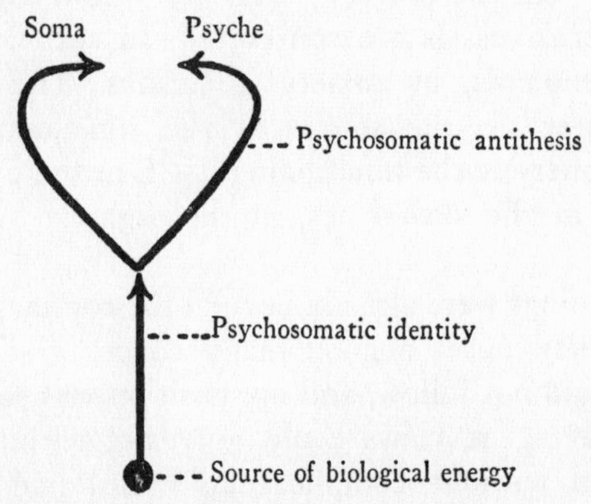

Diagram: Psychosomatic identity and antithesis.

Back in 1924, I had assumed that in the orgasm an excitation concentrates at the *periphery* of the organism, especially at the genital organs, and then flows back to the *vegetative center* where it ebbs away. Unexpectedly, a cycle of ideas was completed. What formerly had appeared as psychic excitation, could now be described as biophysiological current. After all, internal pressure and surface tension of a bladder are nothing but the functions of the *center* and the *periphery* of an organism. They are functionally opposed to each other. Their reciprocal strength determines the "fate" of the bladder, just as balance of sexual energy determines psychic health. "*Sexuality*" could be nothing else than *the biological function of expansion* ("out of the self") *from center to periphery*. Conversely, *anxiety* could be nothing but the reverse direction *from periphery to center* ("back into the self"). Sexuality and anxiety are one and the same process of excitation, only in opposite directions.

Soon, the connection of this theory with a multitude of clinical facts became clear. In sexual excitation, the peripheral vessels are dilated; in anxiety, one feels a tension within one—(in the center)—as if one were going to burst; the peripheral vessels are contracted. In sexual excitation, the penis expands, in anxiety it shrinks. The "biological energy center" is the source of the functioning energy; at the periphery is the functioning itself, in the contact with the world, in the sexual act, in the orgastic discharge, in work, etc.

These findings were already beyond the confines of psychoanalysis. They upset a good many concepts. The psychoanalysts could not follow, and my position was so prominent that my divergent views could not exist within the same organization without complication. Freud had refused to accept my attempt to view the processes of libido as part of the autonomic system. Being in the front line of psychoanalysis, I was not on the best terms with the official psychiatrists and other clinicians. Due to their mechanistic and unanalytic thinking, they would have understood little of what I said. Thus, the new-born theory of sex found itself alone, in a wide and empty space. I was encouraged by the multitude of confirmatory findings which experimental physiology provided for my theory. It seemed to reduce to a common denominator the unrelated findings amassed by generations of physiologists. A central point in these findings was the antithesis of sympathetic and parasympathetic.

4. WHAT IS "BIOPSYCHIC ENERGY"?

After sixty years of sexology, forty years of psychoanalysis, and almost twenty years of my own work against the background of the orgasm theory, this unanswered question still confronted the clinician who was called upon to treat human sexual disturbances. Let us recall the starting point of the orgasm theory. Neuroses and functional psychoses are maintained by excessive, not properly discharged sexual energy. "Psychic energy", it used to be called. What it really was, nobody knew. Doubtless, psychic disturbances had their root in the "somatic realm". What nourished the pathological psychic growths could only be the damming-up of energy. Only the elimination of *this energy source of the neurosis* by way of establishing full orgastic potency seemed to protect the patient against future relapse. Prevention of psychic disturbances on a mass basis without a knowledge of their somatic basis was inconceivable. The correctness of the statement, "with a satisfactory sex life, there are no neurotic disturbances", could not be doubted. This contention, naturally, has individual as well as social consequences; the significance of its implications is obvious. But, in spite of Freud, official science refused to concern itself with sexuality. Psychoanalysis itself eschewed the question more and more. Preoccupation with this question also bordered too much upon all the ordinary effusions of a pathological, distorted kind of sexuality, with that somewhat pornographic coloring which is typical of today. Only the sharp distinction between natural and pathological sexual manifestations, between "primary" and "secondary" drives, made it possible to persevere and to stick to the problem. Cogitation alone would not have led to a solution, nor the integration of all the excellent and pertinent data which appeared in increasing numbers in the modern physiological literature after about 1925 and were collected in Müller's *"Die Lebensnerven"*.

As always, clinical observation led on in the right direction. In Copenhagen, 1933, I treated a man who put up especially strong resistances against the uncovering of his passive-homosexual phantasies. This resistance was manifested in an extreme attitude of stiffness of the neck ("stiffnecked"). After an energetic attack upon his resistance he suddenly gave in, but in a rather alarming manner. For three days, he presented severe manifestations of vegetative shock. The color of his face kept changing rapidly from white to yellow or blue; the skin was mottled and of various tints; he had severe pains in the neck and the occiput; the heart-beat was rapid; he had diarrhea, felt worn out, and seemed to have lost hold. I was disturbed. True, I had often seen similar symptoms, but never that violent. Something had happened here that was somehow inherent in the therapeutic process but was at first unintelligible. *Affects had broken through somatically after the patient had yielded in a psychic defense attitude.* The stiff neck, expressing an attitude of tense masculinity, apparently had bound vegetative energies which now broke loose in an uncontrolled and disordered fashion. A person with a balanced sex-economy would be incapable of producing such a reaction. Such a reaction presupposes a continuous inhibition and damming-up of biological energy. It was the musculature that served this inhibitory function. When the muscles of the neck relaxed, powerful impulses broke through, as if propelled by a spring. The alternating pallor and redness of the face could be nothing but a movement to and fro of the body fluids, an alternating contraction and relaxation of the blood vessels. That fitted in very well with my concept of the functioning of the biological energy. The direction of "out of the self—toward the world" kept alternating rapidly with the opposite direction of "away from the world—back into the self". The musculature can, by contracting, inhibit the blood flow; it can, in other words, reduce the movement of the body fluids to a minimum.

This finding checked with earlier observations and those in recent cases. Soon, I had a multitude of facts which could be summed up in the formulation: *Sexual energy can be bound by chronic muscular tensions. The same is true of anger and anxiety.* I found that, whenever I dissolved a muscular inhibition or tension, one of the three basic biological excitations made its appearance: *anxiety, anger or sexual excitation.* True, I had been able to bring this about before, by way of dissolving purely characterological inhibitions and attitudes. The difference lay in the fact that now the break-through of biological energy was more complete, more forceful, more thoroughly experienced, and it occurred more *rapidly.* Also, it was accompanied in many patients by a spontaneous dissolution of the characterological inhibitions. These findings, though first made in 1933, were not published until 1935 in a preliminary form, and in 1937 in a more definite form.[1] Soon, some decisive questions of the mind-body problem clarified themselves:

The character armor now showed itself to be *functionally identical* with muscular hypertension, the muscular armor. The concept of "functional identity" which I had to introduce, means nothing but the fact that muscular and character attitudes serve the same function in the psychic apparatus; they can influence and replace each other. Basically, they cannot be separated; in their function they are identical.

Concepts which are arrived at by the unification of facts immediately lead on to other things. If the character armor expressed itself through the muscular armor and vice versa, then the unity of psychic and somatic functions was comprehended and became capable of being *influenced* in a practical way. From now on, I was able to make *practical use* of this unity. When a character inhibition would fail to respond to psychic influencing, I would work at the corresponding somatic attitude. Conversely, when a disturbing muscular attitude proved difficult of access, I would work on

---

[1]Wilhelm Reich, Psychischer Kontakt und Vegetative Strömung. Beitrag zur Affektlehre und charakteranalytischen Technik. Sex-Pol-Verlag, 1935.

Wilhelm Reich, Orgasmusreflex, Muskelhaltung und Körperausdruck. Zur Technik der charakteranalytischen Vegetotherapie. Sex-Pol-Verlag, 1937.

its characterological expression and thus loosen it up. A typical friendly smile, e.g., which impeded the work, could be eliminated by describing the expression as well as by disturbing the muscular attitude. That was an enormous step forward. The further development of this technique into the vegetotherapy of today took another six years.

The loosening of the rigid muscular attitudes resulted in peculiar somatic sensations: involuntary trembling, jerking of muscles, sensations of hot and cold, itching, crawling, prickling sensations, goose flesh, and the somatic perception of anxiety, anger and pleasure. To comprehend these manifestations, I had to break with all the old concepts of psychosomatic interrelationship. These manifestations were not the "result", the "causes", or the "accompaniment" of "psychic" processes; they were simply *these processes themselves in the somatic sphere.*

I brought together into one concept as *"vegetative currents"* all those somatic manifestations which—in contrast to the rigid muscular armor—are characterized by movement. Immediately the question arose: *Are these vegetative currents only movements of body fluids, or more than that?* Purely mechanical movements of fluids, it is true, could account for the sensations of hot and cold, for pallor and blushing, but they could not account for such manifestations as formication, prickling sensations, shuddering, or the "sweet", "melting" quality of preorgastic sensations of pleasure, etc. The problem of orgastic impotence was still unanswered: *the genital may be filled with blood, and yet, any trace of pleasurable excitation may be absent.* That means, sexual excitation is by no means identical with, or produced by, blood flow. Furthermore, there are anxiety states without any special pallor of the face or the rest of the body. The feeling of constriction in the chest (anxiety, *angustiae*), the feeling of "oppression", could not be ascribed solely to congestion in the central organs. Otherwise, one would experience anxiety after a good meal, when the blood is concentrated in the abdomen. *There must be something in addition to the blood flow, something that, according to its biological function, produces anxiety, anger or pleasure.* The blood flow can only play the role of an essential means. Perhaps this unknown "something" does not occur when the flow of the body fluids is somehow impeded. This marks an unformed stage in my thinking on the problem.

5. THE ORGASM FORMULA: TENSION → CHARGE → DISCHARGE → RELAXATION

The unknown "something" I was looking for could be nothing but *bio-electricity.* This occurred to me one day when I tried to understand the physiology of the sexual friction between penis and vaginal mucous membrane. Sexual friction is a fundamental biological process; it occurs whereever in the animal kingdom procreation takes place by means of two separate sexes. In this process, two body surfaces are in mutual friction; this results in biological excitation as well as in congestion, expansion, "erection". The Berlin internist Kraus, on the basis of pioneering experiments, found the body to be governed by electrical processes. The body consists of innumerable "border surfaces" between membranes and electrolytic fluids of various densities and compositions. According to a well-known law of physics, electrical tensions develop at the border between conducting fluids and membranes. As there are differences in density and in the structure of the membranes, there are differences in the tensions at the border surfaces and, consequently, differences of potentials of various intensity. Potential differences may be likened to the difference in energy of two bodies at different heights. In falling, the higher one can perform more work than the lower one. The same weight, say, of 1 kilogram, will drive a pile deeper into the ground when falling from a height of 3 meters than when falling from a height of 1 meter. The "potential energy of position" is greater, and consequently the "kinetic energy" is greater when this potential energy is released. The principle of difference of potential can be applied without difficulty to the differences in electrical tensions. When a highly charged body is connected by a wire with a less highly charged one, a current will flow from the former to the latter; static electrical energy changes into current (i.e., moving) energy. There occurs an equalization between the two charges, just as the level of water in two containers becomes the same when they are connected by a pipe. This equalization of energy always presupposes a *difference* in potential energy. Now, our body consists of innumerable inner surfaces with different potential energies. Consequently, the electrical energy in the body is in constant motion from places of higher potential to places of lower potential. The carriers of the electrical charges in this continuous process of equalization are the particles of the body fluids, the ions. They are atoms carrying a certain amount of electrical charge; according to whether they move towards the negative or positive pole, they are called kations or anions. What has all this to do with the problem of sexuality? A great deal!

Sexual tension is felt in the whole body, but particularly strongly at the heart and in the abdomen. Gradually, the excitation concentrates at the genitals. They fill with blood, and electrical charges occur at the surface of the genitals. We know that a delicate touch of one sexually excited part of the body produces excitation in other parts. Tension or excitation increases with friction. It reaches its peak in the *orgasm*, a state in which *involuntary contractions of the musculature of the genitals and the body as a whole* take place. It is a well-known fact that muscular contraction is accompanied by the discharge of electrical energy. This discharge can be measured and represented in the form of a graphic curve. Some physiologists think that the nerves store up energy which is discharged in the muscular contraction; not the nerve, but only the muscle, which is capable of contraction, can discharge energy. With sexual friction, energy is first stored up in both bodies, and then discharged in the orgasm. *Orgasm must then be a phenomenon of electrical discharge.* The structure of the genitals is peculiarly adapted for this; great vascularity, dense nerve ganglia, erectibility, and a musculature particularly capable of spontaneous contractions.

On closer investigation of the process, one discovers a peculiar four-beat:

1. The organs fill with fluid: erection with *mechanical tension.*
2. This leads to an intense excitation, which I assumed to be of an electrical nature: *electrical charge.*
3. In the orgasm, the electrical charge or sexual excitation is discharged in muscular contractions: *electrical discharge.*
4. This is followed by a relaxation of the genitals through a flowing back of the body fluids: *mechanical relaxation.*

This four-beat: MECHANICAL TENSION → ELECTRICAL CHARGE → ELECTRICAL DISCHARGE → MECHANICAL RELAXATION I termed the *orgasm formula.*

The process described by it we can picture to ourselves in a simple way. I come back here to the functioning of a filled elastic bladder about which I had been thinking some six years previous to the discovery of the orgasm formula. Let us compare two spheres, a rigid one of metal, and an elastic one, say, a pig's bladder, or an ameba.

The metal sphere would be hollow, the pig's bladder, however, would contain a complex system of fluids and membranes of different densities and conductivity. Furthermore, the metal sphere would receive its electrical charge *from without,* say, from a static machine; the pig's bladder, on the other hand, would contain an automatically working charging apparatus in the center, that is, it would spontaneously be charged *from within.* According to fundamental laws of physics, the charge of the metal sphere would be equally distributed over the surface, and only the surface. The pig's bladder, however, would be charged through and through; due to the differences in density and the variety of fluids and

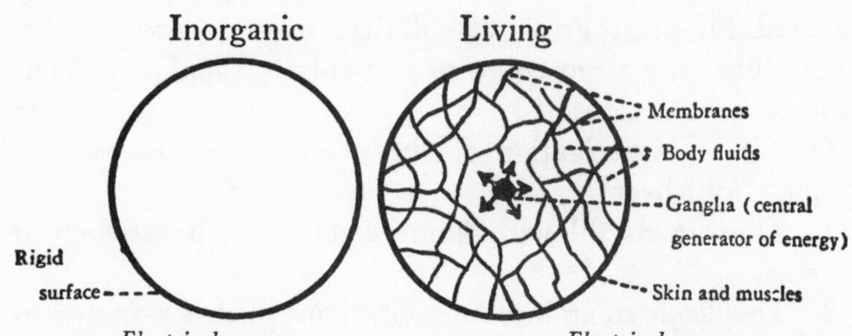

Electrical energy on surface only, evenly distributed, supplied from outside; whole system rigid.	*Electrical energy* in the whole body, unevenly distributed, supplied from inside source; whole system capable of expanding and contracting.

Diagram of inorganic and organic, living, sphere.

membranes, the charge would vary from one place to another; furthermore, the charges would be in continuous motion from places of higher potential to places of lower potential. But, generally speaking, one direction would predominate: that *from the center,* the source of the electrical energy, *to the periphery.* For this reason, the bladder would more or less continually expand and contract. From time to time it would—like the vorticella—return to the spherical shape in which—the content remaining the same—the surface tension is lowest. In case of too great an inner energy production, the bladder would discharge the energy by way of a few contractions, that is, it would be able to *regulate* the energy. This discharge of energy would be extremely pleasurable, because it eliminates dammed-up tension. In the state of longitudinal expansion, the bladder could execute various rhythmical movements, such as an alternating expansion and contraction, the motion of a *worm* or of intestinal peristalsis:

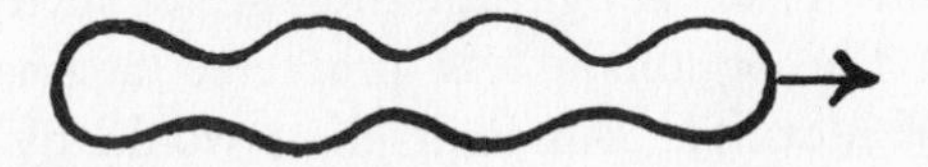

Or the whole body might make a *serpentine* motion:

In these motions, the organism of the electrical bladder would form a *unity*. If it could feel, it would experience this *rhythmic alternation* of expansion and contraction as pleasurable; it would feel like an infant that hops up and down rhythmically with joy. In the course of these movements, the bio-electrical energy would constantly be in a state of tension—charge and discharge—relaxation. It could be converted into heat, mechanical, kinetic energy, or into work. Such a bladder, like the infant, would feel one with the environment, the world, objects. Various bladders, if there were such, would have immediate contact with each other, as each would identify the experience of its own rhythm and motion with that of the others. They would not be able to understand the contempt for natural movements, nor would they understand unnatural behavior. The continuous inner energy production would *guarantee development,* as is the case with the budding of plants or with progressive cell division after the addition of energy by fertilization. More than that, there would be no end to development. Work would take place within the framework of general biological activity, *and not against it.*

Longitudinal expansion over long periods of time would tend to make the bladder maintain this shape and might lead to the development of a supportive apparatus (skeleton) in the organism. This would make impossible a return to the spherical shape, but *flexion and extension* would still be entirely feasible; that is, the energy metabolism would still be present. True enough, the presence of such a skeleton would make the organism less protected against harmful inhibitions of motility. But in itself it would by no means constitute an inhibition. Such an inhibition could be compared only with the tying down of a snake at *one* point of its body. A snake, if tied down at any point of its body, would lose the rhythm and the unity of the organic wave-like motion even in those parts of the body that are still free:

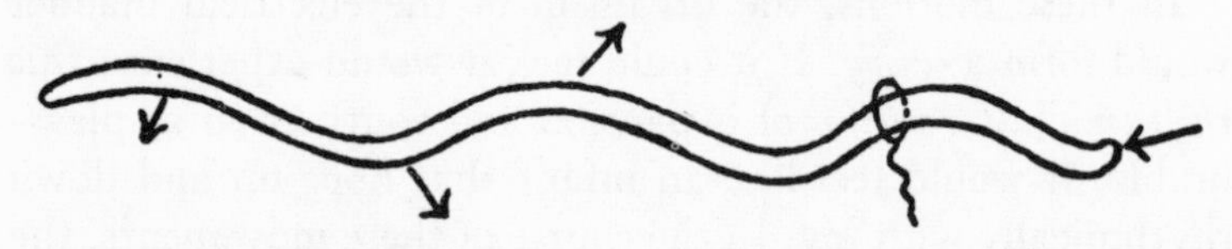

The animal and human body in fact resembles this bladder we just described. To complete the picture, we have to introduce an automatically working pump mechanism which makes the fluid circulate in a steady rhythm *from center to periphery and back:* the cardiovascular system. Even in the lowest developmental stages, the animal body possesses a central apparatus for the production of bio-electricity. In the metazoa, this apparatus consists of the so-called *vegetative ganglia,* conglomerations of nerve cells which are placed at regular intervals and are connected by fine strands with all organs and their parts. They regulate the involuntary life functions and are the organs of *vegetative feelings and sensations.* They form a connected unit, a so-called "syncytium", and are at the same time divided into two groups with an opposite function: *sympathetic and parasympathetic.*

Our imaginary bladder can expand and contract. It could expand to an extreme degree and then relax by way of a few contractions. It could be limp or tense, relaxed or excited.

It could concentrate the electric charges together with the fluids carrying them at one time more in one place, at another time in another. It could keep certain parts constantly tense, and others in constant motion. If one were to compress it in one place, it would immediately show increased tension and charge in another place.

If one were to compress it over its entire surface, i.e., to make expansion impossible while at the same time its inner production of energy would continue, it would experience constant *anxiety,* i.e., a feeling of oppression and constriction. If it could talk, it would implore us to "deliver" it from this painful state. It would not care what would happen to it, provided *one* thing; that *motion* and *change* would replace its rigid, compressed state. As it could not bring this about itself, somebody else would have to do this *for it.* This might be done by being thrown around in space (gymnastics), by being kneaded (massage), if need be by being pricked open (phantasy of being made to burst), by being injured (masochistic beating phantasy, harakiri), and, if everything else fails, by melting, dissolution (nirvana, sacrificial death).

A society consisting of such bladders would create the most perfect philosophies about the ideals of the "state of painlessness". As every expansion caused by pleasure or tending towards pleasure could be experienced only as painful, the bladder would develop fear of pleasurable excitation (*pleasure anxiety*) and, in addition, evolve theories about the "evil", "sinful", "destructive" quality of pleasure. In short, it would be the image of the ascetic of the twentieth century. As time went on, it would come to dread any thought of the possibility of the relaxation so much longed for; then it would hate it, and finally punish it with death. It would band together with others of its kind into a society of peculiarly stiff creatures and think up rigid rules of life. The only function of these rules would be to keep the inner production of energy at a minimum; in other words, to maintain the adherence to a quiet, well-trodden path and to accustomed reactions. Any surplus of inner energy which could not find its natural outlet in pleasure or motion, they would try to master in some inadequate way. They would, for example, introduce sadistic behavior and ceremonials with much conventionality and little sense to them (e.g., religious compulsive behavior). *Realistic* goals are reached by their own appropriate pathways and for this reason compel motion and unrest in those who seek them.

The bladder might be overtaken by sudden convulsions in which the dammed-up energy is discharged; i.e., it might develop *hysterical* or *epileptic* seizures. It also might become completely rigid and dried up like a catatonic *schizophrenic*. Whatever else it might show, this bladder would always be suffering from *anxiety*. Everything else is the inevitable result of this anxiety, be it religious mysticism, belief in a Führer or senseless readiness to die. Since everything in nature moves, changes, develops, expands and contracts, this *armored* bladder would behave towards nature in a strange and antagonistic way. It would think of itself as "something very special", as belonging to a "better race", e.g., because of wearing a stiff collar or a uniform. It would represent "a culture" or "a race" which are incompatible with "nature". It would consider nature as "low", "demoniacal", "animal", "unrestrained" or "undignified". But since it could not help feeling some last traces of this nature in itself, it would also gush over it, sentimentalize it, e.g. as "sublime love". To think of nature in terms of bodily contractions would mean blasphemy. At the same time this bladder would create pornography without a sense of contradiction.

The formula of tension and charge gathered together thoughts that had cropped up earlier during the study of classical biology. Its theoretical soundness had to be checked. On the part of physiology, my theory was substantiated by the well-known fact of *spontaneous contractions* occurring in muscles. The muscle contraction can be produced by electrical stimuli. But it occurs also when one—as did Galvani—injures the muscle and connects the severed end of the nerve with the muscle at the point of injury. The contraction is accompanied by a measurable *action current.* There is also a normal current in an injured muscle. It shows itself when the middle of the muscle surface is connected with the injured end by way of a conductor, say, a copper wire.

The study of muscle contractions has been an important field of physiological investigation for decades. I could not understand why muscle physiology failed to make the connection with the facts of *general* animal electricity. If one puts two nerve-muscle preparations together in such a way that the muscle of one touches the nerve of the other, and if one then makes the first muscle contract by applying an electric current, the second muscle also contracts. This first muscle contracts in response to the electrical stimulus and develops itself a biological action current. This in turn acts as an electrical stimulus for the second muscle, which responds with a contraction, thereby developing another biological action current. Since the muscles in the animal body are in contact with each other and are connected through the body fluids with the *total organism,* every muscle action is bound to have a stimulating influence upon the total organism. This influence, of course, will vary according to the site of the muscle, the initial stimulus and its strength; but there is always an influence upon the total organism. A prototype of this influence is the orgastic contraction of the genital musculature; a contraction which is so powerful that it transmits itself to the whole organism. Nothing about this was to be found in the literature; yet, it seemed to be of decisive significance.

Detailed examination of the cardiac action curve confirmed my assumption that the tension-charge process governs the cardiac function also, in the form of an electric wave which runs from the auricle to the apex. Prerequisite for the beginning of the contraction is the *filling* of the auricle with blood. The result of the charge and discharge is the propulsion of the blood through the aorta due to the contraction of the heart.

Drugs that gain bulk in the intestine have a cathartic effect. This gaining in bulk acts upon the muscles like an electrical stimulus. They contract and relax in a rhythmical wave, thus emptying the intestines. The same is true of the urinary bladder; it fills up with fluid; this leads to contraction and emptying of the content.

This description contains an extremely important fundamental fact which may serve as a paradigm for the refutation of teleological thinking in biology. The urinary bladder does not contract "in order to fulfill the function of micturition" due to some divine will or supernatural biological power; it contracts by reason of a very simple *causal principle: because its mechanical filling produces contraction.* This principle holds for any other function. One does not have sexual intercourse "in order to produce children", but because fluid congestion produces a bio-electric charge in the genital organs and presses for discharge. This is accompanied by the expulsion of the sexual substances. In other words, not "sexuality is in the service of procreation", but procreation itself is an incidental result of the tension-charge process in the genitals. This fact is disappointing to the adherents of an eugenic moral philosophy, but it is, nevertheless, a fact.

In 1933, I happened upon an experimental paper by the Berlin biologist Hartmann. In special experiments concerning the sexuality of gametes, he showed that the male and the female function in copulation is not fixed. That is, a week male gamete may act like a female towards a male stronger than itself. Hartmann did not answer the question as to what determines the grouping of gametes of the same sex, their "copulation", if you will. He assumed "certain, as yet unknown, substances". I realized that it was a matter of electrical processes. A few years later, I was able to demonstrate the mechanism of the grouping by way of an electrical experiment with the bions. It is *bio-electrical* forces that are responsible for the fact that the grouping in the copulation of the gametes takes place in a certain way and not otherwise. At the same time somebody sent me a newspaper clipping about experiments done in Moscow. Some scientist (I am unable to locate his name) had succeeded in demonstrating that egg- and sperm cells result in male and female individuals, respectively, depending on their electrical charge.

Procreation, then, is a function of sexuality, and not vice versa, as heretofore assumed. Freud had postulated this with regard to psychosexuality, when he separated the concepts of "sexual" and "genital". But for reasons which I never understood, he again placed "genitality in puberty" in the "service of procreation". Hartmann provided the proof for the fact that procreation is a function of sexuality and not vice versa, in the field of biology. The consequence of these findings for a moralistic evaluation of sexuality is evident. It is no longer possible to consider sexuality an unwelcome by-product of the preservation of the race. I was able to add a third argument, based on experimental studies by various biologists: the division of the egg, too, like cell division in general, is an orgastic process; it follows the law of tension and charge.

When the egg is fertilized and has taken up the *energy* of the sperm, it at first becomes *tensed.* It takes up fluid, its membrane becomes taut. That means, internal pressure and surface tension increase simultaneously. The greater the pressure within this bladder represented by the egg, the more difficult it becomes for the surface to "keep it together". These are still entirely processes originating from the antithesis between internal pressure and surface tension. A purely physical bladder, if further expanded, would *burst*. In the egg cell, on the other hand, a process begins to take place which is characteristic of the functioning of the living substance: *the stretching results in contraction*. The growth of the egg cell is due to the taking up of fluid and can proceed only up to a certain point. The nucleus begins to "radiate", i.e. to produce energy. Gurwitsch termed this phenomenon "*mitogenetic radiation*" (mitosis means division of the nucleus). Later on, I learned to judge the vitality of bion cultures by observing the degree of certain kinds of radiation in their center. In the cell, extreme filling, that is, mechanical tension, is accompanied by an *electrical charge*. At a certain point, the membrane begins to contract; this takes place at the greatest circumference of the sphere, and at the point of maximal tension; this is the equator, or any meridian, of the sphere. As can easily be observed, the contraction is not a gradual and steady, but a struggling, conflictful process. The tension in the membrane opposes the pressure from within which thus becomes increasingly intense. It can easily be seen how internal pressure and surface tension mutually increase each other. This results in a visible vibrating, undulation and contracting:

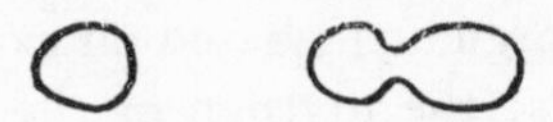

The indentation goes farther and farther, the inner tension continues to increase. If the cell could talk, it would express *anxiety*. There is only one way of relieving this inner pressure (aside from bursting): the *division* of the *one big bladder* with its taut surface *into two smaller bladders in which the same volume content is surrounded by a much larger and consequently less taut membrane*. Egg division, thus, *corresponds to a process of relaxation*. The nucleus, in its spindle formation, has previously gone through the same process. Spindle formation is regarded by many biologists as an electrical phenomenon. If we were able to measure the electric condition of the nucleus after cell-division, we would most likely find a discharge. The "reduction division" in which half the chromosomes (which had been doubled in the process of spindle formation) are extruded, would point in that direction. Each of the daughter cells now contains the same number of chromosomes. Reproduction is complete.

Cell division, thus, also follows the four-beat of the orgasm formula: tension → charge → discharge → relaxation. It is the most significant biological process. The orgasm formula, then, can be called the *"life formula"*.

In those years, I did not want to publish anything about this. I limited myself to hints in clinical presentations and only published a little paper, *"Die Fortpflanzung als Funktion der Sexualität"* (1935), based on the experiments of Hartmann. The subject seemed of such decisive importance that I did not want to publish it without special experiments which would either confirm or disprove my hypothesis.

6. PLEASURE (EXPANSION) AND ANXIETY (CONTRACTION): BASIC ANTITHESIS OF VEGETATIVE LIFE

By 1933, my concepts of the unity of psychic and somatic functioning had clarified themselves in the following direction: The fundamental biological function of *pulsation,* i.e., of expansion and contraction can be demonstrated in the psychic as well as the somatic sphere. There were two series of antithetical phenomena, the elements of which corresponded to different depths of biological functioning.

Impulses and sensations are not created by the nerves, but only transmitted by them. They are biological manifestations of the organism as a whole. They are present in the organism long before the development of an organized nervous tissue. Protozoa show the same fundamental actions and impulses as metazoa, though they possess as yet no organized nervous system.[1] Kraus and Zondek succeeded in demonstrating the important fact that chemical substances can not only stimulate or depress the functions of the autonomic nervous system, but also *can take their place.* Kraus, on the basis of his experiments, arrives at the conclusion that the action of the nerves, of drugs and of the electrolytes can replace each other in the biological system with regard to hydration and dehydration of the tissues (as we have seen, the basic functions of living substance).

The following table shows the action of the sympathetic and parasympathetic from the point of view of the total function:

VEGETATIVE GROUP	GENERAL EFFECT ON TISSUES	CENTRAL EFFECT	PERIPHERAL EFFECT
Sympathetic Calcium (group) Adrenalin Cholesterin H-ions	Decreased surface tension Dehydration *Striated muscle: paralyzed or spastic* Decreased electrical irritability Increased O_2-consumption Increased blood pressure	Systolic Heart muscle stimulated	Vasoconstriction
Parasympathetic Potassium (group) Cholin Lecithin OH-ions	Increased surface tension Hydration (tumescence of tissues) *Muscle: increased tonicity* Increased electrical irritability Decreased O_2-consumption Decreased blood pressure	Diastolic Heart muscle relaxed	Vasodilatation

The findings tabulated here show the following facts:

1. The antithesis between the potassium (*parasympa-*

[1] *Translator's note:* It may be argued here that the finding of a "silver line system" in ciliates is at variance with this statement. Though the silver line system "may well be a mechanism whereby coordination is effected throughout the organism (Calkins)", and while a unitary functioning of the organism is hardly conceivable without some kind of coordinating mechanism, the silver line system, nevertheless, is not a nervous system.

thetic) group and the calcium (*sympathetic*) group: expansion and contraction;

2. The antithesis of *center* and *periphery* with regard to excitation;

3. The functional identity of sympathetic and parasympathetic functions with those of chemical stimuli;

4. The dependency of the innervation of the individual organs on the functional unity and antithesis of the total organism.

As has been stated, all biological impulses and sensations can be reduced to the fundamental functions of *expansion* (elongation, dilatation) and *contraction* (constriction). *What is the relationship between these two fundamental functions and the autonomic nervous system?* Upon detailed examination of the highly complicated vegetative innervation of the organs, one finds the *parasympathetic* operative wherever there is *expansion, elongation, hyperemia, turgor and pleasure.* Conversely, the *sympathetic* is found functioning wherever the organism *contracts,* withdraws blood from the periphery, where it shows pallor, *anxiety or pain.* If we go one step further, we see that the parasympathetic represents the direction of expansion, "out of the self—toward the world", pleasure and joy; the sympathetic, on the other hand, represents the direction of contraction, "away from the world—back into the self", sorrow and pain. The life process takes place in a constant alternation of expansion and contraction.

Further consideration shows the *identity* on the one hand of parasympathetic function and *sexual* function; on the other hand of sympathetic function and the function of *unpleasure* or anxiety. We may see that the blood vessels during pleasure dilate at the periphery, the skin reddens, pleasure is felt from mild pleasurable sensations to sexual ecstasy; while in a state of anxiety, pallor, contraction of the blood vessels and unpleasure go hand in hand. In pleasure, "the heart expands" (parasympathetic dilatation), the pulse is full and quiet. In anxiety, the heart contracts and beats rapidly and forcibly. In the first case, it drives the blood through wide blood vessels, its work is easy; in the second case, it has to drive the blood through constricted blood vessels, and its work is hard. In the first case, the blood is predominantly distributed in the peripheral vessels; in the second case, the constricted blood vessels dam it up in the direction of the heart. This makes it immediately evident why anxiety is accompanied by the sensation of oppression, and why cardiac oppression leads to anxiety. It is the picture of cardiovascular hypertension, which plays such an important role in organic medicine. This hypertension *corresponds to a general condition of sympatheticotonic contraction in the organism.*

	Anxiety syndrome	*Pleasure syndrome*
Peripheral vessels	Constricted	Dilated
Heart action	Accelerated	Retarded
Blood pressure	Increased	Decreased
Pupil	Dilated	Constricted
Secretion of saliva	Decreased	Increased
Musculature	Paralyzed or spastic	In a state of tonus, relaxed

On the highest, i.e, psychic level, biological expansion is experienced as pleasure, contraction as unpleasure. On the instinctual level, expansion and contraction function as sexual excitation and anxiety, respectively. On a deeper physiological level, expansion and contraction correspond to the function of the parasympathetic and sympathetic, respectively. According to the discoveries of Kraus and Zondek, the parasympathetic function can be replaced by the potassium ion group, the sympathetic function by the calcium ion group. We thus get a convincing picture of a *unitary functioning in the organism, from the highest psychic sensations down to the deepest biological reactions.*

The following table presents the two series of functions according to their depth:

Pleasure	*Unpleasure and anxiety*
Sexuality	Anxiety
Parasympathetic	Sympathetic
Potassium	Calcium
Lecithin	Cholesterin
OH-ions, cholin (hydrating bases)	H-ions, adrenalin (dehydrating acids)
Function of expansion	*Function of contraction.*

On the basis of this formula of unitary-antithetical psychosomatic functioning, some seeming contradictions of automatic innervation became clear. Previously, the autonomic innervation of the organism had seemed to lack order. Muscles are made to contract one time by the parasympathetic, the other time by the sympathetic. Glandular function is one time stimulated by the parasympathetic (genital glands), another time by the sympathetic (sweat glands). A table showing the opposition of sympathetic and parasympathetic innervation of the autonomically functioning organs will make this apparent lack of order even clearer:

Functioning of the Autonomic Nervous System

Sympathetic Action	*Organ*	*Parasympathetic Action*
Inhibition of m.sphincter pupillae: *Dilatation of pupils*	Musculature of iris	Stimulation of m.sphincter pupillae: *Narrowing of pupils*
Inhibition of lachrymal glands: *"Dry eyes"*	Lachrymal glands	Stimulation of lachrymal glands: *"Bright eyes"*
Inhibition of salivary glands: *"Dry mouth"*	Salivary glands	Stimulation of salivary glands: *"Mouth waters"*
Stimulation of sweat glands: *"Cold sweat"*	Sweat glands	Inhibition of sweat glands: *Dry skin*
Contraction of arteries: *"Cold sweat"; pallor*	Arteries	Dilatation of arteries: *Redness of skin, increased turgor,* without sweating
Stimulation of arrectores pilorum: *Hair is "raised". "Gooseflesh"*	Arrectores pilorum	Inhibition of arrectores pilorum: *Skin smooth*

Sympathetic Action	*Organ*	*Parasympathetic Action*
Inhibition of contracting musculature: *Relaxation of bronchi*	Bronchial musculature	Stimulation of contracting musculature: *Bronchial spasm*
Stimulates heart action: *Palpitation, tachycardia*	Heart	Depresses heart action: *Heart quiet, pulse slow*
Inhibits peristalsis. Reduces secretion of digestive glands	Gastrointestinal tract; liver, pancreas, kidneys; all digestive glands	*Stimulates peristalsis and secretion of digestive glands*
Stimulates secretion of adrenalin	Adrenals	*Inhibits secretion of adrenalin*
Inhibits musculature which opens bladder, stimulates sphincter: *Inhibits micturition*	Urinary bladder	Stimulates musculature which opens bladder, inhibits sphincter: *Stimulates micturition*
Stimulates smooth musculature, reduces secretion of all glands, decreases blood supply: *Decreased sexual sensation*	Female sex organs	Relaxes smooth musculature, stimulates secretion of all glands, increases blood supply: *Increased sexual sensation*
Stimulates smooth musculature of the scrotum, reduces glandular secretion, decreases blood supply: *Flaccid penis. Decreased sexual sensation*	Male sex organs	Relaxes smooth musculature of the scrotum, stimulates glandular secretion, increases blood supply: *Erection. Increased sexual sensation*

In the course of the demonstration of the two directions of biological energy, a fact has become apparent to which until now we have paid little attention. Up to now, we have a clear picture of the *vegetative periphery*. However, the place is not defined where the biological energy becomes concentrated as soon as an anxiety state occurs. There must be a *vegetative center*, from which the bio-electric energy originates and to which it returns. This question brings us to certain well-known facts of physiology. The abdominal cavity, the well-known seat of the emotions, contains the generators of biological energy. They are large centers of the autonomic nervous system, particularly the solar plexus, the hypogastric plexus and the lumbosacral or pelvic plexus.

A glance at the diagram of the vegetative nervous system (p. 352) shows that the vegetative ganglia are densest in the abdominal and genital regions. The following diagrams show the functional relationships between *center* and *periphery:*

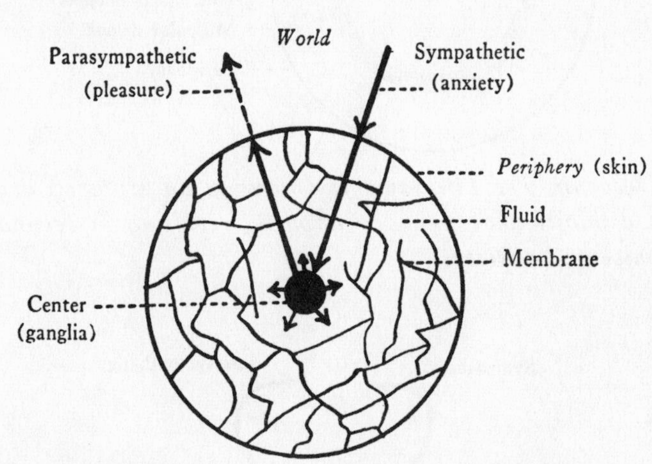

Parasympathetic	*Sympathetic*
Swelling, expansion	Shrinking
Increased turgor (surface tension)	Decreased turgor (surface tension)
Central tension low	Central tension high
Opening up	Closing up
"Toward the world, out of the self"	*"Away from the world, back into the self"*
Sexual excitation; skin warm, red	*Anxiety,* pallor, cold sweat
"Streaming" from center to periphery	"Streaming" from periphery to center

Parasympatheticotonia, relaxation ⟵ Life process oscillating between ⟶ *Sympatheticotonia, hypertension*

Diagram a): The basic functions of the vegetative nervous system.

The attempt to bring order into what seemed a chaos was successful when I began to examine the vegetative innervation of each organ in terms of the biological functions of expansion and contraction *of the total organism.* In other words, I asked myself how this or that organ would normally function in pleasure and anxiety, respectively; and what

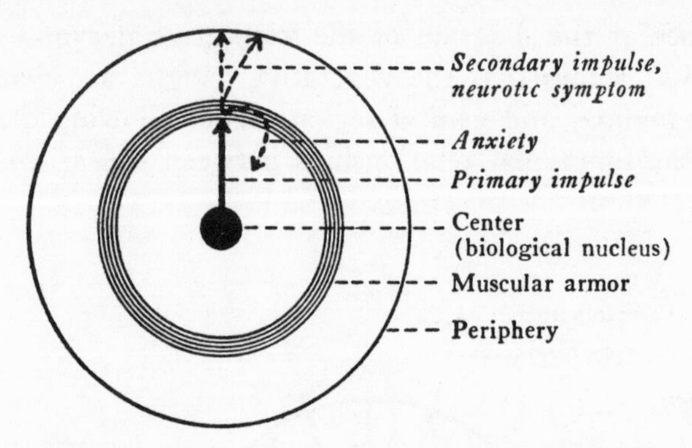

Diagram b): The same functions in an armored *organism. Inhibition of primary impulse, resulting in secondary impulse and anxiety.*

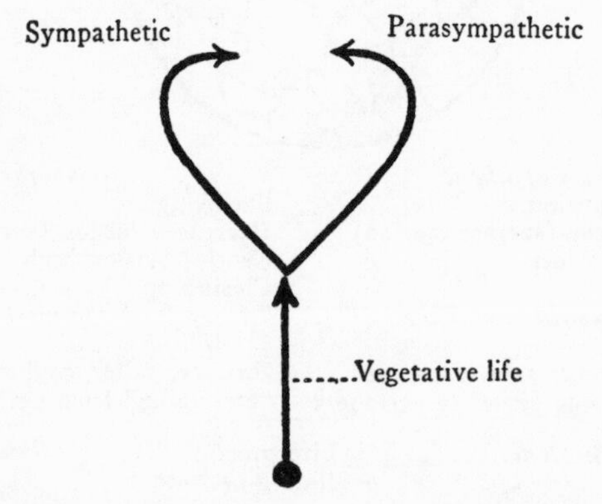

Diagram c): Unity and antithesis in the vegetative nervous system.

kind of autonomic innervation would be found in each case. Thus, the seemingly contradictory innervation, when examined *in terms of the function of the total organism,* revealed itself as entirely orderly and understandable.

This can be most convincingly demonstrated by the antagonistic innervation of the "center", the heart, and the "periphery", the blood vessels and muscles. The parasympathetic stimulates the blood flow in the periphery by dilating the blood vessels, but inhibits the heart action; conversely, the sympathetic inhibits the blood flow in the periphery by contracting the vessels, but stimulates the heart action. In terms of the total organism, this antagonistic innervation is understandable, for in anxiety the heart has to overcome the peripheral constriction, whereas in pleasure it can work peacefully and slowly. There is a *functional antithesis between center and periphery.*

The fact that the same nerve (the sympathetic) inhibits the salivary glands and simultaneously stimulates the outpouring of adrenalin, and thus produces anxiety, is meaningful in terms of the unitary sympathetic anxiety function. Similarly, we see in the case of the urinary bladder that the sympathetic stimulates the muscle that prevents micturition; the action of the parasympathetic is the reverse. Similarly, in terms of the whole, it is meaningful that, in a state of pleasure, the pupils, as a result of parasympathetic action, are contracted, acting like the diaphragm of a camera, and thus increase acuity of vision; conversely, in a state of anxious paralysis, the acuity of vision is diminished through a dilatation of the pupils.

The reduction of autonomic innervation to the basic biological functions of expansion and contraction of the total organism was, of course, an important step forward and at the same time a good test of my biological hypothesis. The parasympathetic, then, always stimulates the organs—regardless of whether it is in the sense of tension or relaxation—when the *total organism* is in a state of pleasurable expansion. Conversely, the sympathetic stimulates the organs in a biologically meaningful way when the total organism is in a state of anxious contraction. The life process, in especial respiration, can thus be understood as a constant state of pulsation in which the organism continues to alternate, pendulum-like, between parasympathetic expansion (expiration) and sympathetic contraction (inspiration). In formulating these theoretical considerations, I had in mind the rhythmic behavior of an ameba, a medusa or a heart. The function of respiration is too complicated to be briefly presented here in terms of these new insights.

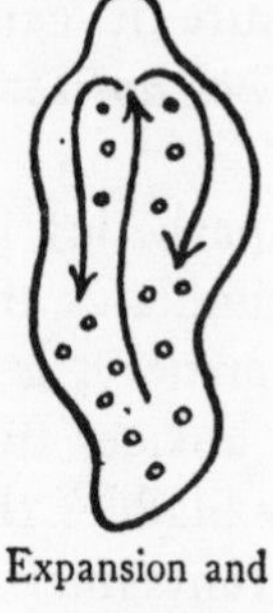

Expansion and movement

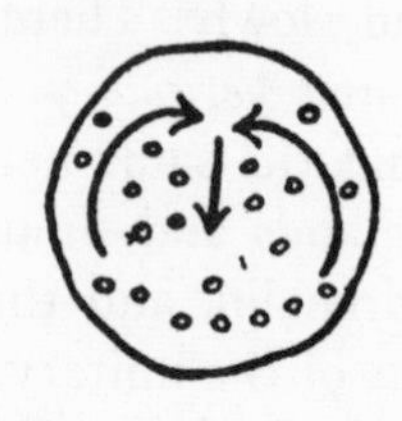

Return to spherical shape upon a strong electrical stimulus.

Plasma currents in the ameba with expansion and contraction.

If this biological state of pulsation is disturbed in one or the other direction, that is, if either the function of expansion or that of contraction predominates, then a disturbance of the biological equilibrium in general is inevitable. Long continuation in a state of expansion is synonymous with general *parasympatheticotonia;* conversely, long continuation in a state of anxious contraction is synonymous with *sympatheticotonia.* Thus, all somatic conditions which are clinically known as cardiovascular hypertension, become understandable as conditions of a chronically fixed sympatheticotonic attitude of anxiety. In the center of this general sympatheticotonia is orgasm anxiety, that is the fear of expansion and involuntary contraction.

The physiological literature contained a wealth of data regarding the complicated mechanisms of autonomic innervation. The achievement of my sex-economic theory was not that of having discovered new facts in this field, but, to begin with, only that of having reduced generally known innervations to a generally valid basic biological formula. The orgasm theory could claim to have made an essential contribution to an understanding of the physiology of the organism. This unification led to the discovery of new facts.

I published a résumé of these findings under the title *"Der Urgegensatz des vegetativen Lebens"* in the "Zeitschrift für Politische Psychologie und Sexualökonomie" which was founded in Denmark in 1934, after the break with the International Psychoanalytic Association. It was not until several years later that this article was taken cognizance of in biological and psychiatric circles.

The painful incidents at the 13th International Psychoanalytic Congress in Lucerne, 1934, were reported in some detail in the periodical just mentioned, so that I shall give here only the highlights for general orientation. When I arrived in Lucerne, I learned from the secretary of the German Psychoanalytic Society, of which I was a member, that I had already been expelled in 1933, after moving to Vienna. Nobody had found it necessary to inform me of the reasons for this expulsion; more than that, I had not even been notified of the fact. Finally, I found out that my book on Fascist irrationalism[1] had placed me in such a position, through the publicity involved, that my membership in the International Psychoanalytic Association seemed no longer desirable. Four years later, Freud had to flee from Vienna to London, and the psychoanalytic groups were smashed by the Fascists. In the interest of my independence, I later did not avail myself of the possibility of becoming again a member of the International Association by joining the Norwegian society.

---

[1]Wilhelm Reich, Massenpsychologie des Faschismus. Verlag für Sexualpolitik, 1933. Pp. 292.

Chapter VIII

THE ORGASM REFLEX AND THE TECHNIQUE OF CHARACTER-ANALYTIC VEGETOTHERAPY

1. MUSCULAR ATTITUDE AND BODILY EXPRESSION

In character-analytic work, we attempt to isolate the variously interwoven character attitudes, and to show to the patient that each of them serves a definite defensive function *in the immediate situation.* In thus loosening the character incrustations, we set free the affects which had previously undergone inhibition and fixation. Every successful dissolution of a character incrustation results first of all, in the liberation of anger or of anxiety. By treating these liberated affects also as defense mechanisms, we finally succeed in restoring to the patient his sexual motility and biological sensitivity. In other words, *by loosening up chronic character attitudes we are able to bring about reactions in the vegetative system.* The break-through into the vegetative is all the more complete and powerful the more thoroughly we treat not only the character attitudes, but—simultaneously—the muscular attitudes that correspond to them. Thus, part of the work shifts from the psychological and characterological to the immediate dissolution of the *muscular armor.* The fact that muscular rigidity is not by any means a "result", an "expression" or an "accompaniment" of the mechanism of repression had been evident for some time. I finally could not avoid the impression that the physical rigidity, actually, represents the most essential part of the process of repression. Without exception, patients relate that they went through periods in their childhood when they learned to suppress their hatred, anxiety or love by way of certain practices which influenced their vegetative functions (such as holding their breath, tensing their abdominal muscles, etc.). Analytic psychology paid attention only to *what* the children suppressed and to the reasons for the suppression. However, no attention was paid to the *manner* in which they fight against their emotions. It is, nevertheless, just this *physiological* side of the process of repression which merits our closest attention. Again and again it is striking to find how the dissolution of a muscular rigidity not only liberates vegetative energy, but, in addition, also brings back into memory the very infantile situation in which the repression had taken effect. We can say: *Every muscular rigidity contains the history and the meaning of its origin.* It is thus not necessary to deduce from dreams or associations the way in which the muscular armor developed; rather, the armor itself is the form in which the infantile experience continues to exist as a harmful agent. The neurosis is by no means only the expression of a disturbed psychic equilibrium; much more correctly and significantly, it is the *expression of a chronic disturbance of the vegetative equilibrium and of natural motility.*

The term "psychic structure" assumed a special connotation during the recent years of my work. It connotes the character of an individual's *spontaneous* reactions, the condition that is typical of him as the result of all the synergistic and antagonistic forces within him. That is, *a certain psychic structure is at the same time a certain biophysiological structure;* it is a representation of the interplay of the vegetative forces within a person. There is no doubt that most of what is today considered "*Anlage*" or "instinctual make-up" will one day be shown to be *acquired vegetative behavior*. The change in structure which we bring about by our therapy is nothing but a change in the interplay of vegetative forces in the organism.

The muscular attitudes have a particular significance for character-analytic technique. Namely, they make it possible, if necessary, to avoid the devious approach via the psychic manifestations, and to break through to the affects directly, from the bodily attitude. If this is done, the repressed affect appears *before* the corresponding memory. In this way, the discharge of affect is guaranteed, provided that the chronic muscular attitude was well understood and properly dissolved. If one attempts to produce the affects by a purely psychological approach, the discharge of affects is left to chance. The character-analytic work on the layers of the character incrustations is the more effective, the more completely it brings about a dissolution of the corresponding muscular attitudes. In a great many cases, psychic inhibitions give way only to a direct loosening of the muscular tensions.

The muscular attitude is identical with what we call "bodily expression". Very often one is unable to tell whether or not a patient is muscularly hypertonic. Nevertheless, one can tell that he is "expressing something", either in his whole body or in individual parts of his body. The forehead, for instance, may appear "perplexed", or the pelvis may express sexual incapacity, "deadness"; or the shoulders give the impression of being "rigid" or "yielding". It is difficult to say what enables us to have such an immediate feeling of a person's bodily expression and to give adequate words to this feeling. One is reminded of the loss of spontaneity ("*Erkalten*") in children, the first and most important sign of final sexual suppression at the age of four or five. This loss of spontaneity is at first always experienced as a "going dead" or "being walled in", "being put into an armor". Later on this feeling of "being dead" may partly be covered up by compensating psychic behavior, such as superficial hilarity or contactless sociability.

The rigidity of the musculature is the somatic side of the process of repression, and the basis for its continued existence. It is never a matter of individual muscles that become spastic, but of muscle *groups forming a functional unit from a vegetative point of view.* If, e.g., an impulse to cry is to be suppressed, not only the lower lip becomes tense, but also the whole musculature of the mouth, the jaw and the throat; that is, all the muscles which, as a functional unit, become active in the process of crying. One is reminded here of the well-known phenomenon that hysterical individuals produce their somatic symptoms not on an anatomical basis, but on a functional one. A hysterical blushing, for example, does not follow the ramifications of a certain artery, but appears, e.g., exclusively on the neck or the forehead. The vegetative function does not know the anatomical demarcations.

The total bodily expression can usually be put into a formula which sooner or later in the course of the character-analytic work appears spontaneously. Peculiarly enough, such a formula is usually derived from the animal kingdom, like "fox", "pig", "snake", "worm", etc.

The function of a spastic muscle group is really not disclosed until the work of unravelling has reached it "logically". It would be useless to try, e.g., to dissolve an abdominal tension right at the beginning. The dissolution of the muscular spasms follows a law which cannot as yet be completely formulated. Usually, the dissolution of the muscular armor begins at the places that are farthest from the genital apparatus, mostly at the head. The facial attitude impresses itself first of all upon us. Facial expression and the character of the voice are also those functions which the patient himself is most likely to be aware of; he rarely is aware of his muscular attitudes in the pelvis, the shoulders or the abdomen.

In the following, I shall describe the signs and mechanisms of some typical muscular attitudes; this description is far from exhaustive.

Head and neck: Violent headaches are a very common symptom. Their localization is very often just above the neck, above the eyes, or in the forehead. In psychopathology, these headaches are customarily referred to as "neurasthenic symptoms". How do they come about? If one tries to tense the muscles of the neck strongly for a considerable length of time, as if one were defending oneself against a threatened blow in the back of the neck, one soon becomes aware of an occipital pain; it appears *above* the place at which the musculature is tensed. That is, occipital headaches are due to a hypertonus in the musculature of the neck. This muscular attitude expresses a continuous fear that something dangerous may happen from the rear, being beaten on the head, etc.

The frontal headache above the eyebrows which is felt as "a band around the head" is the result of a chronic raising of the eyebrows, as everybody can find for himself if he keeps his eyebrows raised for some length of time. In so doing, one will find that the whole musculature of the forehead as well as that of the scalp becomes tense. This attitude expresses chronic anxious anticipation in the eyes. Fully developed, this expression would correspond to the opening wide of the eyes which is characteristic of fright.

Really, these two attitudes—tension in forehead and scalp, and raised eyebrows—belong together. In sudden fright the eyes are opened wide, and simultaneously the scalp muscles are tensed. There are patients with a facial expression which one might call "haughty". When this expression is dissolved, it turns out to be a defense against the expression of a frightened or anxious attentiveness in the face. Other patients present the forehead of a "serious thinker". There is hardly ever one among them who in childhood has not had the phantasy of being a genius. This attitude has usually developed as a defense against anxiety, mostly about masturbation; the frightened facial expression was turned into the "thoughtful attitude". Again, in other cases the forehead looks "smooth", "flat", or "expressionless". The fear of being hit on the head is always behind this expression.

Much more important and also more frequent, are the spasms of the *mouth, chin and neck.* Many people have a mask-like facial expression. The chin is pushed forward and looks broad; the neck below the chin is "lifeless". The lateral neck muscles which go to the breastbone stand out as thick cords; the muscles under the chin are tense. Such patients often suffer from nausea. Their voice is usually low, monotonous, "thin". This attitude, too, one can reproduce in oneself. One only has to imagine that one is trying to suppress an impulse to cry; one will find that the muscles of the floor of the mouth become very tense, the muscles of the whole head become tense, the chin is pushed forward and the mouth becomes small.

In this condition, one will try in vain to talk with a loud and resonant voice. Children acquire such conditions often at a very early age, when they are forced to suppress violent impulses to cry. Lasting concentration of attention on a certain part of the body always results in a fixation of the corresponding innervation. If the attitude taken is the same as one that one would take in a different emotional situation, the two functions may become coupled. Particularly frequently I have found a coupling of *nausea* and the *impulse to cry.* Closer examination revealed the fact that both result in a very similar attitude in the muscles of the floor of the mouth. In such cases it is quite hopeless to try to eliminate the nausea if one does not discover the tension in the muscles of the floor of the mouth. For the nausea is the result of the curbing of another impulse, namely, the impulse to cry. Only the complete liberation of the impulse to cry will eliminate the chronic nausea.

In the region of head and face, the expressive peculiarities of speech are of particular significance. They are mostly the result of spasms in the musculature of the jaw and the throat. In two patients I found a violent defensive reaction which promptly appeared as soon as one, ever so gently, touched the region of the larynx. Both patients had phantasies of having their throats injured by being choked or cut.

The facial expression *as a whole*—independently of the individual parts—has to be observed carefully. We know the depressed face of the melancholic patient. It is peculiar how the expression of flaccidity can be associated with a severe chronic tension of the musculature. There are people with an always artificially beaming face; there are "stiff" and "sagging" cheeks. Usually, the patients are able to find the corresponding expression themselves, if the attitude is repeatedly pointed out and described to them, or shown to them by imitating it. One patient with "stiff cheeks" said: "My cheeks are as if heavy with tears". Suppressed crying easily leads to a mask-like stiffness of the facial musculature. At an early age, children develop a fear of the "faces" which they used to delight in making; they are afraid because they are told that if they make a face "it'll stay that way", and because the very impulses they express in their grimaces are impulses for which they are likely to be reprimanded or punished. Thus, they check these impulses and hold their faces "rigidly under control".

2. THE ABDOMINAL TENSION

I shall postpone the description of the symptoms in chest and shoulders until after the description of the abdominal musculature. There is no neurotic individual who does not show a tension in the abdomen. A mere enumeration of the symptoms, without an understanding of their function in the neurosis, would be of little use.

So important has the treatment of the abdominal tension become in our work that today it seems incomprehensible to me how it was possible to bring about even partial cures in neuroses without knowing the symptomatology of the *solar plexus*. The respiratory disturbances in neurotics are the result of abdominal tensions. Let one imagine that one is frightened, or in anticipation of great danger. Instinctively, one will draw in one's breath and remain in this attitude. As one cannot continue to do this one will soon breathe out again. However, expiration will be incomplete and shallow; one does not breathe out completely in one breath, but in fractions, in steps, as it were. In a state of anxious anticipation, one instinctively draws the shoulders forward and remains in a rigid attitude; sometimes the shoulders are pulled upward. If this attitude is maintained for some time, a pressure in the forehead appears. I have had several patients in whom it was not possible to eliminate the pressure in the forehead until I discovered their attitude of anxious anticipation in the chest musculature.

What is the function of this attitude of "shallow respiration"? If we look at the position of the inner organs and their relation to the solar plexus (p. 352), we see immediately what we are dealing with. In fright, one involuntarily breathes in; as for instance in drowning, where this very inspiration leads to death; the diaphragm contracts and compresses the solar plexus from above. A full understanding of this muscular action is provided by the results of the character-analytic investigation of early infantile mechanisms. Children fight lasting and painful anxiety states, which are accompanied by typical sensations in the "stomach", by holding their breath. They do the same thing when they have pleasurable sensations in the abdomen or in the genitals and are afraid of them.

Holding the breath and keeping the diaphragm contracted is one of the earliest and most important mechanisms for suppressing sensations of pleasure in the abdomen as well as for nipping in the bud "belly anxiety". This mechanism of holding the breath is aided by abdominal pressure which has a similar effect. Everyone knows these vegetative sensations in the abdomen, though they are described in diverse ways. Patients complain of an intolerable "pressure" in the stomach, or of a girdle which "restricts". Others have a certain spot in the abdomen which is very sensitive. Everybody is afraid of getting punched in the belly. This fear becomes the center of very rich phantasies. Others have the feeling that "there is something in the belly that can't get out"; "it feels like a dinnerplate in my belly"; "my belly is dead"; "I have to hold on to my belly", etc., etc. Most of the phantasies of small children about pregnancy and childbirth center around the vegetative sensations in their abdomen.

If, without frightening the patient, one slowly presses with two fingers about an inch below the sternum, one notices sooner or later a reflex-like tension or a constant resistance. *The abdominal content is being protected.* Patients whose complaint is that of a chronic feeling of pressure or of a girdle show a board-like rigidity in the upper abdominal musculature. That is, the musculature here exerts a pressure from in front against the solar plexus, just as the diaphragm exerts a pressure from above. On direct pressure as well as with deep inspiration, the electrical potential of the skin of the abdomen drops by an average of 10 to 30 MV.[1]

I once had a patient who was on the verge of a severe melancholia. Her musculature was highly hypertonic, and during a

---

[1] Cf. the following chapter.

whole year she could not be brought to the point of showing any emotional reaction. For the longest time, I could not understand how she managed to meet the most aggravating situations without any affective reaction. Finally the situation became clear. At the merest sign of an affect she would "adjust something in her belly", hold her breath and stare out of the window as if looking into the distance. Her eyes assumed an empty expression, as if turned inward. The abdominal wall became tense and the buttocks were drawn in. As she said later: "I make the belly dead, then I don't feel anything any more; otherwise my belly has a bad conscience". What she meant was, "Otherwise, it has sexual sensations *and therefore* a bad conscience".

The way in which our children accomplish this "blocking off of sensations in the belly" by way of respiration and abdominal pressure is typical and universal. This technique of emotional control, a kind of universal Yoga method, is something which vegetotherapy has difficulty in combatting.

How can the mechanism of holding the breath suppress or eliminate affects? That was a question of decisive importance. For it had become clear that the inhibition of respiration was *the* physiological mechanism of the suppression and repression of emotion, and consequently, *the basic mechanism of the neurosis* in general. Simple consideration said: The biological function of respiration is that of introducing oxygen and of eliminating carbon dioxide from the organism. The oxygen of the introduced air accomplishes the combustion of the digested food in the organism. Chemically speaking, combustion is everything that consists in the formation of compounds of body substance with oxygen. In combustion, energy is created. Without oxygen, there is no combustion and consequently no production of energy. In the organism, energy is created through the combustion of food stuffs. In this process, heat and kinetic energy are created. Bio-electricity, also, is created in this process of combustion. If respiration is reduced, less oxygen is introduced; only as much as is needed for the maintenance of life. If a smaller amount of energy is created in the organism, the vegetative impulses are less intense and consequently easier to master. The inhibition of respiration, as it is found regularly in neurotics, has, biologically speaking, the function of reducing the production of energy in the organism, and thus, of reducing the production of anxiety.

3. THE ORGASM REFLEX. A CASE HISTORY

For a presentation of the direct liberation of the sexual (vegetative) energies from the pathological muscular attitudes I am choosing a case in which the establishment of orgastic potency succeeded particularly quickly and easily. I should like to stress the fact that—for this reason—this case does not illustrate the considerable difficulties which are commonly encountered in the attempt to overcome disturbances of the orgasm.

The case is that of a technician, 27 years of age, who consulted me because of excessive drinking. He could hardly resist getting severely intoxicated every day; he was afraid he would soon completely ruin his health and his ability to work. His marriage was exceedingly unhappy. His wife was a rather difficult hysteric who made life quite a problem for him; it was easy to see that the misery of his marriage was an important factor in his escape into alcoholism. In addition, his complaint was that he "did not feel alive". Though his marriage was very unhappy, he was not able to establish a relationship with another woman. His work gave him no pleasure, he did it mechanically, without any interest. If this went on, he said, he would soon collapse completely. This condition had already lasted for many years and had become considerably worse during the past few months.

One of his most obvious pathological traits was his complete inability to show any aggression. He felt in himself the compulsion always to be "nice and polite", to agree with everything people said, even if his own opinion was diametrically opposite. His superficiality made him suffer. He was unable to give himself over fully to any cause, any idea or work. His spare time he spent in restaurants and pool rooms, with empty talk and silly jokes. He felt somehow that this was a pathological attitude, but as yet he was unaware of the full pathological significance of these traits. He suffered from compulsive contactless sociability, a disturbance of widespread occurrence.

The general impression the patient made was characterized by his uncertain movements; he walked with a forced stride, so that his gait was somehow clumsy. His posture was not erect, but expressed submissiveness; as if he were being constantly on guard. His facial expression was empty and meant nothing in particular. The skin of his face was somewhat shiny, drawn taut and looked like a mask. His forehead looked "flat". His mouth was small, tight and hardly moved when he spoke; his lips were thin, as if pressed together. The eyes were expressionless.

In spite of this obviously severe impairment of his vegetative motility one felt, behind all this, a very lively intelligent being. It is probably to this fact that we can attribute the great energy with which he attempted to eliminate his difficulties.

The ensuing treatment lasted six and a half months with daily sessions. I shall try to present the most important steps of its course:

As early as the first session I was confronted by the question as to whether I should start with his psychic reserve or his very striking facial expression. I decided to do the latter and to leave to the further development the decision as to when and how I would tackle the problem of his psychic reserve. As a result of a repeated description on my part of the rigid attitude of his mouth, there appeared a slight and then steadily increasing clonic tremor in his lips. He was surprised by the involuntary character of this tremor and tried to fight it. I urged him to give in to any impulse he might feel. Whereupon his lips began to be protruded and retracted in a rhythmic fashion and to remain for a few seconds in the protruded state as if in a tonic spasm. While this was going on, the patient's face took on the unmistakable expression of an infant at the breast. He was surprised and asked anxiously what this was going to lead to. I reassured him and urged him to keep on giving in consistently to any impulse and to tell me about any inhibition of an impulse he would become aware of.

In the following sessions the various manifestations in his face became more and more distinct and gradually aroused the patient's interest. This, he thought, must indicate something of great importance. Yet, peculiarly enough, it all did not seem to touch him; rather, after such clonic or tonic spasms in his face, he continued to talk with me calmly as if nothing had happened. In one of the following sessions, the twitching of the mouth increased to a suppressed weeping. He emitted sounds which resembled the breaking out of a long-suppressed, painful sobbing. My continued request to give in to every muscular impulse was successful. The activity in his face became more manifold. True, his mouth became distorted into a spasm of weeping. However, this expression did not result in weeping, but, to our surprise, passed over into a distorted expression of anger. Peculiarly enough, the patient did not feel the least bit angry, although he knew immediately that what he was expressing was anger.

At the times when these muscular phenomena became particularly intense, so that his face would become blue, the patient would get restless and anxious. He continued to ask what this was going to lead to and what was going to happen to him. Now, I began to point out to him that his fear of some unforeseen happening fully corresponded to his general character attitude; that he was dominated by a vague fear of something unexpected, something that suddenly might befall him.

Since I did not want to relinquish the consistent investigation of a somatic attitude once it was tackled, I had first to become clear in my own mind as to what was the connection between the muscular actions in his face and his general character defense. Had the muscular rigidity been less outspoken, I would have started by working on the character defense which presented itself in the form of his reserve. I was forced to the conclusion that his dominating psychic conflict was split up in the following manner. The defensive function at this time was contained in his psychic reserve, whereas that against which he defended himself, that is, the vegetative impulse, revealed itself in the muscular actions of his face. Just in time I remembered that the muscular attitude itself contained not only the warded-off affect, but also the defense. The smallness and tightness of his mouth could, indeed, be nothing else but the expression of the *opposite,* of the mouth that was protruded, twitching, weeping. I made it a point now to carry to a conclusion the experiment of destroying the defensive forces consistently from the muscular, and not from the psychic side.

Thus, I proceeded to work on all those muscular attitudes in the face which I assumed to be spasmodic contractions, that is, hypertonic defenses against the corresponding muscular actions. In the course of a few weeks, the actions of the musculature of face and neck developed into the following picture: The tightness of the mouth first gave way to a clonic twitching and then to a protrusion of the lips. This protrusion changed into weeping, which, however, did not break out fully. The weeping, in turn, gave way to the facial expression of an extremely intense anger. With this, the mouth became distorted, the musculature of the jaws became hard as a board, there was grinding of the teeth. There were further expressive movements. The patient half sat up, shook with anger, and raised his fist, as if for a blow, *without, however, really striking*. Then he fell back on the couch, exhausted; the whole thing dissolved itself into a sort of whimpering. These actions expressed "*impotent rage*", as it is so often experienced by children toward adults.

After this seizure had subsided, he talked about it calmly, as if nothing had happened. There was no doubt: there was an interruption, some place, between his vegetative muscular impulses and his psychic awareness of these impulses. Of course, I kept discussing with him not only the sequence and the content of his muscular actions, but also this peculiar phenomenon of his psychic detachment with regard to these. What struck him as well as me was the fact that—in spite of this psychic detachment—he had an immediate grasp of the function and the meaning of these seizures. There was no need for me to interpret them to him. On the contrary, he kept surprising me by the explanations which were *immediately evident* to him. This was a highly gratifying state of affairs. I was reminded of the many years of painstaking work of interpreting symptoms, in the course of which one would deduce anger or anxiety from symptoms or associations, and then would try, for months and years, to get the patient into some contact with it. How rarely and to what small degree had it been possible in those years to get further than a purely intellectual understanding! Thus, I had good reason to be pleased with my patient who, without any explanation on my part, had an immediate feeling for the meaning of his actions. He knew that he was expressing an immense anger which he had kept back for decades. The psychic detachment disappeared when one of the seizures reproduced the memory of his older brother who used to bully and maltreat him badly when he was a child.

Spontaneously, he now understood that at that time he had repressed his hatred of his brother who was his mother's favorite.

As an overcompensation of his hatred he developed a particularly nice and loving attitude toward his brother, an attitude which was in violent contradiction to his true feelings. He had done this in order to keep on good terms with his mother. This hatred, which at that time had not been expressed, came out now in his muscular actions, just as if decades had not altered it in the least.

At this point in the story, it may be well to stop for a moment to consider the psychic situation with which we are dealing. With the old technique of free association and symptom-interpretation, it is a matter of chance whether, first, the decisive memories of earlier experiences appear; and second, whether the memories which do appear are really those to which were attached the most intense emotions, and those emotions which had an essential effect on the future life of the patient. In vegetotherapy, on the other hand, the vegetative behavior brings up of necessity that memory which was decisive for the development of the neurotic character trait. As we know, the approach from the psychic memories alone, accomplishes this task in a highly incomplete measure; when one appraises the changes brought about in a patient after years of this treatment, one has to admit that they are not worth the expenditure of time and effort. On the other hand, those patients in whom one succeeds in getting directly at the muscular fixation of the affect, produce the affect *before* they know which affect it is that is repressed. In addition, the memory of the experience which had originally produced the affect, appears afterwards without any effort; as, e.g., in our case the memory of the situation with the older brother whom his mother preferred to him. This fact—which is as important as it is typical—cannot be stressed too much: in this case it is not a matter of a memory which—under favorable circumstances—produces an affect, but the reverse: *the concentration of a vegetative excitation and its breaking through reproduces the memory.*

Freud again and again stressed the fact that in analysis one was dealing only with "derivatives of the unconscious", that the unconscious itself was not really tangible. This statement was correct, but only conditionally, that is, as far as the *method practised at that time* is concerned. Today, by way of a direct approach to the immobilizing of the vegetative energy, we are able to grasp the unconscious not in its derivatives, but in its reality. Our patient, e.g., did not deduce his hatred towards his brother from vague associations charged with little affect; rather, he behaved exactly as he would have behaved in the childhood situation, had not his hatred been curbed by the fear of losing his mother's love. More than that: we know that there are infantile experiences which have never become conscious. The ensuing analysis of our patient showed that, though he had an intellectual knowledge of his envy of his brother, he had never been conscious of the extent and the intensity of his fury. Now, as we know, the effects of a psychic experience are not determined by its content, but by the amount of vegetative energy which was mobilized by the experience and then immobilized by repression. In a compulsion neurosis, for example, even incestuous desires may be conscious; and yet, we are justified in calling them "unconscious", because they have lost their emotional charge; we all have had the experience that by the usual method it is not possible to make the incestuous desire conscious except in an intellectual form. Which means, really, that the lifting of the repression has *not* succeeded. For an illustration, let us return to the further course of this treatment.

The more intense the muscular actions in the face became, the more did the somatic excitation spread toward chest and abdomen; at the same time, the complete psychic detachment persisted. A few weeks later the patient reported new sensations: in the course of the twitchings in the chest, but particularly when they subsided, there were "currents" toward the lower abdomen. At this time, he moved away from his wife, with the intention of entering a relationship with another woman. However, during the ensuing weeks, it turned out that he had not realized this intention. The patient did not even seem to be aware of this inconsistency. Only when I called his attention to it, he began—after first giving a number of rationalisations—to show some interest in the problem; however, it was obvious that some inner inhibition kept him from approaching the question in a really affective manner. As it is a rule in character-analytic work not to enter upon any subject unless the patient has become capable of dealing with it with full emotional participation, even if it seems immediately important, I postponed a discussion of the matter and continued to follow the course which was indicated by the spreading of his muscular actions.

The tonic spasm began to spread to the chest and the upper abdomen; the musculature would become boardlike. In these seizures, it looked as if some inner force were lifting the upper part of his body, against his own will, off the couch and were keeping it in that position. There was an immense tension in the musculature of the chest and abdomen. It took considerable time until I understood why a further spreading downward of the excitation failed to occur. I had expected that now the vegetative excitation would spread from the abdomen to the pelvis; but this did not happen. Instead, there occurred violent clonic twitchings of the musculature of the legs, with an extreme increase of the patellar reflex. To my great surprise, the patient told me that he experienced the twitchings in his legs as extremely pleasurable. This seemed to confirm my previous assumption that the epileptic and epileptiform seizures represent the release of anxiety; as such, they cannot be experienced but as pleasurable. There were periods during the treatment of this patient when I was not quite sure that I was not dealing with a case of genuine epilepsy. At least in outward appearance, his seizures, which began in the form of tonus and often resolved themselves in clonic form, were hardly distinguishable from epileptic seizures.

At this point of the treatment, after about three months, the musculature of the head, the chest and the upper abdomen had become mobile, as well as that of the legs, particularly of the knees and thighs. At the same time, the lower abdomen and the pelvis were and remained immobile. Also, the psychic detachment from the muscular actions remained constant. The patient knew of the seizures. He understood their significance. He felt the affect contained in the seizure. But he still appeared not to be really touched by it. The main question continued to be: what was the obstacle causing this dissociation? It became increasingly clear that the patient was defending himself against comprehending the whole in all its parts. We both knew: *he was very cautious.* This caution expressed itself not only in his psychic attitude. Not only in the fact that his amiability and cooperation in the therapeutic work never went beyond a certain point and that he always became somehow cold or aloof when the work went beyond certain limits. This "caution" was also contained in his muscular behavior; it was, so to speak, maintained in twofold fashion. He himself grasped and described the situation in terms of a boy whom a man was pursuing and trying to beat. In so doing, he took a few steps to one side, as if dodging something, looked anxiously behind him and pulled his buttocks forward, as if to get this region of his body out of the reach of the pursuer. In the usual psychoanalytic language one would have said: behind this fear of being beaten is the fear of a homosexual attack. As a matter of fact, the patient had been in an analysis for about one year, and there his passive homosexuality had constantly been interpreted. "In itself", that had been correct; but from the standpoint of our present knowledge we must say that this interpreting was useless. For, we see what kept that patient from really affectively grasping his homosexual attitude: his characterological caution as well as the muscular fixation of his energy; neither of which were anywhere near dissolved.

I proceeded to tackle his caution, not from the psychic side, as is customary in character-analysis, but from the somatic side. For example, I kept showing him that, although he expressed his anger in his muscular actions, he never continued the action; that, although he raised his fist, he never really let the blow fall. Several times it was shown that at the very moment when the fist wanted to strike the couch, the anger had disappeared. Now, I concentrated the work on the inhibition of completing the muscular action, always guided by the assumption that it was his very caution that was expressed in this inhibition. After some hours' consistent work on the defense against the muscular action, he suddenly remembered the following episode from his fifth year: When he was a little boy, his family lived on top of a cliff which fell precipitously to the sea. He was engaged in making a fire right at the edge of the cliff, and was so much absorbed in his play that he was in danger of falling over the cliff into the sea. His mother appeared at the door of the house which was a few yards away, became frightened and tried to get him away from the cliff. She knew him to be a child with a very lively motility and was all the more afraid. She lured him to her with the kindest words, promising to give him candy. Then as he went to her, she gave him a terrible beating. This experience had made a deep impression on him; but now he understood it in connection with his defensive attitude towards women and the caution which he exhibited in the treatment.

However, this did not settle the matter. The caution remained, as before. One day, in between seizures, he humorously related the following. He was an enthusiastic trout fisherman. In a very impressive manner, he described the pleasure of catching trout; he executed the corresponding motions, described how one catches sight of the trout, how one casts the line; in giving this description, his face had an enormously avid, almost sadistic expression. What struck me was that, although he described the whole procedure in great detail, he omitted one detail, namely the moment at which the trout bites at the line. I understood the connection, but saw also that he was not aware of omitting this detail. With the customary analytic technique, one would have told him the connection or encouraged him to find it himself. But to me it was more important first to have the patient become aware of his omission of the trout getting caught, and the motives for this omission. It took about four weeks until the following took place: the twitchings in the body lost more and more their spastic tonic character; the clonus also decreased, and peculiar *twitchings appeared in the abdomen.* These in themselves were not new to me; I had seen them in other patients. But I had not seen them in the connection in which this patient now presented them. *The upper part of the body (shoulders and chest) jerked forward, the middle of the abdomen remained quiet, and the lower part of the body (pelvis and thighs) jerked towards the upper part.* In these seizures the patient would suddenly half raise himself, while the lower part of the body came upward. The whole thing was an *organic, unitary* movement. There were hours when these movements occurred continually. Alternating with these jerks of the body as a whole there were sensations of currents, particularly in legs and abdomen, which sensations the patient experienced as pleasurable. The attitude of face and mouth changed somewhat; in one of these seizures the face had unmistakably the expression of a fish. Even before I had called this to his attention, the patient stated spontaneously: "I feel like a primitive animal", and then: "I feel like a fish". What were we dealing with here? Quite unknowingly, without having worked out any connection by way of associations, the patient, in his bodily movements, was representing a fish, apparently a fish that was caught and flapping on the line. In the language of analytic interpretation one would say: he "acted out" the trout on the line. This was expressed in various ways: the mouth was protruded, stiff and distorted. The body jerked from head to foot. The back was stiff as a board. What was not quite understandable at this stage was the fact that for some time he would, in the seizure, stretch out his arms as if embracing somebody. I do not remember whether I called the patient's attention to the connection with the story of the trout, or whether he grasped it spontaneously (nor is this particularly important in this connection); at any rate, he had an *immediate* feeling of the connection and did not doubt in the least that he represented the trout as well as the trout fisherman.

Of course, the whole episode had an immediate connection with the disappointments with respect to his mother. From a certain point in his childhood she had neglected him, had treated him badly and often beaten him. Often he would expect something beautiful and good from her and the exact opposite would happen. His caution now became understandable. He trusted nobody, he did not want to be caught. This was the ultimate basis of his superficiality, of his fear of surrender, his fear of responsibility, etc. When this connection was worked out, he underwent a striking change. His superficiality disappeared, he became serious. The seriousness made its appearance quite suddenly during a session. The patient said, verbatim: "I don't understand. Suddenly everything has become so very serious". That is, he had not just remembered the earnest emotional attitude that he had had at a certain period of his early life; rather, he actually changed from the superficial to the earnest. It became clear that his pathological attitude toward women, i.e., his fear of entering a relationship with a woman, to give himself to a woman, was a result of *this fear which had become structuralized.* He was very attractive to women, and yet made peculiarly little use of this attractiveness.

From then on there was a marked and rapid increase in the sensations of currents, at first in the abdomen, then in the legs and the upper part of the body. He described these sensations not only as currents, but as voluptuous, as "melting", particularly after the abdominal jerks had been strong and lively and had occurred in quick succession.

At this point it may be well to stop for a moment in order to take stock of the situation in which the patient found himself.

The abdominal jerks were nothing but the expression of the fact that the tonic tension of the abdominal wall was relaxing. The whole thing operated like a reflex. A slight tap on the abdominal wall would immediately result in a jerk. After several jerks had taken place, the abdominal wall became soft and could easily be pressed in with the fingers; before, it had been tight and had shown a condition which I would like for the moment to refer to as *abdominal defense.* This phenomenon can be found, without exception, in all neurotic individuals. If one has a patient exhale deeply and then exerts a slight pressure on the abdominal wall about one inch below the sternum, one either feels a violent resistance inside the abdomen, or the patient experiences a pain similar to that when the testicle is squeezed. A glance at the position of the abdominal organs and the solar plexus of the vegetative nervous system—taken together with other phenomena discussed later—shows us that the *abdominal tension has the function of exerting a pressure on the solar plexus.* The same function is fulfilled by the tense *diaphragm* in its position of downward pressure. This symptom, too, is typical. *In all neurotic individuals, without exception, one can find a tonic contracture of the diaphragm;* this contracture shows itself in the fact that the patients *can exhale only in a shallow and jerky manner.* In expiration, the diaphragm is raised, and the amount of pressure on the organs below it—including the solar plexus—diminishes. When, in the course of treatment, we bring about a decrease in the tension of the diaphragm and of the abdominal muscles, the solar plexus is freed of the abnormal pressure to which it was subjected. This is shown by the appearance of a sensation which is like that which one experiences on a roller coaster, in an elevator which suddenly starts going down, or in falling. Clinical experience shows this to be an extremely important phenomenon. Almost all patients come to remember that as children they practised suppressing these abdominal sensations, which were particularly intense when they felt anger or anxiety; *they learned spontaneously to achieve this suppression by way of holding their breath and pulling in their abdomen.*

An understanding of this mechanism of pressure on the solar plexus is indispensable for an understanding of the further course of the treatment in our patient. The ensuing events were in accord with this assumption and confirmed it. The more intensively I had the patient observe and describe the behavior of the musculature in the upper abdomen, the more intensive became the jerks, and the sensation of currents after the jerks, and the more did the wavelike, serpentine movements of the body spread. However, the pelvis remained stiff, until I proceeded to make the patient conscious of the rigidity of his pelvic musculature. During the jerks, the whole lower part of the body moved forward; the pelvis, however, did not move by itself; that is to say, the pelvis partook of the movement of the hips and thighs, but did not move at all as a bodily unit separate from hips and thighs. I asked the patient to pay attention to whatever it was that inhibited the movement of the pelvis. It took him about two weeks to grasp completely the muscular inhibition in the pelvis and to overcome it. Gradually, he learned to include the pelvis in the contraction. *Now there appeared in the genital a sensation of currents which he had never known before.* He had erections during the session and a powerful impulse to have an ejaculation. *Now, the contractions of the pelvis, the upper part of the body and of the abdomen were the same as they are experienced in the orgastic clonus.* From then on, the work was concentrated upon having the patient give a detailed description of his behavior in the sexual act.

This revealed a fact which one finds not only in all neurotics, but in the vast majority of all people of both sexes: *the movements in the sexual act are artificially forced, without the individual's being aware of it.* What moves is, as a rule, not the pelvis by itself, but abdomen, pelvis and thighs as one unit. This does not correspond to the natural vegetative movement of the pelvis in the sexual act; on the contrary, it is an inhibition of the orgasm reflex. It is a voluntary movement, as contrasted with the involuntary movement that takes place when the orgasm reflex is not disturbed. This voluntary movement has the function of diminishing or completely obliterating the orgastic sensation of current in the genital.

Furthermore it was found that the patient always kept the muscles of his pelvic floor pulled up and tense. Not until this case did I realize precisely the nature of the gap in my technique, of which I had been until then only vaguely aware. True, in trying to eliminate the inhibitions of orgasm, I had always paid attention to the contraction of the pelvic floor; but again and again I had felt that the result was somehow incomplete. What I had overlooked was the role played by the tension in the pelvic floor. Now I realized that, while the *diaphragm* compressed the solar plexus from above and the *abdominal wall* compressed it from in front, *the contraction of the pelvic floor served the function of decreasing the abdominal space by pressing from below.* The significance of these findings for the development and maintenance of neurotic conditions will be discussed later on.

After a few more weeks, the complete dissolution of the muscular armor was successful. The isolated abdominal contractions decreased in proportion to the increase in the sensation of current in the genital. With that, the earnest character of his emotional life also increased. In this connection, he remembered an experience from his second year:

He is alone with his mother at a summer resort. It is a bright, starlit night. His mother is asleep and breathing deeply; from the outside he hears the rhythmic sounds of the surf. He feels the same deeply earnest, somewhat sad mood that he felt now. We may say that now he remembered one of the situations in his very early childhood in which he had still permitted his vegetative (orgastic) longing to make itself felt. After the disappointment in his mother, which happened when he was about five years old, he fought against the full experience of his vegetative energies and became cold and superficial; in brief, he developed that character which he presented at the start of the treatment.

From this point in the treatment, he had to an increasing degree the feeling of a "peculiar contact with the world". He assured me of the complete identity of this present earnestness of feeling with the feeling which he used to have as a very small child with his mother, particularly during that night. He described this feeling as follows: "It is as though I had complete contact with the world. It is as if all impressions were registering themselves upon me more slowly, as if in waves. It is like a protective covering around a child. It is unbelievable how I feel the depth of the world now". I did not have to tell him, he comprehended *spontaneously: The closeness to the mother is the same thing as the closeness to nature.* The identification of mother and earth, or universe, has a deeper meaning when it is understood from the point of view of the vegetative harmony between the individual and the world.

During one of the following sessions, the patient had a severe anxiety attack. He suddenly sat up with a painfully distorted mouth; his forehead was covered with perspiration; his whole musculature was tense. He hallucinated an animal, an ape; with this, his hand showed exactly the attitude of a tightly clenched ape's paw, and he emitted sounds which seemed to come out of the depth of his chest, "as if without vocal chords", he said later. He had the feeling that somebody was coming dangerously close to him and was threatening him. Then, as if in a trance, he cried out: "Don't be angry, I only want to suck". After this, he calmed down, and in the following hours we worked it through. He remembered among other things that at the age of about two—which age could be determined by a certain apartment situation—he had seen Brehm's "*Tierleben*"[1] for the first time. He did not remember having experienced the same anxiety at that time. Nevertheless, there was no doubt that this present anxiety corresponded to that experience: he had looked at a *gorilla* with great astonishment and admiration.

Although this anxiety had not become manifest at that time,

---

[1] *Translator's note:* A classic book on animal life.

it had, nevertheless, dominated his whole life. Only now had it broken through. The gorilla represented the father, the threatening figure that tried to keep him from sucking. The relationship to his mother had been fixated on this level. It had broken through at the very beginning of the treatment in the form of the sucking movements with his lips; but it did not become spontaneously evident to him until after the complete dissolution of his muscular armor. It was not necessary to search for years for his sucking experience as an infant; he actually became a suckling infant during the therapeutic session, having the facial expression of the infant and actually experiencing the original anxieties.

The remainder of the story can be told briefly. After the dissolution of the disappointment in his mother and his consequent fear of giving himself, the genital excitability increased rapidly. After only a few days, he made the acquaintance of a young, pretty woman and made friends with her easily and without conflicts. After the second or third sexual act with her he came in beaming and reported with great surprise that his pelvis had moved "so peculiarly *by itself*". On closer investigation, it was shown that he still had a slight inhibition at the moment of ejaculation. But, since the pelvis had become mobile, it was not difficult to eliminate this last remainder. What he still had to overcome was his tendency to hold back at the moment of ejaculation, instead of completely surrendering himself to the vegetative movements. He did not doubt for a moment that the contractions which he had produced during the treatment had been nothing but the *curbed vegetative movements of coitus*. However, as it turned out, the orgasm reflex had not fully developed without any disturbance. The muscular contractions in the orgasm were still jerky; he strongly shied away from letting his neck relax, i.e., assuming the attitude of surrender. Before long, the patient relinquished his resistance against a gentle, harmonic course of the movements. Now, the remainder of his disturbance—which previously had more or less escaped attention—gave way. The hard, jerky form of the muscular contractions corresponded to a psychic attitude which said: "A man is hard and unyielding; any kind of surrender is feminine".

Following this realization, an old infantile conflict with his father was solved. On the one hand, he felt sheltered and protected by his father. He could always be sure that, if things became too difficult, he could "retreat" to the paternal home. But, at the same time, he wanted to stand on his own feet and to be independent of his father; he felt that his need for protection was feminine, and wanted to free himself of it. There was, thus, a conflict between his desire for independence and his passive-feminine need for protection. Both of these tendencies were represented in *the form* of his orgasm reflex. The solution of the psychic conflict occurred hand in hand with the elimination of the hard, jerky form of his orgasm reflex and its being unmasked as a defense against the gentle, surrendering movement. When he experienced the surrender in the reflex itself for the first time, he was gripped by deep amazement: "I never would have thought", he said, "that a man could surrender too. I always thought it was a female sex characteristic". In this way, his own warded-off femininity was linked up with the natural form of orgastic surrender and therefore disturbed the latter.

It is interesting to see how the social double standard of morality was mirrored and anchored in this patient's structure. It is part and parcel of official social ideology to equate surrender with being feminine, and unyielding hardness with being masculine. According to this ideology it is inconceivable that an independent person should be able to give himself, or that a person who gives himself should be able to be independent. Just as women—due to this equation—protest against their femininity and try to be masculine, so men fight against their natural sexual rhythm, for fear of appearing feminine. From this, the different concept of sexuality in man and in woman derives its seeming justification.

In the course of the next few months, every change in the patient consolidated itself. He no longer drank excessively, but neither did he deny himself an occasional drink on social occasions. He was able to put the relationship with his wife on a rational basis, and developed a happy relationship with another woman. Above all, he started a new kind of work and engaged in it with great interest and enthusiasm.

His superficiality had disappeared completely. He was no longer able to engage in empty talk in restaurants or to undertake anything that was not somehow of objective importance. I should like to emphasize the fact that I would not have dreamed of influencing or guiding him in any way morally. I was myself surprised by the spontaneous change in the direction of objectivity and earnestness. He grasped the basic principles of sex-economy not so much on the basis of his treatment—which had been of rather short duration anyhow—but, doubtless, on the basis of his *altered structure, his feeling of his own body, his re-acquired vegetative motility.* In such difficult cases, one is not used to success in such short periods of time. During the ensuing four years—which is as long as I heard from him—the patient continued to consolidate his gains in the form of greater equanimity, capacity for happiness and rational managing of difficult situations.

I have now been practising the vegetotherapeutic technique on students and patients for some six years; it represents a great step forward in the treatment of character neuroses. The results are better than they used to be, and the time required for the treatment is shorter. A number of physicians and teachers have already learned the technique of character-analytic vegetotherapy.

4. THE ESTABLISHMENT OF NATURAL RESPIRATION

Before describing any details of this technique, a brief review of some fundamental facts seems in order. Their knowledge will explain the meaning of each individual technical procedure, which without this knowledge may appear meaningless.

The vegetotherapeutic treatment of muscular attitudes is interwoven in a very definite way with the work on the character attitudes. It does not by any means take the place of the character-analytic work. Instead, it supplements it, or rather: it is the same work taking place in a deeper layer of the biological organism. For, as we know, character armor and muscular armor are completely identical. Thus, vegetotherapy might rightly be called "character-analysis in the realm of biophysical functioning".

However, the identity of character armor and muscular armor has a corrollary. Character attitudes may be dissolved by the dissolution of the muscular armor; and conversely, muscular attitudes by the dissolution of character peculiarities. Once one has experienced the power of muscular vegetotherapy, one is tempted to give up the character-analytic work in its favor. But, everyday practice soon teaches one that it is not permissible to exclude one form of work at the expense of the other. In one type of patient the work on the muscular attitudes will predominate from the start, in another type the work on the character attitudes. In a third type of patient the work on the character will take place simultaneously with that on the musculature, or will alternate with it. However, in all cases, the work on the muscular armor becomes more extensive and more important towards the conclusion of the treatment. Its task is to bring back into functioning the orgasm reflex which is naturally present in any organism, but is disturbed in all patients.

The establishment of the orgasm reflex takes place in many diverse ways. In attempting to free the orgasm reflex from inhibition, one learns a great many details which make one understand the difference between the natural and the unnatural, neurotic movements. The vegetative impulse and its vegetative inhibition may be localized in one and the same muscle group. For example, an attitude of ducking the head may contain the impulse to push the head into somebody's abdomen, as well as the inhibition of this impulse; the conflict between impulse and defense, so well known in the psychic realm, is found in the same way in physiological behavior. In other cases, impulse and inhibition are distributed over different muscle groups. For example, in many patients, the vegetative impulse expresses itself in involuntary contractions of the muscles of the upper abdomen. The inhibition of the vegetative impulse, however, may be found in a spasm of the uterus. In such a case, the uterus can be felt on careful palpation as a well-defined, spherical mass. It is a matter of vegetative hypertonus of the uterine musculature; with the development of the orgasm reflex the mass disappears. It even happens occasionally that the mass appears and disappears repeatedly during one and the same session.

This phenomenon is extremely important. For, the establishment of the orgasm reflex takes place essentially by way of a—temporary—*intensification* of the vegetative inhibitions. The fact has to be kept in mind that the patient knows nothing of his muscular inhibitions. He has to feel them, before he is even capable of turning his attention towards them. To try to intensify his vegetative impulses themselves, without first having dissolved the inhibitions, would prove perfectly useless.

In order to make this clearer, we shall make use of an example. A snake or a worm shows a uniform, wave-like rhythmical movement which involves the whole body. Let us imagine that some segments of the body were paralyzed or somehow restricted, so that they could not participate in the rhythmic motion of the whole body. In this case, the other parts of the body—though not paralyzed or restricted—would be unable to move as previously; rather, the *total rhythm* would be disturbed by the elimination of individual muscle groups. The *completeness* of bodily harmony and motility, therefore, requires that the bodily impulses work *as an undisturbed unity, as a whole*. As mobile as a person may be otherwise, if he inhibits motility in the pelvis, his whole attitude and motility are inhibited. Now, it is the essence of the orgasm reflex that a wave of excitation and movement runs from the vegetative center over head, neck, chest, abdomen and legs. If this wave is blocked in some place, retarded or stopped in its normal course, then the whole reflex becomes "disrupted". As a rule, our patients present not one but *many* such blocks and inhibitions of the orgasm reflex. They occur at various places in the body. There are two places where they are found regularly: the *throat* and the *anus*. It can be surmised that this has to do with the embryonic character of these two openings, since they are the two ends of the primitive intestinal tract.

The technical procedure is that of finding the seat of the inhibition of the orgasm reflex and of intensifying the inhibition; after that, the body of itself seeks to find the pathway prescribed by the natural course of vegetative excitation. It is striking how "logically" the body gathers together the total reflex. For example, when one has dissolved a stiffness in the neck, or a spasm in the throat or the chin, there appears almost regularly some kind of impulse in the chest or the shoulders; before long, this is curbed by the corresponding inhibition. If one dissolves this inhibition, there soon appears some impulse in the abdomen, until this in turn meets an inhibition. Thus one soon convinces oneself that it is *impossible* to bring about vegetative motility in the pelvis *before* the dissolution of the inhibitions in the upper parts of the body has been accomplished.

However, this description should not be taken in a schematic way. True, every dissolution of an inhibition makes possible the appearance of a bit of vegetative impulse "farther down". But, conversely, a throat spasm may become accessible for dissolution only after more intense vegetative impulses have already broken through in the abdomen. As new vegetative impulses break through, inhibitions that had previously remained hidden become unmistakably evident. In many cases it is not possible to discover even severe spasms of the throat until the vegetative excitation in the pelvis has developed to a considerable extent. The heightened excitability mobilizes the remainder of the available inhibitory mechanisms.

In this connection, *substitute movements* are particularly important. Very often, a vegetative impulse is only *simulated* by an acquired, more or less voluntary movement. It is not possible to elicit the basic vegetative impulse before the substitute movement is unmasked as such and eliminated. Many patients, for example, suffer from a chronic tension in the musculature of the jaws, which give to the lower half of their faces a "mean look". In trying to move the chin downward, one becomes aware of a strong resistance, a rigidity; if one asks the patient to open and shut his mouth repeatedly, he does so only after some hesitation and with visible effort. However, one first has to make the patient experience this artificial kind of opening and closing his mouth before it is possible to convince him at all that the motility of his chin is inhibited.

Voluntary movements of certain muscle groups, then, may serve as a defense against involuntary movements. Similarly, involuntary movements may appear as defenses against other involuntary movements, as e.g., a tic of the eyelid as a defense against a sustained staring. Also, voluntary movements may be in the same direction as involuntary ones; the conscious *imitation* of a pelvic movement may induce an involuntary, vegetative pelvic movement.

The basic principle of bringing about the orgasm reflex is: 1. To find the places and mechanisms of the inhibitions which prevent the unitary character of the orgasm reflex. 2. Intensification of the involuntary inhibitory mechanisms and of the involuntary impulses, such as the forward movement of the pelvis, which is capable of inducing the total vegetative impulse.

The most important means of bringing about the orgasm reflex is a *breathing technique* which developed almost by itself in the course of the work. There is no neurotic individual who is capable of exhaling in one breath, deeply and evenly. The patients have developed all conceivable practices which prevent *deep expiration.* They exhale "jerkily", or, as soon as the air is let out, they quickly bring their chest back into the inspiratory position. Some patients describe the inhibition, when they become aware of it, as follows: "It is as if a wave of the ocean struck a cliff. It does not go on".

The sensation of this inhibition is localized in the upper abdomen or in the middle of the abdomen. With deep expiration, there appear in the abdomen vivid sensations of pleasure or anxiety. The function of the respiratory block (inhibition of deep expiration) is exactly that of avoiding the occurrence of these sensations. As a preparation for the process of bringing about the orgasm reflex, I ask my patients to "follow through" with their breathing, to "get into swing". If one asks the patients to breathe deeply, they usually force the air in and out in an artificial manner. This voluntary behavior serves only to prevent the natural vegetative rhythm of respiration. It is unmasked as an inhibition; the patient is asked to breathe without effort, that is, *not to do breathing exercises,* as he would like to do. After five to ten breaths, respiration usually becomes deeper and the first inhibitions make their appearance. With *natural* deep expiration, the head moves *spontaneously* backwards at the end of expiration. Patients are unable to let their heads go back in this spontaneous manner. They stretch their heads forward in order to prevent this spontaneous backward movement, or they jerk it violently to one or the other side; at any rate, the movement is different from that which would come about naturally.

With natural respiration, the shoulders become relaxed and move gently and slightly forward at the end of expiration. Our patients hold their shoulders tight just at the end of expiration, pull them up or back; in brief, they execute various shoulder movements in order not to let the spontaneous vegetative movement come to pass.

Another method in this procedure of bringing about the

orgasm reflex is a gentle pressure on the upper abdomen. I put the fingertips of both hands at about the middle between umbilicus and sternum and have the patient breathe deeply. During expiration, I press the upper abdomen in gradually and gently. This produces widely different reactions in different individuals. In many, the solar plexus proves highly sensitive to pressure. Others show a countermovement, arching the back; they are the same patients who, in the sexual act, suppress any orgastic excitation by pulling back their pelvis and arching their back. In other cases, the pressure on the abdomen results after a while in wave-like contractions in the abdomen. This occasionally induces the orgasm reflex. Continued deep expiration always results in a relaxation of the previously highly tense abdominal wall; it can be more easily pressed in; the patients state that they "feel better" (a statement which has to be taken with a grain of salt). I have adopted a formula which patients grasp spontaneously. I ask them to "give in" completely. The attitude of giving in is the same as that of surrender ("*Hingabe*"): the head glides back, the shoulders move forward and up, the middle of the abdomen draws in, the pelvis is pushed forward, and the legs part spontaneously. *Deep expiration brings about spontaneously the attitude of (sexual) surrender.* We can in this way explain the occurrence, in individuals who are incapable of surrender, of the inhibition of the orgasm by holding the breath when the excitation in the sexual act increases to the acme.

Many patients keep their back arched, so that the pelvis is retracted and the upper abdomen protruded. If one puts a hand under the patient's arched lower back and asks the patient to let it down, one notices an unwillingness to do so: this giving in in posture expresses the same thing as the attitude of surrender in the sexual act or in a state of sexual excitation. Once the patient has grasped the attitude of surrender and has become capable of assuming it, the first prerequisite for the establishment of the orgasm reflex is given. For the establishment of the attitude of surrender, a relaxed opening of the mouth proves helpful. In the course of this work, numerous inhibitions which had previously been hidden, make their appearance; for example, many patients will knit their eyebrows, or extend their legs or feet in a spastic manner, etc. It is thus not possible to eliminate the inhibitions "neatly one after the other" and then find the orgasm reflex established. Rather, it is only in the process of again unifying the disorganized organic rhythm of the total body that all these muscular actions and inhibitions, which previously had impeded the patient's sexual functioning and vegetative motility, disclose themselves.

It is only in the course of this work that the methods come to light which the patients, as children, had practised as a means of mastering their impulses and their "anxieties in the belly". As heroically as they had then fought the "devil", the sexual pleasure in themselves, with just the same absurd valor do they now fight against their capacity for pleasure, the very thing they are striving for. I shall mention only some of the more typical forms of the somatic mechanisms of repression. Many patients, when in the course of the treatment their abdominal sensations become too strong, begin to stare vacantly into a corner or out of the window. If one inquires about such behavior, the patients will remember that, as children, they practised this consciously every time they had to control their anger towards parents, siblings or teachers. To be able to hold one's breath for a long time meant a heroic feat of self-control. Language here clearly portrays the somatic process of self-control; certain phrases commonly heard in everyday education represent exactly what is here described as muscular armoring. "A man has to show self-control"; "a big boy doesn't cry"; "pull yourself together"; "don't let yourself go"; "you shouldn't show that you're afraid"; "it's very bad to lose your temper"; "you must grit your teeth"; "grin and bear it"; "keep your chin up"; "keep a stiff upper lip"; etc., etc. Such typical admonitions are at first rejected by children, then reluctantly adopted as their own and performed. They always impair the child's backbone, break his spirit, destroy the life in him and make a well-behaved puppet of him.

A mother with some background in psychology told me about her eleven year old girl whose bringing up, to the age of five, had included severe prohibition of masturbation. At about the age of nine, she saw a children's play in which there was a magician whose fingers were artificially elongated and of unequal length. She became excited about the enormous index finger, and from then on this magician again and again appeared in her anxiety states. "You know", she said to her mother, "when I get scared, it always starts in the belly" (in saying this, she doubled up as if in pain). "Then I must not move. I must not move any part of me. Only with that little part down there (meaning the clitoris) may I play; that I pull like mad, back and forth, back and forth. The magician says: 'you must not move, only down there, that you may move'. When I get more and more scared, I want to turn the light on. But then I have to move with big movements, and that makes me more scared. Only when I make very small movements does it get better. But then when the light is on and I have pulled enough down there, then I get quieter and quieter, and then it is all over. The magician is like Nana; she also keeps saying: 'Don't move, lie still' (in saying this, she assumes a stern face). If I just had my hands under the cover, she'd come and pull them out".

As she kept her hand on or near her genital almost all day, her mother asked her why she was doing it. It turned out that she was not aware of doing it so often. She then described the various kinds of sensations she had. "Sometimes I just feel like playing, then I don't have to pull. But when I'm scared stiff all over, then I have to pull and tear like mad down there. When everybody is gone and there is nobody with whom I can talk about these things, then I have to do something down there all the time". A little later she added: "When I am scared I get all stubborn. Then I want to fight something, but I don't know what. Don't think that I want to fight the magician (the mother had not mentioned him at all), I'm much too scared of him. It is something else that I don't know".

This child gives a good description of her abdominal sensations and the ways in which—with the aid of a phantasy about a magician—she attempts to control them.

Another example will illustrate the significance of respiration for the activity of the abdominal vegetative ganglia. In one patient there occurred, in the course of repeated deep expirations, a marked sensitivity of the pelvic region. To this he would react with holding his breath. If one touched his thigh or lower abdomen, ever so gently, he would pull himself together with a start. However, if I had him exhale deeply several times, he did not react to being touched at all. When he held his breath again, the irritability of the pelvic region promptly reappeared. This could be repeated *ad libitum.*

This clinical detail is very revealing. Deep inspiration (holding the breath) dams up the biological energy of the vegetative centers and thus increases the reflex irritability. Repeated deep expiration reduces the stasis and with it the anxious irritability. The inhibition of respiration—specifically, of deep expiration—thus creates a conflict: the inhibition serves the purpose of damping the pleasurable excitations of the central vegetative apparatus; but just in doing so, it creates an increased susceptibility for anxiety and increased reflex irritability. Another bit of the problem of the conversion of sexual excitation into anxiety thus became understandable. We also understand the clinical finding that, in our attempts to re-establish the capacity for pleasure, we first come upon physiological anxiety-reflexes. Anxiety is the negative of sexual excitation and at the same time identical with it from the point of view of energy. So-called "nervous irritability" is nothing but a series of short-circuits in the discharge of tissue electricity; it is caused by the damming-up of energy which is blocked from orgastic discharge.

In one of my patients, the central character resistance manifested itself for a long time in his talkativeness. At the same time, he felt his mouth as "alien", "dead", "not belonging to him". At times, he would pass his hand over his mouth as if to make sure that it was still there. It was shown that his delight in telling gossipy stories really was an attempt to overcome the feeling of the "dead mouth". When this defensive function was dissolved, his mouth spontaneously began to take on an infantile attitude of sucking; this alternated with a mean, hard, facial expression. At the same time, the head was turned obliquely to the right. One day I touched the patient's neck, in order to check up on the muscular tension. To my great surprise, the patient immediately assumed the attitude of a hanged man; his head fell limp to one side, the tongue protruded, the mouth stayed rigidly open. All this happened after I had just barely touched his neck. From there, we arrived in a straight line at his early infantile fear of death; its content was that of being *hanged* for sins he had committed, that is, for masturbation. This reflex occurred only when at the same time the breath was held and deep exhaling was avoided. It disappeared as the patient began to overcome his fear of breathing deeply.

The neurotic inhibition of respiration, thus, is a central part of the neurotic mechanism in general, in two ways: It blocks the normal vegetative activity of the organism; and thus it creates the source of energy for all kinds of neurotic symptoms and phantasies. Talking is one of the favorite means of suppressing vegetative excitations. This explains neurotic compulsive talking. In such cases I have the patient stop talking until he shows signs of restlessness.

Another patient suffered from an extreme "feeling of worthlessness". He felt he was a "swine". His neurosis consisted chiefly in his—always unsuccessful—attempts to overcome this feeling of worthlessness by being importunate toward others. His pathological behavior constantly provoked people into calling him down. This confirmed to him his feeling of worthlessness and increased his lack of self-confidence. He began to ruminate: what were people saying about him, why did they treat him so badly, how could he improve matters, etc. At the same time he felt a pressure in his chest, which became all the more intense the more he tried to overcome his feeling of worthlessness by compulsive rumination. It took a long time before we discovered the connection between his compulsive rumination and the "pressure in the chest". The whole thing was preceded by a bodily sensation of which he had never been conscious: "Something begins to stir in my chest, then it shoots into the head; I feel as if my head were going to burst. It is as if a mist came over my eyes. I'm no longer able to think. I lose the feeling for what is going on around me. I am going to be submerged, going to lose myself and everything around me". Such states always occurred when an excitation did not get through to the genital and was diverted "upward". This is the physiological basis for what the psychoanalysts call "displacement from below upward". With this neurotic condition, there were phantasies of being a genius, daydreams about a great future, etc.; these were all the more grotesque the less they were in keeping with his real achievement in daily life.

There are people who claim never to have experienced the well-known gnawing feeling or feeling of longing in the upper abdomen. They are usually hard, cold characters. Two of my patients had developed a pathological eating compulsion for the purpose of suppressing their abdominal sensations; as soon as a feeling of anxiety or depression made itself felt, they would immediately proceed to fill their stomachs to the bursting point. Many women (thus far I have not observed this in men) have to "push something down in the abdomen" after an unsatisfactory sexual act, as one of these patients expressed it. Others have sensations of "having something in the stomach that can't get out".

5. THE MOBILIZATION OF THE "DEAD PELVIS"

The orgasm reflex does not appear in its complete form at once, but develops by an integration of its parts, as it were. At first, there is only a wave running from the neck over the chest and upper abdomen down to the lower abdomen. Many patients describe this as follows: "It is as if the wave got stopped at a certain point down there". The pelvis does not participate in this wave-like movement. In trying to locate the inhibition, one usually finds that the pelvis is fixed in a *retracted* position. Sometimes, an arching of the spinal column goes with this retraction, the abdomen being pushed out. A hand can be placed easily between the lower back and the couch. The immobility of the pelvis gives the impression of deadness. In the majority of cases, this is subjectively felt as an "emptiness in the pelvis" or a "weakness of the genitals". This is especially true in cases suffering from chronic constipation. This becomes understandable when we remind ourselves of the fact that chronic constipation corresponds to a hypertonus of the sympathetic; so does the holding back in the pelvis. The patients are unable to move the pelvis. If they try to, they move *abdomen, pelvis and thighs in one piece.* Thus, the therapeutic task is first that of making the patient fully aware of the vegetative emptiness in the pelvis. As a rule, they fight intensely against moving the pelvis by itself, particularly against moving it forward and upward. In comparing cases of genital anesthesia, one finds that the lack of sensation, the feeling of emptiness and weakness, are all the more intense, the more the pelvis has lost its natural motility. Such patients always suffer from a severe disturbance of the sexual act. The women lie motionless, or else they try to overcome the blocking of their vegetative motility by forced movements of trunk and pelvis together. In men, the same disturbance takes the form of quick, hasty and voluntary movements of all of the lower body. In none of these cases is the vegetative orgastic sensation of current present.

Some details of this syndrome deserve special mention. The genital musculature (bulbo-cavernosus and ischio-cavernosus) is tense, so that the contractions which normally take place as a response to friction cannot occur. The musculature of the buttocks is also tense. The un-responsiveness of these muscles can often be overcome by the patient's trying to bring about *voluntary* contractions and relaxations in them.

The pelvic floor is pulled up. This mechanism prevents a free vegetative current in the abdomen, just as it is prevented from above by the downward fixation of the diaphragm and from in front by the contraction of the musculature of the abdominal wall.

This typical position of the pelvis, as just described, is always found to have originated in childhood and arises in the course of two typical disturbances of development. The groundwork is prepared in the customary brutal training for cleanliness when the demand is made on the child to control its bowels at a very early age; similarly, severe punishment for bedwetting leads to this contracture of the pelvis. But much more important is the contracture of the pelvis which the child institutes when it begins to suppress the high-pitched genital excitations which give the incentive towards infantile masturbation.

For, it is possible to deaden any genital pleasure sensation by a chronic contracture of the pelvic musculature. Proof of this can be seen in the fact that genital sensations of current make their appearance as soon as one succeeds in bringing about a relaxation of this pelvic contracture. In order to accomplish this, the patient first of all, has to feel the way he is holding his pelvis, that is, he must have the immediate feeling that he "holds his pelvis still". Furthermore, all voluntary movements must be elicited which *prevent* the *natural* vegetative movement of the pelvis. The most important and most common of these voluntary movements is that of moving abdomen, pelvis and thighs *in one piece.* It is perfectly useless to have the patient do exercises with his pelvis, as many gymnastics teachers intuitively do. As long as the concealing and defensive attitudes and actions are not discovered and eliminated, the natural pelvic movement cannot develop.

The more intensively the inhibition of the movement of the pelvis is worked on, the more completely does the pelvis begin to take part in the wave of excitation. As it does so, it moves—without any effort on the part of the patient—forward and up. The patient feels as if the pelvis were being drawn up toward the umbilicus as if by an external force. At the same time, the thighs remain still. It is extremely important to make the proper distinction between the natural vegetative movement of the pelvis and those other movements that are a defense against it. As soon as the wave runs from the neck down over the chest and abdomen right down to the pelvis, the character of the total reflex undergoes a change. Whereas up to now the reflex was essentially unpleasant, occasionally even painful, now it begins to become pleasurable. Whereas up to now there were defensive movements such as pushing out the abdomen with arching of the back, now the whole trunk arches forward, reminiscent of the way a fish moves. The pleasurable sensations in the genital and the sensations of current in the whole body which now, increasingly, accompany the movements, leave no doubt that we are dealing with natural, vegetative coitus movements. Their character differs basically from that of the previous reflexes and bodily reactions. The sensation of emptiness in the genital, more or less rapidly, gives way to a sensation of fullness and urgency. Thus develops spontaneously the capacity for orgastic experience in the sexual act.

The very same motions which, appearing in individual muscle groups, represent pathological reactions of the body in the service of warding off sexual pleasure, are—in their *totality*, in the form of a wave-like movement of the *total* body—*the* basis of spontaneous vegetative capacity for pleasure. Thus we understand the nature of the *arc de cercle*, that hysterical symptom in which chest and abdomen are thrown forward, while the shoulders and the pelvis are pulled back; it is the *exact opposite of the orgasm reflex.*

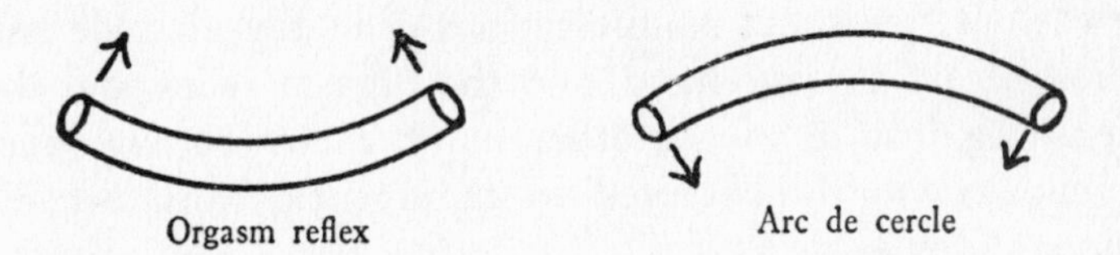

Orgasm reflex

Arc de cercle

Before I knew these facts, I was forced to let the patients overcome their inhibition of the pelvic movement partially by way of "exercises". The incompleteness of the results made me give up such artificial measures and made me look, instead, for the *inhibitions* of natural motility. The defense against the orgasm reflex causes a series of vegetative disturbances, as e.g., chronic constipation, muscular rheumatism, sciatica, etc. In many cases, constipation, though it may have been present for decades, disappears with the development of the orgasm reflex. Its full development is often preceded by nausea and vertigo, spastic conditions in the throat, isolated contractions in the abdominal musculature, the diaphragm, the pelvis, etc. All of these symptoms, however, disappear as soon as the full development of the orgasm reflex succeeds. The "stiff, dead, retracted" pelvis is one of the most common vegetative disturbances in the human. It accounts for lumbago as well as for hemorrhoidal disturbances. Its relationship to another common disease, the cancer of the genital in women, will have to be demonstrated elsewhere.

This mechanism of "making the pelvis dead" thus was shown to have the same function as that of "making the belly dead", namely, the avoidance of sensations, in particular those of pleasure and anxiety. It is brought about by a tight circumvallation of the "vegetative center". In the course of the treatment, the vegetative center is made free by a relaxation of this tight circumvallation.

At this time, when the connection became clear between the various forms and manifestations of bodily attitude and expression on the one hand, and the orgasm reflex and the defense against it on the other hand, many obscure phenomena previously observed in therapeutic work became understandable.

I was reminded of a case[1] of tic of the diaphragm in a woman of 45 whom I had treated at the Vienna Psychoanalytic Clinic fourteen years previously and whom I had partially cured by making masturbation possible for her. From the time of puberty, i.e., for over 30 years, the patient had suffered from a very disturbing tic of the diaphragm, accompanied by noticeable sounds. When it became possible for her to masturbate, the tic decreased to a far-reaching degree. Today it is clear that the improvement was due to a partial dissolution of the spasm of the diaphragm. At that time I was only able to say in a general way that the sexual gratification had partly removed the sexual stasis and had thus diminished the tic. But I did not know then in what way the stasis had become permanent, at what place it had found discharge, or in what manner the sexual gratification reduced the stasis. The respiratory tic corresponded to involuntary contraction of the diaphragm which represented a neurotic attempt to reduce the spasm.

These new insights also recalled those cases of epilepsy with *abdominal aura,* in which I would not have known just where the convulsions took place, and what was their function and their connection with the vegetative nervous system. It became clear now that the epileptic seizures represent convulsions of the vegetative apparatus in which the dammed-up biopsychic energy is discharged exclusively by

[1] Cf. Reich, Wilhelm, "Der Tic als Onanieäquivalent". Ztschr. f. Sexualwissenschaft, 1924.

way of the musculature—with exclusion of the genital. The epileptic seizure is an extragenital, muscular orgasm.[1]

Similarly, those cases became clear now in which one observes "*Bauchflattern*" in the course of the treatment, that is, involuntary, uncoordinated spasms of the abdominal musculature; they represent attempts of the organism to relax the abdominal tension.

In ever so many patients I had had the feeling of a hidden meanness which never came into the open. I could not have said where this meanness was localized. The treatment of the vegetative behavior, however, makes it possible to localize this meanness definitely in one or another part of the body. Some patients express friendliness in their eyes and cheeks, while the expression in chin and mouth is in strict contradiction to this; the expression in the lower part of the face is entirely different from that in the upper part. The analysis of the muscular attitude in mouth and chin sets free an unbelievable amount of anger.

In other cases one senses the falsity of the patient's conventional politeness; it covers up a cunning malice, which may be expressed in a constipation of many years' standing. The bowels do not function and have to be kept open by the constant use of cathartics. Such patients, when they were children, had to control their outbursts of anger and had to "imprison their naughtiness in the belly". The manner in which patients describe their bodily sensations is almost always in terms of often-heard phrases from the nursery. For example, "the belly is bad when it makes a 'poop'." When the child is being "well brought up", the temptation is great to reply to these attempts at education with a "poop". But the child soon has to break this tendency, and the only way of doing that is to "imprison the poop in the belly". This, the child cannot do without suppressing *every* excitation

---

[1] Cf. Reich, Wilhelm, "Ueber den epileptischen Anfall". Internat. Zeitschr. f. Psychoan. 17, 1931, 263.

which makes itself felt in the abdomen, and that includes the genital sexual excitations; this suppression is achieved by the child's withdrawing into himself and "making his belly crawl into itself". The abdomen becomes hard and tense, and has "imprisoned the naughtiness".

It would be worthwhile to present in great detail, from a historical and functional point of view, the complicated development of such pathological bodily attitudes as they are found in diverse cases. I must content myself with indicating a few typical facts.

It is extremely illuminating to see how the body—while it can function as a total organism—is also able to split up into parts, one part functioning in the sense of the parasympathetic, the other in the sense of the sympathetic. One of my women patients showed the following phenomenon in a certain phase of her treatment; the upper abdomen was already completely relaxed; she had the typical sensations of current, the abdominal wall could easily be pressed in, etc. There was no longer any interruption in the sensations in upper abdomen, chest and neck. However, the lower abdomen, as if a line of demarcation had been drawn, behaved quite differently. Here, a hard mass of about the size of an infant's head could be palpated. It would be impossible to state, in terms of anatomy, just how this mass came about, i.e., what organs participated in its formation, but there could be no doubt about the finding itself. In a later phase of the treatment there were days when the mass would alternatingly appear and disappear. It would always appear when the patient was afraid of a beginning genital excitation and suppressed it; it would disappear when the patient was able to allow the genital excitation to make itself felt.

The somatic manifestations of schizophrenia, especially of catatonia, will have to be discussed in a special treatise on the basis of further material. The stereotypies, perseverations and automatisms of all kinds in schizophrenia are the result of muscular armoring and the breaking through of vegetative energy; this is particularly evident in the case of the catatonic seizure of rage. In an ordinary neurosis, the inhibition of vegetative motility is only superficial; beneath this superficial armor, there is still the possibility of inner excitation and of a certain discharge of energy in "phantasy". If, however, as in catatonia, the armoring process extends into deeper strata, so that it blocks the central parts of the biological organism and extends to the *whole* musculature, only two possibilities are left: either a violent breaking through of the vegetative energy (attack of rage, which is experienced as relief), or gradual and complete deterioration of the vital apparatus.

Other problems that will have to be followed from this point are a series of organic diseases, such as peptic ulcer, rheumatism, and cancer.

Doubtless, psychotherapists can observe such symptoms in great numbers in their everyday clinical work. However, these symptoms cannot be analyzed or understood individually, but only in connection with the biological functioning of the body as a whole, and in relation to the functions of pleasure and anxiety. It is impossible to master the manifold problems of bodily attitudes and somatic expression if one considers anxiety only as the cause of sexual stasis, and not, first and above all, as a *result* of sexual stasis. *"Stasis" really means nothing but an inhibition of vegetative expansion and a blocking of the activity and motility of the central vegetative organs.* In this case, the discharge of biological energy is blocked, and the energy becomes bound.

The orgasm reflex is a unitary contraction of the body as a whole. In the orgasm, we are nothing but a convulsing mass of protoplasm. After fifteen years of study of the orgasm problem, the *biological core* of psychic disturbances finally had been found. The orgasm reflex is found in all copulating organisms. In the more primitive organisms, such as the protozoa, it is found in the form of plasma contractions.[1] The lowest level on which it can be found is the process of cell division.

Some difficulties were presented by the question as to what, in more highly organized organisms, takes the place of the contracting into a spherical shape which is characteristic of protozoa. From a certain stage in evolution, the metazoa possess a bony framework. This prevents the occurrence of the movement which is characteristically found in molluscs and protozoa, namely, that of assuming spherical shape in contracting. Let us imagine an elastic tube into which our biological bladder has developed. Let us assume that it contains a longitudinal rod which can bend only lengthwise, representing the spinal column. If now, the elastic tube has the impulse to contract, we see that—if it is going to contract, in spite of its inability to assume the spherical shape—it has only one possibility of doing so: *it must bend,* as quickly and completely as it is possible:

Biologically speaking, the orgasm is nothing but this movement. The corresponding bodily attitude is apparent in many insects and in the embryonic attitude.

In hysterical individuals, muscular spasms occur with particular predilection in parts of the organism which have annular musculature, particularly in the *throat* and the *anus.* These two places correspond, from the point of view of embryology, to the two openings of the primitive gastrointestinal tract:

---

[1]Cf. Reich, Wilhelm, Die Bione. Sexpol-Verlag, 1938, Pp. 205.

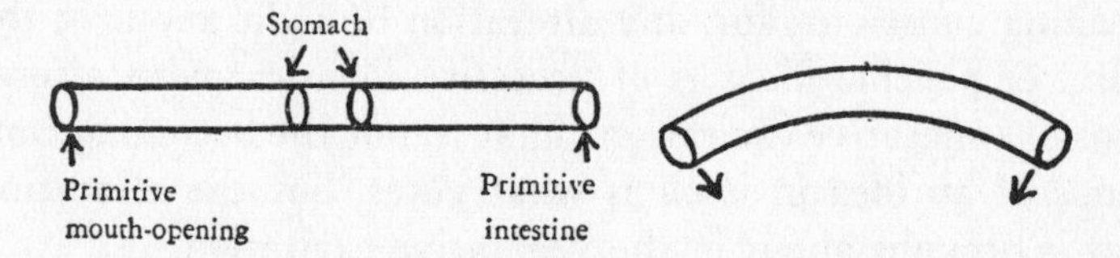

Of similar importance is the annular musculature at the entrance to and the exit from the stomach. Here, hysterical spasms with serious consequences for the general systemic condition are frequent. These places of the body which have a special disposition to lasting contractures and which correspond to very primitive levels of development, are most frequently the seat of neurotic spastic conditions. When there is a spasm at the throat or the anus, orgastic contraction becomes impossible. The somatic "holding back" is expressed in an attitude which is the opposite of that of the orgasm reflex: the back is arched, the neck stiff, the anus tight, the chest stuck out, the shoulders tense. The *arc de cercle* in hysteria is the exact opposite of the orgasm reflex and is the prototype of defense against sexuality.

Every psychic impulse is functionally identical with a definite somatic excitation. The concept that the psychic apparatus functions by itself and influences the somatic apparatus—which also functions by itself—is not in keeping with the facts. A jump from the psychic into the somatic is inconceivable; for, the assumption of two separate fields is erroneous. Nor can an idea, such as that of going to sleep, exert a somatic influence unless it is itself already the expression of a vegetative impulse. The development of an idea from a vegetative impulse is one of the most difficult problems confronting psychology. Clinical experience leaves no doubt that the somatic symptom as well as the unconscious idea are *results* of a conflicting vegetative innervation. This finding does not contradict the fact that one may be able to eliminate a somatic symptom by way of making its psychic meaning conscious; for, any alteration brought about in the realm of psychic ideas is of necessity identical with alterations of vegetative excitation. That is, not the becoming conscious of an idea in itself is what cures, but the alteration that is brought about in the vegetative excitation.

Thus, we find the following succession of functions in the course of the influence of an idea upon the somatic sphere:

a. The psychic excitation is identical with the somatic excitation.

b. The fixation of a psychic excitation occurs as a result of the establishment of a definitive vegetative state of innervation.

c. The alteration of the vegetative state alters the functioning of the organ.

d. The "psychic meaning of the organic symptom" is nothing but the somatic attitude in which the "psychic meaning" expresses itself. (Psychic reserve expresses itself in a vegetative holding back; psychic hatred expresses itself in a definite vegetative attitude of hatred; the two are identical and cannot be separated).

e. The established vegetative state in turn acts on the psychic state.

The perception of an actual danger functions identically with a sympatheticotonic innervation; this in turn increases the anxiety; the increased anxiety calls for an armoring process which is synonymous with binding of vegetative energy in the muscular armor; this armor, in turn, reduces the possibility of discharging energy and thus increases the tension, etc.

The psychic and the somatic operate, from the point of view of biopsychic energy, as two systems which are *unitary* as well as *conditioning each other*.

The following clinical case may serve as an illustration:

An extremely pretty and sexually attractive young woman complained about the feeling that she was ugly, as she did not have a unitary feeling of her body. She described her condition as follows: "Every part of my body acts on its own. My legs are here and my head is there, and I never really know where my hands are. I don't have my body together". That is, she suffered from the well-known disturbance of self-perception, the extreme form of which is schizoid depersonalization. During the vegetotherapeutic work, she showed a very peculiar connection between the various functions of the muscular attitudes in her face. From the very start of the treatment, the "indifferent" expression in her face was striking. This expression of "indifference" gradually became so intense that the patient began to suffer keenly from it. When one would talk to her, even about serious subjects, she would always stare into a corner of the room or out of the window. With this, her face would wear an indifferent expression and her eyes would have an empty, "lost" look. As this indifferent expression was thoroughly analyzed and dissolved, a different facial expression appeared clearly of which one had seen only a trace before. The region of mouth and chin had a different expression from eyes and forehead. As this new expression became more distinct, it became clear that mouth and chin were *"angry"*, while eyes and forehead were *"dead"*. These were the words that expressed the inner perception that the patient had of these attitudes. I proceeded first to work out separately the expression in mouth and chin. In the course of this work there developed incredibly violent reactions of inhibited impulses to bite; they had developed towards her father and her husband, without, however, being lived out. The impulses of violent anger which were thus expressed in the attitude of her mouth and chin had been covered up by an attitude of indifference in the whole face; it was only after the elimination of the indifference that the angry expression at the mouth came to light. The function of the indifference was that of keeping the patient from constantly being exposed to the painful perception of the hatred that would have been expressed by her mouth. After about two weeks' work at the mouth region, the angry expression disappeared completely in connection with the analysis of a very intense reaction of disappointment. One of her outstanding character traits was the compulsion to demand love constantly and to become angry when her impossible demands were not satisfied. After the attitude of mouth and chin was dissolved, there appeared preorgastic contractions in the whole body, at first in the form of a wave-like serpentine movement which also took in the pelvis.

However, genital excitation was inhibited at a definite place. During the search for the inhibitory mechanism, the expression of eyes and forehead gradually became more pronounced. The expression became one of an angry, observing, critical and attentive gaze. Only now did the patient become aware of her attitude "never to lose her head"; she always had to be "on guard".

The way in which vegetative impulses come to light and become more distinct is one of the most peculiar phenomena which we see in vegetotherapy. It cannot really be described; it has to be experienced clinically.

In this patient, the "dead" forehead had covered up the "critical" one. The next question was the function of the "critical, angry" forehead. An analysis of the details of her mechanism of genital excitation revealed the fact that her forehead "watched closely what the genital was doing." Historically, the severe expression of eyes and forehead derived from an identification with her father who was a very moral person with a strict ascetic attitude. At a very early age, her father had again and again impressed on her the danger of giving in to sexual desires; in particular, he had pictured the ravages of the body by syphilis. Thus, the forehead had taken the place of the father in guarding against the temptation of giving in to a sexual desire.

The interpretation that she had identified herself with her father is in no way sufficient. The question is, first, why did this identification take place just where it did, namely *at the forehead;* and second, *what maintained this function in the immediate present?* We have to make a strict distinction between the historical explanation of a function and the dynamic explanation in terms of the immediate present. These are two entirely different things. We do not eliminate a somatic symptom by making it historically understandable. We cannot do without the knowledge of the function which an attitude serves in the immediate present. (This is not to be confused with the present-day conflict!) The derivation of the watchful forehead from the identification with the severe father would not budge the orgastic disturbance in the least.

The further course of the treatment proved the correctness of this view. For, to the same extent to which the "dead" expression was replaced by the "critical" expression, the defense against genitality became accentuated. Following this, the critical, severe expression began to alternate with a cheerful, somewhat child-like expression in forehead and eyes. That is, one time the patient felt in harmony with her genital desire, the other time she had a critical, defensive attitude toward it. With the final disappearance of the critical attitude of the forehead and its replacement by the cheerful attitude, the inhibition of genital excitation disappeared also.

This case is presented in some detail because it illustrates a number of disturbances of the process of tension and charge at the genital apparatus. The defensive attitude of "keeping one's head", for example, which this patient showed so clearly, is a common phenomenon.

This patient had the sensation of a body that was divided, not integrated, not united. This is why she lacked the consciousness and the feeling of her sexual and vegetative gracefulness.

How is it possible that an organism which, after all, forms a unitary whole, can "fall apart" as far as its perception is concerned? The term "depersonalization" means nothing, for it needs itself to be explained. How is it possible, we must ask ourselves, that parts of the organism, as if separated from it, can function on their own? Psychological explanations will not get us anywhere here, for, the psychic depends, in its emotional function, completely on the functions of expansion and contraction in the vegetative vital apparatus. This apparatus is a non-homogeneous system. Clinical and experimental evidence show that the process of tension and charge may occur in the body as a whole as well as in individual groups of organs alone. The vegetative apparatus is capable of showing parasympathetic excitation in the upper abdomen and at the same time sympatheticotonic excitation in the lower abdomen. Similarly, it may produce tension in the muscles of the shoulders, and at the same time relaxation or even flaccidity in the legs. This is possible only because, as stated before, the vegetative apparatus is not a homogeneous structure. In an individual engaged in sexual activity, the region of the mouth may be excited, while at the same time the genital may be completely unexcited or even in a negative state, or *vice versa.*

These facts provide a sound basis for an evaluation of *what is "healthy" and what is "sick" from a sex-economic point of view.* There is no doubt that *the basic criterion of psychic and vegetative health is the ability of the organism to act and react,* as a unit and as a totality, *in terms of the biological functions of tension and charge.* Conversely, we have to consider as pathological any non-participation of single organs or organ-groups in the unity and totality of the vegetative function of tension and charge, if it is chronic and represents a lasting disturbance of the total functioning of the organism.

Clinical experience shows, furthermore, that disturbances of self-perception really disappear only after the orgasm reflex is fully developed. Then, it is as if all organs and organ systems of the body were gathered into one single experiential unit, with regard to contraction as well as to expansion.

From this point of view, depersonalization becomes understandable as a *lack of charge,* i.e., as a disturbance of the vegetative innervation of individual organs or organ systems, of the fingertips, the arms, the head, the legs, the genital, etc. Disunity of the perception of one's own body also is caused by the interruption, in this or that part of the body, of the current of excitation. This is particularly true of two regions: one is the neck, where a spasm blocks the progression of the wave of excitation from chest to head; the other is the musculature of the pelvis, which, when spastic, interrupts the course of the excitation from abdomen to genitals and legs.

Every disturbance of the ability to fully experience one's own body, damages self-confidence as well as the unity of the bodily feeling. At the same time, it creates the need for compensation. The perception of one's vegetative wholeness, which is the natural and the only safe basis for a strong self-confidence, is disturbed in all neurotic individuals. This disturbance manifests itself in the most diverse ways; its extreme degree is the complete *splitting of the personality*. There is no fundamental difference between the simple sensation of being emotionally cold and stiff on the one hand, and schizophrenic dissociation, lack of contact and depersonalization on the other hand; there is only a quantitative difference, though it shows itself also qualitatively. The feeling of wholeness is connected with the feeling of an immediate contact with the world. When, in the course of therapy, the unity of the orgasm reflex is established, the feeling of *depth* and *earnestness*, which was lost long ago, comes back. In this connection, patients recall that period in their early childhood in which the unity of their bodily sensations was as yet undisturbed. Deeply moved, they relate how, as small children, they felt one with nature, with everything around them, how they felt "alive"; and how all this was subsequently broken to pieces and destroyed by their training. This breaking up of the unity of bodily feelings through sexual suppression, and the constant longing to re-establish contact with the self and with the world, is the subjective basis of all sex-negating religions. "God" is the mystical idea of the vegetative harmony of the self with nature. If and when God represents nothing but the personification of the natural laws which govern man and make him part of the universal natural process, then—and only then—can natural science and religion come to terms.

Man has made great strides in the building and mastery of machines. It is hardly forty years that he has tried to understand himself. The psychic plague which characterizes our times will prove insuperable without a planned economy of human biological energy. The path of scientific investigation and of mastery of vital questions is long and hard; it is the exact opposite of the politico's impertinence which is based on ignorance. There is ground for hope that one day science will succeed in handling biological energy as today it masters electrical energy. Not until then will the psychic plague find its master.

6. TYPICAL PSYCHOSOMATIC DISEASES: RESULTS OF CHRONIC SYMPATHETICOTONIA

We have gained a sufficient orientation concerning sympatheticotonia to undertake a cursory review of a series of organic diseases which owe their existence to the orgastic impotence of man. Orgasm anxiety creates chronic sympatheticotonia; this in turn creates orgastic impotence; and this, in a vicious circle, maintains the sympatheticotonia. The basic characteristic of sympatheticotonia is the chronic inspiratory attitude of the thorax and the limitation of full (parasympathetic) expiration. The function of this sympatheticotonic inspiratory attitude is essentially that of preventing those affects and bodily sensations from arising which would appear with normal respiration.

Following are some of the results of the chronic attitude of anxiety:

1. *Cardiovascular hypertension.* The peripheral blood vessels are chronically contracted and their amplitude of expansion and contraction is limited; thus, having to move the blood through rigid blood vessels, the heart has continually an excessive task to fulfill. Tachycardia, high blood pressure and feelings of oppression in the chest, or even full cardiac anxiety, are also symptoms of *hyperthyroidism.* The question seems justified as to whether the disturbance of thyroid function is primary, or in how far it is itself only a secondary symptom of a general sympatheticotonia. *Arteriosclerosis,*

in which a calcification of the blood vessels takes place, is also found with surprising frequency in individuals who had previously suffered from a long-standing functional hypertension. It is highly probable that even valvular disease and other forms of organic heart disease represent a reaction of the organism to chronic hypertension of the vascular system.

2. *Muscular rheumatism.* The chronic inspiratory attitude of the thorax proves in the long run insufficient to master the biological excitations in the autonomic system. It is aided by the chronic tension of the muscles, the muscular armor. If hypertension of the muscles exists over a period of years and decades, it leads to chronic contracture and the formation of rheumatic nodules as a result of the deposit of solid substances in the muscle bundles. In this last stage, the rheumatic process has become irreversible. During the vegetotherapeutic treatment of rheumatism one finds that it affects, in a typical manner, those muscle groups which play a dominant role in the suppression of affects and bodily sensations. It is particularly often localized in the musculature of the *neck* ("stiffnecked", "headstrong"), and *between the shoulderblades,* where the typical muscular action is that of pulling back the shoulders, i.e., character-analytically speaking, of "self-control" and "holding back". Further, in the two thick muscles of the neck which run from the occiput to the clavicle (Mm. sternocleidomastoidei). These muscles are in a state of chronic hypertension when the unconscious suppression of anger is chronic. A rheumatic patient trenchantly designated these muscle-groups as "spite muscles". To these must be added the masseters (jaw muscles) the chronic hypertension of which gives the lower half of the face a stubborn and bitter expression.

In the lower parts of the body, those muscles are particularly frequently affected which retract the pelvis, thus producing a lordosis. As we know, the chronic retraction of the pelvis has the function of suppressing genital excitation. In this connection, the syndrome of *lumbago* needs detailed investigation. It is found very frequently in patients who keep the muscles of their buttocks in chronic hypertension for the purpose of suppressing anal sensations. Another muscle group in which rheumatism is of frequent occurrence is that of the superficial and deep adductors of the thigh, which cause the "pressing together of the legs". Their function, more clearly observable in women, is that of suppressing genital excitation. In vegetotherapeutic work, their function is so obvious that they came to be called "morality-muscles". The Viennese anatomist Tandler jokingly used to refer to them as "*custodes virginitatis*". In rheumatic patients, but also in a great majority of character-neurotics, these muscles are palpable as thick, sensitive rolls which cannot be made to relax. In the same category belong the flexors of the knee which run from the lower surface of the pelvis to the upper end of the tibia. They are in chronic contraction if the individual suppresses sensations in the pelvic floor.

The large anterior chest muscles (pectorales) are in chronic hypertension, hard and prominent, if the inspiratory attitude of the chest is chronically maintained. It often results in intercostal neuralgias which disappear with the muscular hypertension of the thorax.

3. There is every reason to assume that *pulmonary emphysema* with the accompanying barrel chest is a result of an extreme chronic inspiratory attitude of the thorax. The fact must be considered that any chronic fixation of a certain muscular attitude impairs the elasticity of the tissues, as is true in the case of emphysema with regard to the elastic fibres of the bronchi.

4. The connections between *nervous bronchial asthma* and sympatheticotonia are as yet unclear.

5. *Peptic ulcer*. According to the table on p. 259, chronic sympatheticotonia is accompanied by a preponderance of acidity, which is also reflected in excessive gastric acidity.

Alkalization is decreased. The mucous membrane of the stomach is exposed to the effect of the acid. The typical localization of peptic ulcer is in the middle of the posterior wall of the stomach, just in front of the pancreas and the solar plexus. Everything points to the assumption that the vegetative nerves at the posterior wall retract in the state of sympatheticotonia and thus reduce the resistance of the mucous membrane against attack by the acid. Peptic ulcer has been recognized so thoroughly as an accompaniment of chronic affective disturbance that its psychosomatic nature can no longer be doubted.

6. *Spasms of annular muscles of all kinds.*

a. Spastic attacks at the entrance to the stomach, *cardiospasm,* and at the exit of the stomach, *pylorospasm.*

b. Chronic *constipation,* as a result of the diminution or cessation of the function of tension and charge in the intestines. It is always accompanied by general sympatheticotonia and chronic inspiratory attitude of the chest. It is one of the most widespread chronic diseases.

c. *Hemorrhoids,* as a result of a chronic spasm of the anal sphincter. The blood in the veins peripherally from the anus is mechanically dammed up, and the vessel walls undergo dilation in places.

d. *Vaginismus,* as a result of a contraction of the annular musculature of the vagina.

7. A series of *blood diseases,* such as chlorosis and certain forms of anemia, are described by Müller, in his work *"Die Lebensnerven"*, as sympatheticotonic diseases.

8. *Carbon dioxide excess in the blood and the tissues.* In connection with the fundamental work of the Viennese scientist Warburg on the CO_2-excess in cancer tissue, it becomes clear that the chronically reduced expiration due to sympatheticotonia represents an essential part of the disposition toward cancer. The reduced external respiration results in poor internal respiration. Organs with chronically poor respi-

ration and insufficient bio-electric charge are more susceptible to cancer-producing stimuli than are organs with good respiration. The connection between the expiratory inhibition of the sympatheticotonic character neurotics and Warburg's discovery of the respiratory disturbance of cancerous organs was the starting point of the sex-economic study of cancer. This subject cannot be entered upon here. The following, eminently important fact, however, belongs in the context of this book: cancer in women is predominantly

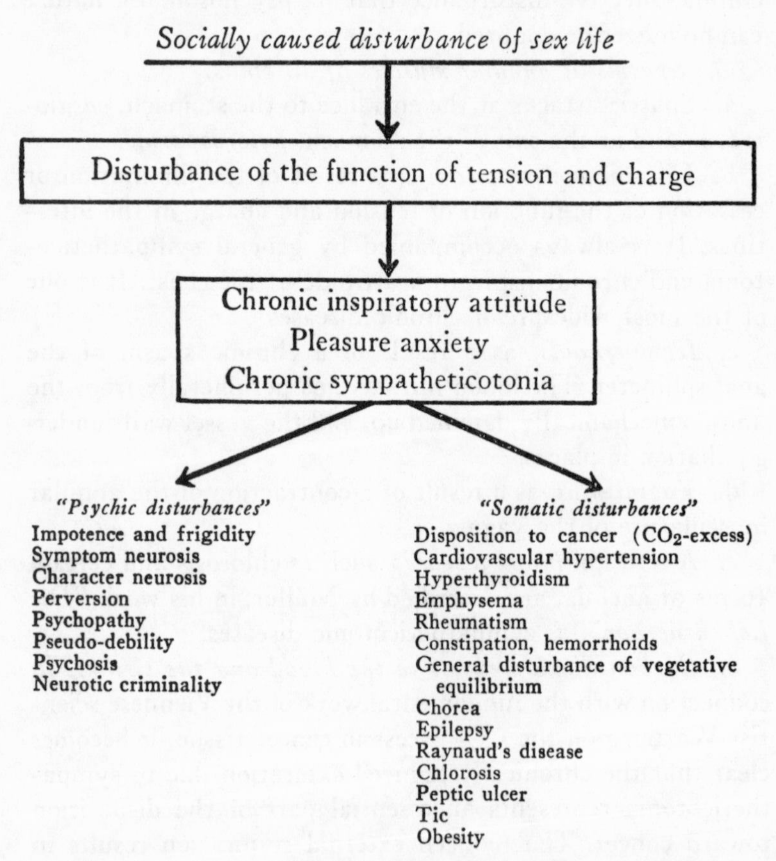

The social causation of disease through disturbance of the function of tension and charge.

localized in the sexual organs. The connection with frigidity is obvious and is known to many gynecologists. Furthermore, chronic constipation is, as a rule, in the background of cancer of the intestinal tract.

It goes without saying that this cursory tabulation is not meant to take the place of a detailed elaboration which would be an impossible task for an individual, which, rather, requires the collaboration of a great many physicians and research workers. All it intended to do was to point to an enormous field of pathology which has the closest relation to the function of the orgasm. It was to stress connections that had hitherto been overlooked and was to make an appeal to the conscience of the medical profession to take the sexual disturbances of man as seriously as they deserve to be taken; and to see to it that medical students obtain a correct knowledge of the orgasm theory and general sexology in order to be able to meet an enormous need of the population. It is necessary that the medical man should not remain absorbed in a microscopic slide, but should be able to bring that which he sees in the microscope into the proper relation with the autonomic life function of the *total organism;* he should have a mastery of this total function in its biological and psychic components; and finally, he should comprehend that the influence which society exerts upon the function of tension and charge of the organism and its organs is of decisive significance for health or disease in those he has to take care of. Then, *psychosomatic medicine,* today a preoccupation of especially interested individuals and specialists, could soon become what it promises to become: *the general framework of the medicine of the future.*

It goes without saying that this framework remains unattainable as long as the normal sexual function of the living organism continues to be confused with the pathological manifestations of neurotic humans and the productions of the pornographic industry.

Chapter IX

FROM PSYCHOANALYSIS TO BIOGENESIS

1. THE BIO-ELECTRIC FUNCTION OF PLEASURE AND ANXIETY

Up to 1934, I had merely applied my clinical theory, derived from the field of sex-economy, to the general biophysiological field. This did not conclude the work. On the contrary, now more than ever, it seemed absolutely essential to establish *experimental* proof of the correctness of the orgasm formula. In the summer of 1934, Dr. Schjelderup, director of the Psychological Institute of the University of Oslo, came to Denmark to participate in a course I was giving to Scandinavian, German and Austrian colleagues. He wanted to learn the technique of character-analysis. As he could not continue the work in Denmark, he suggested that I might continue my experiments at the Psychological Institute of the University of Oslo. I went there to teach character-analysis, and in return was given the opportunity to carry out my physiological experiments.

I knew that at the beginning I would need the help of technical specialists at every step. In talking things over with the assistant at the Oslo Physiological Institute, I found that we had no difficulty in understanding each other. My theory made sense to him. The fundamental question was, whether the sexual organs, in a state of excitation, would show an increase in their bio-electric charge. Based on my theoretical data, the physiologist designed an apparatus. The magnitude of the phenomena to be measured was unknown. Such experiments had never been done before. Would the surface charges of the sexual zones be one thousandth of a volt or half a volt? The physiological literature contained no data for answering such questions. More than that, the very fact of an electrical charge on the surface of the body was not generally known. When, in December, 1934, I asked the chief of a physiological institute in London how one could measure the charge of the skin, he thought the very question quite peculiar. As early as before the turn of the century, Tarchanoff and Veraguth had discovered the "psychogalvanic phenomenon", i.e., changes in the electrical potential of the skin as a result of emotions. Sexual pleasure had never been measured.

After a few months' deliberation, it was decided to build an apparatus consisting of a chain of electron tubes. The electrical charges of the body were to disturb the normal current ("anode current") of the tubes, to be amplified by the apparatus, transmitted to an electromagnetic oscillograph, and to be made visible on a strip of paper by way of a mirror. The apparatus was finished by February, 1935. The experimental subjects were some of my Norwegian friends and students, and myself.

It was surprising to find that the curves representing the cardiac action currents were extremely small compared with the changes in the surface charges. After a series of tentative preliminary experiments the prospects became clear. I shall omit here all the details of trial and error and only present the essential findings. The experiments took about two years. The results were published in a monograph[1] to which the

---

[1]Experimentelle Ergebnisse über die elektrische Funktion von Sexualität und Angst. Sexpol Verlag, 1937.

reader who is interested in the technical set-up and in the control experiments is referred.

The total surface of the organism forms a "porous membrane". This membrane shows an electrical potential with respect to any area of the body at which the epidermis is scratched away. Under ordinary circumstances, the uninjured skin shows a *basal or normal potential.* This represents the biological normal potential of the body surface. It is symmetrical on both sides of the body and approximately the same all over the body (cf. Fig. 2, p. 346). In different individuals, it varies within narrow limits (10-20 MV). In the electrogram, it appears as an even, horizontal line. Superimposed on it one sees, at regular intervals, the peaks of the electrocardiogram. The cardiac peaks correspond to a change in the normal potential of the skin through the electrical pulsations of the heart.

There are certain areas of the surface which show a fundamentally different behavior from the rest of the surface. They are the *erogenous zones:* lips, anus, nipples, penis, mucous membrane of the vagina, earlobe, tongue, palms, and—peculiarly enough—the forehead. The charge of these areas may be within the range of the potential of the other parts of the skin; but they also may show a much higher or much lower normal potential than the ordinary skin. In vegetatively free individuals, the potential of one and the same sexual zone is rarely constant; the same zones may show variations up to 50 MV or more. This corresponds to the fact that the sexual zones are characterized by an extremely variable intensity of sensation and capacity of excitation. Subjectively, the excitation of the sexual zones is experienced as a current, as itching, as flushes, waves of sensation, pleasurable warmth or "sweet", "melting" sensations. Those areas of the skin that are not specifically erogenous show these characteristics to a far smaller degree or not at all.

While the ordinary skin registers its bio-electrical charge in the form of a practically even, horizontal line (cf. Fig. 1, p. 346), the sequence of the different potentials of an erogenous zone registers as a wave-like line, going up or down more or less steeply. Let us call this steady change of potential "wandering" (cf. Fig. 3, p. 347).

The potential of the erogenous zones—unless it is within the range of that of the rest of the skin—*wanders,* that is, it increases and decreases. The ascent of the wavy curve indicates an increase, its descent a decrease of the charge at the surface. *The potential at the erogenous zones does not increase unless there is a pleasurable feeling of current at the respective zones.* A nipple, e.g., may become erect without an increase in potential taking place. An increase in potential at a sexual zone is always accompanied by an increase in pleasure sensation; conversely, a decrease of the potential always goes with a decrease of the pleasure sensation. In several experiments, the subject was able, on the basis of his or her sensations, to tell what the apparatus in the adjoining room was showing.

These experimental findings confirm the formula of tension and charge. They show that a congestion or tumescence in an organ does not by itself suffice to produce the vegetative sensation of pleasure. *In order to make the pleasure sensation perceptible, there is necessary, in addition to the mechanical congestion of the organ, an increase in bio-electrical charge. The psychic intensity* of the pleasure sensation corresponds to the *physiological quantity* of the bio-electrical potential.

Control experiments with non-living material showed that this slow, organic "wandering" of the potential is a specific characteristic of living substance. Non-living substances either give no reaction at all, or they produce, as, e.g., electrically charged bodies, such as a flashlight, mechanically angular, jerky, irregular jumps in potential (cf. Figs. 6 and 7, p. 348).

Let us call the ascending "wandering" potential the *pre-orgastic potential.* It varies at different times in one and the same organ. It also varies in different individuals in the same organ. It corresponds to the pre-orgastic excitation or streaming in the vegetatively active organ. The *increase* in charge is the response of the organ to a *pleasurable* stimulus.

If an erogenous zone, connected with an electrode which is applied evenly and without pressure, is tickled with a dry pledget of cotton, so that a pleasure sensation arises, the potential shows a wave-like oscillation, the so-called "*tickling phenomenon*" (K to * in Fig. 8, p. 349). Tickling is a variant of sexual friction. The latter is a basic phenomenon in the realm of the living. The sensation of itching also belongs here; for it results automatically in the impulse to scratch or to rub. These have an essential relationship to sexual friction.

We know from vegetotherapeutic clinical experience that sensations of sexual pleasure cannot always be brought about consciously. Similarly, an electro-biological charge cannot be provoked at an erogenous zone merely by pleasurable stimuli. Whether or not an organ responds with excitation to a stimulus, depends entirely on the attitude of the organ. This phenomenon has to be carefully taken into consideration in the course of the experiments.

The tickling phenomenon can be found in every region of the surface of the organism. It is not found when moist inorganic material is rubbed with dry cotton. The positive ascending portions of the tickling oscillation are usually steeper than the descending portions. The wavy line of the tickling phenomenon obtained at others than specifically sexual zones is more or less horizontal. At the sexual zones, the tickling oscillation is superimposed on the "wandering" electrical wave, just like the cardiac peaks.

Pressure of any kind decreases the charge of the surface. If the pressure is released, the charge returns exactly to its previous level. If a pleasurable ascending "wandering" of the potential is interrupted by pressure, the potential drops sharply; after release of the pressure, the wandering continues at the level where it had broken off (cf. Fig. 9, p. 349).

The increase in potential at a sexual zone depends on the *gentleness* of the stimulus; the more gentle the stimulus, the steeper the increase. It depends, furthermore, on the psychophysical readiness to respond to the stimulus. The greater this readiness, the steeper, i.e., the more rapid, is the increase.

Pleasurable stimuli, resulting in sensations of pleasure, regularly lead to an increase in potential; on the other hand, stimuli resulting in *anxiety* or *unpleasure,* decrease the surface charge more or less rapidly and intensely. Of course, the extent of this reaction also depends on the organism's readiness to react. *Emotionally blocked and vegetatively rigid individuals,* as for example catatonics, *show no or only very slight reactions.* With them, the biological excitation of the sexual zones lies within the range of that of the rest of the surface of the body. For this reason, the investigation of these electrical oscillation phenomena requires the choice of suitable experimental subjects. Reactions to anxiety in the form of rapid decreases of the surface charge were found at the mucous membranes of vagina and tongue, and at the palm. The best stimulus is an unexpected shock by shouting at the subject, the explosion of a balloon, a sudden violent stroke of a gong, etc.

Just as anxiety and pressure decrease the bio-electrical charge at the sexual zones, so does *annoyance.* In a state of *anxious anticipation,* all electrical reactions are decreased; increases in potential cannot be brought about. Anxiety reactions are, as a rule, easier to provoke than pleasure reactions. The most outspoken decrease of charge occurs with fright (cf. Figs. 10 and 11, p. 350).

The penis, in a flaccid state, may show a much lower potential than the ordinary skin. *Compression of the root of the penis and consequent congestion of blood in the penis does not result in an increase of the potential.* This control experiment shows that only pleasurable excitation, and not mechanical congestion by itself, is accompanied by an increased bio-electrical charge.

After a reaction of fright, pleasure reactions are much more difficult to produce. It is as if the vegetative excitation had become "cautious". If a concentrated sugar solution is used as electrode fluid at the tongue, the potential increases rapidly. If immediately afterwards, a salt solution is applied, the potential drops (cf. Figs. 12 and 13, p. 351).

If now, after the experiment with salt, sugar is again applied, there is no longer an increase of the potential. The tongue reacts as if "cautious" or "disillusioned". If sugar alone is applied to the tongue several times in succession, one finds that the increase in potential is less with each succeeding trial. It is as if the tongue had become "accustomed" to the pleasurable stimulus. Organs which have become disillusioned or accustomed react sluggishly even to pleasurable stimuli.

If the electrode is not connected with the sexual zone being tested, but, instead, an *indirect lead* is used, the results are the same. If, e.g., one lets a male and a female subject put a finger of one hand simultaneously into electrode fluids connected with the oscillograph, the touching of their lips in a kiss produces a marked increase in potential (cf. Fig. 14, p. 351). That is, the phenomenon occurs regardless of where the electrode is being applied. The same results are obtained when the subjects touch each other's free hand. Gentle stroking produces an increase, pressure or violent friction of the palms a decrease of charge. If a subject is averse to engaging in the activities required by the experiment, the same stimulus, instead of producing an increase in potential (pleasure reaction), results in a decrease (unpleasure reaction).

What is the manner of conduction of the bio-electric energy from the vegetative center to the periphery and vice-versa? According to traditional views, the bio-electric energy would move along the pathways of the nerve fibres, the assumption being that these fibres are non-contractile. On the other hand, all observations led of necessity to the assumption that the syncytial vegetative nervous *plexuses are themselves contractile,* i.e., capable of expanding and contracting. This assumption was later confirmed by microscopic observation. In small, translucent worms, movements of expansion and contraction in the autonomic nerve and ganglia apparatus can be readily observed under the miscroscope. These movements are independent of the movements of the total body and usually precede them. According to this observation, the ameba continues to exist in the higher animals and in man in the form of the contractile autonomic nervous system.

If one lets a subject take a deep breath or press as if at stool, and puts the differential electrode on the abdominal skin above the umbilicus, one finds that *with deep inspiration the surface potential decreases more or less sharply and that with expiration it increases again.* In a great number of subjects, the same result was found again and again; however, it could not be obtained in individuals who were strongly blocked emotionally or who showed a marked muscular rigidity. This finding, combined with the clinical finding that inspiration decreases affects, led to the following assumption:

With *inspiration,* the diaphragm descends, exerting a pressure on the abdominal organs; in other words, it constricts the abdominal cavity. On the other hand, with *expiration* the diaphragm is elevated, the pressure on the abdominal organs is decreased; the abdominal cavity is *expanded.* The thoracic and the abdominal cavities alternatingly expand and contract with respiration; the significance of this fact is discussed elsewhere. Since pressure always decreases the potential, its decrease with inspiration is not anything peculiar in itself. What is peculiar, however, is the fact that the potential decreases *although the pressure is not exerted at the skin surface but in the center of the organism.*

The fact that the *internal* pressure manifests itself externally, on the abdominal skin, can be explained only by the assumption of a *continuous bio-electric field of excitation between center and periphery.* The transmission of bioenergy cannot be limited to the nerve-tracts alone; rather, it must be thought of as following all membranes and fluids of the body. This assumption fits in with our concept of the organism as a membranous bladder, and confirms the theory of Fr. Kraus.[1]

Further confirmation for this assumption was provided by the finding that emotionally disturbed individuals with restricted expiration show only minimal fluctuations of charge in the abdominal skin, or none at all.

Summarizing the findings described, in terms of our basic problem, we can say the following:

Increase in bio-electric charge occurs only with biological pleasure accompanied by the feeling of current. All other excitations, pain, fright, anxiety, pressure, annoyance, depression, *are accompanied by a decrease in surface charge of the organism.*

There are, basically, four different kinds of decrease of charge at the periphery of the organism:

1. A retraction of the surface charge *previous to* an intended strong charge. This reaction may be compared to the coiled-up tension of a tiger previous to jumping.

[1] Cf. chapter VII.

2. The *orgastic discharge,* which, in contrast to pre-orgastic excitation, results in a decrease of the potential.

3. In *anxiety,* the charge in the periphery decreases.

4. In the process of *dying,* the tissues lose their charge; we obtain negative reactions; *the source of energy becomes extinguished.*

Surface charge

Increased	*Decreased*
Pleasure of any kind	Central tension previous to action
	Peripheral orgastic discharge
	Anxiety, annoyance, pain, pressure, depression
	Death (energy source being extinguished)

Sexual excitation thus is identical with bio-electrical charge of the periphery of the organism. Freud's concept of the libido as a measure of psychic energy is no longer a mere simile. It covers actual bio-electrical processes. Sexual excitation alone represents bio-electrical functioning in the direction of the periphery ("toward the world—out of the self").

Pleasure and anxiety are the basic excitations or emotions of the living substance. Their bio-electric functioning makes them part of the general electric process of nature.

Individuals who are not psychically disturbed and who are capable of orgastic sensations, individuals, in other words, who are not vegetatively rigid, are able, in our experiments, to state what is taking place at the apparatus in the adjoining room. The intensity of the pleasure sensation corresponds to the intensity of the bio-electric charge of the surface, and vice-versa. The sensations of "being cold", "being dead", "having no contact" which are experienced by neurotic individuals, are the expression of a deficiency in bio-electric charge in the body periphery.

The formula of *tension and charge,* a clinical finding, thus found its experimental confirmation. Biological excitation is a process which, in addition to mechanical tumescence, requires bio-electrical charge. *Orgastic gratification is a bio-electrical discharge, followed by a mechanical relaxation (detumescence).*

The biological process of expansion, as exemplified in the erection of an organ or the putting out of peudopodia in the ameba, *is the outward manifestation of the movement of bio-electric energy from the center to the periphery of the organism.* What is moving here is—in the psychic as well as the somatic sense—the bio-electrical charge itself.

Since only vegetative pleasure sensations are accompanied by an increased charge of the body surface, *pleasurable excitation must be considered the specifically productive process in the biological system.* All other affects, such as pain, annoyance, anxiety, depression, as well as pressure, are antithetical to it from the point of view of energy, and consequently represent functions negative to life. Thus, *the process of sexual pleasure is the life process* per se. This is not just a manner of speaking, but an experimentally proven fact.

Anxiety, as the fundamental functional antithesis of sexuality, is concurrent with death. It is, however, not identical with death. For, in death the central source of energy becomes extinguished; in anxiety, however, the energy is withdrawn from the periphery and dammed up in the center, creating the subjective sensation of oppression (*angustiae*).

These facts give the concept of *sex-economy* a concrete meaning in terms of natural science. It means *the manner of regulation of bio-electric energy,* or, what is the same thing, of *the economy of the sexual energies of the individual.* "Sex-economy" means the manner in which an individual handles his bio-electric energy; how much of it he dams up and how much of it he discharges orgastically. As we have to take the bio-electric energy of the organism as our basic point of departure, a new avenue of approach to the understanding of organic disease is opened.

The neuroses now appear to us in a fundamentally different light than to the psychoanalysts. They are by no means just the result of unresolved psychic conflicts and infantile fixations. *Rather, these fixations and conflicts cause fundamental disturbances of the economy of the bio-electrical energy and thus become anchored somatically.* For this reason, a separation of psychic from somatic processes is not possible or tenable. Psychic illnesses are biological disturbances, manifesting themselves in the somatic as well as in the psychic sphere. The basis of the disturbances is a deviation from the natural modes of discharge of biological energy.

Psyche and soma form a functional unity, having at the same time an antithetical relationship. Both function on the basis of biological laws. Deviation from these biological laws is a result of social factors in the environment. *The psycho-somatic structure is the result of a clash between social and biological functions.*

The function of the orgasm becomes the measuring rod of psychophysical functioning because in it the function of biological energy is expressed.

2. THE THEORETICAL SOLUTION OF THE CONFLICT BETWEEN MECHANISM AND VITALISM

When it was found that the formula of tension and charge applied to all involuntary functions of living substance, the question suggested itself as to whether it also applies to processes occurring in inanimate nature. Neither the literature nor discussions with physicists revealed the existence of an inorganic function in which a mechanical tension (through filling up with fluid) would lead to an electric charge, and then to an electric discharge and mechanical relaxation (through evacuation of fluid). It is true that in inorganic nature all the physical elements of the formula can be found. One finds mechanical tension through filling up with fluids and relaxation through evacuation of fluids; one finds electric charge and discharge. But these elements are found only separately and not in the particular sequence in which they are found in the living substance.

The inevitable conclusion was that the *particular combination of mechanical and electrical functions was the specific characteristic of living functioning.* I was now in a position to make an essential contribution to the age-old dispute between the vitalists and the mechanists. The vitalists had always contended that there was a fundamental difference between living and non-living substance. To make living functioning comprehensible, they always adduced some metaphysical principle, such as "entelechy". The mechanists, on the other hand, contended that living matter, physically and chemically, differed in no way from non-living matter; that it simply was as yet not sufficiently investigated. That is, the mechanists denied a fundamental difference between living and non-living matter. The formula of tension and charge showed both schools to be right, though not in the way they had thought.

As a matter of fact, living matter does function on the basis of the same physical laws as non-living matter, as is contended by the mechanists. It is, at the same time, fundamentally different from non-living matter, as is contended by the vitalists. For, in living matter, *the functions of mechanics* (tension—relaxation) *and those of electricity* (charge—discharge) *are combined in a specific manner which does not occur in non-living matter.* This difference of living matter, however, is not to be ascribed—as the vitalists believe—to some metaphysical principle beyond matter and energy. Rather, it is itself to be understood on the basis of laws of matter and energy. *The living is in its function* at one and the same time *identical with the non-living and different from it.*

It is to be expected that the vitalists and spiritualists will argue against this statement by pointing out that the phenomena of *consciousness* and *self-perception* are still unexplained. Correct as this is, it does not justify the assumption of a metaphysical principle; and besides, it seems likely that we are already within sight of a final clarification of this problem. The electrical experiments have demonstrated the fact that the biological excitation of pleasure and anxiety is functionally identical with its perception. The assumption is justified, therefore, that even the most primitive organisms possess the ability to perceive pleasure and anxiety.

3. "BIOLOGICAL ENERGY" IS ATMOSPHERIC (COSMIC) ORGONE ENERGY

I have arrived at the close of my description of the orgasm theory. In conclusion, I can give no more than a glimpse of the vast field into which the investigation of the orgasm was to lead. The bio-electrical experiments raised a question which was as unexpected as its importance was of the first magnitude: the question as to the nature of the bio-electrical energy which manifested itself in these experiments. It became clear that it could not be any of the known forms of energy.

For example, the speed of electromagnetic energy is that of light, i.e., about 186,000 miles per second. Observation of the curves and the time intervals shows that *the movement of bio-electric energy is, in manner and speed, fundamentally different from the known movement of electromagnetic energy*. The movement of bio-electric energy is exceedingly *slow*, measurable in millimeters per second. (The speed is indicated by the number of cardiac peaks; cf., e.g., Fig. 8,

p. 349). The form of the movement of biological energy is that of a slow undulation, reminiscent of the movements of an intestine or a snake. It also corresponds to the slow rise of an organic sensation or a vegetative excitation. One might try to find an explanation in the fact that it is the high resistance of the animal tissues which reduces the speed of electric energy in the organism. This explanation is wrong; if an electric stimulus is applied to the body, it is immediately perceived and responded to.

Quite unexpectedly, the knowledge of the biological function of tension and charge led me to the discovery of hitherto unknown energy processes in bions, in the human organism and in the radiation of the sun.

In the summer of 1939, I published a short communication[1] reporting on the following observations: A certain bion culture derived from sea sand influenced rubber or cotton in such a manner that these substances produced a marked movement of the indicator of a static electroscope. In the same way rubber and cotton are influenced by the human body, provided it is vegetatively undisturbed, most strongly by the abdomen and the genitals; that is, if rubber or cotton, which in themselves give no reaction measurable by the electroscope, are in contact with the body for fifteen to twenty minutes, they then produce a deflection of the electroscope. The sand from which the bions originated is nothing but immobilized sun energy. This suggested the experiment of exposing rubber or cotton to the bright sunlight after having made sure that they were not producing a deflection of the electroscope. It was shown that the sun emits a form of energy which influences cellulose, rubber and cotton in the same manner as the bion culture just mentioned and the human organism in a state of physiological respiration and in a vegetatively undisturbed condition. This energy, which

[1] Drei Versuche am statischen Elektroskop. Klinische und experimentelle Berichte, Nr. 7. Sexpol Verlag, 1939.

is capable of charging non-conducting substances, I termed *orgone.*

The *bions* are microscopic vesicles charged with orgone energy ("energy vesicles"). They can be produced from organic and inorganic material by a process of disintegration and swelling up. They propagate like bacteria. They also develop spontaneously in the soil, or, as in cancer, from disintegrating tissues. My book, *"Die Bione"* (1938), shows the significance which the formula of tension and charge assumed for the experimental investigation of the natural organization of living substance out of non-living substance.

The orgone energy can be demonstrated visually, thermically and electroscopically in the soil, the atmosphere and in plant and animal organisms. The flickering in the sky which many physicists ascribe to terrestrial magnetism, and the flickering of the stars, are the immediate expression of the motion of the atmospheric orgone. The "electrical storms" which disturb electrical apparatus at times of increased sun spot activity, are, as can be shown experimentally, an effect of the atmospheric orgone energy. Thus far, it is tangible only as a *disturbance* of electric currents.

The color of the orgone is *blue* or bluish gray. In our laboratory, the atmospheric orgone is accumulated by means of especially constructed apparatus. A special arrangement of materials allows to make it visible. The stoppage of the kinetic energy of the orgone expresses itself as a temperature rise. The concentration of the orgone energy is reflected in the varying speed of discharge in the static electroscope. The orgone contains three different kinds of radiation: bluish gray fog-like formations; deep blue-violet expanding and contracting dots; and whitish, rapidly moving dots and lines. The color of the atmospheric orgone is apparent in the blue sky and the bluish haze which one sees in the distance, particularly on hot summer days. Similarly, the blue-gray Northern lights, the so-called St. Elmo's Fire and the bluish formations which astronomers recently observed during a period of increased sun spot activity, are manifestations of the orgone energy.

Cloud formation and thunderstorms—phenomena which to date have remained unexplained—depend on changes in the concentration of atmospheric orgone. This can be simply demonstrated by measuring the speed of discharge of the electroscope.

The living organism contains orgone energy in every one of its cells, and keeps charging itself orgonotically from the atmosphere by the process of breathing. The "red" blood corpuscles, at a magnification of over 2000x, show a bluish glimmer; they are vesicles charged with orgone energy which they transport from the lungs to the body tissues. The plant chlorophyl, which is related to the iron-containing protein of the animal blood, contains orgone which it takes up directly from the atmosphere and the sun radiation.

In cells and colloids, if viewed with a magnification of over 2000x, the orgone energy shows itself in the bluish coloration of the protoplasm and of the content of organic vesicles. All cooked foods consist of blue, orgone-charged vesicles. Similarly charged with orgone are the vesicles in humus and all bions obtained by heating inorganic substances to incandescence and making them swell. Similarly, all gonadal cells, protozoa, cancer cells, etc., consist of orgone-charged, bluish energy vesicles.

The orgone energy has a parasympatheticotonic effect and charges living tissues, in particular red blood corpuscles. It kills cancer cells and many kinds of bacteria. Our therapeutic experiments in cancer are based on these biological effects of the orgone. Many biologists (like Meisenheimer, Linné and others) have observed the blue coloration of frogs in sexual excitation, or a bluish light emanating from flowers; we are dealing here with biological (orgonotic) excitation of the organism.

The human organism is surrounded by an orgonotic field which varies in range according to the individual's vegetative motility. The demonstration of this fact is simple. The orgone charges organic substances, such as cellulose. Thus, if we set up a cellulose plate of about one square foot at a distance of about 2 inches from a silver electrode which is connected with an oscillograph, we find the following: If inorganic material is moved back and forth in front of the cellulose plate, there is no reaction at the oscillograph (provided it is done in such a manner as not to move any part of our body in front of the plate). If, however, we move our fingers or hand back and forth in front of the plate, at a distance of ½ to 3 meters—without any metallic connection between body and apparatus—we find vivid oscillographic reactions. If the cellulose plate is removed, this effect disappears completely or almost completely. *In contradistinction to electromagnetic energy, the orgone energy is transmitted exclusively by non-conducting organic material.*

The second volume of this book will have to show the way in which the bion research led to the discovery of the atmospheric orgone energy, the ways in which the orgone can be objectively demonstrated, and the significance of its discovery for the understanding of biophysical functioning. Arrived at the conclusion of the present volume, the reader, like the writer himself, will not be able to escape the feeling that the investigation of the orgasm, the Cinderella of the natural sciences, has led us far into deeply stirring secrets of nature. The investigation of living matter went beyond the confines of depth psychology and physiology; it entered biological territory as yet unexplored. The subject of "sexuality" became one with that of "the living". It opened a new avenue of approach to the problem of biogenesis. Psychology came to be *biophysics* and genuine, experimental natural science. Its center remains always the same: the enigma of love, to which we owe our being.

The human organism is surrounded by an energy field which [illegible] according to the [illegible] vegetative [illegible] the [illegible] of [illegible]. The [illegible] used [illegible]. Through water [illegible] plates [illegible] at a distance of about [illegible] inches from a silver [illegible] which is connected with an oscillograph, we find the following: (1) moving one's [illegible] back and forth in front of the [illegible] plate, there is no reaction at the oscillograph [illegible] in such a [illegible] not to move any part of any body in front of the plate. If, however, we move our fingers [illegible] back and forth in front of the plate, at a distance of [illegible] meters—[illegible] connection between body and apparatus—we find [illegible] oscillograph reactions. In the [illegible] plates [illegible], the effect disappears completely [illegible] or [illegible] resonance of [illegible] energy [illegible] of [illegible].

The second volume of this book will [illegible] the way in which the [illegible] led to the discovery of the [illegible] energy, the ways in which the energy can be [illegible], and the significance of its discovery for the understanding of [illegible]. [illegible] of the present volume, the [illegible] will [illegible] able to [illegible] that [illegible] natural sciences has [illegible] far into [illegible] secrets of nature. The [illegible] of living matter [illegible] beyond the [illegible] of [illegible] and physiology [illegible]. The [illegible] of [illegible] opened a new [illegible] approach to the problem [illegible]. [illegible] and [illegible] science. [illegible] the same [illegible] of [illegible] which [illegible] being [illegible].

Amplifier and silver electrodes.

Oscillograph, paper film apparatus and electrode.

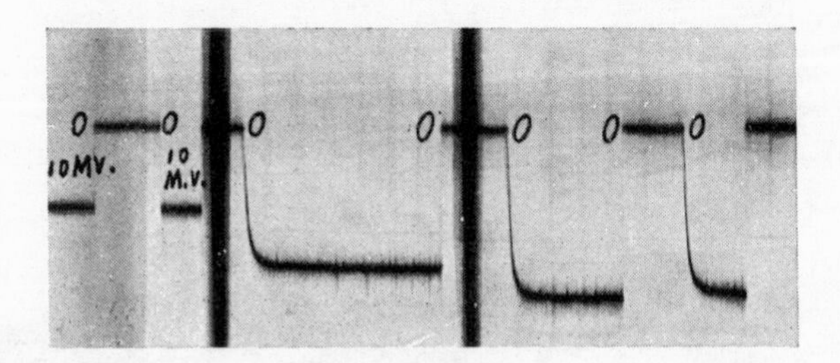

Fig. 1. *Average skin potential* (skin of the abdomen, right and left).

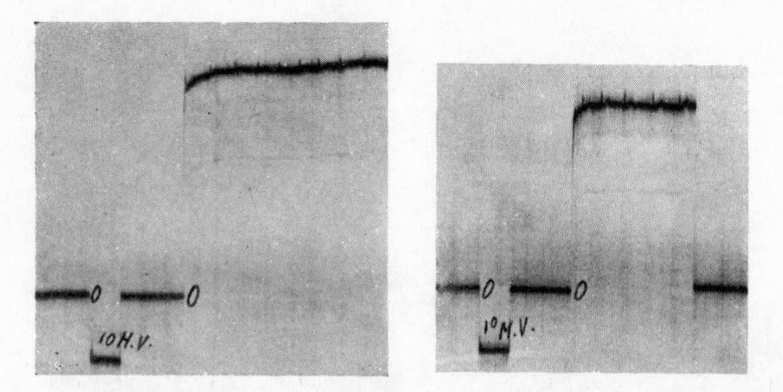

Fig. 2. *Symmetrical normal potentials* of a right and left palm.

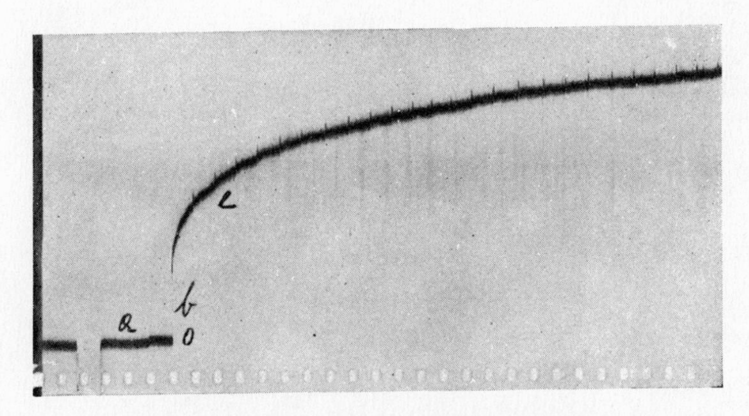

Fig. 3. "Wandering" of the potential of a palm.

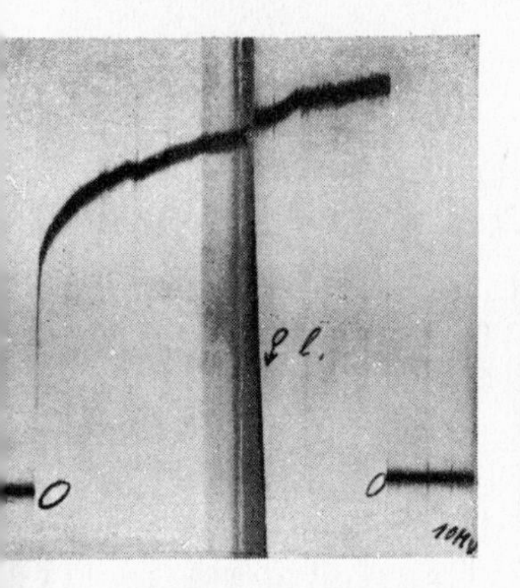

ig. 4. Mucous membrane of the nus in a woman in a state of sexual excitation.

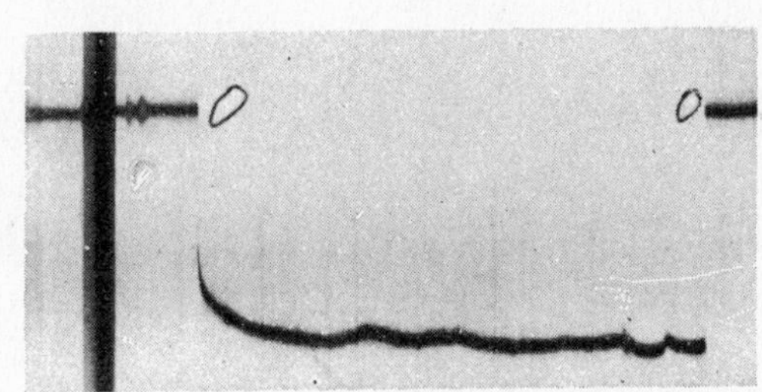

Fig. 5. The same mucous membrane in a state of depression (menstruation).

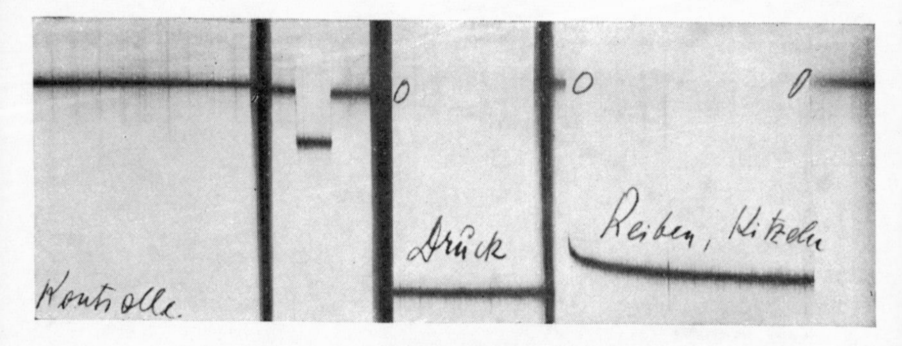

Fig. 6. Control experiment with wet towel.

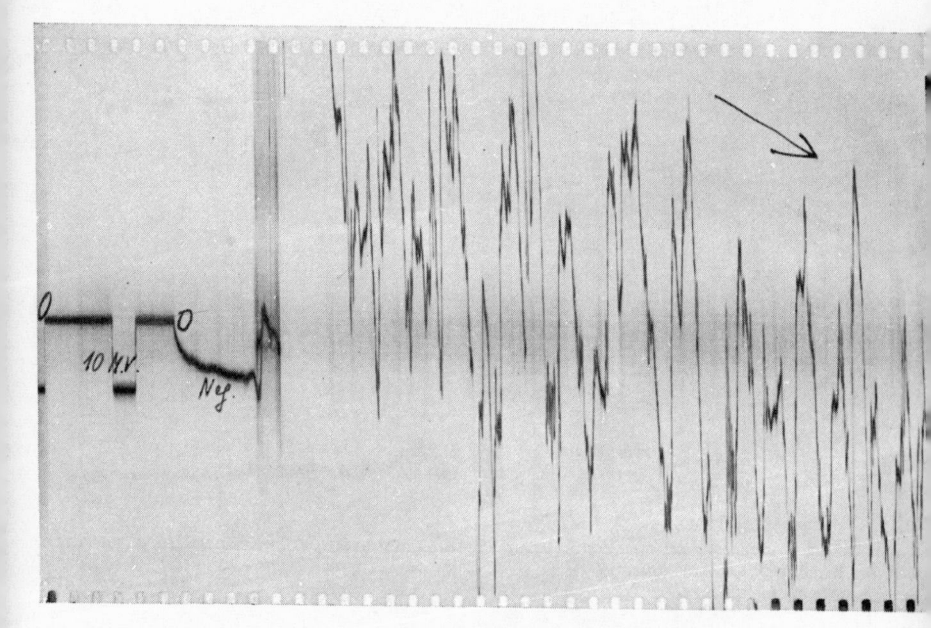

Fig. 7. Changes of potential produced by an electric flashlight.

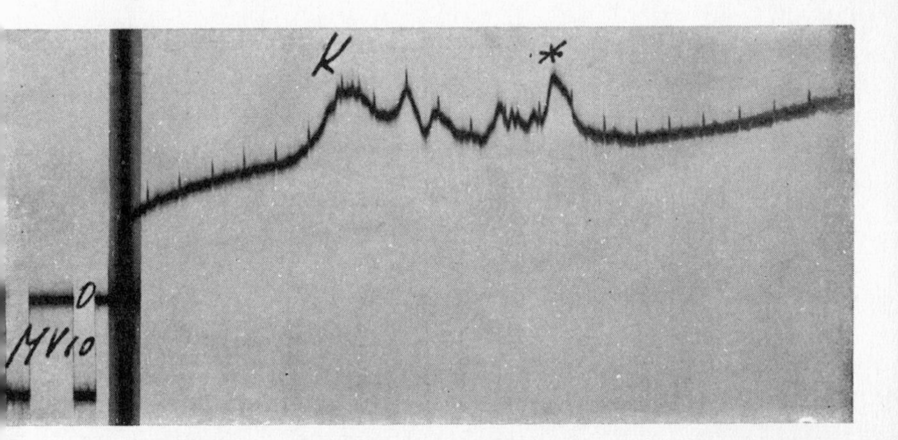

Fig. 8. *Mucous membrane of the lip. K to * = tickling phenomenon.* (The cardiac peaks are visible at regular intervals).

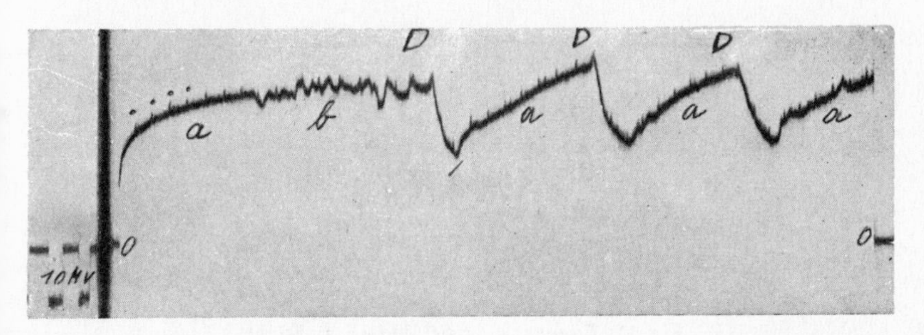

Fig. 9. *Mucous membrane of the tongue.* a = wandering; b = tickling phenomenon; D = pressure.

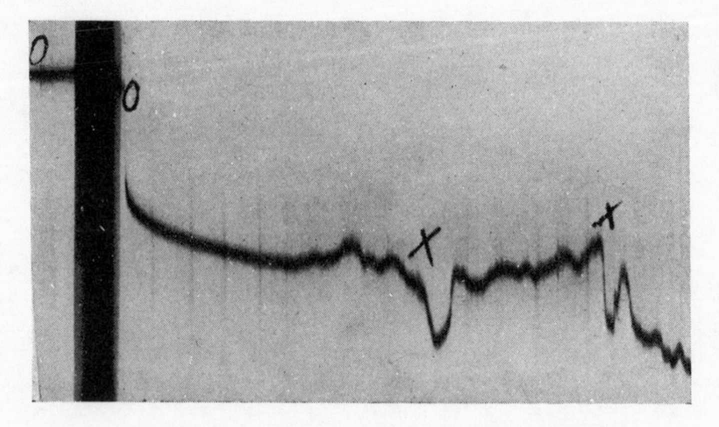

Fig. 10. x = reaction of vaginal mucous membrane to a stimulus of annoyance.

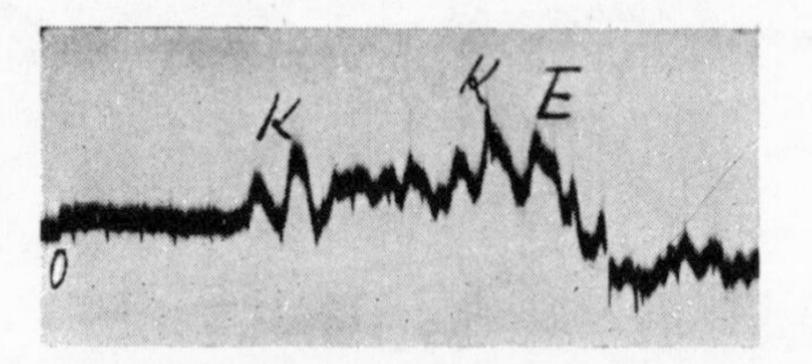

Fig. 11. *Tongue.* K = tickling; E = fright.

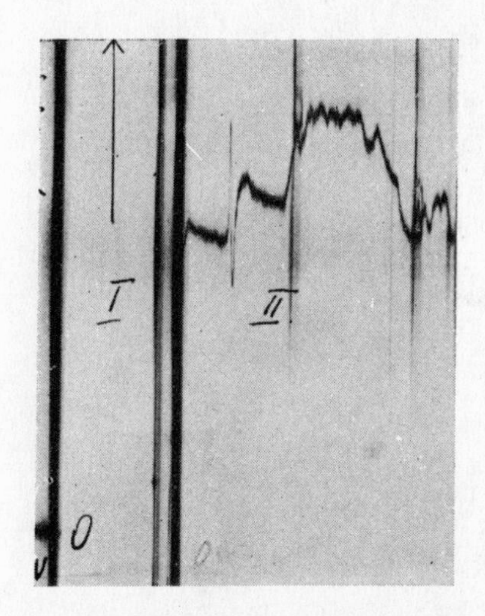

Fig. 12. *Reaction of tongue to sugar* (about + 70 MV; in this experiment, the first application of sugar resulted in a reaction way out of the field: I, arrow).

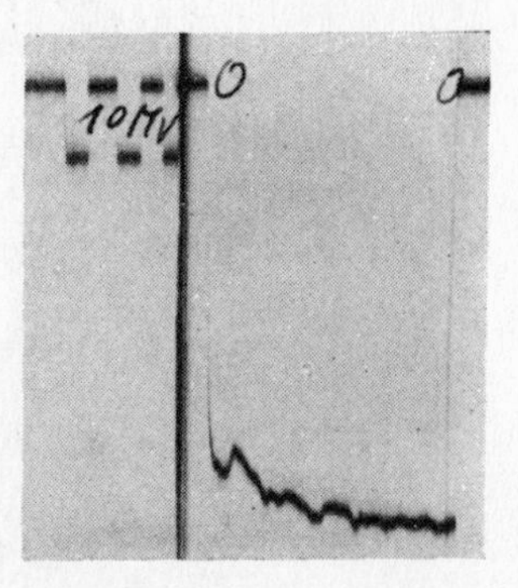

Fig. 13. *Reaction of same tongue to salt* (— 60 MV).

Fig. 14. *Excitation with a kiss* (changes in the bio-electrical excitation of the lips, up to 40 MV).

Anatomy of the vegetative nervous system
(adapted from Müller, Die Lebensnerven).

TABLE OF EVENTS*

1861 *Bachofen's standard work on *Mutterrecht.*

1870 *Morgan's *"Ancient Society"*.

1873 Comstock Law in the U.S.A. A deplorable piece of federal legislation which in turn led to the enactment of a number of other repressive federal and State laws which make it possible to this day for the authorities to detain or seize scientific books and periodicals on sexual matters and literature containing birth control information.

1879 *Bebel's *"Woman and Socialism"* (translated into fourteen languages; published in fifty-one editions).

1890 *First volume of Frazer's *"Golden Bough"*.

1893 Breuer and Freud, *"Ueber den psychischen Mechanismus hysterischer Phänomene. Vorläufige Mitteilung.*

1895 Freud, *"Ueber die Berechtigung, von der Neurasthenie einen bestimmten Symptomenkomplex als 'Angstneurose' abzutrennen"*. In this article, Freud laid the basis for a psychosomatic comprehension of the neuroses. However, he never followed this line of investigation and later repudiated his original, clinically correct, concept of anxiety, as did practically all psychoanalysts.

1898 Freud, *"Die Sexualität in der Aetiologie der Neurosen"*.

*Havelock Ellis' volume on *Auto-eroticism* (published in U.S.A.)

Translator's note: While working on this manuscript, I came across Max Hodann's History of Modern Morals, where every chapter is followed by a table of events. I felt that the addition of such a table to the present volume might prove useful, and Dr. Reich approved of the idea. The items marked with an asterisk are taken from the book of Max Hodann. The responsibility for this Table is the translator's.

1900 *Freud's *Traumdeutung.*

1901 *Brupbacher initiates mass meetings on birth control in Zürich.

1904 *Forel's *Question sexuelle.*

1905 Freud, "*Drei Abhandlungen zur Sexualtheorie*".

1908 *First International Psychoanalytic Congress in Salzburg.

1909 *Frank Wedekind's "*Frühlingserwachen*" gives the signal for the widest discussion on Sex Enlightenment in Continental Europe.

1912 Adler leaves Freudian group, because of his denial of the sexual etiology of the neuroses. First conflict between the sociological and the biological comprehension of the neuroses.

1913 Jung leaves Freudian group. First conflict between the scientific and the mystical comprehension of the libido.

**Zeitschrift für Sexualwissenschaft* founded in Berlin.

1915 *Castberg Law in Norway gives equal rights to illegitimate children.

1916 *First American Birth Control Clinic in New York.

1917 **Birth Control Review* begins publication in New York.

*Margaret Sanger imprisoned.

1919 First Sex Consultation Center at the Institute for Sexual Science in Berlin. Devoted mainly to the struggle for the recognition of the pathological instead of the criminal nature of sexual perversions.

Founding of the *Wiener Studentenseminar für Sexuologie.*

1920 *Anti-Birth Control Law in France.

Freud, "*Jenseits des Lustprinzips*". First hypothetical attempt at a psychoanalytic comprehension of the biological basis of the instincts.

1921 *First British Birth Control Clinic founded by Marie Stopes.

1922 Founding of the Psychoanalytic Clinic in Vienna. First attempt at a shift from individualistic private practice to mass practice, bringing into focus the problem of the prophylaxis of the neuroses.

Founding of the *"Viennese Seminar for Psychoanalytic Therapy"*.

1923 Freud, *"Das Ich und das Es"*. Second hypothetical attempt to comprehend the biological basis of the psychic apparatus.

Reich's paper on *"Die Genitalität vom Standpunkte der psychoanalytischen Prognose und Therapie"*. First formulation of the sex-economic theory of the neuroses.

1924 Psychoanalytic Congress in Salzburg. Reich introduces the concept of *"orgastic potency"*, formulating the economic factor in the neurosis.

Reich elected leader of the Technical Seminar.

*Birth Control Clinics founded in Scandinavia.

1925 Reich's book *"Der triebhafte Charakter"*, showing the necessity of extending symptom-analysis to character-analysis, and the possibility of making certain types of schizoid characters accessible to psychoanalytic therapy which previously had been considered as inaccessible.

*Mussolini penalizes contraception in Italy.

1926 Freud, *"Hemmung, Symptom und Angst"*. Freud refutes his own clinical theory of anxiety. Neurotic anxiety becomes a metapsychological concept, "a signal of the ego"; the question as to the stuff of which anxiety is made has "lost its interest". Anxiety comes to be considered as only the *cause* of repression, and not also as the *result* of repression.—The clinically correct investigation of anxiety was one of the starting points of Reich's sex-economy.

Van de Velde's *"Vollkommene Ehe"* and B. Lindsey's *"Companionate Marriage"*. Examples of how the problems of sexual and mental hygiene should *not* be approached.

Freud, on his seventieth birthday, warns his pupils not to trust the world; that psychoanalysis was being accepted only in order to be destroyed all the more easily.

Freud, *"Die Zukunft einer Illusion"*. First depth-psychological criticism of religion.

Fr. Kraus, *"Allgemeine und spezielle Pathologie der Person"*. The first successful attempt to introduce, on the basis of experimental findings, the functional nature of the nervous system in contrast to mechanistic concepts. Introduction of the concept of "vegetative current".

1927 Max Hodann's *"Geschlecht und Liebe"*. First attempt to present the sexual mass neurosis in its actual every-day manifestations, as contrasted with depth-psychological description.

Reich, *"Die Funktion des Orgasmus"*. The clinical foundation of sex-economy.

1928 *World League for Sexual Reform (W.L.S.R.) founded at Copenhagen during Second Congress for Sexual Reform.

*Sexual Consultations introduced into Scandinavian countries.

Founding of the *Gesellschaft für Sexualberatung und Sexualforschung* in Vienna by Reich. Founding of sex hygiene clinics in which, for the first time, the problem of the neuroses is attacked as a mass problem.

Reich's paper, *"Zur Technik der Deutung und der Widerstandsanalyse"*. First formulation of the principles of character-analysis.

1929 Reich's talk on the prophylaxis of the neuroses in one of the monthly meetings at Freud's home brings the issue of "psychoanalysis and culture" into the open.

Malinowski, *"The Sexual Life of Savages"*. His ethnological research proves beyond any doubt the social origin of the Oedipus complex.

1930 *Reich's *"Geschlechtsreife, Enthaltsamkeit, Ehemoral"*. The first affirmative analysis of the problems of Sex Education.

Reich's paper on *"Neurose als soziales Problem"* at the Third Congress for Sexual Reform.

1931 Freud, *"Das Unbehagen in der Kultur"*. Freud attempts

to present the rational goal of human happiness as impossible of attainment.

Reich, "*Der Einbruch der Sexualmoral. Zur Geschichte der sexuellen Oekonomie*". Clarification of the socio-economic origin of sexual repression.

1932 *Evang founds *Tidskrift for Sexuell Upplysning* (Periodical for Sexual Enlightenment) in Oslo; simultaneous editions in Stockholm and Copenhagen.

1933 Nazis destroy the Institute of Sexual Science in Berlin, and Reich's *Verlag für Sexualpolitik*.

*German Law of compulsory sterilization.

*Hitler régime suppresses birth control in Germany.

**Riksförbund for seksuell upplysning* (Swedish Sex Education Society) founded under the direction of Elise Ottesen Jensen.

Reich's book, "*Charakter-Analyse*". First comprehensive presentation of the character-analytic technique of the therapy of the neuroses.

Reich's book, "*Massenpsychologie des Faschismus*". First application of sexual sociology to the problems of irrationalism in politics.

1934 Founding of the *Zeitschrift für Politische Psychologie und Sexualökonomie* in Copenhagen.

Fascist "*Gleichschaltung*" of the German Psychoanalytic Societies.

*Massacre of Homosexuals in Germany.

*Leunbach stands as candidate for Danish Riksdag on a Sex-political platform.

*Law suit against Sex Education Press in Sweden. Acquittal on charge of pornography.

Reich's paper on "*Psychischer Kontakt und vegetative Strömung*" at the International Psychoanalytic Congress in Lucerne: first break-through of characterological investigation into the biological basis of the neurosis. Reich's expulsion from the International Psychoanalytical Association.

1935 *W.L.S.R. dissolved.

1936 Reich's book, *"Die Sexualität im Kulturkampf"*. Attempt at a sexual sociology of our times on a sex-economic basis.

1937 Reich, *"Experimentelle Ergebnisse über die elektrische Funktion von Sexualität und Angst"*. Experimental confirmation of the antithesis between sexuality and anxiety.

1938 Reich's book, *"Die Bione. Zur Entstehung des vegetativen Lebens"*. First comprehensive presentation of the experimental findings concerning the process of biogenesis.

Hodann's book, *"History of Modern Morals"*. First comprehensive presentation of the history of moral concepts, with inclusion of Freud's psychoanalysis and Reich's sex-economy.

1939 Freud dies in exile, London, September 23rd.

Reich discovers the *orgone radiation* in certain bion cultures.

First number of the *"Klinisk og pedagogisk Tidskrift for Seksualökonomi"* published in Scandinavia.

Reich's preliminary communication, "Bion experiments on the cancer problem".

1940 Reich discovers the existence of the orgone radiation in the atmosphere and the soil.

1941 Reich starts orgone irradiation experiments in human cancer.

GLOSSARY

ACTUAL NEUROSES. Freud's term for certain forms of neuroses —like anxiety neurosis and neurasthenia—which, in contradistinction to the "psychoneuroses," are caused by direct damming-up of "libido." *See* Stasis neuroses.

ARMOR. *See* character armor, muscular armor.

BIONS. Energy vesicles representing transitional stages between non-living and living substance. They constantly form in nature by a process of disintegration of inorganic and organic matter, which process it has been possible to reproduce experimentally. They are charged with orgone energy (q.v.), i.e., *Life Energy* and may develop into protozoa and bacteria.

CHARACTER. An individual's typical structure, his stereotype manner of acting and reacting. The orgonomic concept of character is functional and biological, and not a static, psychological or moralistic concept.

CHARACTER-ANALYSIS. Originally a modification of the customary psychoanalytic technique of symptom analysis, by the inclusion of the *character* and *character resistance* into the therapeutic process. However, the discovery of the *muscular armor* necessitated the development of a new technique, namely vegetotherapy. The later discovery of *organismic orgone energy* ("*bioenergy*") and the concentration of atmospheric orgone energy with an orgone energy accumulator necessitated the further development of character-analytic vegetotherapy into an inclusive, biophysical *orgone* therapy. *See* Orgone Therapy, physical and psychiatric.

CHARACTER ARMOR. The sum total of typical character attitudes, which an individual develops as a blocking against his emotional excitations, resulting in rigidity of the body, lack of emotional contact, "deadness." Functionally identical with the muscular armor.

CHARACTER, GENITAL. The un-neurotic character structure, which does not suffer from sexual stasis and, therefore, is capable of natural self-regulation on the basis of orgastic potency.

CHARACTER, NEUROTIC. The character which, due to chronic bioenergetic stasis operates according to the principle of compulsive moral regulation.

EMOTIONAL PLAGUE. The neurotic character in destructive action on the social scene.

MUSCULAR ARMOR. The sum total of the muscular attitudes (chronic muscular spasms) which an individual develops as a block against the breakthrough of emotions and organ sensations, in particular anxiety, rage, and sexual excitation.

ORGASM. The unitary involuntary *convulsion of the total organism* at the acme of the genital embrace. This reflex, because of its *involuntary* character and the prevailing orgasm anxiety, is blocked in most humans of civilizations which suppress infantile and adolescent genitality.

ORGASTIC IMPOTENCE. The absence of orgastic potency. It is the most important characteristic of the average human of today, and—by damming up biological (orgone) energy in the organism—provides the source of energy for all kinds of biopathic symptoms and social irrationalism.

ORGASTIC POTENCY. Essentially, the *capacity for complete surrender to the involuntary convulsion* of the organism and *complete discharge* of the excitation at the acme of the genital embrace. It is always lacking in neurotic individuals. It presupposes the presence or establishment of the genital character, i.e. absence of a pathological character armor and muscular armor. Orgastic potency is usually not distinguished from erective and ejaculative potency, both of which are only prerequisites of orgastic potency.

ORGONE ENERGY. Primordial Cosmic Energy; universally present and demonstrable visually, thermically, electroscopically and by means of Geiger-Mueller counters. In the living organism: *Bio-energy*, *Life Energy*. Discovered by Wilhelm Reich between 1936 and 1940.

ORGONE THERAPY.

Physical Orgone Therapy: Application of physical orgone energy concentrated in an orgone energy accumulator to increase the natural bio-energetic resistance of the organism against disease.

Psychiatric Orgone Therapy: Mobilization of the orgone energy in the organism, i.e. the liberation of biophysical emotions from muscular and character armorings with the goal of establishing, if possible, orgastic potency.

PLEASURE ANXIETY. The fear of pleasurable excitation. At first sight a paradoxical phenomenon, it is, nevertheless, as the result of a sex-negative upbringing, a dominant characteristic of the civilized human.

SEX-ECONOMY. The body of knowledge within Orgonomy which deals with the economy of the biological (orgone) energy in the organism, with its *energy household*.

STASIS. The damming-up of Life Energy in the organism, thus the source of energy for biopathy and irrationalism.

STASIS ANXIETY. The anxiety caused by the stasis of sexual energy in the center of the organism when its peripheral orgastic discharge is inhibited.

STASIS NEUROSIS. All somatic disturbances which are the immediate result of the stasis of sexual energy, with stasis anxiety at its core.

VEGETOTHERAPY. The sex-economic therapeutic technique. So called because the therapeutic goal is that of liberating the bound-up vegetative energies and thus restoring to the patient his vegetative motility. *See* Character-analysis.

Work Democracy. The functioning of the natural and intrinsically rational work relationships between human beings. The concept of work democracy represents the established *reality* (not the ideology) of these relationships which, though usually distorted because of prevailing armoring and irrational political ideologies, are nevertheless at the basis of all social achievement.

INDEX